HISTORICAL PERSPECTIVES:
A Reader & Study Guide
Volume II, Fourth Edition

HISTORICAL PERSPECTIVES:
A Reader & Study Guide
Volume II, Fourth Edition

Louise A. Mayo
County College of Morris
Randolph, New Jersey

Doug Cantrell
Elizabethtown Community & Technical College
Elizabethtown, Kentucky

Alison Brown
Union County College
Cranford, New Jersey

Lisa Miles Bunkowski
Del Mar College
Corpus Christi, Texas

Abigail Press   **Wheaton, IL 60187**

Design and Production: Abigail Press
Typesetting: Abigail Press
Typeface: AGaramond
Cover Art: Sam Tolia

HISTORICAL PERSPECTIVES:
A Reader & Study Guide
Volume II, Fourth Edition

Fourth Edition, 2004
Printed in the United States of America
Translation rights reserved by the authors
ISBN 1-890919-33-0

ABOUT THE AUTHORS

Louise Mayo is the Chairperson of the Department of History/ Political Science at County College of Morris, Randolph, NJ, where she has been a professor for the past twenty-four years. She is the author of *The Ambivalent Image* (1988) and numerous articles and papers in the fields of women and minority history. She has an M.A. from Cornell University in Modern European and Russian History and a Ph.D. from City University of New York in American History, specializing in immigration and minority history. She teaches courses in Twentieth Century America, History of American Women, History of Minorities, History of American Cities and Suburbs, and Civil War and Reconstruction.

Doug Cantrell is an Associate Professor of History Elizabethtown Community College in Elizabethtown, Kentucky, where he has taught for 13 years. He holds a B.A. from Berea College in History and Political Science, an M.A. from the University of Kentucky, and has completed 30 hours toward the Ph.D. He is the author of numerous journal and encyclopedia articles in the field of immigration and ethnic history. Professor Cantrell also teaches Kentucky and American History courses on the web and is the social science discipline leader for the Kentucky Commonwealth Virtual University. He is listed in *Who's Who in America,* *Who's Who in the World,* and *Who's Who in the South and Southwest,* He is a former editor of the *Kentucky History Journal* and past president of the Kentucky Association of Teachers of History.

Alison P. Brown is an Associate Professor in the Department of Economics, Government and History at Union County College in Cranford, New Jersey where she has taught history and philosophy for the past eight years. She received an M.A. and Ph.D. from Cornell University in Modern European Intellectual History, specializing in German social theory and philosophy. She teaches survey courses in American History, Civil War and Reconstruction, History of Western Civilization, as well as Introduction to Philosophy and Logic and Critical Thinking.

Lisa Miles Bunkowski is a History Instructor in the Social Science Department at Del Mar College in Corpus Christi, Texas where she has taught American History for the past three years. She received an M.A. in History from Emporia State University and a Ph.D. in History from the University of Kansas, specializing in the history of the American West, Latin American history, and the history of gender. She teaches a variety of American History courses in the classroom and on the web, and has worked with several grant projects designed to improve the teaching of American History in public schools. She has published several essays on the impact of the Great Depression and the New Deal on women and youths. She regularly presents her research on violence and vigilantism in the mid-19th Century American West at regional conferences.

Contents in Brief

Chapter Twelve
RECONSTRUCTION: The Turning Point That Never Turned   1

Chapter Thirteen
INDUSTRIALIZATION   24

Chapter Fourteen
THE TRANS-MISSOURI WEST: The Last Frontier   58

Chapter Fifteen
THE IMPERIAL REPUBLIC   88

Chapter Sixteen
PROGRESSIVISM   109

Chapter Seventeen
THE "GREAT" WAR: World War I   135

Chapter Eighteen
THE ROARING TWENTIES   163

Chapter Nineteen
THE DEPRESSION   192

Chapter Twenty
THE "GOOD" WAR: World War II   230

Chapter Twenty-one
THE COLD WAR: The Truman-Eisenhower Years   253

Chapter Twenty-two
HOPE TO DESPAIR: Kennedy-Johnson Years   275

Chapter Twenty-three
THE SEVENTIES: The Crisis of Confidence   301

Chapter Twenty-four
IN OUR TIMES: Reagan to Clinton   329

Contents

CHAPTER TWELVE
RECONSTRUCTION: The Turning Point That Never Turned 1
    Identification 2
    Think About 4
A LETTER "TO MY OLD MASTER," c. 1865 4
THE BLACK CODES 6
    The Black Code of St. Landry's Parish, 1865 6
THE ISSUE OF LAND FOR THE FREED SLAVES 8
    From a speech by Thaddeus Stevens, 1865 8
    New York Times, July 9, 1867 8
    A Conversation between a Freedman and a General at Fort Smith Arkansas 8
EDUCATING THE FREED PEOPLE 10
    Dedicated Teachers, Determined Students, 1869 10
    Sydney Andrews quoted in the Joint Report on Reconstruction 10
    Captain C. M. Hamilton in a letter to the Office of the Adjutant General 10
THE SPLIT BETWEEN ADVOCATES OF WOMEN'S RIGHTS AND BLACK RIGHTS 11
    A petition drafted after the Civil War by Elizabeth Cady Stanton and Susan B. Anthony 11
    Letter to Susan B. Anthony from Gerritt Smith, ... 11
    A Response by Elizabeth Cady Stanton 12
    "Being Persons, Then, Women are Citizens" 12
DIFFERING VIEWS ABOUT BLACKS IN RECONSTRUCTION IN THE SOUTH 13
    From the Novel, *A Fool's Errand*, By Albion Tourgee 13
    From the Novel, *The Clansman*, By Thomas Dixon Jr. 14
    From—*The Autobiography of John Roy Lynch* 14
RETREAT FROM RECONSTRUCTION 16
    An excerpt from the speech of black Congressman Richard Harvey Cain of South Carolina 16
    Political Terrorism by the Ku Klux Klan Testimony by Harriet Hernandez 16
    Excerpts from the original draft of the S. Carolina 1876 Democratic party campaign plan 17
AFTER RECONSTRUCTION 18
    Address to the Louisville Convention (1883) By Frederick Douglass 18
    Self Test 21
    Essays 23
    Optional Activities 23
    Web Site Listings 23

CHAPTER THIRTEEN
INDUSTRIALIZATION 24
    Identification 25
    Think About 27
THE SHERMAN ANTI-TRUST ACT OF 1890 27
EXCERPTS FROM ANDREW CARNEGIE, *THE GOSPEL OF WEALTH* 29
A SELECTION FROM THE CONSTITUTION OF THE KNIGHTS OF LABOR 30
EXCERPTS FROM JOHN MORRISON'S TESTIMONY BEFORE THE U. S. SENATE 32
ANTI-IMPERIALISM: The Views of Grover Cleveland 35
THE WIZARD OF OZ: Industrial Themes in a Child's Story, By Doug Cantrell 36
FORCED LABOR IN WEST VIRGINIA, By Gino C. Speranza 40
THE AWAKENING OF THE NEGRO, By Booker T. Washington 44
"OF THE TRAINING OF BLACK MEN," By W.E.B. Du Bois 48
    Self Test 54
    Essays 55
    Optional Activities 55
    Web Site Listings 56

CHAPTER FOURTEEN
THE TRANS-MISSOURI WEST: The Last Frontier 58
    Identification. 59
    Think About 61
THE HOMESTEAD ACT 61
THE PACIFIC RAILWAY ACT 63
RED CLOUD SPEECH AT COOPER UNION, NEW YORK 64
THE DAWES ACT 66
D. W. C. DUNCAN TESTIMONY 68
REPORT ON WOUNDED KNEE MASSACRE, By Benjamin Harrison 70
BRYAN'S CROSS OF GOLD SPEECH 71
THE PAGE LAW 75
CHINESE EXCLUSION ACT 76
REPUBLICAN PARTY PLATFORM 78
POPULIST PARTY PLATFORM 82
    Self Test 85
    Essays 87
    Optional Activities 87
    Web Site Listings 87

CHAPTER FIFTEEN
THE IMPERIAL REPUBLIC 88
    Identification 89
    Think About 92
JOSIAH STRONG ON ANGLO-SAXON PREDOMINANCE, 1891 92
TRANSCRIPT OF THE DE LOME LETTER, 1898 95
PLATT AMENDMENT 96
PLATFORM OF THE AMERICAN ANTI-IMPERIALIST LEAGUE 98
PRESIDENT MCKINLEY ON THE ACQUISITION OF THE PHILIPPINES 99
THE OPEN DOOR NOTE: Submitted by U. S. Secretary of State, John Hay 101
THE WHITE MAN'S BURDEN, By Rudyard Kipling 103
    Self Test 105

Essays 107
Optional Activities 107
Web Site Listings 107

CHAPTER SIXTEEN
PROGRESSIVISM 109
    Identification 111
    Think About 113
HOW THE OTHER HALF LIVES: Studies Among the Tenements of New York, By Jacob Riis, ... 113
HISTORY OF THE AMERICAN PEOPLE, By Woodrow Wilson, 1902 117
JAMES MONTGOMERY FLAGG CARTOON 118
MONROE TROTTER PROTESTS PRESIDENT WILSON'S SEGREGATION OF FEDERAL
    EMPLOYEES 119
"OF OUR SPIRITUAL STRIVINGS," *The Souls of Black Folk*, By W.E.B. Du Bois, 1903 120
THE JUNGLE, By Upton Sinclair, 1906 124
TRIANGLE MEMORIAL SPEECH, By Rose Schneiderman, 1911 125
A NEW CONSCIENCE AND AN ANCIENT EVIL, By Jane Addams, 1911 126
NAWSA CONVENTION SPEECH, *Remarks on Emotionalism in Politics*, By Anna Howard
    Shaw, 1913 129
*SENATORS VS. WORKING WOMEN, A Reply to New York Senators on Delicacy and Charm
of Women*, By Rose Schneiderman, 1912 130
    Self Test 132
    Essays 133
    Optional Activities 133
    Web Site Listings 134

CHAPTER SEVENTEEN
THE "GREAT" WAR: World War I 135
    Identification 137
    Think About 139
PRESIDENT WOODROW WILSON'S WAR MESSAGE TO THE U. S. CONGRESS 140
AT THE FRENCH FRONT, By Alan Seeger, May 22, 1915 142
*THE BACKWASH OF WAR: The Human Wreckage of the Battlefield as Witnessed by an American
Hospital Nurse*, 1916, By Ellen N. LaMott 144
SECRET INFORMATION CONCERNING BLACK AMERICAN TROOPS 147
MOBILIZING SUPPORT FOR THE WAR EFFORT 149
CONSCRIPTION, By H. J. Glintenkamp, 1917 150
SCHENCK V. UNITED STATES, 1919 152
THE LYNCHING OF ROBERT PRAGER AND THE ACQUITTAL OF HIS MURDERERS 153
    German Enemy of U. S. Hanged By Mob 153
    Jury Finds Prager Defendants Not Guilty and Others are Free 154
PETITION FROM THE WOMEN VOTERS ANTI-SUFFRAGE PARTY, 1917 156
THE NEGRO IN CHICAGO: A Study of Race Relations and a Race Riot, 1922 157
THE NEW MENACE, 1918 159
    Self Test 160
    Essays 161
    Optional Activities 162
    Web Site Listings 162

CHAPTER EIGHTEEN
THE ROARING TWENTIES 163
    Identification 164
    Think About 167
THE RISING TIDE OF COLOR AGAINST WHITE WORLD SUPREMACY 167
ADDRESS IN THE SENATE, By David I. Walsh, April 15, 1924 170
"THE KLAN'S FIGHT FOR AMERICANISM," By Hiram W. Evans, 1926 172
"BIG IDEAS FROM BIG BUSINESS," by Edward Earle Purinton, 1921 175
"IN HIS DISCREET WAY HE TOLD HER," Listerine Ad, 1923 177
"PETTING AND THE CAMPUS," Eleanor Rowland Wembridge, 1925 178
DEBATE ON BIRTH CONTROL, Margaret Sanger and Winter Russell, c. 1921 180
BABBITT, By Sinclair Lewis, 1922 183
THE NEGRO SPEAKS OF RIVERS, Langston Hughes, 1921 186
BLACK SEPARATISM AND THE BACK TO AFRICA MOVEMENT OF MARCUS GARVEY 187
    Marcus Garvey, Editorial, 1925 187
    Marcus Garvey, An Appeal to the Soul of White America: The Solution to the Problem of
    Competition Between Two Opposite Races: Negro Leader Appeals to the Conscience of
    White Race to Save His Own, 1923 187
    Self Test 189
    Essays 190
    Optional Activities 190
    Web Site Listings 191

CHAPTER NINETEEN
THE DEPRESSION 192
    Identification 193
    Think About 195
FRANKLIN D. ROOSEVELT'S FIRST INAUGURAL ADDRESS 195
FRANKLIN D. ROOSEVELT'S SECOND INAUGURAL ADDRESS 198
SHARE OUR WEALTH PLAN, By Huey Long 201
NATIONAL LABOR RELATIONS ACT 203
OKIES: TESTIMONY OF CAREY MCWILLIAMS IN CONGRESS 205
ROOSEVELT'S FIRESIDE CHAT, June 28, 1934 207
REPUBLICAN PARTY PLATFORM, ELECTION OF 1936 210
FOLK SONGS FROM THE GREAT DEPRESSION 214
    Every Man a King 214
    Some More Greenback Dollar 215
    Sunny Cal 215
    Three Crows 215
TWO MANUSCRIPTS FROM THE FEDERAL WRITERS PROJECT OF THE WPA 217
    Begging, by Anne Winn Stevens 217
    Afternoon in a Pushcart Peddlers' Colony, by Frank Byrd 219
THE TOWNSEND PLAN 222
CARTOONS THAT APPEARED IN THE TOWNSEND WEEKLY ON MAY 25, 1940 225
    Self Test 227
    Essays 228
    Optional Activities 228
    Web Site Listings 228

CHAPTER TWENTY
THE "GOOD" WAR: World War II 230
    Identification 231
    Think About 233
  ROOSEVELT'S NEW INTERNATIONALISM 233
    Roosevelt's "Four Freedoms" Speech, January 6, 1941 233
    The Atlantic Charter, August 14, 1941 234
  DAY OF INFAMY 236
    Address to Congress (1941) Franklin D. Roosevelt 236
  INTERNMENT OF JAPANESE AMERICANS 237
    Conditions in the Camps (1942-1945) 237
    Korematsu v. U.S.: The Majority Opinion 239
    Dissent by Justice Frank Murphy 239
  "A LOYAL NEGRO SOLDIER" 240
  SHIPYARD DIARY OF A WOMAN WELDER, 1944 243
  IWO JIMA, Edgar L. Jones, *Atlantic Monthly*, February 1945 245
  U.S. GOVERNMENT ACQUIESCENCE IN THE MURDER OF JEWS 246
  THE DEATH OF ROOSEVELT, April 12-13, 1945, Warm Springs, Georgia 248
  DROPPING THE ATOMIC BOMB 249
    Self Test 250
    Essays 252
    Optional Activities 252
    Web Site Listings 252

CHAPTER TWENTY-ONE
THE COLD WAR: The Truman-Eisenhower Years 253
    Identification 254
    Think About 256
  THE TRUMAN DOCTRINE 257
  HUAC VS. HOLLYWOOD 259
  ADDRESS ON KOREA, By Harry S Truman 263
  BROWN V. TOPEKA, BOARD OF EDUCATION 265
  PRESIDENT EISENHOWER ENFORCES THE *BROWN* DECISION
    IN LITTLE ROCK, 1957 266
  MEMORANDUM OF CONFERENCE WITH THE PRESIDENT 268
  FAREWELL ADDRESS, By President Dwight D. Eisenhower 270
    Self Test 272
    Essays 273
    Optional Activities 273
    Web Site Listings 273

CHAPTER TWENTY-TWO
HOPE TO DESPAIR: Kennedy-Johnson Years 275
    Identification 276
    Think About 278
  SENATOR J. WILLIAM FULLBRIGHT'S REMARKS ON THE CONCEPT OF TOTAL
    VICTORY 279
  CUBAN MISSILE CRISIS, By President John F. Kennedy 281
  THE UNITED STATES AND THE WAR IN VIETNAM 284

Television Interview with Walter Cronkite and President John F. Kennedy 285
U.S. Policy on Vietnam, White House Statement 285
OUR DUTY IN SOUTHEAST ASIA, By President Lyndon B. Johnson 286
AN INVITATION TO ACTION: President's Commission on the Status of Women 291
JONES V. ALFRED MAYER CO. 294
SOCIAL UNREST: The Kerner Commission Report on the Causes of Civil Disorders 295
Self Test 297
Essays 299
Optional Activities 299
Web Site Listings 299

CHAPTER TWENTY-THREE
THE SEVENTIES: The Crisis of Confidence 301
Identification 302
Think About 305
JOHN KERRY "STATEMENT" 305
"PEACE WITH HONOR," By President Richard M. Nixon 308
WHITE HOUSE CONVERSATIONS (1972-1973) 310
PRESIDENTIAL TELEVISION ADDRESS, By President Richard M. Nixon 313
WATERGATE SPECIAL PROSECUTION FORCE 316
GLORIA STEINEM ON CONSTITUTIONAL CHANGE, 1970 318
MK-ULTRA: The CIA and Radiation 320
Self Test 325
Essays 325
Optional Activities 327
Web Site Listings 327

CHAPTER TWENTY-FOUR
IN OUR TIMES: Reagan to Clinton 329
Identification 330
Think About 332
THE "SECOND AMERICAN REVOLUTION," By Ronald W. Reagan 333
THE PLIGHT OF THE HOMELESS 336
LIVING WITH AIDS, By Ryan White 340
ULTIMATUM TO SADDAM HUSSEIN, By George W. Bush 341
CAUSES OF THE L.A. RIOTS, By Maxine Waters 344
"DON'T ASK, DON'T TELL" 345
Policy Concerning Homosexuality in the Armed Forces 345
Pentagon Issues New Guidelines for Gays in Military 346
LET US STRENGTHEN OUR NATION FOR THE 21ST CENTURY, By Bill Clinton 347
Self Test 350
Essays 351
Optional Activities 351
Web Site Listings 352

Chapter Twelve

RECONSTRUCTION: The Turning Point That Never Turned

The Civil War was over. It ended both secession and slavery, but it did not settle the fate of the former slaves or that of the former Confederate states. What labor system would arise in the South to replace slavery? What rights and privileges would be given to the newly freed people? How could governments be reestablished in the South and who would control them?

Unfortunately Lincoln, the man best equipped to deal with these thorny issues, was assassinated. His mantle fell to Andrew Johnson, a southern Democratic Union supporter, a man ill-fitted to handle the give and take of political compromise. The new president and Congress rapidly moved further and further apart on how to reconstruct the South. Johnson supported the establishment of new state governments headed by former Confederate leaders who had been pardoned by the president. The intransigence of these governments was demonstrated by the passage of Black Codes that sought to severely limit the freed slaves. Congress reacted to this challenge by passing the Freedman's Bureau and Civil Rights Bills, both of which were vetoed by Johnson.

The congressional Joint Committee on Reconstruction developed its own reconstruction plan that was based upon acceptance of the Fourteenth Amendment guaranteeing citizenship rights to black Americans. At Johnson's urging, ten of the eleven ex-confederate states rejected the amendment. In the congressional elections of 1866 the president strenuously campaigned against the Republicans. His efforts were a disaster that led to the dominance of radical Republicans in Congress. In 1867, they passed a more demanding Reconstruction Act, dividing the ten recalcitrant states into five military districts. New state governments would be created guaranteeing black men the right to vote and ratifying the Fourteenth Amendment.

President Johnson continued to fight the radicals at every turn and attempted to sabotage their reconstruction efforts. Finally, he challenged Congress by removing Secretary of War Edwin Stanton, violating the Tenure of Office Act. He was impeached by the House, but the Senate narrowly failed to convict him. However, his power was destroyed, and he was followed in office by Republican Ulysses S. Grant, the former commander of the Union Army.

The radical governments in the South, set up by the Reconstruction Act, depended on a fragile alliance of northern "carpetbaggers," southern "scalawags," and the votes of the freedmen. These governments accomplished substantial social and political progress including universal manhood suffrage, the establishment of public school systems, institutions for the poor and handicapped, and the rebuilding of roads and railroads. Their image was tarnished, however, by widespread corruption, which also existed in the North and in the federal government. A more serious limitation was the widely held conviction of the limited role of government and the sanctity of private property. This meant that land would not be distributed to former slaves, limiting their possibilities for economic advancement. The South would have to rely on its own limited resources in dealing with postwar economic adaptations. The economic pattern that developed in the South was based upon sharecropping and one-crop agriculture. This not only obstructed black economic opportunity, it also assured the South's continuing poverty.

Despite the passage of the Fifteenth Amendment that seemed to guarantee the right of blacks to vote, the alliance supporting reconstruction began to disintegrate. Feminists, who had once been ardent supporters of rights for freed people, balked when women's suffrage was not included. The old Radicals, who were committed to racial equality, died out. Most Northerners, themselves firm believers in black inferiority, lost interest in the issue, particularly as economic depression took center stage. Southern Democratic "redeemers" regained control of one state after another utilizing racism, intimidation, and terror. They were aided by terrorist organizations like the Ku Klux Klan that frightened prospective Republican voters.

The disputed presidential election of 1876 undermined the few remaining radical governments in Louisiana, South Carolina, and Florida. Under the "Compromise of 1877," Southerners agreed to withdraw opposition to the election of the Republican, Rutherford B. Hayes, in return for the removal of federal troops from those last few states.

The nation entered an astonishing period of economic progress and vigor. Despite the proclamation of a "New South," the economic and social system of the South remained backward and mired in poverty. "Jim Crow" laws created a rigid system of segregation. The Supreme Court in the *Plessy v. Ferguson* case validated this system of segregation.

Reconstruction was unable to deliver in its promise of permanent change in race relations in America. Although the amendments and civil rights acts passed during this era became the basis for later struggles for equality, blacks remained second-class citizens for many years to come.

IDENTIFICATION: Briefly describe each term.

Andrew Johnson

Thirteenth Amendment

Radical Republicans

Thaddeus Stevens

Black Codes

Freedmen's Bureau

Joint Committee on Reconstruction

Fourteenth Amendment

Reconstruction Act of 1867

Secretary of War Edwin Stanton

Tenure of Office Act

Impeachment of President Johnson

"Waving the bloody shirt"

Ku Klux Klan

Fifteenth Amendment

Carpetbaggers

Scalawags

Sharecropping

Black churches

Credit Mobilier scandal

Whiskey Ring

Elizabeth Cady Stanton

Susan B. Anthony

Civil Rights Act of 1875

Charles Sumner

"redeemers"

Disputed Election of 1876

3

Compromise of 1877

"New South"

Booker T. Washington

Jim Crow

Plessy v. Ferguson

THINK ABOUT:

1. If Lincoln had not been assassinated, would the story of Reconstruction had been different? In what ways? How would the relations between Congress and the president have been affected? Would there have been a different process in reintegrating the South into the union and the former slaves into the South?

2.   If you could have been in charge of Reconstruction, what actions would you have taken? How would these have differed from what was actually done? What do you think the long-term results would have been for the future of America?

A LETTER "TO MY OLD MASTER," c. 1865

The newly freed slaves had struggled for their freedom. They aided the Union cause during the Civil War. At the war's end, they were overjoyed by their hard-won liberty. In this letter, Jourdon Anderson lets his former master know exactly how he really felt about being a slave and what he thinks about his new life.

TO MY OLD MASTER, COLONEL P.H. ANDERSON, BIG SPRING, TENNESSEE

Sir: I got your letter, and was glad to find that you had not forgotten Jourdon, and that you wanted me to come back and live with you again, promising to do better for me than anybody else can. I have often felt uneasy about you. I thought the Yankees would have hung you long before this, for harboring Rebs they found at your house. I suppose they never heard about your going to Colonel Martin's to kill the Union soldier that was left by his company in their stable. Although you shot at me twice before I left you, I did not want to hear of your being hurt, and am glad you are still living. It would do me good to go back to the dear old home again, and see Miss Mary and Miss Martha and Allen, Esther, Green, and Lee. Give my love to them all, and tell them I hope we will meet in the better world, if not in this. I would have gone back to see you all when I was working in the Nashville Hospital, but one of the neighbors told me that Henry intended to shoot me if he ever got a chance.

I want to know particularly what the good chance is you propose to give me. I am doing tolerably well here. I get twenty-five dollars a month, with victuals and clothing; have a comfortable home for Mandy—the folks call her Mrs. Anderson—and the children—Milly, Jane, and Grundy—go to school and are learning well. The teacher says Grundy has a head for a preacher. They go to Sunday school, and Mandy and me attend church regularly. We are kindly treated. Sometimes we overhear others saying, "Them colored people were slaves" down in Tennessee. The children feel hurt when they hear such remarks; but I tell them it was no disgrace in Tennessee to belong to Colonel Anderson. Many darkeys would have been proud, as I used to be, to call you master. Now if you will write and say what wages you will give me, I will be better able to decide whether it would be to my advantage to move back again.

As to my freedom, which you say I can have, there is nothing to be gained on that score, as I got my free papers in 1864 from the Provost-Marshal General of the Department of Nashville. Mandy says she would be afraid to go back without some proof that you were disposed to treat us justly and kindly; and we have concluded to test your sincerity by asking you to send us our wages for the time we served you. This will make us forget and forgive old scores, and rely on your justice and friendship in the future. I served you faithfully for thirty-two years, and Mandy twenty years. At twenty-five dollars a month for me, and two dollars a week for Mandy, our earnings would amount to eleven thousand six hundred and eighty dollars. Add to this the interest for the time our wages have been kept back, and deduct what you paid for our clothing, and three doctor's visits to me, and pulling a tooth for Mandy, and the balance will show what we are in justice entitled to. Please send the money by Adam's Express, in care of V. Winters, Esq., Dayton, Ohio. If you fail to pay us for faithful labors in the past, we can have little faith in your promises in the future. We trust the good Maker has opened your eyes to the wrongs which you and your fathers have done to me and my fathers, in making us toil for you for generations without recompense. Here I draw my wages every Saturday night; but in Tennessee there was never any pay-day for the Negroes any more than for the horses and cows. Surely there will be a day of reckoning for those who defraud the laborer of his hire.

In answering this letter, please state if there would be any safety for my Milly and Jane, who are now grown up, and both good-looking girls. You know how it was with poor Matilda and Catherine. I would rather stay here and starve—and die, if it come to that—than have my girls brought to shame by the violence and wickedness of their young masters. You will also please state if there has been any schools opened for the colored children in your neighborhood. The great desire of my life now is to give my children an education, and have them form virtuous habits.

Say howdy to George Carter, and thank him for taking the pistol from you when you were shooting at me.

FROM YOUR OLD SERVANT,
JOURDON ANDERSON

HOW WELL DID YOU UNDERSTAND THIS SELECTION?

1. What point do you think Jourdon Anderson was trying to make to his old master?

2. Do you think he ever intended to go back? Why or why not?

3. What does this letter tell you about freed people and their aspirations?

At the end of the war, in 1865 and 1866, southern state legislatures passed a series of "Black Codes," supposedly to codify legal rights for newly freed blacks. In reality, most of the codes denied blacks many basic rights. Many Northerners believed that the provisions of the codes foreshadowed an attempt to reinstitute plantation slavery.

The Black Code of
St. Landry's Parish, 1865

Whereas it was formerly made the duty of the police jury to make suitable regulations for the police of slaves within the limits of the parish; and whereas slaves have become emancipated by the action of the ruling powers; and whereas it is necessary for public order, as well as for the comfort and correct deportment of said freedmen, that suitable regulations should be established by their government in their changed condition, the following ordinances are adopted, with the approval of the United States military authorities commanding in said parish, viz:

SECTION *1. Be it ordained by the police jury of the parish of St. Landry,* That no negro shall be allowed to pass within the limits of said parish without a special permit in writing from his employer. Whoever shall violate this provision shall pay a fine of two dollars and fifty cents, or in default thereof shall be forced to work four days on the public road, or suffer corporeal punishment as provided hereinafter.

SECTION *2. Be it further ordained,* That every negro who shall be found absent from the residence of his employer after 10 o'clock at night, without a written permit from his employer, shall pay a fine of five dollars, or in default thereof, shall be compelled to work five days on the public road, or suffer corporeal punishment as hereinafter provided.

SECTION *3. Be it further ordained,* That no negro shall be permitted to rent or keep a house within said parish. Any negro violating this provision shall be immediately ejected and compelled to find an employer; and any person who shall rent, or give the use of any house to any negro, in violation of this section, shall pay a fine of five dollars for each offence.

SECTION *4. Be it further ordained,* That every negro is required to be in the regular service of some white person, or former owner, who shall be held responsible for the conduct of said negro. But said employer or former owner may permit said negro to hire his own time by special permission in writing, which permission shall not extend over seven days at any one time. Any negro violating the provisions of this section shall be fined five dollars for each offence, or in default of the payment thereof shall be forced to work five days on the public road, or suffer corporeal punishment as hereinafter provided.

SECTION *5. Be it further ordained,* That no public meetings or congregations of negroes shall be allowed within said parish after sunset; but such public meetings and congregations may be held between the hours of sunrise and sunset, by the special permission of writing of the captain of patrol, within whose beat such meetings shall take place. This prohibition, however, is not intended to prevent negroes from attending the usual church services, conducted by white ministers and priests. Every negro violating the provisions of this section shall pay a fine of five dollars, or in default thereof shall be compelled to work five days on the public road, or suffer corporeal punishment as hereinafter provided.

SECTION *6. Be it further ordained,* That no negro shall be permitted to preach, exhort, or otherwise declaim to congregations of colored people, without a special permission in writing from the president of the police jury. Any negro violating the provisions of this section shall pay a fine of ten dollars, or in default thereof shall be forced to work ten days on the public road, or suffer corporeal punishment as hereinafter provided.

SECTION *7. Be it further ordained,* That no negro who is not in the military service shall be allowed to carry fire-arms, or any kind of weapons, within the parish, without the special written permission of his employers, approved and indorsed by the nearest or most convenient chief of patrol. Any one violating the provisions of this section shall forfeit his weapons and pay a fine of five dollars, or in default of the payment of said fine, shall be forced to work five days on the public road, or suffer corporeal punishment as hereinafter provided.

SECTION 8. *Be it further ordained,* That no negro shall sell, barter, or exchange any articles of merchandise or traffic within said parish without the special written permission of his employer, specifying the articles of sale, barter or traffic. Any one thus offending shall pay a fine of one dollar for each offence, and suffer the forfeiture of said articles' or in default of the payment of said fine shall work one day on the public road, or suffer corporeal punishment as hereinafter provided.

SECTION 9. *Be it further ordained,* That any negro found drunk within the said parish shall pay a fine of five dollars, or in default thereof shall work five days on the public road, or suffer corporeal punishment as hereinafter provided.

SECTION 10. *Be it further ordained,* That all the foregoing provisions shall apply to negroes of both sexes.

SECTION 11. *Be it further ordained,* That it shall be the duty of every citizen to act as a police officer for the detection of offences and the apprehension of offenders, who shall be immediately handed over to the proper captain or chief of patrol.

SECTION 12. *Be it further ordained,* That the aforesaid penalties shall be summarily enforced, and that it shall be the duty of the captains and chiefs of patrol to see that the aforesaid ordinances are promptly executed.

SECTION 13. *Be it further ordained,* That all sums collected from the aforesaid fines shall be immediately handed over to the parish treasurer.

SECTION 14. *Be it further ordained,* That the corporeal punishment provided for in the foregoing sections shall consist in confining the body of the offender within a barrel placed over his or her shoulders, in the manner practiced in the army, such confinement not to continue longer than twelve hours, and for such time within the aforesaid limit as shall be fixed by the captain or chief of patrol who inflicts the penalty.

HOW WELL DID YOU UNDERSTAND THIS SELECTION?

1. What do you think was the real purpose of this Black Code?

2. Which provisions would be most troubling to freedmen? To northern public opinion?

It was clear to some Radical Republicans that the only way freed people could expect to achieve real independence was if they could have their own land to farm. This land would have to be taken from plantation owners and Confederate leaders. Most Americans believed that such a policy was contrary to deeply-held ideas about economic rights. Radical Republican congressman, Thaddeus Stevens argued in favor of confiscation and redistribution of southern land. The New York **Times** *opposed such redistribution, while the former slaves expressed their deep desire to own their own land.*

From a speech by THADDEUS STEVENS, 1865
Published in the Congressional Record

We especially insist that the property of the chief rebels should be seized and appropriated to the payment of the national debt, caused by the unjust and wicked war they instigated [started] .... There are about 6,000,000 of freedmen in the South. The number of acres of land is 465,000,000. Of this those who own above 200 acres each number about 70,000 persons, holding in the aggregate—together with the states—about 394,000,000 acres. By forfeiting the estates of the leading rebels the government would have 394,000,000 of acres besides their town property, and yet nine-tenths of the people would remain untouched. Divide the land into convenient farms. Give, if you please, forty acres to each adult male freedman. Suppose there are 1,000,000 of them. That would require 40,000,000 acres, which deducted from 394,000,000 leaves 354,000,000 acres for sale. Divide it into suitable farms, and sell it to the highest bidders. I think it, including town property, would average at least $10 per acre. That would produce $3,540,000.

The whole fabric of southern society must be changed and never can it be done if this opportunity is lost. Without this, this government can never be, as it has never been, a true republic.... How can republican institutions, free schools, free churches, free social intercourse exist in a mingled community of nabobs [men of wealth and high position] and serfs [tillers of the land]? If the South is ever made a safe republic let her lands be cultivated by the toil of .. free labor....

Nothing is so likely to make a man a good citizen as to make him a freeholder. Nothing will so multiply the production of the South as to divide it into small farms. Nothing will make men so industrious and moral as to let them feel that they are above want and are the owners of the soil which they till.... No people will ever be republican in spirit and practice where a few own immense manors and the masses are landless. Small and independent land-holders are the support and guardians of republican liberty.

NEW YORK TIMES, July 9, 1867:

[Land confiscation] is a question not of humanity, not of loyalty, but of fundamental relation of industry to capital; and sooner or later, if begun at the South, it will find its way into the cities of the North.... An attempt to justify the confiscation of Southern land under the pretense of doing justice to the freedmen, strikes at the root of property rights in both sections. It concerns Massachusetts as much as Mississippi.

A Conversation between a Freedman and a General at Fort Smith Arkansas
Reported by the JOINT CONGRESSIONAL COMMITTEE ON RECONSTRUCTION, 1867:

FREEDMAN: Sir, I want you to help me in a personal matter.
GENERAL: Where is your family?
FREEDMAN: On the Red River.

GENERAL: Have you not everything you want?

FREEDMAN: No sir.

GENERAL: You are free!

FREEDMAN: Yes sir, you set me free, but you left me there.

GENERAL: What do you want?

FREEDMAN: I want some land; I am helpless; you do nothing for me but give me freedom.

GENERAL: Is not that enough?

FREEDMAN: It is enough for the present; but I cannot help myself unless I get some land; then I can take care of myself and my family; otherwise I cannot do it.

HOW WELL DID YOU UNDERSTAND THIS SELECTION?

1. What was Thaddeus Steven's plan? To whom do you think the plan would appeal?

2. What are the grounds for his argument that his plan would strengthen democracy and agricultural production? Do you agree?

3. What is the basis for the *New York Times'* opposition to confiscation and redistribution of southern lands? Who would find its argument convincing? Why?

4. How does the freedman look at this issue?

Most Americans believed in a close connection between education and democracy. Under slavery laws, masters had been prohibited from teaching reading and writing to slaves. Now that they were free, blacks thirsted for the knowledge that had once been denied to them.

Dedicated Teachers,
Determined Students, 1869

RALEIGH, N.C., FEB 22, 1869

It is surprising to me to see the amount of suffering which many of the people endure for the sake of sending their children to school. Men get very low wages here—from $2.50 to $8 per month usually, while a first-rate hand may get $10, and a peck or two of meal per week for rations—and a great many men cannot get work at all. The women take in sewing and washing, go out by day to scour, etc. There is one woman who supports three children and keeps them at school; she says, "I don't care how hard I has to work, if I can only send Sallie and the boys to school looking respectable." Many of the girls have but one decent dress; it gets washed and ironed on Saturday, and then is worn until the next Saturday, provided they do not tear it or fall in the mud; when such an accident happens there is an absent mark on the register.... One may go into their cabins on cold, windy days, and see daylight between every two boards, or feel the rain dropping through the roof; but a word of complaint is rarely heard. They are anxious to have the children "get on" in their books, and do not seem to feel impatient if they lack comforts themselves. A pile of books is seen in almost every cabin, though there be no furniture except a poor bed, a table and two or three broken chairs.

>   MISS M. A. PARKER
>   In *American Freedman, April 1869*

SYDNEY ANDREWS quoted in the Joint Report
on Reconstruction, 39th (U.S.) Congress, 1st Session, 1866:

Many of the negroes ... common plantation negroes, and day laborers in the towns and villages, were supporting little schools themselves. Everywhere I found among them a disposition to get their children into schools, if possible. I had occasion very frequently to notice that porters in stores and laboring men in warehouses, and cart drivers on the streets, had spelling books with them, and were studying them during the time they were not occupied with their work. Go into the outskirts of any large town and walk among the negro inhabitants, and you will see children and in many instances grown negroes, sitting in the sun alongside their cabins studying.

CAPTAIN C. M. HAMILTON in a letter to the Office
of the Adjutant General in Washington, D.C., 1866:

The night school has been frequently disturbed. One evening a mob called out of the school house, the teacher, who upon presenting himself was confronted with four revolvers, and menacing expressions of shooting him, if he did not promise to quit the place, and close the school. The freedmen promptly came to his aid and the mob dispersed.

About the 18th or 19th of the month, I was absent ... when a formidable disturbance took place at the school. The same mob threatened to destroy the school that night, and the freedmen, learning this, assembled... at their place of instruction in a condition of self-defense.

I understand that not less than forty colored men armed to protect themselves, but the preparation becoming known to the *respectable, rowdies,* they only maneuvered about in small squads, and were wise enough to avoid a collision.

HOW WELL DID YOU UNDERSTAND THIS SELECTION?

1. What evidence do the documents in this section show about the significance of education for freed people?

2. What barriers did these blacks have to overcome to get some education?

3. What is meant by "respectable rowdies"? Why would they assault a school?

THE SPLIT BETWEEN ADVOCATES OF WOMEN'S RIGHTS AND BLACK RIGHTS

The close alliance between women reformers and abolitionists was seriously tested by the dispute over universal suffrage. The women expected to see the right to vote extended to women, as well as blacks. Many advocates of rights for the freed people, however, argued that it was "the Negro's hour, not the woman's."

A petition drafted after the Civil War by ELIZABETH CADY STANTON and SUSAN B. ANTHONY, leaders of the women's movement and also abolitionists:

To the Senate and House of Representatives in Congress Assembled:
The undersigned citizens of the State of _____ earnestly but respectfully request that in any change or amendment of the Constitution you may propose to extend or regulate Suffrage, there shall be no distinction made between men and women.

Letter to Susan B. Anthony from abolitionist and advocate of suffrage for ex-slaves GERRITT SMITH, December 30, 1868

My Dear Susan B. Anthony: I this evening received your earnest letter. It pains me to be obliged to disappoint you. But I cannot sign the petition you sent me. Cheerfully, gladly can I sign a petition for the enfranchisement [granting the right to vote] of women. But I cannot sign a paper against the enfranchisement of the Negro man, unless at the same time woman shall be enfranchised. The removal of the political disabilities of race is my first desire, of sex my second. If put on the same level and urged in the same connection, neither will be soon accomplished. The former will very soon be, if untrammeled by the other, and its success will prepare the way for the other.

A Response by Elizabeth Cady Stanton

[Gerritt Smith] does not clearly read the sign of the times, or he would see that there is to be no reconstruction of this nation, except on the basis of Universal Suffrage, as the natural, inalienable right of every citizen to its exercise....

As the aristocracy of this country is the "male sex" and as Mr. Smith belongs to the privileged order, he naturally considers it important, for the best interests of the nation, that every type and shade of degraded, ignorant manhood should be enfranchised, before even the higher classes of womanhood should be admitted to the polls.

This does not surprise us. Men always judge more wisely of objective wrongs and oppressions, than of those in which they themselves are involved. Tyranny on a southern plantation is far more easily seen by white men... [in] the north than the wrongs of the women of their own households....

Again, Mr. Smith refuses to sign the petition because he thinks that to press the broader question of "Universal Suffrage" would defeat the partial one of "Manhood Suffrage"; in other words to demand protection for women against her oppressors would jeopardize the black man's chances for securing protection against his oppressors. If it is a question of precedence merely, on what principle of justice or courtesy should woman yield her right of enfranchisement to the Negro? If men cannot be trusted to legislate for their own sex, how can they legislate for the opposite sex, of whose wants and needs they know nothing! It has always been considered good philosophy in pressing any measure to claim the uttermost in order to get something .... Henry Ward Beecher advised abolitionists, right after the war, to demand "Universal Suffrage" if they wished to secure the ballot for the new made freedmen. "Bait your hooks," said he, "with a woman and perhaps you will catch a Negro." But their intense interest in the Negro blinded them, and they forsook principle for policy. In giving woman the cold shoulder they raised a more deadly opposition to the Negro than any we had encountered, creating an antagonism between him and the very element most needed, especially in the South, to be propitiated in his behalf...

... There is no other ground on which to debate the question. Every argument for the Negro is an argument for woman and no logician can escape it....

Although those who demand "Women's Suffrage" on principle are few, those who would oppose "Negro suffrage" from prejudice are many, hence the only way to secure the latter is to end all this talk of class legislation, bury the Negro in the citizen, and claim suffrage for all men and women as a natural, inalienable right.
- ELIZABETH CADY STANTON, January 14, 1869

"Being Persons, Then, Women are Citizens"

Though the words persons, people, inhabitants, electors, citizens, are all used indiscriminately in the national and State constitutions, there was always a conflict of opinion, prior to the war, as to whether they were synonymous terms, but whatever room there was for doubts, under the old regime, the adoption of the Fourteenth Amendment settled that question forever in its first sentence:

All persons born or naturalized in the United States, and subject to the jurisdiction thereof, are citizens of the United States wherein they reside.

The second settles the equal status of all citizens:

No state shall make or enforce any law which shall abridge the privileges or immunities of citizens of the United States; nor shall any State deprive any person of life, liberty, or property without due process of law; nor deny to any person within its jurisdiction the equal protection of the laws.

The only question left to be settled now is: Are women persons? I scarcely believe that any of our opponents will have the hardihood to say that they are not. Being persons, then, women are citizens and no State has a right to make any new law, or to enforce any old law, which shall abridge their privileges and immunities. Hence, every discrimination against women in the constitutions and laws of the several States is today null and void, precisely as is every one against Negroes.
- SUSAN B. ANTHONY, November 1872

HOW WELL DID YOU UNDERSTAND THIS SELECTION?

1. Why wouldn't Gerritt Smith sign the petition? Why did he want to separate the issues of women and blacks getting the vote?

2. How does Elizabeth Cady Stanton respond to his argument? What aspect of her response do you find most troubling?

3. What is the basis of Susan B. Anthony's claim that the Fourteenth Amendment also guaranteed women's rights?

4. Why did the women's movement split with their former abolitionist allies?

DIFFERING VIEWS ABOUT BLACKS IN RECONSTRUCTION IN THE SOUTH

Most white Southerners saw the Reconstruction era as a time period in which blacks, drunk with new-found power, lorded it over the oppressed white population. The reality, of course, was far different. Blacks never had real power in any state and were very moderate in their demands and votes. Albion Tourgee was a Northerner who served as a judge in the South, propelled by idealism. He was eventually disillusioned by the level of resistance to rights for freed people he found among southern whites. Thomas Dixon's bestselling novel, **The Clansman,** *reflected the attitudes of southern whites. (It later became the basis for the popular movie,* **Birth of a Nation,** *which was instrumental in disseminating negative images of black-actions in Reconstruction.) The final document in this segment relates the experiences of a black man who gained some measure of authority during Reconstruction.*

From the Novel, *A Fool's Errand*
By the "carpetbagger," Albion Tourgee (1879)

When the second Christmas come, Metta wrote again to her sister:

"The feeling is terribly bitter against Comfort on account of his course towards the colored people. There is quite a village of them on the lower end of the plantation. They have a church, a sabbath school, and are to have next year a school. You can not imagine how kind they have been to us, and how much they are attached to Comfort.... I got Comfort to go with me to one of their prayer meetings a few nights ago. I had heard a great deal about them, but had never attended one before. It was strangely weird. There were, perhaps, fifty present, mostly middle-aged men and women. They were singing in a soft, low monotone, interspersed with prolonged exclamatory notes, a sort of rude hymn, which I was surprised to know was one of their old songs in slave times. How the chorus came to be endured in those days I can not imagine. It was—

'Free! free! free, my Lord, free!
An' we walks de hebben-ly way!'

"A few looked around as we came in and seated ourselves; and Uncle Jerry, the saint of the settlement, came forward on his staves, and said, in his soft voice, "'Ev'nin', Kunnel! Sarvant, Missus! Will you walk up, an' hev seats in front?'

'We told him we had just looked in, and might go in a short time; so we would stay in the back part of the audience.

"Uncle Jerry can not read nor write; but he is a man of strange intelligence and power. Unable to do work of any account, he is the faithful friend, monitor, and director of others. He has a house and piece of land, all paid for, a good horse and cow, and, with the aid of his wife and two boys, made a fine crop this season. He is one of the most promising colored men in the settlement: so Comfort says, at least. Everybody seems to have great respect for his character. I don't know how many people I have heard speak of his religion. Mr. Savage used to say he had rather hear him pray than any other man on earth. He was much prized by his master, even after he was disabled, on account of his faithfulness and character."

From the Novel, *The Clansman*
By Thomas Dixon Jr. (1905)

At noon Ben and Phil strolled to the polling-place to watch the progress of the first election under Negro rule. The Square was jammed with shouting, jostling, perspiring negroes, men, women, and children. The day was worm, and the African odour was supreme even in the open air....

The negroes, under the drill of the League and the Freedman's Bureau, protected by the bayonet, were voting to enfranchise themselves, disfranchise their former masters, ratify a new constitution, and elect a legislature to do their will. Old Aleck was a candidate for the House, chief poll-holder, and seemed to be in charge of the movements of the voters outside the booth as well as inside. He appeared to be omnipresent, and his self-importance was a sight Phil had never dreamed. He could not keep his eyes off him....

[Aleck] was a born African orator, undoubtedly descended from a long line of savage spell-binders, whose eloquence in the palaver houses of the jungle had made them native leaders. His thin spindle-shanks supported an oblong, protruding stomach, resembling an elderly monkey's, which seemed so heavy it swayed his back to carry it.

The animal vivacity of his small eyes and the flexibility of his eye-brows, which he worked up and down rapidly with every change of countenance, expressed his eager desires.

He had laid aside his new shoes, which hurt him, and went barefooted to facilitate his movements on the great occasion. His heels projected and his foot was so flat that what should have been the hollow of it made a hole in the dirt where he left his track.

He was already mellow with liquor, and was dressed in an old army uniform and cap, with two horse-pistols buckled around his waist. On a strap hanging from his shoulder were strung a half-dozen tin canteens filled with whiskey.

From—*The Autobiography of JOHN ROY LYNCH*,
an ex-slave appointed justice-of-the peace in Natchez, Mississippi at age 22
(he later was elected a three-term congressman)

[A] case of some significance that came before me was that of a white man that I knew unfavorably and well. He had cursed, abused, and threatened the life of an inoffensive old colored man on account of a misunderstanding over a small business transaction. Upon the complaint of the colored man, a warrant was issued for the arrest of the party against whom the complaint was made. When he was brought before the court and the charges had been read to him and he was asked whether or not he was guilty as charged, he seemed to be somewhat surprised. "Why," he remarked, "do you mean to tell me that it is a crime for a white man to curse a nigger?" "Yes," the court replied. "It is a crime for a white man to curse a Negro as it is for a Negro to curse a white man." "Well," he exclaimed, "that's news to me. You certainly must be mistaken. If there is such a law, I never heard of it." The court then handed him the code and told him where he could find the section bearing upon the point at issue and requested him to read it for himself, which he did.

When he had finished, he exclaimed in a somewhat subdued tone: "Well, I'll be damned." The court then admonished him that if that remark should be repeated, he would be committed to the county jail for contempt of court. He quickly apologized and assured the court that no disrespect was intended. He said that he could not deny having used the language set forth in the affidavit, but he hoped the court would not be severe because he did not know and did not believe that in using that language he was violating any law. Since it was his first offense, he was let off with a fine of five dollars and costs which he promptly paid. It was the first and only time he was brought before me.

HOW WELL DID YOU UNDERSTAND THIS SELECTION?

1. What are the differences in the ways Tourgee and Dixon (in selections A and B) see freed people and their conduct? Why do you think there are such great differences in their points of view?

2. Whose description do feel is most accurate? Why?

3. Why do you think John Lynch considers his case to be "of some significance"? Do you agree or disagree?

4. What does his experience tell you about changes in the South during the era of Reconstruction?

Eventually, Americans grew weary with the struggle to maintain the rights of black people. The Civil Rights Act of 1875 was the last attempt to guarantee such rights. Northern white commitment faded as other issues, such as economic depression and political scandals, drew their attention. Southern white violence, directed at white and black Republicans and any blacks asserting their rights, was carried out by groups such as the Ku Klux Klan. Democratic opponents of Reconstruction returned to political control of the South.

**An excerpt from the speech of black Congressman Richard Harvey Cain of South Carolina
on the floor of the House in support of the Civil Rights Act of 1875.**

All we ask is that you, the legislators of this nation, shall pass a law so strong and so powerful that no one shall be able to elude it and destroy our rights under the Constitution and laws of our country. That is all we ask....

We do not want any discriminations to be made. If discriminations arc made in regard to schools, then there will be accomplished just what we are fighting against. If you say that the schools in the State of Georgia, for instance, shall be allowed to discriminate against colored people, then you will have discriminations made against us. We do not want any discriminations. I do not ask any legislation for the colored people of this country that is not applied to the white people. All that we ask is equal laws, equal legislation, and equal rights throughout the length and the breadth of this land.

[Another congressman] says that the colored men should not come here begging at the doors of Congress for their rights. I agree with him. I want to say that we do not come here begging for our rights. We come here clothed in the garb of American citizenship. We come demanding our rights in the name of justice. We come, with no arrogance on our part, asking that this great nation, which laid the foundations of civilization and progress more deeply and more securely than any other nation on the face of the earth, guarantee us protection from outrage. We come here, five millions of people—more than composed this entire nation when it had its great tea-party in Boston Harbor, and demanded its rights at the point of a bayonet—asking that unjust discriminations against us be forbidden. We come here in the name of justice, equity, and law, in the name of our children, in the name of our country, petitioning for our rights.

Source: Congressional Record, 43rd Cong., 1st session, Vol. II, pg. 1

**Political Terrorism by the Ku Klux Klan
Testimony by Harriet Hernandez**

The following account by Harriet Hernandez, a former slave of Spartanburg, South Carolina, describes how the Klan used threats and violence to intimidate black Republican voters in the region. It is excerpted from her testimony in December 1871 before a congressional committee appointed to investigate Klan activities.

Question: Did the Ku-Klux ever come to your house at any time?
Answer: Yes, Sir; twice.
Q.: Go on to the second time....
A.: They came in; I was lying in bed. Says he, "Come out here, Sir; Come out here, Sir!" They took me out of bed; they would not let me get out, but they took me up in their arms and toted me out—me and my daughter Lucy. He struck me on the forehead with a pistol, and here is the scar above my eye now. Says he, "Damn you, fall!" I fell. Says

he, "Damn you, get up!" I got up. Says he, "Damn you, get over this fence!" And he kicked me over when I went to get over; and then he went to a brush pile, and they laid us right down there, both together. They laid us down twenty yards apart, I reckon. They had dragged and beat us along. They struck me right on the top of my head, and I thought they had killed me; and I said, "Lord o' mercy, don't, don't kill my child!" He gave me a lick on the head, and it liked to have killed me; I saw stars. He threw my arm over my head so I could not do anything with it for three weeks, and there are great knots on my wrist now.

Q: What did they say this was for?

A: They said, "You can tell your husband that when we see him we are going to kill him."

Q: Did they say why they wanted to kill him?

A: They said, "He voted the radical ticket, didn't he?" I said, "Yes, that very way."

Q: When did your husband get back after this whipping? He was not at home, was he?

A: He was lying out; he couldn't stay at home, bless your soul

Q: Has he been afraid for any length of time?

A: He has been afraid ever since last October. He has been lying out. He has not laid in the house ten nights since October.

Q: Is that the situation of the colored people down there to any extent?

A: That is the way they all have to do—men and women both.

Q: What are they afraid of?

A: Of being killed or whipped to death.

Q: What has made them afraid?

A: Because men that voted radical tickets they took the spite out on the women when they could get at them.

Q: How many colored people have been whipped in that neighborhood?

A: It is all of them, mighty near.

Source: Report of the Joint Select Committee to Inquire into the Condition of Affairs in the Late Insurrectionary States (1872)

Excerpts from the original draft of the South Carolina 1876 Democratic party campaign plan formulated by ex-Confederate general MARTIN W. GARY

[It is decreed] That the Democratic Military Clubs are to be armed with rifles and pistols and such other arms as they may command. They are to be divided into two companies, one of the old men, the other of the young; an experienced captain or commander to be placed over each of them. That each company is to have a first and second lieutenant. That the number of ten privates is to be the unit of organization. That each captain is to see that his men are well armed and provided with at least thirty rounds of ammunition. That the Captain of the young men is to provide a Baggage wagon in which three days rations for the horses and three days rations for the men are to be stored on the day before the election in order that they may be prepared at a moment's notice to move to any point in the County when ordered by the Chairman of the Executive Committee....

Every Democrat must feel honor bound to control the vote of at least one Negro, by intimidation, purchase, keeping him away or as each individual may determine, how he may best accomplish it....

Never threaten a man individually. If he deserves to be threatened, the necessities of the times require that he should die. A dead Radical is very harmless—a threatened Radical or one driven off by threats from the scene of his operations is often very troublesome, sometimes dangerous, always vindictive [vengeful]....In the month of September, we ought to begin to organize Negro [Democratic] clubs, or pretend that we have organized them.... Those who join are to be taken on probation and are not to be taken into full fellowship until they have proven their sincerity by voting our ticket.

HOW WELL DID YOU UNDERSTAND THIS SELECTION?

1. What is the basis for Congressman Cain's pleas for the passage of the Civil Rights Act of 1875?

2. What was the purpose of Klan threats and violence as shown by Harriet Hernandez's testimony? What do you think would be the result of such tactics?

3. What were the key elements of South Carolina Democratic Party's 1876 election plan? In what way did it intend to "control the vote" of freedmen? Why do you think the plan included an organization of "Negro Democratic" clubs?

AFTER RECONSTRUCTION

Frederick Douglass had great hopes that his fellow blacks would gain full rights as American citizens after the Civil War. He had helped the Republican Party to win black votes and was rewarded by various government appointments. It soon became clear, however, that the hard-won gains of the Reconstruction era were rapidly being lost. In this keynote address to a convention of blacks, Douglass describes the discrimination faced by his people and hopes for its eventual elimination.

Address to the Louisville Convention (1883)
FREDERICK DOUGLASS

Born on American soil in common with yourselves, deriving our bodies and our minds from its dust, centuries having passed away since our ancestors were torn from the shores of Africa, we, like yourselves, hold ourselves to be in every sense Americans, and that we may, therefore, venture to speak to you in a tone not lower than that which becomes earnest men and American citizens. Having watered your soil with our tears, enriched it with our blood, performed its roughest labor in time of peace, defended it against war, and at all times been loyal and true to its best interests, we deem it no arrogance or presumption to manifest now a common concern with you for its welfare, prosperity, honor and glory ...

18

It is our lot to live among a people whose laws, traditions, and prejudices have been against us for centuries, and from these they are not yet free. To assume that they are free from these evils simply because they have changed their laws is to assume what is utterly unreasonable and contrary to facts. Large bodies move slowly. Individuals may be converted on the instant and change their whole course of life. Nations never. Time and events are required for the conversion of nations. Not even the character of a great political organization can be changed by a new platform. It will be the same old snake though in a new skin. Though we have had war, reconstruction and abolition as a nation, we still linger in the shadow and blight of an extinct institution. Though the colored man is no longer subject to be bought and sold, he is still surrounded by an adverse sentiment which fetters all his movements. In his downward course he meets with no resistance, but his course upward is resented and resisted at every step of his progress. If he comes in ignorance, rags, and wretchedness, he conforms to the popular belief of his character, and in that character he is welcome. But if he shall come as a gentleman, a scholar, and a statesman, he is hailed as a contradiction to the national faith concerning his race, and his coming is resented as impudence. In the one case he may provoke contempt and derision, but in the other he is an affront to pride, and provokes malice. Let him do what he will, there is at present, therefore, no escape for him. The color line meets him everywhere, and in a measure shuts him out from all respectable and profitable trades and callings. In spite of all your religion and laws he is a rejected man.

He is rejected by trade unions, of every trade, and refused work while he lives, and burial when he dies, and yet he is asked to forget his color, and forget that which everybody else remembers. If he offers himself to a builder as a mechanic, to a client as a lawyer, to a patient as a physician, to a college as a professor, to a firm as a clerk, to a Government Department as an agent, or an officer, he is sternly met on the color line, and his claim to consideration in some way is disputed on the ground of color.

Not even our churches, whose members profess to follow the despised Nazarene, whose home, when on earth, was among the lowly and despised, have yet conquered this feeling of color madness, and what is true of our churches is also true of our courts of law. Neither is free from this all pervading atmosphere of color hate. The one describes the Deity as impartial, no respecter of persons, and the other the Goddess of Justice as blindfolded, with sword by her side and scales in her hand held evenly between high and low, rich and low, white and black, but both are the images of American imagination, rather than American practices.

Taking advantage of the general disposition in this country to impute crime to color, white men color their faces to commit crime and wash off the hated color to escape punishment. In many places where the commission of crime is alleged against one of our color, the ordinary processes of law are set aside as too slow for the impetuous justice of the infuriated populace. They take the law into their own bloody hands and proceed to whip, stab, shoot, hang, or burn the alleged culprit, without the intervention of courts, counsel, judges, juries, or witnesses. In such cases it is not the business of the accusers to prove guilt, but it is for the accused to prove his innocence, a thing hard for him to do in these infernal Lynch courts. A man accused, surprised, frightened, and captured by a motley crowd, dragged with a rope about his neck in midnight-darkness to the nearest tree, and told in the coarsest terms of profanity to prepare for death, would be more than human if he did not, in his terror-stricken appearance, more confirm suspicion of guilt than the contrary. Worse still, in the presence of such hell-black outrages, the pulpit is usually dumb, and the press in the neighborhood is silent or openly takes side with the mob. There are occasional cases in which white men are lynched, but one sparrow does not make a summer. Every one knows that what is called Lynch law is peculiarly the law for colored people and for nobody else. If there were no other grievance than this horrible and barbarous Lynch law custom, we should be justified in assembling, as we have now done, to expose and denounce it. But this is not all. Even now, after twenty years of so-called emancipation, we are subject to lawless raids of midnight riders, who, with blackened faces, invade our homes and perpetrate the foulest of crimes upon us and our families. This condition of things is too flagrant and notorious to require specifications or proof. Thus in all the relations of life and death we are met by the color line.

While we recognize the color line as a hurtful force, a mountain barrier to our progress, wounding our bleeding feet with its flinty rocks at every step, we do not despair. We are a hopeful people. This convention is a proof of our faith in you, in reason, in truth and justice our belief that prejudice, with all its malign accomplishments, may yet be removed by peaceful means; that, assisted by time and events and the growing enlightenment of both races, the color line will ultimately become harmless. When this shall come it will then only be used, as it should be, to distinguish one variety of the human family from another. It will cease to have any civil, political, or moral significance, and colored conventions will then be dispensed with as anachronisms, wholly out of place, but not till then. Do not marvel that we are discouraged. The faith within us has a rational basis, and is confirmed by facts. When we consider how deep-seated this feeling against us is; the long centuries it has been forming; the forces of avarice which have been marshaled to sustain it; how the language and literature of the country have been pervaded with it; how the church, the press, the play-house, and other influences of the country have been arrayed in its support, the progress toward its extinction must be considered vast and wonderful....

We do not believe, as we are often told, that the Negro is the ugly child of the national family, and the more he is kept out of sight the better it will be for him. You know that liberty given is never so precious as liberty sought for and fought for. The man outraged is the man to make the outcry. Depend upon it, men will not care much for a people who do not care for themselves. Our meeting here was opposed by some of our members, because it would disturb the peace of the Republican party. The suggestion came from coward lips and misapprehended the character of that party. If the Republican party cannot stand a demand for justice and fair play, it ought to go down. We were men before that party was born, and our manhood is more sacred than any party can be. Parties were made for men, not men for parties.

The colored people of the South are the laboring people of the South. The labor of a country is the source of its wealth; without the colored laborer today the South would be a howling wilderness, given up to bats, owls, wolves, and bears. He was the source of its wealth before the war, and has been the source of its prosperity since the war. He almost alone is visible in her fields, with implements of toil in his hands, and laboriously using them to-day.

Let us look candidly at the matter. While we see and hear that the South is more prosperous than it ever was before and rapidly recovering from the waste of war, while we read that it raises more cotton, sugar, rice, tobacco, corn, and other valuable products than it ever produced before, how happens it, we sternly ask, that the houses of its laborers are miserable huts, that their clothes are rags, and their food the coarsest and scantiest? How happens it that the land-owner is becoming richer and the laborer poorer?

The implication is irresistible that where the landlord is prosperous the laborer ought to share his prosperity, and whenever and wherever we find this is not the case there is manifestly wrong somewhere....

Flagrant as have been the outrages committed upon colored citizens in respect to their civil rights, more flagrant, shocking, and scandalous still have been the outrages committed upon our political rights by means of bull-dozing and Kukluxing, Mississippi plans, fraudulent courts, tissue ballots, and the like devices. Three States in which the colored people outnumber the white population are without colored representation and their political voice suppressed. The colored citizens in those States are virtually disfranchised, the Constitution held in utter contempt and its provisions nullified. This has been done in the face of the Republican party and successive Republican administrations....

This is no question of party It is a question of law and government. It is a question whether men shall be protected by law, or be left to the mercy of cyclones of anarchy and bloodshed. It is whether the Government or the mob shall rule this land; whether the promises solemnly made to us in the constitution be manfully kept or meanly and flagrantly broken. Upon this vital point we ask the whole people of the United States to take notice that whatever of political power we have shall be exerted for no man of any party who will not, in advance of election, promise to use every power given him by the Government, State or National, to make the black man's path to the ballot-box as straight, smooth and safe as that Of any other American citizen....

We hold it to be self-evident that no class or color should be the exclusive rulers of this country. If there is such a ruling class, there must of course be a subject class, and when this condition is once established this Government of the people, by the people, and for the people, will have perished from the earth.

Source: *The Life and Writings of Frederick Douglass*, Philip Foner, ed., vol. IV (1955).

HOW WELL DID YOU UNDERSTAND THIS SELECTION?

1. To whom do you think Douglass is directing his speech?

2. What are five specific injustices he sees in the period following Reconstruction?

3. What does he believe the solution should be?

4. What does his description tell you about Reconstruction and its results?

SELF TEST

MULTIPLE CHOICE: Circle the correct response. The correct answers are given at the end.

1. Slavery was finally prohibited in all the states and territories of the United States by the
    a. Thirteenth Amendment.
    b. Fourteenth Amendment.
    c. Emancipation Proclamation.
    d. treaty ending the Civil War.

2. The Black Codes established in the South after the Civil War demonstrated that Southerners
    a. understood the need the newly freed people had for education.
    b. were happy to leave the future of blacks in the hands of blacks themselves.
    c. hoped to limit black rights and to restrict blacks to a servile position.
    d. were happy to grant blacks their full equality under the law.

3. The most important disagreement between President Johnson and Congress concerned
    a. how many representatives each state would be given.
    b. what to do with land seized from the Confederate leaders.
    c. how to demobilize the opposing armies.
    d. what the position of the former slaves would be in the reconstructed states.

4. After the Civil War, freed slaves
    a. upset Northerners due to their disinterest in any kind of education.
    b. put most of their efforts into creating racially integrated school systems.
    c. demonstrated a great desire for education as a means of upward mobility.
    d. felt that primary schools were more than adequate to meet their needs.

5. The three constitutional amendments that were ratified after the Civil War were designed to
    a. limit the powers of the federal government that had expanded during the war.
    b. grant the basic rights of citizenship to black Americans.
    c. punish the Confederates for their treason to their country.
    d. restore the country to exactly where it had been before the war.

6. Since most congressmen in the Reconstruction era were firm believers in laissez-faire, they resisted suggestions that
    a. plantation land be appropriated and redistributed to former slaves.
    b. former Confederate states be readmitted to the union.
    c. Northerners invest capital in southern railroads and industry.
    d. former slaves be given rights as citizens of the United States.

7. By the 1870s, northern public opinion
    a. continued to strongly back protection of the rights of blacks in the South.
    b. grew increasingly disinterested in black rights and southern Reconstruction.
    c. continued to strongly favor congressional reconstruction plans.
    d. grew increasingly angry at the political leaders who had led the nation into the Civil War.

8. By the end of Reconstruction most blacks worked as
    a. sharecroppers
    b. small farmers on their own land.
    c. domestic servants on their former plantations.
    d. industrial wage workers.

9. The most significant, long-lasting failure of southern Reconstruction governments was their
    a. unwillingness to rebuild and promote industrial development.
    b. failure to provide any support for a system of public education.
    c. inability to raise any taxes to support the needs of state budgets.
    d. failure to try to change the social and economic structure of southern society.

10. The Supreme Court, in the *Plessy v. Ferguson* case, authorized
    a. the prohibition of racial intermarriages.
    b. denying blacks the right to vote.
    c. state-mandated racial segregation.
    d. state efforts to create equal rights for all.

Answers:: 1-a; 2-c; 3-d; 4-c; 5-b; 6-a; 7-b; 8-a; 9-d; 10-c.

ESSAYS:

1. Describe the conflict between the president and Congress over Reconstruction and discuss the long and short-term consequences of this conflict.

2. Explain the following statement: "Reconstruction changed southern society in important but limited ways." What were the most important accomplishments of Reconstruction? Its failures? How would you evaluate its overall impact?

3. After the Civil War, the nation appeared to commit itself to equality for freed slaves through laws and constitutional amendments. Describe these laws and amendments. What caused the nation to retreat from this commitment?

OPTIONAL ACTIVITIES: (Use your knowledge **and** imagination.)

1. You are the prosecutor of Andrew Johnson in his impeachment trial **OR** his defense attorney. Write a two-page brief of the prosecution/defense strategy you would follow. What do you feel is the strongest point of your argument?

2. You live in a small southern town during Reconstruction. In a 2-3 page paper describe how a freedman/woman and a klansman would view the same events.

WEB SITE LISTINGS:

Harper's Weekly – America's Leading Magazine During Reconstruction
http://www.harpweek.com

Library of Congress
http://lcweb.loc.gov/exhibits/africa/intro.html
http://memory.loc.gov/ammem/aaohtml/exhibit/aopart5.html
http://scriptorium.lib.duke.edu/collections/african-american-women.html
                                        /franklin/af-am-mss.collections53.html

Many Specific Events
http://www.channelone.com/fasttrack/ushistory/1800-1877/

Primary Sources including a Black Code and Sharecropper's Contract
http://longman.awl.com/history/activities_16_20.htm

Report of the Joint committee on Reconstruction
http://odur.let.rug.nl/~usa/usa.htm

Making of America – hundreds of articles and books in search
www.hti.umcih.edu/m/moagrp
http://moa.cit.cornell.edu/moa

Chapter Thirteen

INDUSTRIALIZATION

America's Industrial Revolution kicked into high gear about 1880. For the next forty years everything about the United States changed, including government, society, politics, work, and, most of all, the economy. The machine age embodied optimism and opportunity. Technological adaptation of existing devices, such as the steam engine and the sewing machine, as well as new discoveries and inventions in electricity, chemistry, physics, engineering, manufacturing, and agriculture, enabled the United States to move to the forefront of industrial nations. No people were more inventive and innovative than were Americans during this time. Between 1790 and 1860 the U. S. Patent Office granted a total of 36,000 patents. In 1897 alone it granted 22,000; by 1920, it had granted about 1.4 million patents.

Despite the optimism, industrialization did not proceed without problems. Cities experienced tremendous growth. Areas that before the Civil War had been, at best, small towns became bustling metropolitan areas almost overnight. New buildings had to be built, police forces enlarged, fire brigades created, streets enlarged, and new neighborhoods to house the growing population had to be constructed. Mayors and city councils sometimes struggled to find financing to pay for these projects.

Workers also experienced problems. Before the Industrial Revolution most products sold in the United States were produced by craftspeople working in shops near their houses. They set their own hours and worked when they had orders to fill. Mechanization changed methods of production, destroying time-honored crafts, such as glassmaking and iron molding, and subjecting workers to rigid schedules and repetitive routines they had never before experienced. Although mechanization created new jobs, it also produced low wages because most machines were labor saving devices that enabled fewer workers to produce more products. This created a situation workers had never experienced—unemployment and low wages. Workers responded by organizing unions such as the Knights of Labor and the American Federation of Labor. Their goals were generally to improve the lives of workers and eliminate evils like child labor.

Imperialism also came with industrialization. In 1898 the United States acquired its first overseas colonies and fought a war of seven years duration to prevent the Philippine Islands from gaining independence. Many Americans believed imperialism sullied America's reputation around the world and protested against it. Despite the protests, industrialists demanded that the United States acquire colonies so they could market products to additional populations.

Racism and Jim Crow segregation continued to play a prominent role in the South. Efforts by African Americans to overcome the racism, prejudice, and discrimination that were part of their everyday life generally centered on education. African-American leaders hoped that an educated population would be able to surmount racial barriers that white society had erected. Unfortunately, this was not reality.

IDENTIFICATION: Briefly describe each term.

Joseph Pulitzer

William Randolph Hearst

Andrew Carnegie

John D. Rockefeller

J. Pierpont Morgan

Cornelius Vanderbilt

Henry Huntington

Leland Stanford

Robber Barons

Standard Oil of Ohio

James Duke

Thomas Edison

Alexander Graham Bell

Vertical Integration

Horizontal Integration

Sherman Silver Purchase Act

Sherman Anti-Trust Act

Interstate Commerce Act

Queen Liliuokalani

Spanish-American War

Rough Riders

Emilio Aguinaldo

Gospel of Wealth

Ida B. Wells

Theodore Dreiser

Jacob Riis

Knights of Labor

Chinese Exclusion Act

Haymarket Square Bombing

American Federation of Labor

Mary Harris "Mother" Jones

Pullman Strike

Booker T. Washington

W.E.B. Du Bois

Women's Suffrage Movement

Lucy Stone

Susan B. Anthony

Elizabeth Cady Stanton

Francs Willard

Jane Addams

THINK ABOUT:

1.   How did the Industrial Revolution change America? Could historians argue that modern America began with the Industrial Revolution? Why or why not? If not, when did modern America begin? What characteristics are part of modern America?

2.   How did imperialism and the Spanish-American War change American foreign policy? What impact throughout the twentieth century did the Spanish-American War and imperialism have on American history?

3.   What role did problems created by industrialism play in governmental regulation of the economy?

4.   How did wealthy Americans deal with contradictions in American society produced by the concentration of wealth in the hands of a few while the masses remained poor? Does the same economic gap between rich and poor exist in the United States today? Why or why not?

THE SHERMAN ANTI-TRUST ACT OF 1890

Industrialization during the last half of the nineteenth century created the problem of trusts and monopolies. Big business faced cutthroat competition. They produced vast quantities of products and sold them quickly for small profits. To overcome the cutthroat competition, industrialists developed the pool, trust, and holding company. The purpose of these forms of business organizations was to eliminate or limit competition and thus raise profit margins. This was best done by getting rival businesses to cooperate or by driving competitors out of business. The first trust formed was Standard Oil in 1882. John D. Rockefeller's attorney, Samuel Dodd, thought of the idea. He created a board of trustees to control all companies Standard Oil had acquired, which allowed them to function as one company. Later, Rockefeller and Standard Oil created the Holding Company to serve the same purpose. Other corporations emulated Rockefeller, forming trusts of their own to restrain competition and raise prices.

By the mid 1880s the American public was fed up with monopolistic companies who drove up prices for products and services they produced. In 1888 both Democratic and Republican candidates for president promised to restrain the mo-

nopolies. This restraint occurred in 1890 when Congress passed the Sherman Anti-Trust Act by a vote of 51 to 1 in the Senate and 242 to 0 in the House of Representatives. President Harrison signed the bill into law, and trusts and monopolies became illegal forms of business.

SECTION ONE:

Every contract, combination in the form of trust or otherwise, or conspiracy, in restraint of trade or commerce among the several States, or with foreign nations, is declared to be illegal. Every person who shall make any contract or engage in any combination or conspiracy hereby declared to be illegal shall be deemed guilty of a felony, and, on conviction thereof, shall be punished by fine not exceeding ten million dollars if a corporation, or, if any other person, three hundred and fifty thousand dollars, or by imprisonment not exceeding three years, or by both said punishments, in the discretion of the court.

SECTION TWO:

Every person who shall monopolize, or attempt to monopolize, or combine or conspire with any other person or persons, to monopolize any part of the trade or commerce among the several States, or with foreign nations, shall be deemed guilty of a felony, and, on conviction thereof, shall be punished by fine not exceeding ten million dollars if a corporation, or, if any other person, three hundred and fifty thousand dollars or by imprisonment not exceeding three years, or by both said punishments, in the discretion of the court.

HOW WELL DID YOU UNDERSTAND THIS SELECTION?

1. What was the penalty corporations faced for violating the Sherman Anti-Trust Act?

2. What penalties did individuals face for violating the Sherman Anti-Trust Act?

3. Does the Sherman Anti-Trust Act define what a monopoly is? If so, what is a monopoly?

4. What weaknesses can you find in the Sherman Anti-Trust Act?

5. Look at the Constitution in the appendix to your textbook? What part of the Constitution gives Congress the power to pass the Sherman Anti-Trust Act?

Andrew Carnegie, a poor immigrant from Scotland, became one of the world's wealthiest men. He made his vast fortune in the steel industry, which he dominated through vertical integration until he sold the Carnegie Steel Company to J. P. Morgan, a New York financier, for nearly half a billion dollars. Carnegie felt guilty about acquiring such a vast fortune, especially when he had been poor in his native land and because workers who produced his vast wealth lived little better than animals. To ease his conscious, Carnegie devised an idea called the gospel of wealth. Late in life, he gave away much of his fortune, especially to libraries and churches.

The problem of our age is the administration of wealth, so that the ties of brotherhood may still bind together the rich and poor in harmonious relationship. The conditions of human life have not only been changed, but revolutionized, within the past few hundred years. In former days there was little difference between the dwelling, dress, food, and environment of the chief and those of his retainers.... The contrast between the…millionaire and the…laborer…today measures the change which has come with civilization.... This change, however, is not to be deplored, but welcomed as highly beneficial....

There are but three modes in which surplus wealth can be disposed of. It can be left to the families of the descendents; or it can be bequeathed for public purposes; or finally it can be administered during life by its possessors.... Let us consider each of these modes. The first is the most injudicious. In monarchial countries, the estates and the greatest portion of the wealth are left to the first son, that the vanity of the parent may be gratified by the thought that his name and title are to descend to succeeding generations unimpaired. The condition of this class in Europe today teaches the futility of such hopes or ambitions. The successors have become impoverished through their follies or from the fall in the value of land.... Why should men leave great fortunes to their children? If this is done from affection, is it not misguided affection? Observation teaches that, generally speaking, it is not well for the children that they be so burdened. Neither is it well for the state....

As to the second mode, that of leaving at death for public uses, it may be said that this is only a means for the disposal of wealth, provided a man is content to wait until he is dead before it becomes of much good....

The growing disposition to tax more and more heavily large estates left at death is a cheering indication of the growth of a salutary change in public opinion.... Of all forms of taxation, this seems the wisest. Men who continue hoarding great sums all their lives, the proper use of which for public ends would work good to the community, should be made to feel that the community, in the form of the state, cannot thus be deprived of its proper share. By taxing estates heavily at death, the state marks its condemnation of the selfish millionaire's unworthy life.

Source: Andrew Carnegie, "Wealth," *North American Review*, 1889

HOW WELL DID YOU UNDERSTAND THIS SELECTION?

1. How does Carnegie feel about the economic gap between rich and poor?

2. What does he think the problem of his (the industrial) age was?

3. What does Carnegie think caused the great disparity of wealth?

4. How does Carnegie define wealth? How does he define competence?

5. How does Carnegie believe wealth should be disposed of?

6. Why does Carnegie want to heavily tax large estates left at death?

A SELECTION FROM THE CONSTITUTION OF THE KNIGHTS OF LABOR

American workers faced numerous problems created by the Industrial Revolution. These included: low wages, long hours, unsafe working conditions, no job security, no health insurance, and few fringe benefits like paid vacations and sick leave. Laborers attempted to solve these and other problems by forming unions. An early and important union was the Knights of Labor. Initially the Knights of Labor practiced secret rituals much like fraternal lodges did, but Terence V. Powderly, who assumed the organization's presidency in 1879, moved the Knights away from fraternalism to unionism. Under Powderly's leadership the Knights of Labor advocated an eight-hour work day, a graduated income tax, and abolition of child labor. Membership approached one million in the mid-1880s. The Knights of Labor Constitution defines many of the objectives of the organization. Unlike most unions active in the nineteenth century, the Knights of Labor organized on an industry-wide basis rather than by crafts and accepted both skilled and unskilled workers as well as women. Philosophically the Knights opposed strikes in favor of organized boycotts, mediation and arbitration, and political involvement. Ultimately Powderly wanted to create a political party that would represent labor. He hoped workers could improve their economic situation by electing candidates to governmental office who would support labor issues. Ironically, the downfall of the Knights of Labor came as a result of their involvement in a strike against the McCormick Reaper Company and the Haymarket Square incident it produced.

PREAMBLE

The recent alarming development and aggression of aggregated wealth, which, unless checked, will invariably lead to the pauperization and hopeless degradation of the toiling masses, render it imperative, if we desire to enjoy the blessings of life, that a check should be placed upon its power and upon unjust accumulation, and a system adopted which will secure to the laborer the fruits of his toil, and as this much-desired object can only be accomplished by the thorough unification of labor, and the united efforts of those who obey the divine injunction that "in the sweat of thy brow shalt thou eat bread," we have formed the Knights of Labor with a view of securing the organization and direction, by cooperative effort, of the power of the industrial classes; and we submit to the world the objects sought to be accomplished by our organization, calling upon all who believe in securing "the greatest good to the greatest number" to aid and assist us:

I. To bring within the folds of organization every department of productive industry, making knowledge a stand-point for action, and industrial and moral worth, not wealth, the true standard of individual and national greatness.

II. To secure to the toilers a proper share of the wealth that they create: more of the leisure that rightfully belongs to them, more societary advantages; more of the benefits, privileges, and emoluments of the world: in a word, all those rights and privileges necessary to make them capable of enjoying, appreciating, defending and perpetuating the blessings of good government.

III. To arrive at the true condition of the producing masses in their educational, moral, and financial condition, by demanding from the various governments the establishment of bureaus of Labor Statistics.

IV. The establishment of co-operative institutions, productive and distributive.

V. The reserving of the public lands—the heritage of the people—or the actual settler—not another acre for railroads or speculators.

VI. The abrogation of all laws that do not bear equally upon capital and labor, the removal of unjust technicalities, delays, and discriminations in the administration of justice, and the adopting of measures providing for the health and safety of those engaged in mining, manufacturing, or building pursuits.

VII. The enactment of laws to compel chartered corporations to pay their employes weekly, in full, for labor performed during the preceding week, in the lawful money of the country.

VIII. The enactment of laws giving mechanics and laborers a first lien on their work for their full wages.

IX. The abolishment of the contract system on national, State, and municipal work.

X. The substitution of arbitration for strikes, whenever and wherever employers and employees are willing to meet on equitable grounds.

XI. The prohibition of the employment of children in workshops, mines and factories before attaining their fourteenth year.

XII. To abolish the system of letting out by contract the labor of convicts in our prisons and reformatory institutions.

XIII. To secure for both sexes equal pay for equal work.

XIV. The reduction of the hours of labor to eight per day, so that the laborers may have more time for social enjoyment and intellectual improvement, and be enabled to reap the advantages conferred by the labor-saving machinery which their brains have created.

XV. To prevail upon governments to establish a purely national circulating medium, based upon the faith and resources of the nation, and issued directly to the people, without the intervention of any system of banking corporations, which money shall be a legal tender in payment of all debts…

Source: Terence V. Powderly, *Thirty Years of Labor*, 1899

HOW WELL DID YOU UNDERSTAND THIS SELECTION?

1. What is the primary objective of the Knights of Labor?

2. Why do the Knights of Labor want state governments to create Bureaus of Labor Statistics?

3. How do the Knights of Labor propose to solve problems between labor and management?

4. What are the Knights of Labor's views regarding female workers? Does this surprise you?

5. What were the Knights of Labor's ideas regarding money and banks?

6. What problems did workers have that the Knights of Labor tried to address?

EXCERPTS FROM JOHN MORRISON'S TESTIMONY BEFORE THE UNITED STATES SENATE

John Morrison was one of hundreds of workers who testified before the Senate Committee upon the Relations between Labor and Capital in 1884 and 1885. This committee, which was convened to investigate the cause of strikes, concluded that strikes resulted because industrialization caused the workers' status to decline. Morrison, at the time of his testimony, was a young machinist in New York City. His testimony supports the conclusions about strikes drawn by the committee.

Q: Is there any difference between the conditions under which machinery is made now and those that existed ten years ago?

A: A great deal of difference.

Q: State the differences as well as you can.

A: Well, the trade has been subdivided and those subdivisions have been again subdivided, so that a man never learns the machinist's trade now. Ten years ago he learned, not the whole of the trade, but a fair portion of it. Also, there is more machinery used in the business, which again makes machinery. In the case of making the sewing-machine, for instance, you find that the trade is so subdivided that a man is not considered a machinist at all. Hence it is merely laborers' work and it is laborers that work at that branch of our trade. The different branches of the trade are divided and subdivided so that one man may make just a particular part of a machine and may not know anything whatever about another part of the same machine. In that way machinery is produced a great deal cheaper than it used to be formerly, and in fact through this system of work, 100 men are able to do now what it took 300 or 400 men to do fifteen years ago. By the use of machinery and the subdivision of the trade they so simplify the work that it is made a great deal easier and put together a great deal faster. There is no system of apprenticeship, I may say, in the business. You simply go in and learn whatever branch you are put at, and you stay at that unless you are changed to another.

Q: Does a man learn his branch very rapidly?

A: Yes, sir, he can learn his portion of the business very rapidly. Of course he becomes very expert at it, doing that all the time and nothing else, and therefore he is able to do a great deal more work in that particular branch than if he were a general hand and expected to do everything in the business as it came along.

Q: Do you know from reading the papers or from your general knowledge of the business whether there are other places in other cities or other parts of the country that those men could have gone and got work?

A: I know from general reports of the condition of our trade that the same condition existed throughout the country generally.

Q: Then those men could not have bettered themselves by going to any other place, you think?

A: Not in a body.

Q: I am requested to ask you this question: dividing the public, as is commonly done, into the upper, middle, and lower classes, to which class would you assign the average workingman of your trade at the time when you entered it, and to which class you would assign him now?

A: I now assign them to the lower class. At the time I entered the trade I should assign them as merely hanging on to the middle class, ready to drop out at any time.

Q: What is the character of the social intercourse of those workingmen? Answer first with reference to their intercourse with other people outside of their own trade—merchants, employers, and others.

A: Are you asking what sort of social intercourse exists between the machinists and the merchants? If you are, there is none whatever, or very little if any.

Q: What sort of social intercourse exists among the machinists themselves and their families, as to visiting, entertaining one another, and having little parties and other forms of sociability, those little things that go to make up the social pleasures of life?

A: In fact with the married folks that has died out—such things as birthday parties, picnics, and so on. The machinists today are on such small pay, and the cost of living is so high, that they have very little, if anything, to spend for recreation, and the machinist has to content himself with enjoying himself at home, either fighting with his wife or licking his children

Q: I hope that is not a common amusement in the trade. Was it so ten years ago?

A: It was not, from the fact that they then sought enjoyment in other places, and had a little more money to spend. But since they have had no organization worth speaking of, of course their pay has gone down. At that time they had a form of organization in some way or other which seemed to keep up the wages, and there was more life left in the machinist then, he had more ambition, he felt more like seeking enjoyment outside, and in reading and such things, but now it is changed to the opposite, the machinist has no such desires.

Q: What is the social air about the ordinary machinist's house? Are there evidences of happiness, and joy, and hilarity, or is the general atmosphere solemn, and somber, and gloomy?

A: To explain that fully, I would first of all state, that machinists have got to work ten hours a day in New York, and that they are compelled to work very hard. In fact the machinists of America are compelled to do about one-third more work than the machinists do in England in a day. Therefore, when they come home they are naturally played out from shoving the file, or using the hammer or the chisel, or whatever it may be, such long hours. They are pretty well played out when they come home, and the first thing they think of is having something to eat and sitting down, and resting, and then of striking a bed. Of course when a man is dragged out in that way he is naturally cranky, and he makes all around him cranky; so, instead of a pleasant house it is every day expecting to lose his job by competition from his fellow workman, there being so many out of employment, and no places for them, and his wages being pulled down through their competition, looking at all times to be thrown out of work in that way, and staring starvation in the face makes him feel sad, and the head of the house being sad, of course the whole family are the same, so the house looks like a dull prison instead of a home.

Q: Where do you work?

A: I would rather not have it in print. Perhaps I would have to go Monday morning if I did. We are so situated in the machinist's trade that we daren't let them know much about us. If they know that we open our mouths on the labor question, and try to form organizations, we are quietly told that "business is slack," and we have got to go.

Q: Do you know of anybody being discharged for making speeches on the labor question?

A: Yes, I do know of several. A little less than a year ago several members of the organization that I belong to were discharged because it was discovered that they were members of the organization.

Q: Do you say those men were members of the same organization that you belong to?

A: Yes sir; but not working in the same place where I work. And in fact many of my trade have been on the "black list," and have had to leave town to find work.

Q: Are the machinists here generally contented, or are they in a state of discontent and unrest?

A: There is mostly a general feeling of discontent, and you will find among the machinists the most radical workingmen, with the most revolutionary ideas. You will find that they don't so much give their thoughts simply to trades unions and other efforts of that kind, but they go far beyond that; they only look for relief through the ballot or through a revolution, a forcible revolution....

Q: You say they look for relief through a forcible revolution. In the alternative of a forcible revolution have they considered what form of government they would establish?

A: Yes; some of them have and some of them have not.

Q: What kind of government would they establish?

A: …They want to form a government such as this was intended to be, a government "of the people, for the people, and by the people"—different entirely from the present form of government.

Source: Report of the Committee of the Senate upon the Relations between Labor and Capital, 48th Congress, 1885

HOW WELL DID YOU UNDERSTAND THIS SELECTION?

1. What does Morrison think has happened to the machinist's trade?

2. What does Morrison say has happened to machinists as a result of the Industrial Revolution? What is their economic status?

3. How does Morrison describe the life of workers?

4. What would likely happen if workers joined a union?

5. What is a black list?

6. How does Morrison say workers will seek relief?

The Spanish-American War generated much controversy within the United States. Many Americans opposed going to war with Spain to acquire colonies because they believed it violated one of America's founding principles, that of self-determination. Americans had maintained for years that they believed all people should have the right to determine their own government. After all, this is why Americans had fought England for independence during the American Revolution. An organization called the Anti-Imperialist League was organized. Grover Cleveland, who served two nonconsecutive terms as president from 1885 to 1889 and from 1893 to 1897, was a member of this group, as well as other notable Americans, such as the author Mark Twain, the Supreme Court Justice Morfield Story, and Speaker of the House of Representatives Thomas Reed, who resigned after serving forty years in Congress because he believed the acquisition of colonies soiled America. Former President Cleveland served as vice president of the Anti-Imperialist League and spoke out forcefully against imperialism as the following speech indicates.

When our Government entered upon a war for the professed purpose of aiding self-government and releasing from foreign rule a struggling people whose cries for liberty were heard at our very doors, it rallied to its enthusiastic support a nation of freemen, in whose hearts and minds there was deeply fixed by heredity and tradition the living belief that all just powers of government are derived from the consent of the governed.

It was the mockery of fate that led us to an unexpected and unforeseen incident in this conflict, and placed in the path of our Government, while professing national righteousness, representing an honest and liberty-loving people, and intent on a benevolent, self-sacrificing errand, the temptation of sordid aggrandizement and the false glitter of world-power.

No sincerely thoughtful American can recall what followed without amazement, nor without sadly realizing how the apathy of our people's trustfulness and their unreflecting acceptance of alluring representations can be played upon.

No greater national fall from grace was ever known than that of the Government of the United States, when in the midst of high design, while still speaking words of sympathy with the weak who struggled against the strong, and while still professing to exemplify before the world a great Republic's love for self-government and its impulse to stay the bloody hand of oppression and conquest, it embraced an opportunity offered by the exigencies of its beneficent undertaking, to possess itself of territory thousands of miles from our coast, and to conquer and govern, without pretense of their consent, millions of resisting people—a heterogeneous population largely mixed with elements hardly within the light of civilization, and all far from the prospect of assimilation with anything American.

.... Refusing to accept the shallow and discreditable pretense that our conquest in the Philippines has gone so far beyond recall or correction, we insist that a nation as well as an individual is never so magnanimous or great as when false steps are retraced and the path of honesty and virtue is regained.

The message of the Democracy to the American people should courageously enjoin that, in sincere and consistent compliance with the spirit and profession of our interference in behalf of Cuba's self-government, our beneficent designs toward her should also extend to the lands which, as an incident of such interference, have come under our control; that the people of the Philippine Islands should be aided in the establishment of a government of their own; and that when this is accomplished our interference in their domestic rule should cease.

Source: "Ex-President Grover Cleveland on the Philippine Problem," Boston: Anti-Imperialist League, 1904

HOW WELL DID YOU UNDERSTAND THIS SELECTION?

1. What does President Cleveland consider wrong about America's acquisition of colonies such as the Philippines?

2. What does he think the United States government should do regarding the Philippines?

3. Where does Cleveland think government is derived from?

4. Would Cleveland think America's acquisition of colonies was hypocritical? Why or why not?

THE WIZARD OF OZ: Industrial Themes in a Child's Story
By Doug Cantrell

Practically everyone has either read the child's story, **The Wizard of Oz,** *by L. Frank Baum or viewed the movie starring Judy Garland. On the surface, this tale of witches and wizards appears to be a simple child's story complete with magic, intrigue, and good triumphing over evil. Beneath the simple tale, however, lies political metaphor. While it might appear that* **The Wizard of Oz** *is a child's story, it is really a potent story about the industrial revolution and its impact on workers and farmers. Contained within the child's story are powerful images and symbols drawn from the presidential election of 1900 pitting Republican William McKinley against Democrat William Jennings Bryan, the former Populist. These symbols and images reflect many of the issues facing Americans that arose during the Industrial Revolution. The following pages will examine* **The Wizard of Oz** *from the perspective of the Industrial Revolution, beginning with its author L. Frank Baum.*

Baum by profession was a journalist who experienced the Industrial Revolution first hand as a printer in the West and then a newspaper reporter in Chicago. As a printer in South Dakota, a state in which Populists were very active, Baum came to understand the problem farmers in the Great Plains states faced during the Industrial Revolution. He became aware of the importance farmers and Populists placed on inflation through their advocacy of the free coinage of silver. He also realized that the Industrial Revolution created a situation in which farmers saw their real incomes and social status decline because developments in agricultural technology enabled farmers to produce such a surplus that the market became glutted, driving down prices. It seemed as if the harder farmers worked the less compensation they received. As a printer, Baum experienced first hand the impact the Industrial Revolution had on skilled workers. Baum lost his printing business in South Dakota and had to move to Chicago and work for a big city newspaper (the equivalent of a blacksmith or tailor moving to the city to work in a factory). Like most skilled workers who were driven out of business by the factory, Baum's move to the city resulted in less income and a lowered social status. In the 1896 and 1900 presidential elections Baum actively supported the Populist/Democratic candidate, William Jennings Bryan. He wrote **The Wizard of Oz** *in the context of the 1900 presidential election, incorporating themes from the Industrial Revolution and issues in the 1896 and 1900 elections. An analysis of the story will reflect those themes.*

The story begins in Kansas, a farming state whose residents had experienced a decline in income and social status as a result of the Industrial Revolution. Baum describes everything in Kansas as gray. The sky is gray, people are gray, animals are gray, the landscape is gray. This image of gray is a metaphor for the negative impact the Industrial Revolution had on farmers in Kansas and elsewhere. Farmers have little to smile about. They are heavily in debt and are facing declining prices for farm produce as a result of the glut created by the use of industrial technology (machinery, fertilizer, hybrid seed, etc.) on the farm. Then, along comes a cyclone. The cyclone is symbolic of the presidential election of 1900. Baum believes that voters in the 1900 election will cleanse the political landscape much as a tornado cleanses the physical landscape. Everything will be swept clean in its path and Bryan's election to the presidency will represent a new beginning for Americans.

Dorothy, the central character in the story, and her little dog, Toto, hide in a farmhouse that is lifted high into the sky by the cyclone and deposited in a wonderful, magical land called Oz. There is much symbolism in this scene. Baum takes the name for his magical land, Oz, from the silver/gold issue so important to farmers and workers during the 1890s. Oz is the abbreviation for ounce and is taken from the formula Populists and workers urged the federal government to adopt to inflate the currency supply. They wanted sixteen ounces of silver to be equal to one ounce of gold. The fact that Oz is a magical land is also symbolic. Many farmers and workers believed that if the sixteen to one ratio was adopted and the nation got inflation many of their problems would magically disappear. Farmers would receive higher prices for their produce and could more easily pay debts with inflated currency while factory workers would see higher wages.

Dorothy's house had accidentally landed on a character called the Wicked Witch of the East, killing her. Dorothy emerges from the house and is greeted by small people called Munchkins who are dancing around the house expressing joy that Dorothy has killed the Wicked Witch of the East and hailing Dorothy as their liberator. Dorothy is taken aback. She quickly assures everyone that she did not mean to kill anyone, that it was an accident. The Wicked Witch of the East is symbolic for eastern capitalists, the so-called Robber Barons, the Rockefellers, the Carnegies, the Henry Fords, the corporations that oppressed workers and farmers. The witch's death represents what Baum believes will happen to the oppressors of workers and farmers when Bryan becomes president. He will crush them much as Dorothy's house crushed the Wicked Witch of the East. Munchkins, of course, are the common people who are oppressed by capitalism and conditions created by the Industrial Revolution.

Dorothy, after expressing remorse at the witch's death, becomes concerned about her family in Kansas. She asks the Munchkins if they can tell her how to return to Kansas. The Munchkins feel badly. They can't help their liberator. Suddenly, one of them has an idea. He tells Dorothy to see the Wizard. Dorothy is puzzled. She has never heard of the Wizard. The Munchkins explain that they have heard that a Wizard descended out of the clouds in Emerald City and that he is a good wizard who uses his magical powers to help common people. Dorothy agrees to see the Wizard but doesn't know how to get to Emerald City. The Munchkins tell her to take the yellow brick road. Dorothy, being a Midwestern farm girl, is bare footed (most rural residents did not wear shoes during warm months because leather was too expensive). The Munchkins tell her to take the shoes from the feet of the Wicked Witch of the East; after all, she is dead and will not need them. Dorothy takes the shoes from the witch's feet, which are made of silver (in the movie the slippers are ruby red because that color shows up better on the screen than does silver). She then proceeds to walk down the yellow brick road toward Emerald City wearing the silver slippers. There is a powerful metaphor here. Yellow is the color of gold. Dorothy wearing silver slippers walking down a golden road signifies the relationship between silver and gold so important to workers and farmers and the major issue in the 1896 and 1900 presidential elections.

After walking for a long time Dorothy and Toto stop to rest near a cornfield. As they are resting they hear a voice speaking to them. At first they can't figure out where the voice is coming from but finally determine it is that of the Scarecrow. The Scarecrow is in bad shape. He has had the straw that composed his body torn out by crows. Dorothy puts the straw back into the Scarecrow's body and he tells his tale. He says that the crows became so bold that they attacked him, the corn's guardian. After tearing out his stuffing, the crows stole the corn. The Scarecrow represents the American farmer and the fact that the stuffing is torn out of his body is symbolic of the negative impact the Industrial Revolution had on farmers. They were not in good shape. The crows are the factories that buy the farmer's produce—the canneries, the meat processors, and the tobacco companies. Farmers often believed that these companies stole from farmers by paying prices below what it cost to produce crops and livestock. The Scarecrow decides to go to Emerald City with Dorothy and Toto because he wants the Wizard to give him a brain. The journey to Emerald City represents the trek many farmers made to the city when their farms failed, as did the Scarecrows' when the crows stole his corn. Many farmers, like the Scarecrow, leave their farms, move to the city and become factory workers. The brain the Scarecrow wants is symbolic of prejudices rural people faced as a result of the Industrial Revolution. Farmers were often viewed as "hicks," "hayseeds," and "country bumpkins" who were not as smart or sophisticated as city residents. Before the Industrial Revolution almost everybody was a farmer and farmers were the backbone of American society; afterward, their social status had fallen.

Dorothy, Toto, and the Scarecrow proceed down the yellow brick road toward Emerald City. On the way they encounter the Tin Woodsman. Like the farmer, the Tin Woodsman is in a bad way. He is rusted over. Dorothy and the Scarecrow apply oil to the Tin Woodsman's joints, loosening the rust. He then tells them his story. He says that once he was human until the Wicked Witch of the East cast a spell on him that caused him to cut off an appendage every time he swung his ax. Fortunately, however, tinsmiths in Oz can replace human parts with metal. Like other scenes in the *Wizard of Oz*, there are powerful metaphors in this one. The Tin Woodsman is the American worker. Metal (the steel industry) represents the American Industrial Revolution. The rust is symbolic of the impact the Industrial Revolution had on workers, low wages, long hours, and horrible working conditions and depressions the United States experienced in 1873 and 1893. His metal body reflects the impact the Industrial Revolution had on workers. Once he had been human but factory work had dehumanized him. He was no longer a man but a machine. Severing limbs by swinging the ax reflects the high rate of accidents industrial workers experienced. The application of oil represents what Baum thinks will happen once Bryan becomes president; he will institute policies that will benefit the worker and break the hold industrial capitalism has on them. The Tin Woodsman decides to join Dorothy, Toto, and the Scarecrow on their journey to Emerald City. He wants a heart, again symbolic of the dehumanizing affect the Industrial Revolution had on workers. Getting a heart will make the worker human again.

The group set off down the yellow brick road toward Emerald City. Taken together, they represent the political coalition Baum thinks will be important to Bryan's election. Of course, the Scarecrow represents farmers and the Tin Woodsman represents workers. Dorothy and Toto are part of the coalition too. Dorothy represents a feminist and Toto is short for a teetotaler (someone who does not believe in consuming alcoholic beverages). Both the feminist movement and the prohibition movement were active in the United States around the turn of the twentieth century. Women reformers were campaigning for suffrage, more liberal divorce laws and birth control while prohibitionists wanted to make the country dry. Bryan himself advocated national prohibition and was a teetotaler. All these groups, farmers, workers, feminists, and prohibitionists must unite behind Bryan before he can win the presidency, or so Baum thinks.

While traveling down the yellow brick road toward Emerald City the group next encounters the Cowardly Lion. He roars but frightens nobody; he scratched the Tin Woodsman but dulled his claws on the tin man's body. The Cowardly Lion is William Jennings Bryan. The roar is symbolic of his oratorical abilities. Bryan was often called the "boy orator from the Platt." He had crisscrossed the country making speech after speech during the 1896 campaign while his opponent, McKinley, had stayed home. Bryan's speeches appeared to have little effect. They had not persuaded workers to vote for him. He had dulled his claws on their armor. The Cowardly Lion wants courage. This reflects Baum's belief that Bryan needs to be more courageous in persuading workers to vote for him. He needs to promise workers more in the 1900 campaign than he promised in 1896.

The political coalition continues down the yellow brick road until finally it reaches Emerald City. A gatekeeper meets Dorothy and her friends and makes them put on green goggles (glasses), which they are required to wear while in Emerald City. They are told that they must not take the goggles off. The goggles make everything appear to be a bright shiny green. Curious, Dorothy lifts one corner of the goggles and peeks at the city through the naked eye. What she sees is not a city that is bright and shiny but one that is a dull, dirty white. Emerald City, the capitol of Oz, represents Washington, D.C., America's political capitol, during the Gilded Age. Just as America on the surface during the Gilded Age appeared to be bright and shiny, if one takes off the glasses and looks beneath the surface, corruption will be found in the government. Industrialists often bribed government officials. Things, as Mark Twain pointed out when he coined the term Gilded Age, were not what they appeared to be.

When the group gets an audience with the Wizard he appears to be all powerful and promises Dorothy and her friends what each one wants if they will do something for him—kill the Wicked Witch of the West. The Wizard represents President McKinley. A political deal has been struck. To gain the support of feminist, workers, farmers and others in the upcoming election, McKinley has made numerous promises that he will have trouble keeping, typical behavior for a politician.

Dorothy and her entourage head west where they are told they will find the Wicked Witch of the West. The Wicked Witch of the West, like her sister in the east, is the capitalist who oppresses common people. Dorothy, Toto, the Scarecrow, the Tin Woodsman, and the Cowardly Lion encounter the Wicked Witch of the West through characters identified as Flying Monkeys. The Flying Monkeys and their king appear to be vicious creatures. They take Dorothy to the Wicked Witch of the West where she is imprisoned. One day, while taking a bath, Dorothy splashes water on the witch, which causes her to melt. The water is symbolic that the drought, which had hurt farmers in the west during the 1880s, finally came to an end in the 1890s. Dorothy has destroyed the Wicked Witch of the West, freeing the Flying Monkeys from her spell. Again, when Bryan wins the 1900 election, Baum thinks the power of the capitalist will be broken over workers and farmers. The Flying Monkeys represent the American Indian confined to western reservations. The Flying Monkeys turn out to be good people who have been oppressed just as Native Americans were oppressed in the West. Dorothy asks the Flying Monkeys to return with her to Emerald City but they reply that they can't because they are bound to the land. The Indian was confined to the reservation.

Dorothy and her friends return to Emerald City, seeking an audience with the Wizard. He cannot believe that the group has destroyed the Wicked Witch of the West. He thought that task was impossible to achieve. Baum is saying here that Bryan has overcome impossible obstacles to win the 1900 election, defeating McKinley, the Wizard. At first, the Wizard tries to avoid Dorothy, the Scarecrow, the Tin Woodsman, and the Cowardly Lion. When they force an audience with him, he then tries to avoid keeping the promise he made to each of them, typical behavior for politicians who promise voters many things they can't deliver. Toto doesn't like the Wizard and knocks down a screen in the throne room. Instead of concealing a powerful wizard, the screen hides a short bald headed man that Baum describes as a humbug. McKinley has no real power. He is a fake, a fraud, and a ventriloquist who makes people believe he is a powerful man. This reflects the view many Americans had that President McKinley had no real power but was controlled by his handlers, such as the industrialists Mark Hanna. The Wizard attempts to keep his promise to Dorothy and each of her friends. Even here, he is a fake. Instead of giving the Scarecrow a real brain he fills his head with needles which will prick the skin and make him believe he has a brain. The lion's courage is merely a dose of cod liver oil and the Tin Woodsman gets a paper heart rather than a real one. Since the Wizard had been a carnival barker in the United States who drew a crowd by ascending aloft in a hot air balloon he decides he wants to return home with Dorothy. He makes a balloon that he and Dorothy plan to use to transport them home. Unfortunately, the balloon gets loose from its moorings while Dorothy is hunting for Toto and the Wizard leaves without her. Before departing the Wizard made some changes. He makes the Scarecrow the ruler of Oz; thus the farmer is restored to his lofty position at the top of society before the Industrial Revolution knocked him from that perch. The Wizard's departure is symbolic of McKinley leaving power after having lost the 1900 election.

Since the Wizard has left without her, Dorothy appears to be stuck in Oz. She encounters Glinda, the Good Witch of the North. Glinda tells Dorothy that the silver slippers she is wearing have magical powers that can be used to transport her anywhere in the world. This reflects the magical power of silver to solve the problems of farmers and workers. They believed their problems would magically disappear if America's currency were inflated by use of silver. Dorothy clicks her heels together, says magical words and is transported back to Kansas. When she arrives, the sun is shining and things are looking up for farmers and workers. Bryan is president and the power of the robber barons and corporations they control is broken. A new day has dawned for workers and farmers.

HOW WELL DID YOU UNDERSTAND THIS SELECTION?

1. What figures do the characters in *The Wizard of Oz* represent?

2. What themes from the Industrial Revolution are present in this child's story?

3. Can you find symbolism, other than the themes discussed by Cantrell in the above essay, reflected in issues or events from the Industrial Revolution?

4. Do politicians behave much like the Wizard?

5. What is a political coalition? Has Baum correctly identified the coalition needed to sweep Bryan into the White House?

6. Do you think Baum was disappointed when Bryan did not defeat McKinley in the 1900 election? Why or why not?

FORCED LABOR IN WEST VIRGINIA
By Gino C. Speranza

Gino C. Speranza was head of the Society for the Protection of Italian Immigrants in the United States. This organization existed to improve the lives of Italian immigrants in the United States. He wrote the following article for **The Outlook** *after conducting an investigation of working conditions and debt peonage in West Virginia coal mining and lumber camps.*

It is a far cry from Harmon's Camp in the lonely mountains of Raleigh County, West Virginia to New York City, yet it speaks well for the unceasing vigilance of our militant philanthropy that a cry from that camp in the wilderness was heard and heeded. The adventures of the twenty-three Italian laborers who were sent to Raleigh County from New York reads like a page from the history of the Middle Ages, except that the splendid animal courage of those days is replaced here by the all-absorbing sordid interest of money-making.

In the early part of March, 1903, twenty-three Italians were shipped (I use the word advisedly) from New York by one of those numberless "bankers" who infest the Italian colony, to Beckley, West Virginia, to work on a railroad in process of building in the Piney Creek District. They were told, as is often done and as must be done to induce men to go to that region, that Beckley was a few hours from New York and the approximate cost of transportation would be eighty cents. When they arrived at Beckley, after a journey of nearly two days, hungry, bewildered, and conscious already that they had been betrayed, they were driven to Harmon's Camp, some four miles from town. Those who have not been to the West Virginian labor camps can hardly understand how lonely and isolated some of them are. Even though geographically near each other, they are completely shut in by high mountains, and the surrounding country is practically uninhabited. Conscious of having been sold by the agents in New York, the lonesomeness of the camp naturally increased the apprehension of the laborers. But they started in on the work of drilling and grading, even thought the work was not as it had been represented. Perhaps they worked because the presence of some armed guards and the sight of the contractor with a revolver ostentatiously stuck in his breast pocket was not reassuring. Moreover, to make matters worse, though they were at liberty to "buy anywhere," they had to buy from the camp commissary, no matter how extortionate the prices were, as the nearest store was miles away. The day came when such conditions grew unbearable and the men left; they were not paid, but it seemed better to lose money than to remain. The contractor, however, having advanced transportation, was not going to stand a loss if he could help it. It is true that the Governor of West Virginia, stirred by constant complaints of abuse, had urged the use of legal process in such cases rather than a recourse to force. However hampered legally the contractor might be, the storekeeper had a ready remedy under the "Boarding-House Law" of West Virginia, which gives the right of arrest for non-payment of board. It did not matter that it applied with doubtful propriety to shanty board in a camp, once an accommodating squire could be found to grant a warrant. And so the twenty-three "insurgents" were arrested and locked over night in the Grand Jury room at the County Court House at Beckley, on the charge of non-payment of board. The next morning enters the contractor; he is a private citizen, he in not an officer, he is not even a party of record to the proceedings. What right has he in that Grand Jury room used as a jail? And when the prisoners, in the actual custody of the law, refuse to go back to his camp, he and his henchman, in that room set apart for what has been called "the bulwark of Anglo-Saxon liberty," proceed to bind six of the prisoner with ropes. I cite from the sworn statement of one of the men, "He had tied my wrists and had thrown the rope around my neck, when I shouted to the storekeeper, who was present and spoke Italian, "Not this, not this!" "It is Holy Week and I know Christ's hands were tied, but there was no rope around his neck." Thereupon the contractor, convinced that the binding of the arms was sufficient bunched together six of the bound men and marched them out into the public street. There, before "the whole town," not excluding certain sworn officers of the law, seeing that the prisoners still refused to march back to camp, the contractor hitched the rope by which they were tied to a mule, urging it on. The squire who had issued the warrant of arrest fortunately appeared then and cut the men free. Praise be to him for this act! But why did he urge these men to go back, as he did, with that brute of a contractor, and why did he, instead of trying the prisoners then and there according to law, go back to camp with them and help to induce them to "work out" their "board" and transportation? Why did he not take action against the contractor caught *in flagrante?* Why was there no entry made in his official docket of the disposition of this case till months after? Why did not the Prosecuting Officer at Beckley, who knew of this barbarity, take any action until two months after the event, when a society six hundred miles away submitted to him evidence which he could have gathered fifty yards from his office; and even then why did he merely promise to submit "this small matter" to the next Grand Jury?

Of the twenty-two men who worked out their "debts," one escaped and cannot be traced; eleven walked practically all the way from Charleston, West Virginia, to Washington, District of Columbia; two I found in a Washington hospital; the others had money enough to return to New York.

I have given this case at length, not because it is an example of exceptional cruelty and lawlessness, but because it is an uncommonly well substantiated and corroborated case of the system of intimidation in force in some labor camps of West Virginia, ranging from the silent intimidation of armed guards to an active terrorism of blows and abuse, of which the general public knows nothing.

It was in the latter part of April, 1903, that I was sent by the Society for the Protection of Italian Immigrants of New York to investigate a large number of complaints of alleged maltreatment suffered by Italians in certain counties of West Virginia. That State is developing her splendid resources of coal and lumber, and this necessitates the building of railroads for the transportation of such products. The demand for labor is tremendous and the supply totally inadequate. If it is true that too many immigrants come to our shores, it hardly holds good for West Virginia.

There capital is in danger of becoming paralyzed from lack of the labor supply. To supply the feverish demands, laborers of all conditions and classes have been literally dumped into that State by the brokers in human flesh in the cities—not only men unfit for the hard work required, but a lawless and criminal element as well. The problem for the contractor does not end with getting the men to West Virginia; an even harder task is to keep them there, for the isolation of the camps, the absence of human intercourse, and the hardships of life create a feeling of discontent among the laborers almost from the first day. It is not strange, under these circumstances, therefore, that contractors should resort to methods both to get and to keep laborers which are in defiance of law and repugnant to the moral sense. The temptation to illegitimate practices is further strengthened by the method employed of advancing transportation for the men. Thus, two hundred laborers at $10 each means an investment of $2,000; if the men become dissatisfied and leave, it means a clear loss to the contractor. Yet, however strong the temptation, it cannot justify acts of restraint which in practice amount to white slavery. The use of armed guards around the camps is notorious. Worse yet, the evidence seems to show that the men are charged for the expense of such unlawful surveillance.

Cases of brutality are frequent and inexcusable. One may find some palliation for the unlawful restraint exercised over men who wish to escape before they have "worked out" their transportation. But what can be said in extenuation of such acts of brutality as those of men felled with blows from iron bars or gun butts, or marched at the point of rifles and cursed and beaten if unable to keep up with the pace of the mounted overseers? I have before me the sworn declaration of one Girardi—a bright young Piedmontese, who had been employed by Boxley & Co. near Kayford. He was ordered to lift a heavy stone, and asked a negro co-laborer to help him. His was not, evidently, a permissible request, as his foreman, on hearing it, called him a vile name and thrust a revolver in his face. Thereupon Girardi lifted the stone, at the cost of a very bad rupture. That man to this day has had no redress.

"Tired of abuse," reads the sworn statement of another laborer, "we decided to escape from the camp; we had proceeded but a short distance when we were overtaken by several men armed with rifles and revolvers, who drove us back. One of the pursuing band took from me an iron rod which I held over my shoulder, over which I had slung my valise, and with it repeatedly struck several of my companions." Another, a splendid type of hardy Calabrian, described under oath the following picture: "My attention was drawn to the other side of the creek, where an Italian was shouting for help—appealing to us as fellow-countrymen to aid him. He had been felled by a blow of a heavy stick dealt him by one of the guards. Cervi, my friend, and I tried to cross over to help him, but were prevented by our boss, who drove us back at the point of a pistol; all I dared do was to shout to him not to resist or he would be killed, and to go back; the man who had struck him lifted him bodily by his coat and pushed him on, striking him every time he stumbled or fell from exhaustion."

These are a few of a number of well-substantiated cases. It will be hard for many of us to believe these facts; it will seem impossible that such barbarities should be allowed in a civilized community. Perhaps they would not be allowed if they were known. Publicity is the great hope for reform; a wide publicity that will, on the one hand, arouse public sentiment and react on the local authorities, and, on the other hand, that will further cut off the supply of laborers, thereby forcing the contractors to reform.

Little, if anything, can be hoped from the local officials. The Chief Executive of West Virginia admitted to me that it was practically impossible to obtain convictions through the local courts, and, however good his intentions, his powers seem very limited. In a recent letter the Governor of that State writes: "I am willing to do anything I can to bring about a better condition of affairs and to co-operate as I have the power in bringing to justice those guilty of the acts complained of, but you see my limitations. . . The executive in West Virginia has practically no power in controlling the administration of justice in our courts. . . .The legislature refused last winter to give me the necessary powers asked for in as grave a matter as lynching."

It is a reasonable presumption that contractors do not engage men with the express purpose of maltreating them, for it is a plain business principle that dissatisfied men make poor workers. I believe, therefore, that, with some few exceptions, these abuses are to a great extent due to that lack of mutual confidence and more especially of mutual understanding which is the basis of much of the unrest and spirit of reprisal in the labor situation. This lack of mutual understanding is especially evident in the relations between American employers and Italian laborers. It is not merely ignorance of the language, it is rather a lack of clear-sightedness and perception as regards what counts with these foreign laborers. Employers of Italian labor too often forget that their employees are proverbially sensitive, but are also susceptible to kind treatment. Courtesy and kindness will hold these men even in distant and isolated camps much better than curses and forcible threats. As a purely business proposition, the employment of a capable and honest interpreter or confidential secretary who knows both Italian and American ways, to whom laborers could go, would be a better and cheaper investment for contractors than the maintenance of armed guards or brutal foremen. As it is, not only in West Virginia but wherever Italian labor is employed the Italian is at the mercy of the middleman, without any right of appeal. Whether it be the fraud of his own countryman, the banker-agent who sells his labor under false pretenses, or the extortion of his countryman, the camp storekeeper to whom the contractor lets the commissary privileges, whether it be the "rake-off" of the foreman or the peculations of the paymaster, whether it be the brutality of the boss or the unlawful order of the gang-foremen—no matter what the injustice may be, the laborer has no opportunity to appeal to his employer, either because the employer recognizes the decision of his middleman as final or because he will not "bother with details." While this system, popularly called the "pardone system," is tolerated by contractors, abuses will continue. Much, however, can be done to lessen its evils by institutions like the Society for the Protection of Italian Immigrants, a society administered by Americans, which aims to destroy the padrone system by competing with padrone, using legitimate methods in supplying laborers and safeguarding their rights.

The responsibility, in the last instance, however, rests on the employers. Their duty to the men should not cease with the payment of agreed wages; without the careful, businesslike, and humane supervision, workmen are very likely to be abused by the middlemen. Especially is this true of the foreign workman whose helplessness in the face of unlawful and brutal treatment such as that in West Virginia would almost justify an extra-judicial reprisal. Certainly it is of vital importance that these numberless foreign laborers who come to us should learn, as a first step towards assimilation, that Americanism means honesty, regard for law, fair play, and plain dealing.

Source: *The Outlook*, June 13, 1908

HOW WELL DID YOU UNDERSTAND THIS SELECTION?

1. Who is Gino Speranza?

2. What is labor peonage?

3. What does Speranza find in West Virginia?

4. How are immigrant workers treated in West Virginia if they don't pay transportation charges?

5. What is "on transportation"?

6. What is the padrone system?

7. What does Speranza think will solve the problem of labor peonage?

Booker T. Washington was an African-American leader who founded Tuskegee Institute in Alabama. A pioneer in education, he thought African Americans would best be served by obtaining a practical education in mechanical skills and agriculture. Washington was often accused of being an "Uncle Tom" because he was willing to accept racism and discrimination for slow economic gains for African Americans.

When a mere boy, I saw a young colored man, who had spent several years in school, sitting in a common cabin in the South, studying a French grammar. I noted the poverty, the untidiness, the want of system and thrift that existed about the cabin, notwithstanding his knowledge of French and other academic subjects. Another time, when riding on the outer edges of a town in the South, I heard the sound of a piano coming from a cabin of the same kind. Contriving some excuse, I entered, and began a conversation with the young colored woman who was playing, and who had recently returned from a boarding-school, where she had been studying instrumental music among other things. Despite the fact that her parents were living in a rented cabin, eating poorly cooked food, surrounded with poverty, and having almost none of the conveniences of life, she had persuaded them to rent a piano for four or five dollars per month. Many such instances as these, in connection with my own struggles, impressed upon me the importance of making a study of our needs as a race, and applying the remedy accordingly. Some one may be tempted to ask, Has not the negro boy or girl as good a right to study a French grammar and instrumental music as the white youth? I answer, Yes, but in the present condition of the negro race in this country there is need of something more. Perhaps I may be forgiven for the seeming egotism if I mention the expansion of my own life partly as an example of what I mean. My earliest recollection is of a small one-room log hut on a large slave plantation in Virginia. After the close of the war, while working in the coal-mines of West Virginia for the support of my mother, I heard in some accidental way of the Hampton Institute. When I learned that it was an institution where a black boy could study, could have a chance to work for his board, and at the same time be taught how to work and to realize the dignity of labor, I resolved to go there. Bidding my mother good-by, I started out one morning to find my way to Hampton, though I was almost penniless and had no definite idea where Hampton was. By walking, begging rides, and paying for a portion of the journey on the steam-cars, I finally succeeded in reaching the city of Richmond, Virginia. I was without money or friends. I slept under a sidewalk, and by working on a vessel next day I earned money to continue my way to the institute, where I arrived with a surplus of fifty cents. At Hampton I found the opportunity — in the way of buildings, teachers, and industries provided by the generous — to get training in the class-room and by practical touch with industrial life, to learn thrift, economy, and push. I was surrounded by an atmosphere of business, Christian influence, and a spirit of self-help that seemed to have awakened every faculty in me, and caused me for the first time to realize what it meant to be a man instead of a piece of property.

While there I resolved that when I had finished the course of training I would go into the far South, into the Black Belt of the South, and give my life to providing the same kind of opportunity for self-reliance and self-awakening that I had found provided for me at Hampton. My work began at Tuskegee, Alabama, in 1881, in a small shanty and church, with one teacher and thirty students, without a dollar's worth of property. The spirit of work and of industrial thrift, with aid from the State and generosity from the North, has enabled us to develop an institution of eight hundred students gathered from nineteen States, with seventy-nine instructors, fourteen hundred acres of land, and thirty buildings, including large and small; in all, property valued at $280,000. Twenty-five industries have been organized, and the whole work is carried on at an annual cost of about $80,000 in cash; two fifths of the annual expense so far has gone into permanent plant.

What is the object of all this outlay? First, it must be borne in mind that we have in the South a peculiar and unprecedented state of things. It is of the utmost importance that our energy be given to meeting conditions that exist right about us rather than conditions that existed centuries ago or that exist in countries a thousand miles away. What are the cardinal needs among the seven millions of colored people in the South, most of whom are to be found on the plantations? Roughly, these needs may be stated as food, clothing, shelter, education, proper habits, and a settlement of race relations. The seven millions of colored people of the South cannot be reached directly by any missionary agency, but they can be reached by sending out among them strong selected young men and women, with the proper training of head, hand, and heart, who will live among these masses and show them how to lift themselves up.

The problem that the Tuskegee Institute keeps before itself constantly is how to prepare these leaders. From the outset, in connection with religious and academic training, it has emphasized industrial or hand training as a means of finding the way out of present conditions. First, we have found the industrial teaching useful in giving the student a chance to work out a portion of his expenses while in school. Second, the school furnishes labor that has an economic value, and at the same time gives the student a chance to acquire knowledge and skill while performing the labor. Most of all, we find the industrial system valuable in teaching economy, thrift, and the dignity of labor, and in giving moral backbone to students. The fact that a student goes out into the world conscious of his power to build a house or a wagon, or to make a harness, gives him a certain confidence and moral independence that he would not possess without such training.

A more detailed example of our methods at Tuskegee may be of interest. For example, we cultivate by student labor six hundred and fifty acres of land. The object is not only to cultivate the land in a way to make it pay our boarding department, but at the same time to teach the students, in addition to the practical work, something of the chemistry of the soil, the best methods of drainage, dairying, the cultivation of fruit, the care of livestock and tools, and scores of other lessons needed by a people whose main dependence is on agriculture. Notwithstanding that eighty-five per cent of the colored people in the South live by agriculture in some form, aside from what has been done by Hampton, Tuskegee, and one or two other institutions practically nothing has been attempted in the direction of teaching them about the very industry from which the masses of our people must get their subsistence. Friends have recently provided means for the erection of a large new chapel at Tuskegee. Our students have made the bricks for this chapel. A large part of the timber is sawed by students at our own sawmill, the plans are drawn by our teacher of architecture and mechanical drawing, and students do the brick-masonry, plastering, painting, carpentry work, tinning, slating, and make most of the furniture. Practically, the whole chapel will be built and furnished by student labor; in the end the school will have the building for permanent use, and the students will have a knowledge of the trades employed in its construction. In this way all but three of the thirty buildings on the grounds have been erected. While the young men do the kinds of work I have mentioned, the young women to a large extent make, mend, and launder the clothing of the young men, and thus are taught important industries.

One of the objections sometimes urged against industrial education for the negro is that it aims merely to teach him to work on the same plan that he was made to follow when in slavery. This is far from being the object at Tuskegee. At the head of each of the twenty-five industrial departments we have an intelligent and competent instructor, just as we have in our history classes, so that the student is taught not only practical brick-masonry, for example, but also the underlying principles of that industry, the mathematics and the mechanical and architectural drawing. Or he is taught how to become master of the forces of nature so that, instead of cultivating corn in the old way, he can use a corn cultivator, that lays off the furrows, drops the corn into them, and covers it, and in this way he can do more work than three men by the old process of corn-planting; at the same time much of the toil is eliminated and labor is dignified. In a word, the constant aim is to show the student how to put brains into every process of labor; how to bring his knowledge of mathematics and the sciences into farming, carpentry, forging, foundry work; how to dispense as soon as possible with the old form of ante-bellum labor. In the erection of the chapel just referred to, instead of letting the money which was given us go into outside hands, we make it accomplish three objects: first, it provides the chapel; second, it gives the students a chance to get a practical knowledge of the trades connected with building; and third, it enables them to earn something toward the payment of board while receiving academic and industrial training.

Having been fortified at Tuskegee by education of mind, skill of hand, Christian character, ideas of thrift, economy, and push, and a spirit of independence, the student is sent out to become a centre of influence and light in showing the masses of our people in the Black Belt of the South how to lift themselves up. How can this be done? I give but one or two examples. Ten years ago a young colored man came to the institute from one of the large plantation districts; he studied in the class-room a portion of the time, and received practical and theoretical training on the farm the remainder of the time. Having finished his course at Tuskegee, he returned to his plantation home, which was in a county where the colored people outnumber the whites six to one, as is true of many of the counties in the Black Belt of the South. He found the negroes in debt. Ever since the war they had been mortgaging ir crops for the food on which to live while the crops were growing. The majority of them were living from hand to mouth on rented land, in small, one-room log cabins, and attempting to pay a rate of interest on their advances that ranged from fifteen to forty per cent per annum. The school had been taught in a wreck of a log cabin, with no apparatus, and had never been in session longer than three months out of twelve. With as many as eight or ten persons of all ages and conditions and of both sexes huddled together in one cabin year after year, and with a minister whose only aim was to work upon the emotions of the people, one can imagine something of the moral and religious state of the community.

He took the three months' public school as a nucleus for his work. Then he organized the older people into a club, or conference, that held meetings every week. In these meetings he taught the people in a plain, simple manner how to save their money, how to farm in a better way, how to sacrifice, — to live on bread and potatoes, if need be, till they could get out of debt, and begin the buying of lands.

Soon a large proportion of the people were in condition to make contracts for the buying of homes (land is very cheap in the South), and to live without mortgaging their crops. Not only this: under the guidance and leadership of this teacher, the first year that he was among them they learned how, by contributions in money and labor, to build a neat, comfortable schoolhouse that replaced the wreck of a log cabin formerly used. The following year the weekly meetings were continued, and two months were added to the original three months of school. The next year two more months were added. The improvement has gone on, until now these people have every year an eight months' school.

I wish my readers could have the chance that I have had of going into this community. I wish they could look into the faces of the people and see them beaming with hope and delight. I wish they could see the two or three room cottages that have taken the place of the usual one-room cabin, the well-cultivated farms, and the religious life of the people that now means something more than the name. The teacher has a good cottage and a well-kept farm that serve as models. In a word, a complete revolution has been wrought in the industrial, educational, and religious life of this whole community by reason of the fact that they have had this leader, this guide and object-lesson, to show them how to take the money and effort that had hitherto been scattered to the wind in mortgages and high rents, in whiskey and gewgaws, and concentrate them in the direction of their own uplifting. One community on its feet presents an object-lesson for the adjoining communities, and soon improvements show themselves in other places.

Another student who received academic and industrial training at Tuskegee established himself, three years ago, as a blacksmith and wheelwright in a community, and, in addition to the influence of his successful business enterprise, he is fast making the same kind of changes in the life of the people about him that I have just recounted. It would be easy for me to fill many pages describing the influence of the Tuskegee graduates in every part of the South. We keep it constantly in the minds of our students and graduates that the industrial or material condition of the masses of our people must be improved, as well as the intellectual, before there can be any permanent change in their moral and religious life. We find it a pretty hard thing to make a good Christian of a hungry man. No matter how much our people "get happy" and "shout" in church, if they go home at night from church hungry, they are tempted to find something before morning. This is a principle of human nature, and is not confined to the negro.

The negro has within him immense power for self-uplifting, but for years it will be necessary to guide and stimulate him. The recognition of this power led us to organize, five years ago, what is now known as the Tuskegee Negro Conference, — a gathering that meets every February, and is composed of about eight hundred representative colored men and women from all sections of the Black Belt. They come in ox-carts, mule-carts, buggies, on muleback and horseback, on foot, by railroad: some traveling all night in order to be present. The matters considered at the conferences are those that the colored people have it within their own power to control: such as the evils of the mortgage system, the one-room cabin, buying on credit, the importance of owning a home and of putting money in the bank, how to build schoolhouses and prolong the school term, and how to improve their moral and religious condition.

As a single example of the results, one delegate reported that since the conferences were started five years ago eleven people in his neighborhood had bought homes, fourteen had got out of debt, and a number had stopped mortgaging their crops. Moreover, a schoolhouse had been built by the people themselves, and the school term had been extended from three to six months; and with a look of triumph he exclaimed, "We is done stopped libin' in de ashes!"

Besides this Negro Conference for the masses of the people, we now have a gathering at the same time known as the Workers' Conference, composed of the officers and instructors in the leading colored schools of the South. After listening to the story of the conditions and needs from the people themselves, the Workers' Conference finds much food for thought and discussion.

Nothing else so soon brings about right relations between the two races in the South as the industrial progress of the negro. Friction between the races will pass away in proportion as the black man, by reason of his skill, intelligence, and character, can produce something that the white man wants or respects in the commercial world. This is another reason why at Tuskegee we push the industrial training. We find that as every year we put into a Southern community colored men who can start a brick-yard, a sawmill, a tin-shop, or a printing-office, — men who produce something that makes the white man partly dependent upon the negro, instead of all the dependence being on the other side, — a change takes place in the relations of the races.

Let us go on for a few more years knitting our business and industrial relations into those of the white man, till a black man gets a mortgage on a white man's house that he can foreclose at will. The white man on whose house the mortgage rests will not try to prevent that negro from voting when he goes to the polls. It is through the dairy farm, the truck garden, the trades, and commercial life, largely, that the negro is to find his way to the enjoyment of all his rights. Whether he will or not, a white man respects a negro who owns a two-story brick house.

What is the permanent value of the Tuskegee system of training to the South in a broader sense? In connection with this, it is well to bear in mind that slavery taught the white man that labor with the hands was something fit for the negro only, and something for the white man to come into contact with just as little as possible. It is true that there was a large class of poor white people who labored with the hands, but they did it because they were not able to secure negroes to work for them; and these poor whites were constantly trying to imitate the slave-holding class in escaping labor, and they too regarded it as anything but elevating. The negro in turn looked down upon the poor whites with a certain contempt because they had to work. The negro, it is to be borne in mind, worked under constant protest, because he felt that his labor was being unjustly required, and he spent almost as much effort in planning how to escape work as in learning how to work. Labor with him was a badge of degradation. The white man was held up before him as the highest type of civilization, but the negro noted that this highest type of civilization himself did no labor; hence he argued that the less work he did, the more nearly he would be like a white man. Then, in addition to these influences, the slave system discouraged labor-saving machinery. To use labor-saving machinery intelligence was required, and intelligence and slavery were not on friendly terms; hence the negro always associated labor with toil, drudgery, something to be escaped. When the negro first became free, his idea of education was that it was something that would soon put him in the same position as regards work that his recent master had occupied. Out of these conditions grew the Southern habit of putting off till to-morrow and the day after the duty that should be done promptly to-day. The leaky house was not repaired while the sun shone, for then the rain did not come through. While the rain was falling, no one cared to expose himself to stop the leak. The plough, on the same principle, was left where the last furrow was run, to rot and rust in the field during the winter. There was no need to repair the wooden chimney that was exposed to the fire, because water could be thrown on it when it was on fire. There was no need to trouble about the payment of a debt to-day, for it could just as well be paid next week or next year. Besides these conditions, the whole South, at the close of the war, was without proper food, clothing, and shelter,— was in need of habits of thrift and economy and of something laid up for a rainy day.

This industrial training, emphasizing as it does the idea of economic production, is gradually bringing the South to the point where it is feeding itself. Before the war, and long after it, the South made what little profit was received from the cotton crop, and sent its earnings out of the South to purchase food supplies, — meat, bread, canned vegetables, and the like; but the improved methods of agriculture are fast changing this habit. With the newer methods of labor, which teach promptness and system, and emphasize the worth of the beautiful, — the moral value of the well-painted house, and the fence with every paling and nail in its place, — we are bringing to bear upon the South an influence that is making it a new country in industry, education, and religion.

Source: *Atlantic Monthly*, 1886

HOW WELL DID YOU UNDERSTAND THIS SELECTION?

1. What is the Tuskegee System?

2. What does Washington think is the solution to the problems African Americans face in the South?

3. What influence does Washington maintain Tuskegee Institute has had on the South?

4. What does Washington think is the key to improving race relations?

5. Why does Washington advocate industrial rather than academic training for African Americans?

6. How does Washington think Tuskegee Institute has changed southern attitudes about labor?

OF THE TRAINING OF BLACK MEN" By W.E.B. Du Bois

W.E.B. Du Bois was an African-American leader who often criticized Booker T. Washington, especially his views on race and education. Du Bois disagrees with Washington's idea that industrial training is the most appropriate education for African Americans. He thinks African Americans are suited for higher education, especially college.

From the shimmering swirl of waters where many, many thoughts ago the slave-ship first saw the square tower of Jamestown have flowed down to our day three streams of thinking: one from the larger world here and over-seas, saying, the multiplying of human wants in culture lands calls for the world-wide co-operation of men in satisfying them. Hence arises a new human unity, pulling the ends of earth nearer, and all men, black, yellow, and white. The larger humanity strives to feel in this contact of living nations and sleeping hordes a thrill of new life in the world, crying, If the contact of Life and Sleep be Death, shame on such Life. To be sure, behind this thought lurks the afterthought of force and dominion, — the making of brown men to delve when the temptation of beads and red calico cloys. The second thought streaming from the death-ship and the curving river is the thought of the older South: the sincere and passionate belief that somewhere between men and cattle God created a *tertium quid*, and called it a Negro, — a clownish, simple creature, at times even lovable within its limitations, but straitly foreordained to walk within the Veil. To be sure, behind the thought lurks the afterthought, — some of them with favoring chance might become men, but in sheer self-defense we dare not let them, and build about them walls so high, and hang between them and the light a veil so thick, that they shall not even think of breaking through. And last of all there trickles down that third and darker thought, the thought of the things themselves, the confused half-conscious mutter of men who are black and whitened, crying Liberty, Freedom, Opportunity — vouchsafe to us, O boastful World, the chance of living men! To be sure, behind the thought lurks the afterthought: suppose, after all, the World is right and we are less than men? Suppose this mad impulse within is all wrong, some mock mirage from the untrue?

So here we stand among thoughts of human unity, even through conquest and slavery; the inferiority of black men, even if forced by fraud; a shriek in the night for the freedom of men who themselves are not yet sure of their right to demand it. This is the tangle of thought and afterthought wherein we are called to solve the problem of training men for life. Behind all its curiousness, so attractive alike to sage and dilettante, lie its dim dangers, throwing across us shadows at once grotesque and awful. Plain it is to us that what the world seeks through desert and wild we have within our threshold; — a stalwart laboring force, suited to the semi-tropics; if, deaf to the voice of the Zeitgeist, we refuse to use and develop these men, we risk poverty and loss. If, on the other hand, seized by the brutal afterthought, we debauch the race thus caught in our talons, selfishly sucking their blood and brains in the future as in the past, what shall save us from national decadence? Only that saner selfishness which, education teaches men, can find the rights of all in the whirl of work.

Again, we may decry the color prejudice of the South, yet it remains a heavy fact. Such curious kinks of the human mind exist and must be reckoned with soberly. They cannot be laughed away, nor always successfully stormed at, nor easily abolished by act of legislature. And yet they cannot be encouraged by being let alone. They must be recognized as facts, but unpleasant facts; things that stand in the way of civilization and religion and common decency. They can be met in but one way: by the breadth and broadening of human reason, by catholicity of taste and culture. And so, too, the native ambition and aspiration of men, even though they be black, backward, and ungraceful, must not lightly be dealt with. To stimulate wildly weak and untrained minds is to play with mighty fires; to flout their striving idly is to welcome a harvest of brutish crime and shameless lethargy in our very laps. The guiding of thought and the deft coordination of deed is at once the path of honor and humanity.

And so, in this great question of reconciling three vast and partially contradictory streams of thought, the one panacea of Education leaps to the lips of all; such human training as will best use the labor of all men without enslaving or brutalizing; such training as will give us poise to encourage the prejudices that bulwark society, and stamp out those that in sheer barbarity deafen us to the wail of prisoned souls within the Veil, and the mounting fury of shackled men.

But when we have vaguely said Education will set this tangle straight, what have we uttered but a truism? Training for life teaches living; but what training for the profitable living together of black men and white? Two hundred years ago our task would have seemed easier. Then Dr. Johnson blandly assured us that education was needed solely for the embellishments of life, and was useless for ordinary vermin. Today we have climbed to heights where we would open at least the outer courts of knowledge to all, display its treasures to many, and select the few to whom its mystery of Truth is revealed, not wholly by truth or the accidents of the stock market, but at least in part according to deftness and aim, talent and character. This program, however, we are sorely puzzled in carrying out through that part of the land where the blight of slavery fell hardest, and where we are dealing with two backward peoples. To make here in human education that ever necessary combination of the permanent and the contingent — of the ideal and the practical in workable equilibrium — has been there, as it ever must be in every age and place, a matter of infinite experiment and frequent mistakes.

In rough approximation we may point out four varying decades of work in Southern education since the Civil War. From the close of the war until 1876 was the period of uncertain groping and temporary relief. There were army schools, mission schools, and schools of the Freedmen's Bureau in chaotic disarrangement, seeking system and cooperation. Then followed ten years of constructive definite effort toward the building of complete school systems in the South. Normal schools and colleges were founded for the freedmen, and teachers trained there to man the public schools. There was the inevitable tendency of war to underestimate the prejudice of the master and the ignorance of the slave, and all seemed clear sailing out of the wreckage of the storm. Meantime, starting in this decade yet especially developing from 1885 to 1895, began the industrial revolution of the South. The land saw glimpses of a new destiny and the stirring of new ideals. The educational system striving to complete itself saw new obstacles and a field of work ever broader and deeper. The Negro colleges, hurriedly founded, were inadequately equipped, illogically distributed, and of varying efficiency and grade; the normal and high schools were doing little more than common school work, and the common schools were training but a third of the children who ought to be in them, and training these too often poorly. At the same time the white South, by reason of its sudden conversion from the slavery ideal, by so much the more became set and strengthened in its racial prejudice, and crystallized it into harsh law and harsher custom; while the marvelous pushing forward of the poor white daily threatened to take even bread and butter from the mouths of the heavily handicapped sons of the freedmen. In the midst, then, of the larger problem of Negro education sprang up the more practical question of work, the inevitable economic quandary that faces a people in the transition from slavery to freedom, and especially those who make that change amid hate and prejudice, lawlessness and ruthless competition.

The industrial school springing to notice in this decade, but coming to full recognition in the decade beginning with 1895, was the proffered answer to this combined educational and economic crisis, and an answer of singular wisdom and timeliness. From the very first in nearly all the schools some attention had been given to training in handiwork, but now was this training first raised to a dignity that brought it in direct touch with the South's magnificent industrial development, and given an emphasis which reminded black folk that before the Temple of Knowledge swing the Gates of Toil.

Yet after all they are but gates, and when turning our eyes from the temporary and the contingent in the Negro problem to the broader question of the permanent uplifting and civilization of black men in America, we have a right to inquire, as this enthusiasm for material advancement mounts to its height, if after all the industrial school is the final and sufficient answer in the training of the Negro race; and to ask gently, but in all sincerity, the ever recurring query of the ages, Is not life more than meat, and the body more than raiment? And men ask this to-day all the more eagerly because of sinister signs in recent educational movements. The tendency is here born of slavery and quickened to renewed life by the crazy imperialism of the day, to regard human beings as among the material resources of a land to be trained with an eye single to future dividends. Race prejudices, which keep brown and black men in their "places," we are coming to regard as useful allies with such a theory, no matter how much they may dull the ambition and sicken the hearts of struggling human beings. And above all, we daily hear that an education that encourages aspiration, that sets the loftiest of ideals and seeks as an end culture and character than bread-winning, is the privilege of white men and the danger and delusion of black.

Especially has criticism been directed against the former educational efforts to aid the Negro. In the four periods I have mentioned, we find first boundless, planless enthusiasm and sacrifice; then the preparation of teachers for a vast public school system; then the launching and expansion of that school system amid increasing difficulties; and finally the training of workmen for the new and growing industries. This development has been sharply ridiculed as a logical anomaly and flat reversal of nature. Soothly we have been told that first industrial and manual training should have taught the Negro to work, then simple schools should have taught him to read and write, and finally, after years, high and normal schools could have completed the system, as intelligence and skill were demanded.

That a system logically so complete was historically impossible, it needs but a little thought to prove. Progress in human affairs is more often a pull than a push, surging forward of the exceptional man, and the lifting of his duller brethren slowly and painfully to his vantage ground. Thus it was no accident that gave birth to universities centuries before the common schools, that made fair Harvard the first flower of our wilderness. So in the South: the mass of the freedmen at the end of the war lacked the intelligence so necessary to modern workingmen. They must first have the common school to teach them to read, write, and cipher. The white teachers who flocked South went to establish such a common school system. They had no idea of founding colleges; they themselves at first would have laughed at the idea. But they faced, as all men since them have faced, that central paradox of the South, the social separation of the races. Then it was the sudden volcanic rupture of nearly all relations between black and white, in work and government and family life. Since then a new adjustment of relations in economic and political affairs has grown up, — an adjustment subtle and difficult to grasp, yet singularly ingenious, which leaves still that frightful chasm at the color line across which men pass at their peril. Thus, then and now, there stand in the South two separate worlds; and separate not simply in the higher realms of social intercourse, but also in church and school, on railway and street car, in hotels and theatres, in streets and city sections, in books and newspapers, in asylums and jails, in hospitals and graveyards. There is still enough of contact for large economic and group cooperation, but the separation is so thorough and deep, that it absolutely precludes for the present between the races anything like that sympathetic and effective group training and leadership of the one by the other, such as the American Negro and all backward peoples must have for effectual progress.

This the missionaries of '68 soon saw; and if effective industrial and trade schools were impractical before the establishment of a common school system, just as certainly no adequate common schools could be founded until there were teachers to teach them. Southern whites would not teach them; Northern whites in sufficient numbers could not be had. If the Negro was to learn, he must teach himself, and the most effective help that could be given him was the establishment of schools to train Negro teachers. This conclusion was slowly but surely reached by every student of the situation until simultaneously, in widely separated regions, without consultation or systematic plan, there arose a series of institutions designed to furnish teachers for the untaught. Above the sneers of critics at the obvious defects of this procedure must ever stand its one crushing rejoinder: in a single generation they put thirty thousand black teachers in the South; they wiped out the illiteracy of the majority of the black people of the land, and they made Tuskegee possible.

Such higher training schools tended naturally to deepen broader development: at first they were common and grammar schools, then some became high schools. And finally, by 1900, some thirty-four had one year or more of studies of college grade. This development was reached with different degrees of speed in different institutions: Hampton is still a high school, while Fisk University started her college in 1871, and Spelman Seminary about 1896. In all cases the aim was identical: to maintain the standards of the lower training by giving teachers and leaders the best practicable training; and above all to furnish the black world with adequate standards of human culture and lofty ideals of life. It was not enough that the teachers of teachers should be trained in technical normal methods; they must also, so far as possible, be broad-minded, cultured men and women, to scatter civilization among a people whose ignorance was not simply of letters, but of life itself.

It can thus be seen that the work of education in the South began with higher institutions of training, which threw off as their foliage common schools, and later industrial schools, and at the same time strove to shoot their roots ever deeper toward college and university training. That this was an inevitable and necessary development, sooner or later, goes without saying; but there has been, and still is, a question in many minds if the natural growth was not forced, and if the higher training was not either overdone or done with cheap and unsound methods. Among white Southerners this feeling is widespread and positive. A prominent Southern journal voiced this in a recent editorial: "The experiment that has been made to give the colored students classical training has not been satisfactory. Even though many were able to pursue the course, most of them did so in a parrot-like way, learning what was taught, but not seeming to appropriate the truth and import of their instruction, and graduating without sensible aim or valuable occupation for their future. The whole scheme has proved a waste of time, efforts, and the money of the state." While most far-minded men would recognize this as extreme and overdrawn, still without doubt many are asking, are there a sufficient number of Negroes ready for college training to warrant the undertaking? Are not too many students prematurely forced into this work? Does it not have the effect of dissatisfying the young Negro with his environment? And do these graduates succeed in real life? Such natural questions cannot be evaded, nor on the other hand must a nation naturally skeptical as to Negro ability assume an unfavorable answer without careful inquiry and patient openness to conviction. We must not forget that most Americans answer all queries regarding the Negro *a priori*, and that the least that human courtesy can do is to listen to evidence.

The advocates of the higher education of the Negro would be the last to deny the incompleteness and glaring defects of the present system: too many institutions have attempted to do college work, the work in some cases has not been thoroughly done, and quantity rather than quality has sometimes been sought. But all this can be said of higher education throughout the land: it is the almost inevitable incident of educational growth, and leaves the deeper question of the legitimate demand for the higher training of Negroes untouched. And this latter question can be settled in but one way — by a first-hand study of the facts. If we leave out of view all institutions which have not actually graduated students from a course higher than that of a New England high school, even though they be called colleges; if then we take the thirty-four remaining institutions, we may clear up many misapprehensions by asking searchingly, What kind of institutions are they, what do they teach, and what sort of men do they graduate?

From such schools about two thousand Negroes have gone forth with the bachelor's degree. The number in itself is enough to put at rest the argument that too large a proportion of Negroes are receiving higher training. If the ratio to population of all Negro students throughout the land, in both college and secondary training, be counted, Commissioner Harris assures us "it must be increased to five times its present average" to equal the average of the land.

Fifty years ago the ability of Negro students in any appreciable numbers to master a modern college course would have been difficult to prove. Today it is proved by the fact that four hundred Negroes, many of whom have been reported as brilliant students, have received the bachelor's degree from Harvard, Yale, Oberlin, and seventy other leading colleges. Here we have, then, nearly twenty-five hundred Negro graduates, of whom the crucial query must be made. How far did their training fit them for life? It is of course extremely difficult to collect satisfactory data on such a point, — difficult to reach the men, to get trustworthy testimony, and to gauge that testimony by any generally acceptable criterion of success. In 1900, the Conference at Atlanta University undertook to study these graduates, and published the results. First they sought to know what these graduates were doing, and succeeded in getting answers from nearly two thirds of the living. The direct testimony was in almost all cases corroborated by the reports of the colleges where they graduated, so that in the main the reports were worthy of credence. Fifty-three per cent of these graduates were teachers, — presidents of institutions, heads of normal schools, principals of city school systems, and the like. Seventeen per cent were clergymen; another seventeen per cent were in the professions, chiefly as physicians. Over six per cent were merchants, farmers, and artisans, and four per cent were in the government civil service. Granting even that a considerable proportion of the third unheard from are unsuccessful, this is a record of usefulness. Personally I know many hundreds of these graduates and have corresponded with more than a thousand; through others I have followed carefully the life-work of scores; I have taught some of them and some of the pupils whom they have taught, lived in homes which they have built, and looked at life through their eyes. Comparing them as a class with my fellow students in New England and in Europe, I cannot hesitate in saying that nowhere have I met men and women with a broader spirit of helpfulness, with deeper devotion to their life-work, or with more consecrated determination to succeed in the face of bitter difficulties than among Negro college-bred men.

Strange to relate! for this is certain, no secure civilization can be built in the South with the Negro as an ignorant, turbulent proletariat. Suppose we seek to remedy this by making them laborers and nothing more: they are not fools, they have tasted of the Tree of Life, and they will not cease to think, will not cease attempting to read the riddle of the world. By taking away their best equipped teachers and leaders, by slamming the door of opportunity in the faces of their bolder and brighter minds, will you make them satisfied with their lot? Or will you not rather transfer their leading from the hands of men taught to think to the hands of untrained demagogues? We ought not to forget that despite the pressure of poverty, and despite the active discouragement and even ridicule of friends, the demand for higher training steadily increases among Negro youth: there were, in the years from 1875 to 1880, twenty-two Negro graduates from Northern colleges; from 1885 to 1895 there were forty-three, and from 1895 to 1900, nearly 100 graduates. From Southern Negro colleges there were, in the same three periods, 143, 413, and over 500 graduates. Here, then, is the plain thirst for training; by refusing to give this Talented Tenth the key to knowledge can any sane man imagine that they will lightly lay aside their yearning and contentedly become hewers of wood and drawers of water?

The function of the Negro college then is clear: it must maintain the standards of popular education, it must seek the social regeneration of the Negro, and it must help in the solution of problems of race contact and cooperation. And finally, beyond all this, it must develop men. Above our modern socialism, and out of the worship of the mass, must persist and evolve that higher individualism which the centers of culture protect; there must come a loftier respect for the sovereign human soul that seeks to know itself and the world about it; that seeks a freedom for expansion and self-development; that will love and hate and labor in its own way, untrammeled alike by old and new. Such souls aforetime have inspired and guided worlds, and if we be not wholly bewitched by our Rhine-gold, they shall again.

Source: *Atlantic Monthly*, 1902

HOW WELL DID YOU UNDERSTAND THIS SELECTION?

1. What type of education does Du Bois advocate for African Americans?

2. Compare and contrast the ideas of Du Bois and Booker T. Washington regarding education for African Americans. How do the two men differ? Are there any similarities between them? Explain?

3. What does Du Bois think the ultimate value of college education will be for African Americans?

4. Is Du Bois an optimist or a pessimist?

5. What does Du Bois believe will be the consequence for American society if African Americans continue to be denied the right to a college education?

6. How does Du Bois respond to the white charge that African Americans are criminal?

7. How does Du Bois justify allowing African Americans to receive college education?

8. What are Du Bois' ideas on race relations? What does he think is necessary before improvements in race relations can occur?

MULTIPLE CHOICE: Circle the correct response. The correct answers are given at the end.

1. Who was Andrew Carnegie?
   a. An important financier of the American Revolutionary War.
   b. One of the leaders of the oil refining industry.
   c. A wealthy steel magnet who used vertical integration to control all aspects of his business.
   d. A leader of the Progressive Movement who demanded that government place curbs on big business.

2. Which of the following industries can best be described as the engine that drove the American Industrial Revolution?
   a. Steel.
   b. Railroads.
   c. Oil.
   d. Coal.

3. Which of the following statements best describes the conditions of African Americans during the industrial era?
   a. Most lived in the North and had high paying jobs.
   b. In both the North and South blacks worked in the lowest paying jobs in the worst possible conditions.
   c. Most lived in the West where they worked as cowboys.
   d. Many were able to attend public universities in the South where upon graduation they found high paying jobs.

4. How did big business generally respond to Unions during the Industrial Era?
   a. By refusing to bargain with Unions.
   b. By signing Union contracts beneficial to workers.
   c. By forming company unions that workers could join.
   d. By raising wages to keep union out of factories and mines.

5. How much did immigrant workers earn, on average, during the last decades of the nineteenth century?
   a. $25,000 per year.
   b. $5,000 per year.
   c. $2,500 per year.
   d. $250 to $300 per year.

6. What Presidential candidate in the 1872 election is described as a spiritualist who advocated free love?
   a. Grover Cleveland.
   b. Elizabeth Cady Stanton.
   c. Victoria Woodhull.
   d. Horace Greeley.

7. Why did Congress enact the Sherman Anti-Trust Act?
   a. To encourage companies to become monopolies.
   b. Because monopolies were restricting competition.
   c. Because workers were being abused by large corporations.
   d. So that American companies could expand into overseas markets.

8. One result of American industrialism was:
   a. Safe working conditions in factories.
   b. The location of factories in rural areas.
   c. High wages for women and children.
   d. Explosive population growth in cities.

9. Why did the United States go to war with Spain in 1898?
   a. Because Spain was a barbaric nation.
   b. Because Spain destroyed the American battleship Maine.
   c. Because Spain refused to liberate Cuba.
   d. Because the United States wanted Spanish colonial possessions like Puerto Rico and the Philippines.

10. What did the theory of Social Darwinism hold?
    a. That government should develop affirmative action programs to help minorities.
    b. That an agricultural lifestyle was superior to an industrial lifestyle.
    c. That it was inevitable that a few exceptional people would rise to the top of society.
    d. That the American gene pool was being strengthened by immigration.

ANSWERS:
   1-c; 2-b; 3-b; 4-a; 5-d; 6-c; 7-b; 8-d; 9-d; 10-c

ESSAYS:

1. Discuss the impact the Industrial Revolution had on American politics and government. Pay attention to foreign policy and race relations.

2. Compare and contrast the impact the Industrial Revolution had on farmers and workers. How did both groups respond to industrialism? How successful were workers and farmers in solving problems both groups faced?

3. Should the government have done more to regulate industrialism? Why or why not?

4. Why did Andrew Carnegie and others adopt ideas like the Social Gospel and Social Darwinism? Do these ideas reflect elitism and racism? Why or why not?

OPTIONAL ACTIVITIES: (Use your knowledge **and** imagination.)

1. You are an immigrant in a West Virginia labor camp. Write a letter to a friend in your native country about your experiences in America.

2. You are Booker T. Washington. As president of Tuskegee Institute, you need to hire a new faculty member. Devise a set of interview questions to ask job applicants that reflect your views on African-American education.

3. Read other books in the Oz series written by L. Frank Baum. See if you can find symbolism from other historical periods and events (hint, one Oz book is about feminism).

WEB SITE LISTINGS:

Tsongas Industrial History Center
Educational programs about the American Industrial Revolution. http://www.uml.edu/tsongas/

The Blackstone Valley
The song "Blackstone Valley," written by Charlie Ball and performed by Plainfolk, tells the tale of the river that launched the American Industrial Revolution. http://www.plainfolk.com/BSV.html

Lowell Visitors Bureau
Visit website for historical information on such things as the beginnings of the Industrial Revolution in America. http://www.lowell.org/

Industrial Revolution
(Letsfindout.com) http://www.letsfindout.com/subjects/america/industri.html

Industrial Revolution
(Encyclopedia.com) http://www.encyclopedia.com/articles/06349.html

Carnegie, Andrew
(Encarta® Concise Encyclopedia Article)
http://encarta.msn.com/index/conciseindex/19/019E0000.htm?z=1&pg=2&br=1

Carnegie, Andrew
(Encyclopedia.com) http://www.encyclopedia.com/articles/02322.html

Ford, Henry
http://www.encyclopedia.com/search.asp?target=@DOCTITLE%20Ford%20%20Henry

The Magic of Oz
L. Frank Baum http://sailor.gutenberg.org/etext96/magoz10.txt

Lowell National Historical Park
The official expanded NPS website. Lowell National Historical Park preserves and interprets the history of the American Industrial Revolution in Lowell, MA. The park includes historic cotton textile mills, 5.6 miles of canals, operating gatehouses, and worker housing. http://www.nps.gov/lowe/home.htm

A Historical View of U.S. Immigration Policy
...the U.S. passed the **National Origins Act**. This **act**... www.missouri.edu/~socbrent/immigr.htm

Spotlight Biography: Labor Reformers
As the power and scale of American industry grew during the 19th century, working conditions for most Americans underwent radical change. Mechanized, large-scale factories staffed by unskilled laborers gradually came to replace specialized craftsmen and small workshops. Samuel Gompers, more than any other individual, helped to modernize the unions, organize them on a national scale, and open their doors to unskilled as well as skilled workers. http://educate.si.edu/spotlight/labor.html

United Mine Workers of America
(Encarta® Concise Encyclopedia Article)
http://encarta.msn.com/index/conciseindex/49/0494B000.htm?z=1&pg=2&br=1

The Homestead and Pullman Strikes

In light of the recent depression, the voters of 1896 were concerned with keeping money in their pockets. Within recent public memory lay two major events that led to this unease—the Homestead strike of 1892 and the Pullman Railroad strike of 1894. These two conflicts brought to the surface the deeper issues at work in an age of industrial progress. http://iberia.vassar.edu/1896/strikes.html

Haymarket Square

(Encyclopedia.com) http://www.encyclopedia.com/articles/05722.html

Haymarket Square Riot

(Encarta® Concise Encyclopedia Article)
http://www.encyclopedia.com/search.asp?target=@DOCTITLE%20Haymarket%20Square%20riot

Chapter Fourteen

THE TRANS-MISSOURI WEST: The Last Frontier

Life west of the Mississippi River was vastly different for people living there than it was for people living east of the Mississippi River before the twentieth century. Native Americans were being forced onto reservations and conflict erupted when whites took Native American land by measures such as the Dawes Act. Native American leaders such as Red Cloud and W.C. Duncan protested before Congress and the American public but their words generally fell on deaf ears. After the Civil War thousands of farmers, miners, and outlaws went west seeking their fortune. These people did not care whether they took land from Native Americans; after all, they viewed Indians as standing in the way of progress. This migration was made possible in part by completion of the Transcontinental Railroad after the federal government offered huge subsidies to railroad companies willing to build this line. Life, for most, was difficult. Social mobility was no easier out West than it was back East. Individuals who came west with money had a much better chance of becoming wealthy than poor people. The West was, however, something of a melting pot as people from all over the world intermingled. Despite the multicultural nature of western society, ethnic minorities in western territories faced racism, prejudice, and discrimination. Congress passed the Chinese Exclusion Act to prevent more Chinese immigrants from settling in the West. Tejanos in Texas and other western states saw their land taken by white settlers. Conflict sometimes broke out between whites and Hispanics, between sheep ranchers and cattle barons, between miners and corporations, and between farmers and ranchers. During this time many myths about the West were created and passed down to future generations of Americans. The lonely cowboy, the gun-fighter, the rancher, etc. are all images Americans living today think of when the West is mentioned. While the western myth has some validity, most of it is not true. Ironically, at the very time the western myth was being created, the West was ending. In 1880 the United States Census Bureau declared the frontier to be officially closed.

The Populist Party arose in the West and made a mark on the American political landscape. Its candidate, William Jennings Bryan, ran a spirited campaign in 1896 when he and western farmers indicted the Republicans for standing behind the gold standard. In many respects the 1896 election represents a clash between the old America, a land of farms, ranchers, and independent individuals, with the new America, a land of corporate monoliths, workers enslaved to the factory, and robber barons who made vast fortunes from the sweat of millions of ordinary laborers.

IDENTIFICATION: Briefly describe each term.

Chief Joseph

Buffalo Bill Cody

Blackfeet

Little Crow

Sioux

Quaker Policy

Heroes of Sand Creek

George Armstrong Custer

Crazy Horse

Sitting Bull

Geronimo

Wounded Knee

Ghost Dance

Dawes Act

Chinese Exclusion Act

Workingmen's Party

Santa Fe Ring

Texas Rangers

Exodusters

Buffalo Soldiers

Comstock Lode

Western Federation of Miners

Joseph McCoy

Johnson County War

Code of the West

Lincoln County War

O.K. Coral

Leland Stanford

Homestead Act of 1862

Defeated Legion

Morrill Act

Grange (Patrons of Husbandry)

Wabash Case

Interstate Commerce Commission

Populist Movement

William McKinley

William Jennings Bryan

Yellowstone National Park

Annie Oakley

Mark Twain

THINK ABOUT:

1. Describe Native American societies in the West. What importance did the buffalo play in these societies? What did the slaughter of the buffalo mean for Native Americans living in the West? What role did government policy play in the decline of Native American societies?

2. Describe your life as a Chinese immigrant? How do you feel about your treatment at the hands of the American government?

3. Examine the views of the Grangers, the Populist, and the Republicans. How were they different? How were they similar?

4. How did life in the West differ from life in the East?

5. Describe your life as a homesteader in the West. What process did you have to follow to acquire land?

THE HOMESTEAD ACT

Passage of the Homestead Act by Congress in 1862 created the first program for making public lands available to ordinary Americans. Thousands of Americans went west in search of new lands. By the time the Civil War had ended, about 15,000 homestead claims had been filed with the government. Thousands of additional claims were filed during the two decades following the war. Most people filing claims were poor farmers from the East and Midwest; city dwellers generally lacked the resources and knowledge to farm in the West. The Homestead Act was responsible for Native Americans losing most of their land from 1862 until 1890. Americans who homesteaded in western states usually faced countless hardships, ranging from periodic droughts to erosion and violence. Some preserved while others gave up and went back east.

An act to secure homesteads to actual settlers on the public domain.

Be it enacted, that any person who is the head of a family, or who has arrived at the age of twenty-one years, and is a citizen of the United States, or who shall have filed his declaration of intention to become such, as required by the naturalization laws of the United States, and who has never born arms against the United States Government or given aid and comfort to its enemies, shall, from and after the first of January, eighteen hundred and sixty-three, be entitled to enter one quarter-section or a less quantity of unappropriated public lands, upon which said person may have filed a pre-emption claim, or which may, at the time the application is made be subject to pre-emption at one dollar and twenty-five cents, or less, per acre; or eighty acres or less of such unappropriated lands, at two dollars and fifty cents per acre, to be located in a body, in conformity to the legal subdivisions of the public lands, and after the same shall have been surveyed; Provided, that any person owning or residing on land may, under the provisions of this act, enter other land lying contiguous to his or her said land, which shall not, with the land so already owned and occupied, exceed in the aggregate one hundred and sixty acres.

Section 2. That the person applying for the benefit of this act shall, upon application to the register of the land office in which he or she is about to make such entry, make affidavit before the said register or receiver that he or she is the head of a family, or is twenty-one or more years of age, or shall have performed service in the Army or Navy of the United States, and that he has never born arms against the Government of the United States or given aid and comfort to its enemies, and that such application is made for his or her exclusive use and benefit, and that said entry is made for the purpose of actual settlement and cultivation, and not, either directly or indirectly, for the use or benefit of any other person or persons whomsoever; and upon filing the said affidavit with the register or receiver, and on payment of ten dollars, he or she shall thereupon be permitted to enter the quantity of land specified: Provided, however, that no certificate shall be given or patent issued therefore until the expiration of five years from the date of such entry; and if, at the expiration of such time, or at any time within two years thereafter, the person making such entry—or if he be dead, his widow; or in case of her death, his heirs or devisee; or in case of a widow making such entry, her heirs or devise, in case of her death—shall prove by two credible witnesses that he, she, or they have resided upon or cultivated the same for the term of five years immediately succeeding the time of filing the affidavit aforesaid, and shall make affidavit that no part of said land has been alienated, and that he has born true allegiance to the Government of the United States; then, in such case, he, she, or they, if at that time a citizen of the United States, shall be entitled to a patent, as in other cases provided for by law; And provided, further, that in case of the death of both father and mother, leaving an infant child or children under twenty-one years of age, the right and fee shall inure to the benefit of said infant child or children; and the executor, administrator, or guardian may, at any time within two years after the death of the surviving parent, and in accordance with the laws of the State in which such children for the time being have their domicile, sell said land for the benefit of said infants, but for no other purpose; and the purchaser shall acquire the absolute title by the purchase, and be entitled to a patent from the United States, on payment of the office fees and sum of money herein specified....

Source: U.S. Statutes at Large, Vol. 12

HOW WELL DID YOU UNDERSTAND THIS SELECTION?

1. Why did Congress enact the Homestead Act?

2. How much land could the head of a family acquire?

3. How much did the land cost the homesteader?

4. What effect did the Homestead Act have on settlement in the West? On Native Americans?

Perhaps the most important development in the history of the American West was construction of the transcontinental railroad. This railroad, which connected the East to the West, made it possible for western farmers and ranchers to get their crops and livestock to market. The transcontinental railroad would not likely have been built had the government not given tremendous subsidies to companies engaged in building the railway. The Pacific Railway Act, passed by Congress on July 1, 1862, made possible the construction of a railroad and telegraph line from the Missouri River to the Pacific Ocean.

Section 1. Be it enacted, That...five commissioners to be appointed by the Secretary of the Interior...are...erected into a body corporate...by the name of..."The Union Pacific Railroad Company"...and the...corporation is hereby authorized...to lay out, locate, construct, furnish, maintain and enjoy a continuous railroad and telegraph...from a point on the one hundredth meridian of longitude west from Greenwich, between the south margin of the valley of the Republican River and the north margin of the valley of the Platte River, to the western boundary of Nevada Territory, upon the route and terms hereinafter provided...

Section 2. That the right of way through...public lands be...granted to said company for the construction of said railroad and telegraph line; and the right...is hereby given to said company to take from the public lands adjacent to the line of said road, earth, stone, timber, and other materials for the construction thereof; said right of way is granted to said railroad to the extent of two hundred feet in width on each side of said railroad when it may pass over the public lands, including all necessary grounds, for stations, buildings, workshops, and depots, machine shops, switches, side tracks, turn tables, and water stations. The United States shall extinguish as rapidly as may be the Indian titles to all lands falling under the operation of this act...

Section 3. That there be...granted...for the purpose of aiding in the construction of...railroad and telegraph line, and to secure the safe and speedy transportation of mail, troops, munitions of war, and public stores thereon, every alternate section of public land, designated by odd numbers, to the amount of five alternate sections per mile on each side of said railroad, on the line thereof, and within the limits of ten miles on each side of...road... Provided That all mineral lands shall be excepted from the operation of act; but where the same shall contain timber, the timber thereon is...granted to said company...

Section 5. That for the purposes herein mentioned the Secretary of the Treasury shall...in accordance with the provisions of this act, issue to said company bonds of the United States of one thousand dollars each, payable in thirty years after date, paying six per centum per annum interest...to the amount of sixteen of said bonds per mile for each section of forty miles; and to secure the repayment to the United States...of the amount of said bonds...the issue of said bonds...shall ipso facto constitute a first mortgage on the whole line of the railroad and telegraph...

Section 9. That the Leavenworth, Pawnee and Western Railroad Company of Kansas are hereby authorized to construct a railroad and telegraph line...upon the same terms and conditions in all respects as are provided.... The Central Pacific Railroad Company of California is hereby authorized to construct a railroad and telegraph line from the Pacific coast...to the eastern boundaries of California, upon the same terms and conditions in all respects.

Section 10. ...And the Central Pacific Railroad Company of California after completing its road...is authorized to continue...construction...through the Territories of the United States to the Missouri River...upon the terms and conditions provided in this act...until said roads shall...connect...

Section 11. That for three hundred miles of said road most mountainous and difficult of construction, to wit: one hundred and fifty miles westerly from the eastern base of the Rocky Mountains, and one hundred and fifty miles eastwardly from the western base of the Sierra Nevada mountains...the bonds to be issued to aid in the construction thereof shall be treble the number per mile herein before provided...and between the sections last named of one hundred and fifty miles each, the bonds to be issued to aid in the constructions...shall be double the number per mile first mentioned...

Source: U.S. Statutes at Large, Vol. 12

HOW WELL DID YOU UNDERSTAND THIS SELECTION?

1. Why did Congress enact the Pacific Railway Act?

2. What incentives are railroads given to lay track across the West?

3. How did the government plan to finance the building of the transcontinental railroad?

4. What do you think would be the Populist Party's reaction to the fact that the government gave railroads so much western land? Why?

RED CLOUD SPEECH AT COOPER UNION, NEW YORK

Chief Red Cloud was one of the most important leaders of the Lakota Sioux. He was born in 1822 near the forks of the Platte River near what is now North Platte, Nebraska and died in 1909. Much of his early life was spent fighting whites and other Native American tribes in the West. His exploits as a warrior gave him enormous prominence within the Lakota nation. In 1866 Red Cloud led the Sioux in a war against the United States that represents the most successful conflict ever by a Native American tribe against the American government. The trouble began when the United States Army constructed forts along the Bozeman Trail in Wyoming to protect settlers and miners going to Montana and Colorado. Red Cloud attacked theses forts and defeated American forces, which caused the United States government in 1868 to sign the Fort Laramie Treaty, mandating that the United States would abandon its forts along the Bozeman Trail and guarantee the Lakota possession of the western half of South Dakota.

My brethren and my friends who are here before me this day. God Almighty has made us all, and He is here to bless what I have to say to you today. The Good Spirit made us both. He gave you lands and he gave us lands; he gave us these lands. You came in here, and we respected you as brothers. God Almighty made you but made you all white and clothed you. When he made us he made us with red skins and poor; now you have come.

When you first came we were very many, and you were few. Now you are many, and we are getting very few, and we are poor. You do not know who appears before you today to speak. I am a representative of the original American race, the first people of this continent. We are good and not bad. The reports that you hear concerning us are all on one side. We are always well disposed to them. You are here told that we are traitors and thieves, and it is not so. We have given you nearly all our lands, and if we had any more land to give we would be very glad to give it. We have nothing more. We are driven into a very little land, and we want you now, as our dear friends, to help us with the government of the United States.

The Great Father made us poor and ignorant—made you rich and wise and more skillful in these things that we know nothing about. The Great Father, the Good Father in heaven, made you all to eat tame food—made us to eat wild food—gives us the wild food. You ask anybody who has gone through our country to California; ask those who have settled there and in Utah, and you will find that we have treated them always well. You have children. We have children. You want to raise your children and make them happy and prosperous. We want to raise [ours] and make them happy and prosperous. We ask you to help us to do it.

At the mouth of the Horse Creek, in 1852, the Great Father made a treaty with us by which we agreed to let all that country open for fifty-five years for the transit of those who were going through. We kept this treaty. We never treated any man wrong. We never committed any murder or depredation until after the troops were sent into that country, and the troops killed our people and ill-treated them, and thus war and trouble arose, but before the troops were sent there we were quiet and peaceable, and there was no disturbance. Since that time there have been various goods sent from time to time to us, the only ones that ever reached us. After they reached us the government took them away. You, as good men, ought to help us to these goods.

Colonel Fitzpatrick of the government said we must all go to farm, and some of the people went to Fort Laramie and were badly treated. I only want to do that which is peaceful, and the Great Fathers know it, and also the Great Father who made us both. I came to Washington to see the Great Father in order to have peace and in order to have peace continue. That is all we want, and that is the reason why we are here now.

In 1868 men came out and brought papers. We are ignorant and do not read papers and they did not tell us right what was in these papers. We wanted them to take away their forts, leave our country, would not make war, and give our traders something. They said we had bound ourselves to trade on the Missouri, and we said, no, we did not want that. The interpreters deceived us. When I went to Washington I saw the Great Father. The Great Father showed me what the treaties were; he showed me all these points and showed me that the interpreters had deceived me and did not let me know what the right side of the treaty was. All I want is right and justice…. I represent the Sioux Nation, they will be governed by what I say and what I represent.

Look at me. I am poor and naked, but I am the chief of the Nation. We do not want riches, we do not ask for riches, but we want our children properly trained and brought up. We look to you for your sympathy. Our riches will … do us no good; we cannot take away into the other world anything we have—we want to have love and peace…. We would like to know why commissioners are sent out there to do nothing but rob [us] and get the riches of this world away from us?

I was brought up among the traders and those who came out there in those early times. I had a good time for they treated us nicely and well. They taught me how to wear clothes and use tobacco, and to use firearms and ammunition, and all went on very well until the Great Father sent out another kind of men—men who drank whisky. He sent out whisky men, men who drank and quarreled, men who were so bad that he could not keep them at home, and so he sent them out there.

I have sent a great many words to the Great Father, but I don't know that they ever reach the Great Father. They were drowned on the way, therefore I was a little offended with it. The words I told the Great Father lately would never come to him, so I thought I would come and tell you myself.

And I am going to leave you today, and I am going back to my home. I want to tell the people that we cannot trust his agents and superintendents. I don't want strange people that we know nothing about. I am very glad that you belong to us. I am very glad that we have come here and found you and that we can understand one another. I don't want any more such men sent out there, who are so poor that when they come out there their first thoughts are how they can fill their own pockets.

We want preserves in our reserves. We want honest men, and we want you to help to keep us in the lands that belong to us so that we may not be a prey to those who are viciously disposed. I am going back home. I am very glad that you have listened to me, and I wish you good-bye and give you an affectionate farewell.

Source: *The New York Times*, July 17, 1870

HOW WELL DID YOU UNDERSTAND THIS SELECTION?

1. How does Red Cloud describe Native Americans?

2. How does Red Cloud describe whites?

3. What similarities and differences does Red Cloud see in whites and Native Americans?

4. How does Red Cloud describe relations between Native Americans and the United States government?

5. Who is Red Cloud? What does he want? What is he doing?

THE DAWES ACT

The Dawes Act, passed by Congress in 1887 was designed to impose assimilation on all Native American tribes and enable land-hungry whites to take lands delegated to Indian peoples. By the 1880s most Native Americans were living on reservations. Many whites believed that the reservations were too large and wanted thousands of acres of land encompassed in these reservations taken away from Native Americans and given to white farmers. Congress, bowing to pressure from farmers and ranchers, passed the General Allotment Act (Dawes Act), which gave individual Indian families 160 acres of land. The hundreds of thousands of acres remaining were then sold at bargain prices to whites, many of whom were land speculators. Native Americans felt cheated again by the United States government. The land most were left with was not large enough to support a family. The Dawes Act is partly responsible for the poverty Native Americans living on reservations experienced during the nineteenth and twentieth centuries.

Be it enacted. That in all cases where any tribe or band of Indians has been, or shall hereafter be, located upon any reservation created for their use, either by treaty stipulation or by virtue of an act of Congress or executive order setting apart the same for their use, the President of the United States be, and he hereby is, authorized, whenever in his opinion any reservation or any part thereof of such Indians is advantageous for agriculture and grazing purposes to cause said reservation, or any part thereof, to be surveyed, or resurveyed if necessary, and to allot the lands in said reservation in severally to any Indian located thereon in quantities as follows: To each head of a family, one-quarter of a section; To each single person over eighteen years of age, one-eighth of a section; To each orphan child under eighteen years of age, one-eight of a section; and, To each other single person under eighteen years now living, or who may be born prior to the date of the order of the President directing an allotment of the lands embraced in any reservation, one-sixteenth of a section: .. .

That upon the approval of the allotments provided for in this act by the Secretary of the Interior, he shall ... declare that the United States does and will hold the land thus allotted, for the period of twenty-five years, in trust for the sole use and benefit of the Indian to whom such allotment shall have been made, ... and that at the expiration of said period the United States will convey the same by patent to said Indian, or his heirs as aforesaid, in fee, discharged of such trust and free of all charge or encumbrance whatsoever:...

That upon the completion of said allotments and the patenting of the lands to said allottees, each and every member of the respective bands or tribes of Indians to whom allotments have been made shall have the benefit of and be subject to the laws, both civil and criminal, of the State or Territory in which they may reside, ... And every Indian born within the territorial limits of the United States to whom allotments shall have been made under the provisions of this act or under any law or treaty, and every Indian born within the territorial limits of the United States who has voluntarily taken up, within said limits, his residence separate and apart from any tribe of Indians therein, and has adopted the habits of civilized life, is hereby declared to be a citizen of the United States, and is entitled to all the rights, privileges, and immunities of such citizens, whether said Indian has been or not, by birth or otherwise, a member of any tribe of Indians within the territorial limits of the United States without in any manner impairing or otherwise affecting the right of any such Indian to tribal or other property....

Source: United States Statutes at Large, Vol. 24

HOW WELL DID YOU UNDERSTAND THIS SELECTION?

1. What was the primary purpose of the Dawes Act?

2. How much land did Native Americans receive under the Dawes Act?

3. What effect do you think the Dawes Act had on Native Americans?

4. If you were a Native American, how would you have felt about the Dawes Act?

D. W. C. Duncan was a Cherokee Indian who testified before a United States Senate Committee in 1906 investigating the condition of Native Americans in the West. He testified against the General Allottment Act (the Dawes Act) ,which took land from Native Americans and allowed land speculators and white farmers to buy it at cheap prices from the government. His testimony provides a valuable record of the effect the Dawes Act had on Native Americans in the West. As his testimony makes clear, Native Americans were impoverished by this law.

Senators, just let me present to you a picture; I know this is a little digression, but let me present it. Suppose the Federal Government should send a survey company into the midst of some of your central counties of Kansas or Colorado or Connecticut and run off the surface of the earth into sections and quarter sections and quarter quarter sections and set apart to each one of the inhabitants of that county 60 acres, rescinding and annulling all title to every inch of the earth's surface which was not included in that 60 acres, would the State of Connecticut submit to it? Would Colorado submit to it? Would Kansas brook such an outrage? No! It would be ruin, immeasurable ruin—devastation. There is not an American citizen in any one of those states would submit to it, if it cost him every drop of his heart's blood. That, my Senators, permit me—I am honest, candid, and fraternal in my feelings—but let me ask a question? Who is that hastened on this terrible destruction upon these Cherokee people? Pardon me, it was the Federal Government. It is a fact; and, old as I am, I am not capable of indulging in euphemisms.

Before this allotment scheme was put in effect in the Cherokee Nation we were a prosperous people. We had farms. Every Indian in this nation that needed one and felt that he needed one had it. Orchards and gardens—everything that promoted the comforts of private life was ours, even as you—probably not so extensively—so far as we went, even as you in the States. The result has been, which I now want to illustrate, as I set out, by my own personal experience.

Under our old Cherokee regime I spent the early days of my life on the farm up here of 300 acres, and arranged to be comfortable in my old age, but the allotment scheme came along and struck me during the crop season while my corn was ripening in full ear. I was looking forward to the crop of corn hopefully for some comforts to be derived from it during the months of the winter. When I was assigned to that 60 acres, and I could take no more under the inexorable law of allotment enforced upon us Cherokees, I had to relinquish every inch of my premises outside of that little 60 acres. What is the result? There is a great scramble of persons to find land—the office was located here in our town— to file upon. Some of the friends in here, especially a white intermarried citizen, goes up and files upon a part of my farm—on a part of my growing crop, upon the crop upon which I had spent my labor and my money, and upon which I had based my hopes. I remonstrated with him. I said to him, "Sir, you don't want to treat me that way. We are neighbors and friends. You can't afford to take my property that way. Of course the Dawes Commission and the Curtis law will give you the land, although I have subdued it, and I have fenced it, and cultivated it. But for God's sake, my friend, don't take my crop." "Well," says he, "I had to surrender my crop to a fellow down here. He allotted on me, and I don't know why I should be any more lenient on you than others are on me. If you don't let that corn alone, I will go to the court and get an order." That was new to me, but when I came to examine the Curtis law, and investigated the orders and rules established by the Dawes Commission, I just folded my hands and said, "I give it up." Away went my crop, and if the same rule had been established in your counties in your State you would have lost your dwelling house, you would have lost your improvements. Now, that is what has been done to these Cherokees.

What a condition, I have 60 acres of land left me, the balance is all gone. I am an old man, not able to follow the plow as I used to when a boy. What am I going to do with it? For the last few years, since I have had my allotment, I have gone out there on that farm day after day I have used the ax, the hoe, the spade, the plow, hour for hour, until fatigue would throw me exhausted upon the ground. Next day I repeated the operation, and let me tell you, Senators, I have exerted all my ability, all industry, all my intelligence, if I have any, my will, my ambition, the love of my wife, all these agencies, I have employed to make my living out of that 60 acres, and God be my judge, I have not been able to do it. I am not able to do it. I can't do it. I have not been able to clear expenses. It will take every ear of the bounteous crop on that 60 acres, for this year is a pretty good crop year, it will take every bushel of it to satisfy the debts that I have incurred to eke out a living during the meager years just passed. And I am here today, a poor man upon the verge of starvation, my muscular energy gone. Hope gone I have nothing to charge my calamity to but the unwise legislation of Congress in reference to my Cherokee people.

I am in that fix. Senators, you will not forget now that when I use the word I, I mean the whole Cherokee people. I am in that fix. What am I to do? I have a piece of property that doesn't support me, and is not worth a cent to me under the same inexorable cruel provisions of the Curtis law that swept away our treaties, our system of nationality, our every existence, and wrested out of our possession our vast territory. The same provisions of that Curtis law that ought to have been satisfied with these achievements didn't stop there. The law goes on and that 60 acres of land, it says, shall not be worth one cent to me, although the Curtis law has given me 60 acres as the only inheritance I have in God's world, even that shall not be worth anything. Let me explain.

If you had a horse that you couldn't use, and some competent power ordained that that horse should have no value in any market on the face of the earth, and at the same time you should be compelled to keep that horse as long as he should live, or at least twenty-five years, at your expense, now, in the name of common sense, what would you do with that horse? He is not worth anything, his services are not worth anything to me, I can't ride him, I can't use him. There is no man in the world that will give me a cent for him, the law won't allow me to sell him. I would get rid of that horse somehow sure.

The point I am making here is applicable to every species of property, whether real or personal. Prevent the property from being purchasable in open market and you destroy it. Upon the same principle, my allotment up here is absolutely destroyed. What am I going to do with it? What can any Indian do with his allotment under similar circumstances?

Let me allude to myself again. It is not egotism I will tell you what I am going to do with my allotment. I sat down one day and wrote out my application for the removal of my restrictions. I went to work and pushed it through all the Federal machinery up to the Secretary of the Interior and back again, and a few days ago I was notified my restrictions were raised. Now for the next step. What am I going to do with that worthless piece of properly? I am going to hold it—how long I don't know—but I am going to wait until the white population becomes a little more multitudinous, when the price of real estate will rise. When I can get anything like an adequate value for my farm I am going to sell it. It is worthless to me.

The Government of the United States knows that these allotments of the Indians are not sufficient. Congress recognizes the fact forcibly, by implication, that these allotments are not sufficient. Why, one American citizen goes out on the western plain in North Dakota to make a home. What is the amount of land allotted to him? Isn't it 160 acres? Why, it is the general consensus all over the country that nothing less would be sufficient to support any family, and there are many years when you think, too, that 160 acres is not sufficient. Since this country has been split up, the Cherokee government abolished, and the allotments attained, immigration has come in from the surrounding States, consisting of persons of different kinds. I have tested them, and know what I am talking about, personally. Persons in pursuit of a sufficient quantity of land upon which to rear their families and take care of themselves, I have interrogated them time and again. I have said to them. "Look here, my friend, where are you going?" "To Indian Territory." "What for?" "To get a piece of land." "Did you have any land in Missouri or Kansas?" "Yes, sir; I had some up there, but it was too small and wasn't sufficient." "How much was it?" "Eighty or one hundred acres," as the case may be. "I have leased out my land up there to parties, and thought I would come down here and get a larger piece of ground." Well, now, that is the state of the case. I think, gentlemen, when you investigate the case fully you will find that these people have been put off with a piece of land that is absolutely inadequate for their needs.

Source: U.S. Senate Report 5013, 59th Congress, 2nd Session

HOW WELL DID YOU UNDERSTAND THIS SELECTION?

1. Who is Duncan? What is he reacting to?

2. How does Duncan describe Cherokee life before the Curtis Law took effect?

3. What happened to Duncan as a result of the Curtis Law?

4. What does Duncan want Congress to do?

REPORT ON WOUNDED KNEE MASSACRE, By Benjamin Harrison

Wounded Knee was the last battle fought between American forces and Native Americans in the West. On December 29, 1890, the Seventh Calvary (the unit massacred at Little Big Horn) of the United States Army and a group of Sioux Indians engaged in a skirmish that resulted in 64 casualties. In addition, 51 Indians, most of whom were women and children, were wounded. The battle was precipitated when the Sioux began to follow the prophet Wovoka and perform the Ghost Dance, which they believed would restore the tribe to its former glory. Settlers and Indian agents feared that this dancing might lead to renewed conflict and tried to suppress it. In the suppression the aging chief, Sitting Bull, was killed. The army feared that his death might cause an Indian uprising, and the Seventh Cavalry rounded up over three hundred Sioux who had left the reservation and camped at Wounded Knee, South Dakota. After the army had began the process of disarming the Sioux, one Indian, intentionally or unintentionally (the evidence is unclear) fired a hidden gun. The troops, fearing they were under attack, opened fire on the Sioux. Indians who had not yet been disarmed returned fire at the troops, killing 25 members of the Seventh Calvary. Bodies of the dead Sioux were buried in a mass grave and the wounded were carried to a local missionary church where they lay beneath a banner proclaiming "Peace on Earth; Good Will to Men." President Harrison addressed Congress about the Battle of Wounded Knee on December 9, 1891.

The outbreak among the Sioux which occurred in December last is as to its causes and incidents fully reported upon by the War Department and the Department of the Interior. That these Indians had some just complaints, especially in the matter of the reduction of the appropriation for rations and in the delays attending the enactment of laws to enable the Department to perform the engagements entered into with them, is probably true; but the Sioux tribes are naturally warlike and turbulent, and their warriors were excited by their medicine men and chiefs, who preached the coming of an Indian messiah who was to give them power to destroy their enemies. In view of the alarm that prevailed among the white settlers near the reservation and of the fatal consequences that would have resulted from an Indian incursion, I placed at the disposal of General Miles, commanding the Division of the Missouri, all such forces as we thought by him to be required. He is entitled to the credit of having given thorough protection to the settlers and of bringing the hostiles into subjection with the least possible loss of life. . . .

Since March 4, 1889, about 23,000,000 acres have been separated from Indian reservations and added to the public domain for the use of those who desired to secure free homes under our beneficent laws. It is difficult to estimate the increase of wealth which will result from the conversion of these waste lands into farms, but it is more difficult to estimate the betterment which will result to the families that have found renewed hope and courage in the ownership of a home and the assurance of a comfortable subsistence under free and healthful conditions. It is also gratifying to be able to feel, as we may, that this work has proceeded upon lines of justice toward the Indian, and that he may now, if he will, secure to himself the good influences of a settled habitation, the fruits of industry, and the security of citizenship.

Source: Third Annual Message to Congress, Dec. 9, 1891

HOW WELL DID YOU UNDERSTAND THIS SELECTION?

1. How does Harrison view the Sioux? Did Americans view all Native Americans in this light? Why or Why not?

2. What reason did the Sioux have for fighting American forces at Wounded Knee?

3. What does American policy attempt to force Native Americans to do?

BRYAN'S CROSS OF GOLD SPEECH

William Jennings Bryan was the Populist/Democratic candidate for president in 1896 and again in 1900. He was noted as a spectacular orator. In 1896 he criss-crossed the United States and made hundreds of speeches in attempt to convince voters to support him against William McKinley in the presidential election. He captured the Democratic presidential nomination in 1896 with his famous "Cross of Gold" speech in which he supported inflation of the American currency through the free coinage of silver. This position was important to Westerners, as most silver produced in the United States was mined in the West and farmers and ranchers living west of the Missouri River faced economic difficulties they believed inflation would solve. Bryan did not win the presidency, but the "Cross of Gold" speech is considered one of the best examples of political oratory in American political history.

Mr. Chairman and Gentlemen of the Convention I would be presumptuous, indeed, to present myself against the distinguished gentlemen to whom you have listened if this were a mere measuring of abilities, but this is not a contest between persons. The humblest citizen in all the land, when clad in the armor of a righteous cause, is stronger than all the hosts of error. I come to speak to you in defense of a cause as holy as the cause of liberty—the cause of humanity.

Never before in the history of this country has there been witnessed such a contest as that through which we have just passed. Never before in the history of American politics has a great issue been fought out as this issue has been, by the voters of a great party. With a zeal approaching the zeal which inspired the crusaders who followed Peter the hermit, our silver Democrats went forth from victory unto victory until they are now assembled, not to discuss, not to debate, but to enter up the judgment already rendered by the plain people of this country. In this contest brother has been arrayed against brother, father against son, the warmest ties of love, acquaintance and association have been disregarded, old leaders have been cast aside when they have refused to give expression to the sentiments of those whom they would lead, and new leaders have sprung up to give direction to the cause of truth.

Thus has the contest been waged, and we have assembled here under as binding and solemn instructions as were ever imposed upon representatives of the people.

The gentleman who preceded me [Governor Russell, the former governor of MA.) spoke of the State of Massachusetts, let me assure him that not one present in all this convention entertains the least hostility to the people of the State of Massachusetts, but we stand here representing people who are the equals, before the law, of the greatest citizens in the State of Massachusetts. When you [the gold delegates] come before us and tell us that we are about to disturb your business interests, we reply that you have disturbed our business interests by your course.

We say to you that you have made the definition of a business man too limited in its application. The man who is employed for wages is as much a business man as his employer, the attorney in a country town is as much a business man as the corporation counsel in a great metropolis, the merchant at the cross-roads store is as much a business man as the merchant of New York, the farmer who goes forth in the morning and toils all day—who begins in the spring and toils all summer—and who by the application of brain and muscle to the natural resources of the country creates wealth, is as much a business man as the man who goes upon the board of trade and bets upon the price of grain, the miners who go down a thousand feet into the earth, or climb two thousand feet upon the cliffs, and bring forth from their hiding places the precious metals to be poured into the channels of trade are as much business men as the few financial magnates who, in a back room, corner the money of the world. We come to speak for this broader class of businessmen.

Ah, my friends, we say not one word against those who live upon the Atlantic coast, but the hardy pioneers who have braved all the dangers of the wilderness, who have made the desert to blossom as the rose—the pioneers away out there [in the West], who rear their children near to nature's heart, where they can mingle their voices with the voices of the birds—out there where they have erected schoolhouses for the education of their young, churches where they praise their Creator, and cemeteries where rest the ashes of their dead—these people, we say, are as deserving of the consideration of our party as any people in this country. It is for these that we speak. We do not come as aggressors. Our war is not a war of conquest, we are fighting in the defense of our homes, our families, and posterity. We have petitioned, and our petitions have been scorned, we have entreated, and our entreaties have been disregarded, we have begged, and they have mocked when our calamity came. We beg no longer, we entreat no more, we petition no more. We defy them.

The gentleman [Senator Vilas] from Wisconsin has said that he fears a Robespierre. My friends, in this land of the free you need not fear that a tyrant will spring up from among the people. What we need is an Andrew Jackson to stand, as Jackson stood, against the encroachments of organized wealth.

They tell us that this platform was made to catch votes. We reply to them that changing conditions make new issues, that the principles upon which democracy rests are as everlasting as the hills, but that they must be applied to new conditions as they arise. Conditions have arisen, and we are here to meet those conditions. They tell us that the income tax ought not to be brought in here, that it is a new idea. They criticize us for our criticism of the Supreme Court of the United States. My friends, we have not criticized, we have simply called attention to what you already know. If you want criticisms, read the dissenting opinions of the court. There you will find criticisms. They say that we passed an unconstitutional law, we deny it. The income tax law was not unconstitutional when it was passed, it was not unconstitutional when it went before the Supreme Court for the first time, it did not become unconstitutional until one of the judges changed his mind, and we cannot be expected to know when a judge will change his mind. The income tax is just. It simply intends to put the burdens of government justly upon the backs of the people. I am in favor of an income tax. When I find a man who is not willing to bear his share of the burdens of the government which protects him, I find a man who is unworthy to enjoy the blessings of a government like ours.

They say that we are opposing national bank currency, it is true. If you will read what Thomas Benton said, you will find he said that, in searching history, he could find but one parallel to Andrew Jackson, that was Cicero, who destroyed the conspiracy of Cataline and saved Rome. Benton said that Cicero only did for Rome what Jackson did for us when he destroyed the bank conspiracy and saved America. We say in our platform that we believe that the right to coin and issue money is a function of government. We believe it. We believe that it is a part of sovereignty, and can no more with safety be delegated to private individuals than we could afford to delegate to private individuals the power to make penal statutes or levy taxes. Mr. Jefferson, who was once regarded as good Democratic authority, seems to have differed in opinion from the gentleman who has addressed us on the part of the minority. Those who are opposed to this proposition tell us that the issue of paper money is a function of the bank, and that the Government ought to go out of the banking business. I stand with Jefferson rather than with them, and tell them, as he did, that the issue of money is a function of government, and that the banks ought to go out of the governing business.

They complain about the plank, which declares against life tenure in office. They have tried to strain it to mean that which it does not mean. What we oppose by that plank is the life tenure, which is being built up in Washington, and which excludes from participation in official benefits the humbler members of society.

Let me call your attention to two or three important things. The gentleman from New York says that he will propose an amendment to the platform providing that the proposed change in our monetary system shall not affect contracts already made. Let me remind you that there is no intention of affecting those contracts which according to present laws are made payable in gold, but if he means to say that we cannot change our monetary system without protecting those who have loaned money before the change was made, I desire to ask him where, in law or in morals, he can find justification for not protecting the debtors when the act of 1873 was passed, if he now insists that we must protect the creditors.

He says he will also propose an amendment, which will provide for the suspension of free coinage if we fail to maintain the parity within a year. We reply that when we advocate a policy which we believe will be successful, we are not compelled to raise a doubt as to our own sincerity by suggesting what we shall do if we fail. I ask him, if he would apply his logic to us, why he does not apply it to himself. He says he wants this country to try to secure an international agreement. Why does he not tell us what he is going to do if he fails to secure an international agreement? There is more reason for him to do that than there is for us to provide against the failure to maintain the parity. Our opponents have tried for twenty years to secure an international agreement, and those are waiting for it most patiently who do not want it at all.

And now, my friends, let me come to the paramount issue. If they ask us why it is that we say more on the money question than we say upon the tariff question, I reply that, if protection has slain its thousands, the gold standard has slain its tens of thousands. If they ask us why we do not embody in our platform all the things that we believe in, we reply that when we have restored the money of the Constitution all other necessary reforms will be possible, but that until this is done there is no other reform that can be accomplished.

Why is it that within three months such a change has come over the country? Three months ago, when it was confidently asserted that those who believe in the gold standard would frame our platform and nominate our candidates, even the advocates of the gold standard did not think that we could elect a president. And they had good reason for their doubt, because there is scarcely a state here today asking for the gold standard, which is not in the absolute control of the Republican Party. But note the change. Mr. McKinley was nominated at St. Louis upon a platform, which declared for the maintenance of the gold standard until it can be changed into bimetallism by international agreement. Mr. McKinley was the most popular man among the Republicans, and three months ago everybody in the Republican Party prophesied his election. How is it today? Why, the man who was once pleased to think that he looked like Napoleon—that man shudders today when he remembers that he was nominated on the anniversary of the battle of Waterloo. Not only that, but as he listens he can hear with ever-increasing distinctness the sound of the waves as they beat upon the lonely shores of St. Helena.

Why this change? Ah, my friends, is not the reason for the change evident to any one who will look at the matter? No private character, however pure, no personal popularity, however great, can protect from the avenging wrath of an indignant people a man who will declare that he is in favor of fastening the gold standard upon this country, or who is willing to surrender the right of self-government and place the legislative control of our affairs in the hands of foreign potentates and powers.

We go forth confident that we shall win. Why? Because upon the paramount issue of this campaign there is not a spot of ground upon which the enemy will dare to challenge battle. If they tell us that the gold standard is a good thing, we shall point to their platform and tell them that their platform pledges the party to get rid of the gold standard and substitute bimetallism. If the gold standard is a good thing, why try to get rid of it? I call your attention to the fact that some of the very people who are in this convention today and who tell us that we ought to declare in favor of international bimetallism— thereby declaring that the gold standard is wrong and that the principle of bimetallism is better—these very people four months ago were open and avowed advocates of the gold standard, and were then telling us that we could not legislate two metals together, even with the aid of all the world. If the gold standard is a good thing, we ought to declare in favor of its retention and not in favor of abandoning it, and if the gold standard is a bad thing why should we wait until other nations are willing to help us to let go? Here is the line of battle, and we care not upon which issue they force the fight, we are prepared to meet them on either issue or on both. If they tell us that the gold standard is the standard of civilization, we reply to them that this, the most enlightened of all the nations of the earth, has never declared for a gold standard and that both the great parties this year are declaring against it. If the gold standard is the standard of civilization, why, my friends, should we not have it? If they come to meet us on that issue we can present the history of our nation. More than that, we can tell them that they will search the pages of history in vain to find a single instance where the common people of any land have ever declared themselves in favor of the gold standard. They can find where the holders of the fixed investments have declared for a gold standard, but not where the masses have.

Mr. Carlisle said in 1878 that this was a struggle between "the idle holders of idle capital" and "the struggling masses, who produce the wealth and pay the taxes of the country," and, my friends, the question we are to decide is upon which side will the Democratic party fight; upon the side of "the idle holders of idle capital" or upon the side of "the struggling masses?" That is the question, which the party must answer first, and then it must be answered by each individual hereafter. The sympathies of the Democratic Party, as shown by the platform, are on the side of the struggling masses who have ever been the foundation of the Democratic Party. There are two ideas of government. There are those who believe that, if you will only legislate to make the well to do prosperous, their prosperity will leak through on those below. The Democratic idea, however, has been that if you legislate to make the masses prosperous, their prosperity will find its way up through every class, which rests upon them.

You come to us and tell us that the great cities are in favor of the gold standard, we reply that the great cities rest upon our broad and fertile prairies. Burn down your cities and leave our farms, and your cities will spring up again as if by magic, but destroy our farms and the grass will grow in the streets of every city in the country.

My friends, we declare that this nation is able to legislate for its own people on every question, without waiting for the aid or consent of any other nation on earth, and upon that issue we expect to carry every State in the Union. I shall not slander the inhabitants of the fair State of Massachusetts nor the inhabitants of the State of New York by saying that, when they are confronted with the proposition, they will declare that this nation is not able to attend to its own business. It is the issue of 1776 over again. Our ancestors, when but three millions in number, had the courage to declare their political independence of every other nation, shall we, their descendants, when we have grown to seventy millions, declare that we are less independent than our forefathers? No, my friends, that will never be the verdict of our people. Therefore, we care not upon what lines the battle is fought. If they say bimetallism is good, but that we cannot have it until other nations help us, we reply that, instead of having a gold standard because England has, we will restore bimetallism, and then let England have bimetallism because the United States has it. If they dare to come out in the open field and defend the gold standard as a good thing, we will fight them to the uttermost.

Having behind us the producing masses of this nation and the world, supported by the commercial interests, the laboring interests, and the toilers everywhere, we will answer their demand for a gold standard by saying to them: You shall not press down upon the brow of labor this crown of thorns, you shall not crucify mankind upon a cross of gold.

Source: William Jennings Bryan, *The First Battle: A Story of the Campaign of 1896,* Chicago 1897

HOW WELL DID YOU UNDERSTAND THIS SELECTION?

1. Who was William Jennings Bryan? What does he advocate in the "Cross of Gold" speech?

2. Why was his message in the "Cross of Gold" speech so appealing to many Americans in 1896?

3. What is the gold standard? What is bimetallism?

4. What have critics said about Bryan's ideas? How does he answer the critics?

THE PAGE LAW

The Page Law, passed on March 3, 1875, was designed to prohibit immigration of Chinese women for the purpose of prostitution. This act was part of the racism present in the American West against Asian immigrants. While untrue, it was widely believed by Westerners in cities like San Francisco that Chinese "pimps" were importing Chinese women to supply prostitution services to Asian and American laborers.

Be it enacted by the Senate and House of Representatives of the United States of America in Congress-assembled,

That in determining whether the immigration of any subject of China, Japan, or any Oriental country, to the United States, is free and voluntary, as provided by section two thousand one hundred and sixty two of the Revised Code, title "Immigration," it shall be the duty of the consul-general or consul of the United States residing at the port from which it is proposed to convey such subjects, in any vessels enrolled or licensed in the United States, or any port within the same, before delivering to the masters of any such vessels the permit or certificate provided for in such section, in ascertain for a term of service within the United States, for lewd and immoral purposes; and if there be such contract or agreement, the said consul-general or consul shall not deliver the required permit or certificate....

SEC.3. That the importation into the United States of women for the purposes of prostitution is hereby forbidden; and all contracts and agreements in relation thereto, made in advance or in pursuance of illegal importation and purposes, are hereby declared void; and whoever shall knowingly and willfully hold, or attempt to hold, any woman to such purposes, in pursuance of such illegal importation and contract or agreement, shall be deemed guilty of a felony, and, on conviction thereof, shall be imprisoned not exceeding five years and pay a fine not exceeding five thousand dollars....

SEC.5. That it shall be unlawful for aliens of the following classes to immigrate into the United States, namely, persons who are undergoing sentence for conviction in their own country of felonious crimes other than political or growing out of or the result of such political offenses, and women "imported for the purposes of prostitution." Every vessel arriving in the United States may be inspected under the direction of the collector of the port at which it arrives, if he shall have reason to believe that such obnoxious persons are on board; and the officer making such inspection shall certify the result thereof to the master or other person in charge of such vessel, designating in such certificate are person or persons, if any there be, ascertained by him to be of either of the classes whose importation is hereby forbidden.....

Source: Proceedings of the Forty-third Congress, Second Session

HOW WELL DID YOU UNDERSTAND THIS SELECTION?

1. What does the Page Law do?

2. Why would the American government pass such a law?

3. How does the Page Law fit into the pattern of racism against Chinese immigrants in the United States?

CHINESE EXCLUSION ACT

Passage of the Chinese Exclusion Act represents the first real attempt by the United States government to close its doors to immigrants from any ethnic group. This law was enacted because a small but vocal minority of white Americans, primarily from the Western states, was racist. Westerners who wanted to prevent further immigration of Chinese to the United States were reacting to economic and labor problems that gripped the West during the 1870s and 1880s . White Americans in the West feared that Chinese laborers, who were highly sought after as miners and railroad workers, would take jobs from them. Chinese immigrants made easy scapegoats for western economic problems because, like Native Americans, they were different.

WHEREAS, in the opinion of the Government of the United States the coming of Chinese laborers to this country endangers the good order of certain localities within the territory thereof, Therefore, Be it enacted. That from and after the expiration of ninety days next after the passage of this act, and until the expiration often years next after the passage of this act, the coming of Chinese laborers to the Untied States be, suspended, and during such suspension it shall not be lawful for any Chinese laborer to come, or, having so come after the expiration of said ninety days, to remain within the United States.

SEC 2: That the master of any vessel who shall knowingly bring within the United States on such vessel, and land or permit to be landed, any Chinese laborer, from any foreign port or place, shall be deemed guilty of a misdemeanor, and on conviction thereof shall be punished by a fine of not more than five hundred dollars for each and every such Chinese laborer so brought, and may be also imprisoned for a term not exceeding one year.

SEC 3: That the two foregoing sections shall not apply to Chinese laborers who were in the United States on the seventeenth day of November, eighteen hundred and eighty, or who shall have come into the same before the expiration of ninety days next after the passage of this act,

SEC 6: That in order to the faithful execution of articles one and two of the treaty in this act before mentioned, every Chinese person other than a laborer who may be entitled by said treaty and this act to come within the United States, and who shall be about to come to the United States, shall be identified as so entitled by the Chinese Government in each case, such identity to be evidenced by a certificate issued under the authority of said government, which certificate shall be in the English language or (if not in the English language) accompanied by a translation into English, stating such right to come, and which certificate shall state the name, title, or official rank, if any, the age, height, and all physical peculiarities former and present occupation or profession and place of residence in China of the person to whom the certificate is issued and that such person is entitled conformably to the treaty in this act mentioned to come within the Untied States.

Source: United States Statutes at Large, Vol. 22

HOW WELL DID YOU UNDERSTAND THIS SELECTION?

1. What does the Chinese Exclusion Act do?

2. What penalties will be assessed against violators of the law?

3. What did non-laborers from China have to do to come to the United States?

4. Is the Chinese Exclusion Act racist? Why or why not?

REPUBLICAN PARTY PLATFORM

The 1896 presidential election was a pivotal one in American history. There was a clear difference between the parties and their stand on the issues. The Republican Party represented big business, imperialism, and the gold standard. The Republican candidate, William McKinley, ran a traditional campaign. Rather than crossing the country to ask for votes, he stayed at home in Ohio and let other Republicans, like Theodore Roosevelt, campaign for him. The issues he and his Republican campaigners stressed are summarized in the Republican Party Platform adopted at their St. Louis convention on June 16, 1896.

The Republicans of the United States, assembled by their representatives in National Convention, appealing for the popular and historical justification of their claims to the matchless achievements of thirty years of Republican rule, earnestly and confidently address themselves to the awakened intelligence, experience, and conscience of their countrymen in the following declaration of facts and principles:

For the first time since the Civil War the American people have witnessed the calamitous consequences of full and unrestricted Democratic control of the Government. It has been a record of unparalleled incapacity, dishonor and disaster. In administrative management it has ruthlessly sacrificed indispensable revenue, entailed an unceasing deficit, eked out ordinary current expenses with borrowed money, piled up the public debt by $262,000,000 in time of peace, forced an adverse balance of trade, kept a perpetual menace hanging over the redemption fund, pawned American credit to alien syndicates, and reversed all the measures and results of successful Republican rule. In the broad effect of its policy it has precipitated panic, blighted industry and trade with prolonged depression, closed factories, reduced work and wages, halted enterprise and crippled American production, while stimulating foreign production for the American market. Every consideration of public safety and individual interest demands that the Government shall be rescued from the hands of those who have shown themselves incapable of conducting it without disaster at home and dishonor abroad, and shall be restored to the party which for thirty years administered it with unequalled success and prosperity. And in this connection we heartily endorse the wisdom, patriotism and the success of the Administration of President Harrison.

Allegiance to <u>Protection</u> Renewed.
We renew and emphasize our allegiance to the policy of Protection as the bulwark of American industrial independence and the foundation of American development and prosperity. This true American policy taxes foreign products and encourages home industry; it puts the burden of revenue on foreign goods; it secures the American market for the American producer; it upholds the American standard of wages for the American workingman; it puts the factory by the side of the farm, and makes the American farmer less dependent on foreign demand and prices; it diffuses general thrift and founds the strength of all on the strength of each. In its reasonable application it is just, far and impartial, equally opposed to foreign control and domestic monopoly, to sectional discrimination and individual favoritism.

We denounce the present Democratic tariff as sectional, injurious to the public credit and destructive to business enterprise. We demand such an equitable tariff on foreign imports which come into competition with American products, as will not only furnish adequate revenue for the necessary expenses of the Government, but will protect American labor from degradation to the wage level of other lands. We are not pledged to any particular schedules. The question of rates is a practical question, to be governed by the conditions of the time and of production; the ruling and uncompromising principle is the protection and development of American labor and industry. The country demands a right settlement, and then it wants rest.

Reciprocity Demanded.
We believe the repeal of the reciprocity arrangements negotiated by the last Republican Administration was a national calamity, and we demand their renewal and extension on such terms as will equalize our trade with other nations, remove the restrictions which now obstruct the sale of American products in the ports of other countries, and secure enlarged markets for the products of our farms, forests and factories.

Protection and reciprocity are twin measures of Republican policy and go hand in hand. Democratic rule has recklessly struck down both, and both must be re-established. Protection for what we produce, free admission for the necessaries of life which we do not produce; reciprocal agreements of mutual interest which gain open markets for us in return for our open market to others. Protection builds up domestic industry and trade and secures our own market for ourselves; reciprocity builds up foreign trade and finds an outlet for our surplus.

We condemn the present Administration for not keeping faith with the sugar producers of this country; the Republican party favors such protection as will lead to the production on American soil of all the sugar which the American people use and for which they pay other countries more than $ 100,000,000 annually. To all our products--to those of the mine and the field, as well as those of the shop and the factory--to hemp, to wool, the product of the great industry of sheep husbandry, as well as to the finished woolens of the mill--we promise the most ample protection.

Merchant Marine.

We favor restoring the early American policy of discriminating duties for the upbuilding of our merchant marine and the protection of our shipping in the foreign carrying trade, so that American ships--the product of American labor, employed in American shipyards, sailing under the Stars and Stripes, and manned, officered and owned by Americans--can regain the carrying of our foreign commerce.

The Currency Plank.

The Republican Party is unreservedly for sound money. It caused the enactment of the law providing for the resumption of specie payment in 1879; since then every dollar has been as good as gold.

We are unalterably opposed to every measure calculated to debase our currency or impair the credit of our country. We are, therefore, opposed to the free coinage of silver, except by international agreement with the leading commercial nations of the world, which we pledge ourselves to promote, and, until such agreement can be obtained, the existing gold standard must be preserved. All our silver and paper currency must be maintained at parity with gold, and we favor all measures designed to maintain inviolable the obligations of the United States and all our money, whether coin or paper, at the present standard, the standard of the most enlightened nations of the earth.

Justice to Veterans.

The veterans of the Union armies deserve and should receive fair treatment and generous recognition. Whenever practicable, they should be given the preference in the matter of employment, and they are entitled to the enactment of such laws as are best calculated to secure the fulfillment of the pledges made to them in the dark days of the country in peril. We denounce the practice in the Pension Bureau, so recklessly and unjustly carried on by the present administration, of reducing pensions and arbitrarily dropping names from the rolls, as deserving the severest condemnation of the American people.

Foreign Relations.

Our foreign policy should be at all times firm, vigorous and dignified, and all our interests in the Western hemisphere carefully watched and guarded. The Hawaiian Islands should be controlled by the United States, and no foreign Power should be permitted to interfere with them; the Nicaragua Canal should be built, owned, and operated by the United States, and, by the purchase of the Danish Islands, we should secure a seaport and much-needed naval station in the West Indies.

The massacres in Armenia have aroused the deep sympathy and just indignation of the American people, and we believe that the United States should exercise all the influence it can properly exert to bring these atrocities to an end. In Turkey, American residents have been exposed to the gravest dangers, and American property destroyed. There, and everywhere, American citizens and American property must be absolutely protected at all hazards and at any cost.

We reassert the Monroe Doctrine in its full extent, and we reaffirm the right of the United States to give the doctrine effect by responding to the appeals of any American State for friendly intervention in case of European encroachment. We have not interfered, and shall not interfere, with the existing possessions of any European Power in this hemisphere, but those possessions must not, on any pretext, be extended. We hopefully look forward to the eventual withdrawal of the European Powers from this hemisphere, and to the ultimate union of all the English-speaking part of the continent by the free consent of its inhabitants.

Suffering Cuba.

From the hour of achieving their own independence, the people of the United States have regarded with sympathy the struggles of other American peoples to free themselves from European domination. We watch with deep and abiding interest the heroic battle of the Cuban patriots against cruelty and oppression, and our best hopes go out for the full success of their determined contest for liberty. The Government of Spain, having lost control of Cuba, and being unable to protect the property or lives of resident American citizens, or to comply with its treaty obligations, we believe that the Government of the United States should actively use its influence and good offices to restore peace and give independence to the island.

The Navy.
The peace and security of the Republic, and the maintenance of its rightful influence among the nations of the earth, demand a naval power commensurate with its position and responsibility. We therefore favor the continued enlargement of the navy and a complete system of harbor and seacoast defenses.

Foreign Immigration.
For the protection of the equality of our American citizenship and of the wages of our workingmen against the fatal competition of low-priced labor, we demand that the immigration laws be thoroughly enforced and so extended as to exclude from entrance to the United States those who can neither read nor write.

Civil Service.
The Civil Service law was placed on the statute book by the Republican Party, which has always sustained it, and we renew our repeated declarations that it shall be thoroughly and honestly enforced and extended wherever practicable.

Free Ballot.
We demand that every citizen of the United States shall be allowed to cast one free and unrestricted ballot, and that such ballot shall be counted and returned as cast.

Lynchings.
We proclaim our unqualified condemnation of the uncivilized and barbarous practices well known as lynching and killing of human beings, suspected or charged with crime, without process of law.

National Arbitration.
We favor the creation of a National Board of Arbitration to settle and adjust differences which may arise between employers and employed engaged in inter-State commerce.

Homesteads.
We believe in an immediate return to the free homestead policy of the Republican party, and urge the passage by Congress of the satisfactory free homestead measure which has already passed the House and is now pending in the Senate.

Territories.
We favor the admission of the remaining Territories at the earliest practicable date, having due regard to the interests of the people of the Territories and of the United States. All the Federal officers appointed for the Territories should be selected from bona fide residents thereof, and the right of self-government should be accorded as far as practicable.

We believe the citizens of Alaska should have representation in the Congress of the United States, to the end that needful legislation may be intelligently enacted.

Temperance and the Rights of Women.
We sympathize with all wise and legitimate efforts to lessen and prevent the evils of intemperance and promote morality.

The Republican Party is mindful of the rights and interests of women. Protection of American industries includes equal opportunities, equal pay for equal work, and protection to the home. We favor the admission of women to wider spheres of usefulness, and welcome their co-operation in rescuing the country from Democratic and Populistic mismanagement and misrule.

Such are the principles and policies of the Republican Party. By these principles we will abide, and these policies we will put into execution. We ask for them the considerate judgment of the American people. Confident alike in the history of our great party and in the justice of our cause, we present our platform and our candidates in the full assurance that the election will bring victory to the Republican party and prosperity to the people of the United States.

Source: Proceedings of the Republican National Convention, 1896

HOW WELL DID YOU UNDERSTAND THIS SELECTION?

1. How does the Republican Party Platform criticize the Democratic-controlled government?

2. Identify the various planks within the Republican Party Platform.

3. Does the Republican Party Platform favor business? Why or why not?

4. Does the Republican Party favor giving women the right to vote? Why or why not? What is the Republican stand on the women's rights movement?

5. Discuss Republican views on foreign policy.

The Populist or People's Party was one of the most successful third parties in American history. It elected candidates to many positions in the 1880s and 1890s, including the United States Congress, state governors, and state legislatures. In 1892 and 1896 the Populist Party ran candidates for president. Most supporters of the Populist Party came from the South and West because those states were largely agricultural, and the Populist Party was clearly the party of farmers. The Populist Party largely disappeared after the 1896 election because the Democratic Party "stole" its issues and presidential candidate (William Jennings Bryan) in that year. Even though the People's Party disappeared, most issues it advocated later became law. These issues are summarized in the Populist Platform adopted at its convention in St. Louis on July 24, 1896.

The People's party, assembled in National Convention, reaffirms its allegiance to the principles declared by the founders of the Republic, and also to the fundamental principles of just government as enunciated in the platform of the party in 1892. We recognize that, through the connivance of the present and preceding. Administrations, the country has reached a crisis in its national life as predicted in our declaration four years ago, and that prompt and patriotic action is the supreme duty of the hour. We realize that, while we have political independence, our financial and industrial independence is yet to be attained by restoring to our country the constitutional control and exercise of the functions necessary to a people's government, which functions have been basely surrendered by our public servant to corporate monopolies. The influence of European money changers has been more potent in shaping legislation than the voice of the American people. Executive power and patronage have been used to corrupt our Legislatures and defeat the will of the people, and plutocracy has thereby been enthroned upon the ruins of Democracy. To restore the Government intended by the fathers and for the welfare and prosperity of this and future generations, we demand the establishment of an economic and financial system, which shall make us masters of our own affairs and independent of European control by the adoption of the following:

Declaration of Principles.

FIRST. We demand a national money, safe and sound, issued by the General Government only, without the intervention of banks of issue, to be a full legal tender for all debts, public and private, a just, equitable, and efficient means of distribution direct to the people and through the lawful disbursements of the Government.

SECOND. We demand the free and unrestricted coinage of silver and gold at the present ratio of 16 to 1, without waiting for the consent of foreign nations.

THIRD. We demand the volume of circulating medium be speedily increased to an amount sufficient to meet the demands of the business and population and to restore the just level of prices of labor and production.

FOURTH. We denounce the sale of bonds and the increase of the public interest-bearing debt made by the present Administration as unnecessary and without authority of law, and demand that no more bonds be issued except by specific act of Congress.

FIFTH. We demand such legislation as will prevent the demonetization of the lawful money of the United States by private contract.

SIXTH. We demand that the Government, in payment of its obligations, shall use its option as to the kind of lawful money in which they are to be paid, and we denounce the present and preceding Administrations for surrendering this option to the holders of Government obligations.

SEVENTH. We demand a graduated income tax to the end that aggregated wealth shall bear its just proportion of taxation, and we regard the recent decision of the Supreme Court relative to the Income Tax law as a misinterpretation of the Constitution and an invasion of the rightful powers of Congress over the subject of taxation.

EIGHTH. We demand that postal savings banks be established by the Government for the safe deposit of the savings of the people and to facilitate exchange.

Transportation.

FIRST. Transportation being a means of exchange and a public necessity, the Government should own and operate the railroads in the interest of the people and on a non-partisan basis, to the end that all may be accorded the same treatment in transportation and that the tyranny and political power now exercised by the great railroad corporations, which result in the impairment if not the destruction of the political rights and personal liberties of the citizen, may be destroyed. Such ownership is to be accomplished gradually, in a manner consistent with sound public policy.

SECOND. The interest of the United States in the public highways built with public moneys and the proceeds of extensive grants of land to the Pacific Railroads should never be alienated, mortgaged, or sold, but guarded and protected for the general welfare as provided by the laws organizing such railroads. The foreclosure of existing liens of the United States on these roads should at once follow default in the payment thereof by the debtor companies, and at the foreclosure sales of said roads the Government shall purchase the same if it becomes necessary to protect its interests therein, or if they can be purchased at a reasonable price, and the Government shall operate said railroads as public highways for the benefit of the whole people and not in the interest of the few under suitable provisions for protection of life and property, giving to all transportation interests equal privileges and equal rates for fares and freights.

THIRD. We denounce the present infamous schemes for refunding these debts, and demand that the laws now applicable thereto be executed and administered according to their interest and spirit.

Telegraph.

The telegraph, like the Post-office system, being a necessity for the transmission of news, should be owned and operated by the Government in the interest of the people.

Land.

FIRST. True policy demands that the National and State legislation shall be such as will ultimately enable every prudent and industrious citizen to secure a home, and, therefore, the land should not be monopolized for speculative purposes. All lands now held by railroads and other corporations in excess of their actual needs, should by lawful means be reclaimed by the Government and held for natural settlers only, and private land monopoly as well as alien ownership should be prohibited.

SECOND. We condemn the frauds by which the land grant Pacific Railroad Companies have, through the connivance of the Interior Department, robbed multitudes of actual bona fide settlers of their homes and miners of their claims, and we demand legislation by Congress which will enforce the exception of mineral land from such grants after as well as before the patent.

THIRD. We demand that bona fide settlers on all public lands be granted free homes, as provided in the National Homestead law, and that no exception be made in the case of Indian reservations when opened for settlement, and that all lands not now patented come under this demand.

Direct Legislation.

We favor a system of direct legislation, through the initiative and referendum, under proper constitutional safeguards.

General Propositions.

FIRST. We demand the election of President, Vice-President, and United States Senators by a direct vote of the people.

SECOND. We tender to the patriotic people of the country our deepest sympathies in their heroic struggle for political freedom and independence, and we believe the time has come when the United States, the great Republic of the world, should recognize that Cuba is and of right ought to be a free and independent State.

THIRD. We favor home rule in the Territories and the District of Columbia, and the early admission of the Territories as States.

FOURTH. All public salaries should be made to correspond to the price of labor and its products.

FIFTH. In times of great industrial depression idle labor should be employed on public works as far as practicable.

SIXTH. The arbitrary course of the courts in assuming to imprison citizens for indirect contempt, and ruling them by injunction, should be prevented by proper legislation.

SEVENTH. We favor just pensions for our disabled Union soldiers.

EIGHTH. Believing that the elective franchise and an untrammeled ballot are essential to government of, for, and by the people, the People's party condemn the wholesale system of disfranchisement adopted in some of the States as unrepublican and undemocratic, and we declare it to be the duty of the several State Legislatures to take such action as will secure a full, free and fair ballot and honest count.

NINTH. While the foregoing propositions constitute the platform upon which our party stands, and for the vindication of which its organization will be maintained, we recognize that the real and pressing issue of the pending campaign, upon which the present election will turn, is the financial question, and upon this great and specific issue between the parties we cordially invite the aid and co-operation of all organizations and citizens agreeing with us upon this vital question.

Source: Proceedings of People's Party (Populist) Convention, 1896

HOW WELL DID YOU UNDERSTAND THIS SELECTION?

1. What does the Populist Party appear to be reacting against?

2. Identify the various planks in the Populist Party Platform.

3. Contrast Populist views with those of Republicans in the 1896 election.

4. What is the most significant issue in the Populist Party Platform?

SELF TEST:

MULTIPLE CHOICE: Circle the correct response. The correct answers are given at the end.

1. How much land did the Dawes Act provide for each head of a Native American family?
    a.   Three acres.
    b.   140 acres.
    c.   160
    d.   one-quarter section (60 acres).

2. What does William Jennings Bryan advocated in the "Cross of Gold" speech?
    a.   A strict gold standard.
    b.   A currency that is deflated.
    c.   Government policies that will help corporations but discriminate against agriculture.
    d.   Inflation through the coinage of silver.

3. The final battle between whites and Native Americans in the West was
    a.   Wounded Knee.
    b.   Little Big Horn
    c.   Custer's Last Stand
    d.   Sand's Creek.

4. What was the most significant factor in the destruction of the Plains Tribes?
    a.   Introduction of the horse.
    b.   Destruction of the Buffalo.
    c.   The demise of Salmon populations in the Pacific Northwest.
    d.   The coming of the Railroad into western territories.

5. Why did the United States want to limit Chinese immigration to the United States?
    a.   Because of racist views in the United States.
    b.   Because China was traditionally an enemy of the United States.
    c.   Because there was not enough work for Chinese laborers to do in the United States.
    d.   Because Chinese immigrants were put on the welfare rolls in higher numbers than were other immigrant groups.

6. What was the African-American settlement in northwestern Kansas called?
   a. Exoduster.
   b. Deadeye Dick.
   c. Isom Dart.
   d. Nicodemus.

7. Which of the following did William McKinley and the Republican Party favor in the 1896 election?
   a. The free coinage of silver to create inflation.
   b. Giving 18 year old citizens the right to vote in national elections.
   c. Making Hawaii an independent nation.
   d. Tariffs, big business, and the gold standard.

8. Which of the following was not part of the Populist Party Platform in 1896?
   a. Direct election of United States Senators.
   b. A graduated income tax.
   c. A strict gold standard.
   d. The free coinage of silver.

9. The first great economic boom in the Far West occurred in which of the following industries?
   a. Petroleum.
   b. Farming.
   c. Cattle ranching.
   d. Mining.

10. What was perhaps the worst problem women who lived in the Great Plains faced?
    a. Loneliness and isolation.
    b. Hard labor.
    c. Indian attacks.
    d. Few men to serve as mates.

ANSWERS: 1-c; 2-d; 3-a; 4-b; 5-a; 6-d; 7-d; 8-c; 9-d; 10-a

ESSAYS:

1. There are many myths prevalent in American society about the West. Identify some of these myths and examine their validity.

2. Compare and contrast the views of the Populist Party with those of the Republican Party in the 1896 election.

3. Discuss the mistreatment of Native Americans. How could this mistreatment have been avoided?

4. Examine the racism present in the United States against minority ethnic groups. Why were Americans so racist? How can racism be overcome?

5. Examine the effect the Homestead Act had on the West. What happened to most of the land that was filed on? How was the act abused?

OPTIONAL ACTIVITIES: (Use your knowledge **and** imagination.)

1. You are a Native American confined to a reservation in the West. Keep a diary for the semester in which you compare and contrast your life before and after life on the reservation.

2.   You are a member of a United States Senate Committee investigating conditions and events that led to the massacre at Wounded Knee. Write a report that summarizes the findings of your committee.

3.   You have just been nominated by the Populist Party to run for Congress in a district from South Dakota in 1896. Write and deliver a campaign speech to your class that reflects your views on the issues dominant in American politics in 1896.

WEB SITE LISTINGS:

Populist Party

> http://www.encyclopedia.com/search.asp?target=@DOCTITLE%20Populist%20party
> (Encyclopedia.com)
> http://www.encyclopedia.com/searchpool.asp?target=@DOCTITLE%20Populist%20party

CyberSoup's Wild West

> Colorful educational site covering Western legends and Native Americans. http://www.thewildwest.org/

Bryan, William Jennings

> Essays and speeches about imperialism (1898-1913) by one of the most influential leaders of the Democratic Party during the late 19th and early 20th centuries. http://www.boondocksnet.com/ail/bryan.html

Bryan, William Jennings

> (Encarta® Concise Encyclopedia Article)
> http://encarta.msn.com/index/conciseindex/0C/00C50000.htm?z=1&pg=2&br=1

Biography of Jesse James

> In-depth article about the legendary outlaw and gunman
> http://www.crimelibrary.com/americana/jesse/index.htm

Angel Island Immigration Station

> Historical information about Angel Island State Park in California, site of the Immigration Station, a National Historic Landmark, which played a role in the Chinese Exclusion Act of 1882.
> http://www.angelisland.org/immigr02.html

Women of the West Museum

> An educational organization that traces and interprets the history, contributions, and roles of women of all cultures—past, present, and future in the American West. http://www.wowmuseum.org/

American West Heritage Center

> dedicated to honoring, celebrating, and re-creating the heritage and culture of the American West from the period of 1820 to 1920 http://www.americanwestcenter.org/

Legends of the American West - Wyatt Earp & the Gunfighters

> Reviews on Legends of the American West - Wyatt Earp & the Gunfighters written by consumers at Epinions.com. http://www.epinions.com/mvie_mu-1037468

Ghost Town Museum

> A complete and authentic old western town built from the very buildings abandoned after the Pikes Peak Region's gold mining era and straight out of the days of America's frontier.
> http://www.ghosttownmuseum.com/

Buffalo Soldiers and Indian Wars

> Sixteen photographs of Buffalo Soldiers, 14 of their legendary Native American foes, two mini-videos and 24 story/page links are displayed. Buffalo Soldier battles, skirmishes and background events are given. http://www.buffalosoldier.net

The Buffalo Soldiers on the Western Frontier

> History of the 9th and 10th Cavalry
> http://www.imh.org/imh/buf/buftoc.html

Chapter Fifteen

THE IMPERIAL REPUBLIC

Expansion has been a common theme in American history since its earliest years. Ultimately, through purchase and by force, Americans extended their control westward from the Atlantic seaboard to the Pacific coast. They rationalized this westward movement with ethnocentric notions of entitlement or *Manifest Destiny*. By the end of the nineteenth century, similar ideas dictated expansion beyond the continental borders of the United States.

A variety of groups promoted the cause of American expansion. Some Americans proclaimed it was their duty as Christians to bring their religious ideas to the "ignorant" masses overseas. Others explained that expansion was an economic imperative. As a nation whose level of production far exceeded domestic consumption, continued economic prosperity depended on access to foreign markets. Still others promoted not only expansion into new areas of the globe, but the extension of imperialistic control of those regions. Men like John Fiske stressed the cultural superiority of Americans and spoke of the inevitability that American political and cultural views would one day spread through the world. Grounding their position in Social Darwinism, men like Josiah Strong emphasized the racial superiority of Anglo-Saxon Americans and proclaimed it the destiny of white Americans to dominate all others.

Admiral Alfred Thayer Mahan emphasized the military and strategic need of American imperialism. If America was to be a world power, it was necessary to control bases and fueling stations throughout the globe to support an activist military and merchant marine. American political leaders embraced Mahan's ideas and embarked on a new phase of American expansion. In 1878, James G. Blaine, Secretary of State under President Rutherford B. Hays, obtained rights to Pago Pago, securing access for the United States to a deepwater harbor in the Samoan Islands. Within a few years the area was claimed as a protectorate in order to protect interests in the region of German and British competition. Americans next turned their attention to establishing a naval base in Hawaii, as a result of the Pearl Harbor Treaty of 1887. A forceful presence in Hawaii for decades, American sugar planters pressed for annexation. They began by ousting the king and replacing him with Queen Liliuokalani. When the Queen refused to be controlled, the planters, assisted by the US Navy, ousted her as well. By 1900 Hawaii was officially annexed by the United States.

Economic interests led Americans to intervene in Chinese politics as well. Fearful a weakening of the Manchu dynasty would leave China vulnerable to the imperialist designs of Europe, Russia and Japan, Secretary of State John Hay issued the Open Door Policy in 1899, declaring America's intentions to advance its commercial interests in the region. The situation was compounded by a nationalist rebellion determined to rid China of all foreign occupation. President McKinley sent 5,000 American troops to assist an international effort to quell the rebellion.

The United States was involved in the West as well. Americans had been observing Cuban efforts to gain their independence from Spain since the 1860s. As the fighting intensified and newspapers reported atrocities committed by the Spanish troops under the direction of General Valeriano Weyler, the American public sympathized with the Cuban cause. American sentiment was further inflamed by the sensationalized reporting of the newspapers owned by William Randolph Hearst and Joseph Pulitzer. In response to American pressure Spain removed Weyler from

Cuba. The situation was re-ignited, however, by the American press. The papers published a letter that had been stolen from the Spanish minister, Dupuy de Lome. The letter expressed de Lome's negative opinion of the American president. American outrage was later compounded by reports that Spain was responsible for an explosion on board the *U.S.S. Maine*, which had killed 260 American sailors. The American public demanded action. Anxious for the opportunity to display newly modernized military, the government assented, and the United States declared war with Spain in April 1898. Lasting less than six months, the "splendid little war" witnessed few casualties due to combat. The superiority of the U.S. Navy led to a relatively easy victory at sea. The fighting on land was more intense. The U.S. Army, augmented by regiments of African-American soldiers, secured both Cuba and the Philippines by July. With the Treaty of Paris, December 1898, Spain recognized Cuban independence, ceded Puerto Rico, Guam and the Philippines to the United States.

The failure of the U.S. government to grant immediate independence to Cuba and the Philippines alarmed the American Anti-Imperialist League. Their concerns encompassed a number of issues. Control of the Philippines challenged the American commitment to independence and self-government. The military presence that would be required to administer this control posed a threat, anti-imperialists believed, to political liberties at home. Some feared competition with Filipino sugar producers. Many feared Filipino laborers would relocate to the U.S. and drive down wages. Racist attitudes concerning the alleged "inferiority" of the Filipino people also prevented many Americans from supporting annexation of the Philippines. The anti-imperialist influence proved insufficient. The U.S. committed itself to controlling the islands. For five years the Americans fought to suppress the Filipino war for independence. The guerrilla tactics of the Filipinos led the Americans to employ measures as brutal as those imposed by the Spanish. American control in the Philippines would continue through 1946.

American control of Cuba and Puerto Rico, although peaceful, was nevertheless complete. Although Cuba was technically independent, as a result of the Platt Amendment, Congress ensured that U.S. would have the authority to intervene in Cuban political and economic affairs. Through economic pressure, the U.S. exerted its control until Fidel Castro seized power in 1959. Puerto Rico was denied independence and formally annexed by the U.S. in 1900, as a result of the Foraker Act. Although the Puerto Ricans were later granted citizenship, their rights were limited, and their economic situation continues to be significantly poorer than that of the United States.

Within the span of just twenty years, the U.S. moved from a position of relative isolation to that of a major world power. The concerns of anti-imperialists would be outweighed by a combination of factors including missionary zeal, economic necessity, the notion of racial and cultural superiority, military and strategic requirements, and the sensationalism of the American press, which enabled Americans to feel justified in engaging in imperialistic expansion.

IDENTIFICATION: Briefly describe each item.

Manifest Destiny

Imperialist

Frederick Jackson Turner's "Frontier Thesis"

WASP

John Fiske

Social Darwinism

Josiah Strong

Anglo-Saxonism

Alfred Thayer Mahan

William McKinley

Henry Cabot Lodge

Theodore Roosevelt

James G. Blaine

Pago Pago

Pearl Harbor Treaty

King Kalahaua

Queen Liliuokalani

Sanford B. Dole

John Hay

Open Door Policy

Boxer Rebellion

Jingoism

E.L. Godkin

General Valeriano Weyler

William Randolph Hearst

Joseph Pulitzer

Yellow Journalism

Interventionist

Cuba Libre

De Lome Letter

U.S.S. Maine

Spanish-American War

Commodore George Dewey

Buffalo Soldiers

Rough Riders

Anti-Imperialists

Treaty of Paris, 1898

Emilio Aguinaldo

Teller Amendment

Platt Amendment

Foraker Act

THINK ABOUT:

1. Considering that the United States gained its independence from colonial oppression in 1783, how did Americans justify their own imperialistic actions at the end of the 19th century?

2. Evaluate the anti-imperialist argument to prevent the ratification of the Treaty of Paris. What factors explain the defeat of their position?

3. To what extent was the Open Door Policy responsible for American intervention in China? How successful were American newspapers in promoting the imperialist position? Discuss the role of the press in Spanish American War.

JOSIAH STRONG ON ANGLO-SAXON PREDOMINANCE, 1891

Reverend Josiah Strong, General Secretary of the Evangelical Alliance for the United States, promoted his social Darwinist ideas about Anglo-Saxon American society. Anglo-Saxon Americans, he claimed, were superior to other races, uniquely ordained by God to bring civilization to less-developed people and to govern them.

It is not necessary to argue to those for whom I write that the two great needs of mankind, that all men may be lifted up into the light of the highest Christian civilization, are, first, a pure, spiritual Christianity, and second, civil liberty. Without controversy, these are the forces which, in the past, have contributed most to the elevation of the human race, and they must continue to be, in the future, the most efficient ministers to its progress. It follows, then, that the Anglo-Saxon, as the great representative of these two ideas, the despository of these two greatest blessings, sustains peculiar relations to the world's future, is divinely commissioned to be, in a peculiar sense, his brother's keeper. Add to this the fact of his rapidly increasing strength in modem times, and we have well-nigh a demonstration of his destiny. In 1700 this race numbered less than 6,000,000 souls. In 1800, Anglo-Saxons (I use the term somewhat broadly to include all English speaking peoples) had increased to about 20,500,000, and now, in 1890, they number more than 120,000,000, having multiplied almost six-fold in ninety years. At the end of the reign of Charles 11, the English colonists in America numbered 200,000. During these two hundred years, our population has increased two hundred and fifty-fold. And the expansion of this race has been no less remarkable than its multiplication. In one century the United States has increased its territory ten-fold, while the enormous acquisition of foreign territory by Great Britain-and chiefly within the last hundred years-is wholly unparalleled in history. This mighty Anglo-Saxon race, though comprising only one-thirteenth part of mankind, now rules more than one-third of the earth's surface, and more than one-fourth of its people. And if this race, while growing from 6,000,000 to 120,000,000, thus gained possession of a third portion of the earth, is it to be supposed that when it numbers 1,000,000,000, it will lose the disposition, or lack the power to extend its sway? ...

America is to have the great preponderance of numbers and of wealth, and by the logic of events will follow the scepter of controlling influence. This will be but the consummation of a movement as old as civilization—a result to which men have looked forward for centuries. John Adams records that nothing was "more ancient in his memory than the observation that arts, sciences and empire had traveled westward; and in conversation it was always added that their next leap would be over the Atlantic into America." He recalled a couplet that had been inscribed or rather drilled, into a rock on the shore of Monument Bay in our old colony of Plymouth:

The Eastern nations sink, their glory ends,
And empire rises where the sun descends. . .

Mr. Darwin is not only disposed to see, in the superior vigor of our people, an illustration of his favorite theory of natural selection, but even intimates that the world's history thus far has been simply preparatory for our future, and tributary to it. He says: "There is apparently much truth in the belief that the wonderful progress of the United States, as well as the character of the people, are the results of natural selection; for the more energetic, restless, and courageous men from all parts of Europe have emigrated during the last ten or twelve generations to that great country, and have there succeeded best. Looking at the distant future, I do not think that the Rev. Mr. Zincke takes an exaggerated view when he says: 'All other series of events-as that which resulted in the culture of mind in Greece, and that which resulted in the Empire of Rome-only appear to have purpose and value when viewed in connection with, or rather as subsidiary to, the great stream of Anglo-Saxon emigration to the West.' "

There is abundant reason to believe that the Anglo-Saxon race is to be, is, indeed, already becoming, more effective here than in the mother country. The marked superiority of this race is due, in large measure, to its highly mixed origin. Says Rawlinson: "It is a general rule, now almost universally admitted by ethnologists, that the mixed races of mankind are superior to the pure ones"; and adds: "Even the Jews, who are so often cited as an example of a race at once pure and strong, may, with more reason, be adduced on the opposite side of the argument." The ancient Egyptians, the Greeks, and the Romans, were all mixed races. Among modem races, the most conspicuous example is afforded by the AngloSaxons.... There is here a new commingling of races; and, while the largest injections of foreign blood are substantially the same elements that constituted the original Anglo-Saxon admixture, so that we may infer the general type will be preserved, there are strains of other bloods being added, which, if Mr. Emerson's remark is true, that "the best nations are those most widely related," may be expected to improve the stock, and aid it to a higher destiny. If the dangers of immigration, which have been pointed out, can be successfully met for the next few years, until it has passed its climax, it may be expected to add value to the amalgam which will constitute the new Anglo-Saxon race of the New World. Concerning our future, Herbert Spencer says: "One great result is, I think, tolerably clear. From biological truths it is to be inferred that the eventual mixture of the allied varieties of the Aryan race, forming the population, will produce a more powerful type of man than has hitherto existed, and a type of man more plastic, more adaptable, more capable of undergoing the modifications needful for complete social life. I think, whatever difficulties they may have to surmount, and whatever tribulations they may have to pass through, the Americans may reasonably look forward to a time when they will have produced a civilization grander than any the world has known."

It may be easily shown, and is of no small significance, that the two great ideas of which the Anglo-Saxon is the exponent are having a fuller development in the United States than in Great Britain. There the union of Church and State tends strongly to paralyze some of the members of the body of Christ. Here there is no such influence to destroy spiritual life and power. Here, also, has been evolved the form of government consistent with the largest possible civil liberty. Furthermore, it is significant that the marked characteristics of this race are being here emphasized most. Among the most striking features of the Anglo-Saxon is his money-making powera power of increasing importance in the widening commerce of the world's future. We have seen . . . that, although England is by far the richest nation of Europe, we have already outstripped her in the race after wealth, and we have only begun the development of our vast resources.

Again, another marked characteristic of the Anglo-Saxon is what may be called an instinct or genius for colonizing. His unequaled energy, his indomitable perseverance, and his personal independence, made him a pioneer. He excels all others in pushing his way into new countries. It was those in whom this tendency was strongest that came to America, and this inherited tendency has been further developed by the westward sweep of successive generations across the continent. So noticeable has this characteristic become that English visitors remark it. Charles Dickens once said that the typical American would hesitate to enter heaven unless assured that he could go farther west.

Again, nothing more manifestly distinguishes the Anglo-Saxon than his intense and persistent energy, and he is developing in the United States an energy which, in eager activity and effectiveness, is peculiarly American.

This is due partly to the fact that Americans are much better fed than Europeans, and partly to the undeveloped resources of a new country, but more largely to our climate, which acts as a constant stimulus. Ten years after the landing of the Pilgrims, the Rev. Francis Higginson, a good observer, wrote: "A sup of New England air is better than a whole flagon of English ale." Thus early had the stimulating effect of our climate been noted. Moreover, our social institutions are stimulating. In Europe the various ranks of society are, like the strata of the earth, fixed and fossilized. There can be no great change without a terrible upheaval, a social earthquake. Here society is like the waters of the sea, mobile; as General Garfield said, and so signally illustrated in his own experience, that which is at the bottom today may one day flash on the crest of the highest wave. Every one is free to become whatever he can make of himself; free to transform himself from a rail splitter or a tanner or a canal-boy, into the nation's President. Our aristocracy, unlike that of Europe, is open to all comers. Wealth, position, influence, are prizes offered for energy; and every farmer's boy, every apprentice and clerk, every friendless and penniless immigrant, is free to enter the lists. Thus many causes co-operate to produce here the most forceful and tremendous energy in the world.

What is the significance of such facts? These tendencies infold the future; they are the mighty alphabet with which God writes his prophecies. May we not, by a careful laying together of the letters, spell out something of his meaning? It seems to me that God, with infinite wisdom and skill, is training the Anglo-Saxon race for an hour sure to come in the world's future. Heretofore there has always been in the history of the world a comparatively unoccupied land westward, into which the crowded countries of the East have poured their surplus populations. But the widening waves of migration, which millenniums ago rolled east and west from the valley of the Euphrates, meet to-day on our Pacific coast. There are no more new worlds. The unoccupied arable lands of the earth are limited, and will soon be taken. The time is coming when the pressure of population on the means of subsistence will be felt here as it is now felt in Europe and Asia. Then will the world enter upon a new stage of its history-the *final competition of races, for which the Anglo-Saxon is being schooled.* Long before the thousand millions are here, the mighty *centrifugal* tendency, inherent in this stock and strengthened in the United States, will assert itself. Then this race of unequaled energy, with all the majesty of numbers and the might of wealth behind it-the representative, let us hope, of the largest liberty, the purest Christianity, the highest civilization-having developed peculiarly aggressive traits calculated to impress its institutions upon mankind, will spread itself over the earth. If I read not amiss, this powerful race will move down upon Mexico, down upon Central and South America, out upon the islands of the sea, over upon Africa and beyond. And can any one doubt that the results of this competition of races will be the "survival of the fittest?" "Any people," says Dr. Bushnell, "that is physiologically advanced in culture, though it be only in a degree beyond another which is mingled with it on strictly equal terms, is sure to live down and finally live out its inferior. Nothing can save the inferior race but a ready and pliant assimilation. Whether the feebler and more abject races are going to be regenerated and raised up, is already, very much of a question. What if it should be God's plan to people the world with better and finer material?"

HOW WELL DID YOU UNDERSTAND THIS SELECTION?

1. How does Strong justify American imperialism?

2. What factors make Anglo-Saxons a superior race, according to Strong?

3. Why was his position so popular among Americans in the 1890s?

The de Lôme letter was written by Don Enrigue Dupuy de Lôme, the Spanish Ambassador to the United States. In his note to Don José Canelejas, the Foreign Minister of Spain, de Lôme describes President McKinley as "weak" and pandering to the whims of the public to stay in office. The letter was intercepted by Cuban rebels and published by William Randolph Hearst in the New York **Journal***, 9 February 1898. The remarks helped harden McKinley's attitude toward Spain*

His Excellency
Don José Canalejas.

My distinguished and dear friend:
You have no reason to ask my excuses for not having written to me, I ought also to have written to you but I have put off doing so because overwhelmed with work and nous sommes quittes.

The situation here remains the same. Everything depends on the political and military outcome in Cuba. The prologue of all this, in this second stage (phase) of the war, will end the day when the colonial cabinet shall be appointed and we shall be relieved in the eyes of this country of a part of the responsibility for what is happening in Cuba while the Cubans, whom these people think so immaculate, will have to assume it.

Until then, nothing can be clearly seen, and I regard it as a waste of time and progress, by a wrong road, to be sending emissaries to the rebel camp, or to negotiate with the autonomists who have as yet no legal standing, or to try to ascertain the intentions and plans of this government. The (Cuban) refugees will keep on returning one by one and as they do so will make their way into the sheep-fold, while the leaders in the field will gradually come back. Neither the one nor the other class had the courage to leave in a body and they will not be brave enough to return in a body. The Message has been a disillusionment to the insurgents who expected something different; but I regard it as bad (for us).

Besides the ingrained and inevitable bluntness (grosería) with which is repeated all that the press and public opinion in Spain have said about Weyler, it once more shows what McKinley is, weak and a bidder for the admiration of the crowd besides being a would-be politician (politicastro) who tries to leave a door open behind himself while keeping on good terms with the jingoes of his party.

Nevertheless, whether the practical results of it (the Message) are to be injurious and adverse depends only upon ourselves.

I am entirely of your opinions; without a military end of the matter nothing will be accomplished in Cuba, and without a military and political settlement there will always be the danger of encouragement being give to the insurgents, buy a part of the public opinion if not by the government.

I do not think sufficient attention has been paid to the part England is playing.

Nearly all the newspaper rabble that swarms in your hotels are Englishmen, and while writing for the Journal they are also correspondents of the most influential journals and reviews of London. It has been so ever since this thing began.

As I look at it, England's only object is that the Americans should amuse themselves with us and leave her alone, and if there should be a war, that would the better stave off the conflict which she dreads but which will never come about.

It would be very advantageous to take up, even if only for effect, the question of commercial relations and to have a man of some prominence sent hither, in order that I may make use of him here to carry on a propaganda among the seantors and others in opposition to the Junta and to try to win over the refugees.

So, Amblard is coming. I think he devotes himself too much to petty politics, and we have got to do something very big or we shall fail.

Adela returns your greeting, and we all trust that next year you may be a messenger of peace and take it as a Christmas gift to poor Spain.

Ever your attached friend and servant,
ENRIQUE DUPUY de LÔME.
Source: National Archives & Record Administration

HOW WELL DID YOU UNDERSTAND THIS SELECTION?

1. What is de Lôme's perception of President McKinley?

2. What would motivate Cuban rebels to deliver the intercepted letter to the American press?

3. What effect did the letter have on American attitudes toward Spain?

PLATT AMENDMENT

The Platt Amendment was drafted in 1901 to safeguard American interests in Cuba by limiting Cuban autonomy. American pressure forced the Cuban people to incorporate the terms in their 1902 Constitution. The United States implemented this power several times to assist pro-American leaders and to protect American economic interests. Franklin D. Roosevelt abolished the Platt Amendment as part of his Good Neighbor policy in 1934.

Whereas the Congress of the United States of America, by an Act approved March 2, 1901, provided as follows:

Provided further, That in fulfillment of the declaration contained in the joint resolution approved April twentieth, eighteen hundred and ninety-eight, entitled "For the recognition of the independence of the people of Cuba, demanding that the Government of Spain relinquish its authority and government in the island of Cuba, and withdraw its land and naval forces from Cuba and Cuban waters, and directing the President of the United States to use the land and naval forces of the United States to carry these resolutions into effect," the President is hereby authorized to "leave the government and control of the island of Cuba to its people" so soon as a government shall have been established in said island under a constitution which, either as a part thereof or in an ordinance appended thereto, shall define the future relations of the United States with Cuba, substantially as follows:

"I.-That the government of Cuba shall never enter into any treaty or other compact with any foreign power or powers which will impair or tend to impair the independence of Cuba, nor in any manner authorize or permit any foreign power or powers to obtain by colonization or for military or naval purposes or otherwise, lodgement in or control over any portion of said island."

"II. That said government shall not assume or contract any public debt, to pay the interest upon which, and to make reasonable sinking fund provision for the ultimate discharge of which, the ordinary revenues of the island, after defraying the current expenses of government shall be inadequate."

"III. That the government of Cuba consents that the United States may exercise the right to intervene for the preservation of Cuban independence, the maintenance of a government adequate for the protection of life, property, and individual liberty, and for discharging the obligations with respect to Cuba imposed by the treaty of Paris on the United States, now to be assumed and undertaken by the government of Cuba."

"IV. That all Acts of the United States in Cuba during its military occupancy thereof are ratified and validated, and all lawful rights acquired thereunder shall be maintained and protected."

"V. That the government of Cuba will execute, and as far as necessary extend, the plans already devised or other plans to be mutually agreed upon, for the sanitation of the cities of the island, to the end that a recurrence of epidemic and infectious diseases may be prevented, thereby assuring protection to the people and commerce of Cuba, as well asto the commerce of the southern ports of the United States and the people residing therein."

"VI. That the Isle of Pines shall be omitted from the proposed constitutional boundaries of Cuba, the title thereto being left to future adjustment by treaty."

"VII. That to enable the United States to maintain the independence of Cuba, and to protect the people thereof, as well as for its own defense, the government of Cuba will sell or lease to the United States lands necessary for coaling or naval stations at certain specified points to be agreed upon with the President of the United States."

"VIII. That by way of further assurance the government of Cuba will embody the foregoing provisions in a permanent treaty with the United States."

Source: United States Government Printing Office, Washington D. C.

HOW WELL DID YOU UNDERSTAND THIS SELECTION?

1. In what ways did the Platt Amendment limit the independence of Cuba?

2. What benefits did it provide for the United States?

3. In what ways did the Platt Amendment repudiate the earlier Teller Amendment? How was this justified?

The American Anti-Imperialist League was organized in 1898 to oppose America occupation of Cuba and Puerto Rico, and the acquisition of the Philippines. Although most members of the League favored economic expansion, they claimed it would be better to accomplish this through open trade. American territorial expansion that undermined the autonomy of other nations, they argued was antithetical to the American tradition of political liberty.

We hold that the policy known as imperialism is hostile to liberty and tends toward militarism, an evil from which it has been our glory to be free. We regret that it has become necessary in the land of Washington and Lincoln *to* reaffirm that all men, of whatever race or color, are entitled to life, liberty and the pursuit of happiness. We maintain that governments derive their just powers from the consent of the governed. We insist that the subjugation of any people is "criminal aggression" and open disloyalty to the distinctive principles of our Government.

We earnestly condemn the policy of the present National Administration in the Philippines. It seeks to extinguish the spirit of 1776 in those islands. We deplore the sacrifice of our soldiers and sailors, whose bravery deserves admiration even in an unjust war. We denounce the slaughter of the Filipinos as a needless horror. We protest against the extension of American sovereignty by Spanish methods.

We demand the immediate cessation of the war against liberty, begun by Spain and continued by us. We urge that Congress be promptly convened to announce to the Filipinos our purpose to concede to them the independence for which they have so long fought and which of right is theirs.

The United States have always protested against the doctrine of international law which permits the subjugation of the weak by the strong. A self-governing state cannot accept sovereignty over an unwilling people. The United States cannot act upon the ancient heresy that might makes right.

Imperialists assume that with the destruction of self-government in the Philippines by American hands, all opposition here will cease. This is a grievous error. Much as we abhor the war of "criminal aggression" in the Philippines, greatly as we regret that the blood of the Filipinos is on American hands, we more deeply resent the betrayal of American institutions at home. The real firing line is not in the suburbs of Manila. The foe is of our own household. The attempt of 1861 was to divide the country. That of 1899 is to destroy its fundamental principles and noblest ideals.

Whether the ruthless slaughter of the Filipinos shall end next month or next year is but an incident in a contest that must go on until the Declaration of Independence and the Constitution of the United States are rescued from the hands of their betrayers. Those who dispute about standards of value while the foundation of the Republic is undermined will be listened to as little as those who would wrangle about the small economies of the household while the house is on fire. The training of a great people for a century, the aspiration for liberty of a vast immigration are forces that will hurl aside those who in the delirium of conquest seek to destroy the character of our institutions.

We deny that the obligation of all citizens to support their Government in times of grave National peril applies to the present situation. If an Administration may with impunity ignore the issues upon which it was chosen, deliberately create a condition of war anywhere on the face of the globe, debauch the civil service for spoils to promote the adventure, organize a truth-suppressing censorship and demand of all citizens a suspension of judgment and their unanimous support while it chooses to continue the fighting, representative government itself is imperiled.

We propose to contribute to the defeat of any person or party that stands for the forcible subjugation of any people
. We shall oppose for reelection all who in the White House or in Congress betray American liberty in pursuit of un-

American ends. We still hope that both of our great political parties will support and defend the Declaration of Independence in the closing campaign of the century.

We hold, with Abraham Lincoln, that "no man is good enough to govern another man without that other's consent. When the white man governs himself, that is self-government, but when he governs himself and also governs another man, that is more than self-government-that is despotism." "Our reliance is in the love of liberty which God has planted in us. Our defense is in the spirit which prizes liberty as the heritage of all men in all lands. Those who deny freedom to others deserve it not for themselves, and under a just God cannot long retain it."

We cordially invite the cooperation of all men and women who remain loyal to the Declaration of Independence and the Constitution of the United States.

HOW WELL DID YOU UNDERSTAND THIS SELECTION?

1, What is the Anti-Imperialist League's position on the 1898 situation in the Philippines?

2. What argument does the League employ to support their opposition to American actions there?

3. Why do think the League failed to gain widespread support for this position?

PRESIDENT MCKINLEY ON THE ACQUISITION OF THE PHILIPPINES

President William McKinley outlines the truce agreement between the United States and Spain concluding the war in 1898. McKinley clarifies the American political and economic interests in the Philippines.

By a protocol signed at Washington August 12, 1898 . . . it was agreed that the United States and Spain would each appoint not more than five commissioners to treat of peace, and that the commissioners so appointed should meet at Paris not later than October 1, 1898, and proceed to the negotiation and conclusion of a treaty of peace, which treaty should be subject to ratification according to the respective constitutional forms of the two countries.

For the purpose of carrying into effect this stipulation, I have appointed you as commissioners on the part of the United States to meet and confer with commissioners on the part of Spain.

As an essential preliminary to the agreement to appoint commissioners to treat of peace, this government required of that of Spain the unqualified concession of the following precise demands:

1. The relinquishment of all claim of sovereignty over and title to Cuba.
2. The cession to the United States of Puerto Rico and other islands under Spanish sovereignty in the West Indies.
3. The cession of an island in the Ladrones, to be selected by the United States.
4. The immediate evacuation by Spain of Cuba, Puerto Rico, and other Spanish islands in the West Indies.
5. The occupation by the United States of the city, bay, and harbor of Manila pending the conclusion of a treaty of peace which should determine the control, disposition, and government of the Philippines.

These demands were conceded by Spain, and their concession was, as you will perceive, solemnly recorded in the protocol of the 12th of August. . . .

It is my wish that throughout the negotiations entrusted to the Commission the purpose and spirit with which the United States accepted the unwelcome necessity of war should be kept constantly in view. We took up arms only in obedience to the dictates of humanity and in the fulfillment of high public and moral obligations. We had no design of aggrandizement and no ambition of conquest. Through the long course of repeated representations which preceded and aimed to avert the struggle, and in the final arbitrament of force, this country was impelled solely by the purpose of relieving grievous wrongs and removing long-existing conditions which disturbed its tranquillity, which shocked the moral sense of mankind, and which could no longer be endured.

It is my earnest wish that the United States in making peace should follow the same high rule of conduct which guided it in facing war. It should be as scrupulous and magnanimous in the concluding settlement as it was just and humane in its original action. The luster and the moral strength attaching to a cause which can be confidently rested upon the considerate judgment of the world should not under any illusion of the hour be dimmed by ulterior designs which might tempt us into excessive demands or into an adventurous departure on untried paths. It is believed that the true glory and the enduring interests of the country will most surely be served if an unselfish duty conscientiously accepted and a signal triumph honorably achieved shall be crowned by such an example of moderation, restraint, and reason in victory as best comports with the traditions and character of our enlightened republic.

Our aim in the adjustment of peace should be directed to lasting results and to the achievement of the common good under the demands of civilization, rather than to ambitious designs. The terms of the protocol were framed upon this consideration. The abandonment of the Western Hemisphere by Spain was an imperative necessity. In presenting that requirement, we only fulfilled a duty universally acknowledged. It involves no ungenerous reference to our recent foe, but simply a recognition of the plain teachings of history, to say that it was not compatible with the assurance of permanent peace on and near our own territory that the Spanish flag should remain on this side of the sea. This lesson of events and of reason left no alternative as to Cuba, Puerto Rico, and the other islands belonging to Spain in this hemisphere.

The Philippines stand upon a different basis. It is nonetheless true, however, that without any original thought of complete or even partial acquisition, the presence and success of our arms at Manila imposes upon us obligations which we cannot disregard. The march of events rules and overrules human action. Avowing unreservedly the purpose which has animated all our effort, and still solicitous to adhere to it, we cannot be unmindful that, without any desire or design on our part, the war has brought us new duties and responsibilities which we must meet and discharge as becomes a great nation on whose growth and career from the beginning the ruler of nations has plainly written the high command and pledge of civilization.

Incidental to our tenure in the Philippines is the commercial opportunity to which American statesmanship cannot be indifferent. It is just to use every legitimate means for the enlargement of American trade; but we seek no advantages in the Orient which are not common to all. Asking only the open door for ourselves, we are ready to accord the open door to others. The commercial opportunity which is naturally and inevitably associated with this new opening depends less on large territorial possession than upon an adequate commercial basis and upon broad and equal privileges. . . .

In view of what has been stated, the United States cannot accept less than the cession in full right and sovereignty of the island of Luzon. It is desirable, however, that the United States shall acquire the right of entry for vessels and merchandise belonging to citizens of the United States into such ports of the Philippines as are not ceded to the United States upon terms of equal favor with Spanish ships and merchandise, both in relation to port and customs charges and rates of trade and commerce, together with other rights of protection and trade accorded to citizens of one country within the territory of another. You are therefore instructed to demand such concession, agreeing on your part that Spain shall have similar rights as to her subjects and vessels in the ports of anyterritory in the Philippines ceded to the United States.

Source: United States Department of State, Papers Relating to Foreign Affairs, 1898

HOW WELL DID YOU UNDERSTAND THIS SELECTION?

1. What does President McKinley state should be the American position in the Philippines? Why?

2. To what extent do American economic concerns effect his assessment?

3. Do you find in his speech any indication that the U.S. plans a long-term occupation of the Philippines?

THE OPEN DOOR NOTE: Submitted by U.S. Secretary of State, John Hay, September 6, 1899

By the end of the nineteenth century, American access to trade with China was threatened by the imperialist policies of Britain, France, Germany, Russia, and Japan. These nations sought to divide China into separate spheres of influence, in which each nation could exclude other nations from access Chinese trade within their particular region. In a series of notes Secretary of State John Hay advocated the idea of an "open door," which would allow all nations to have equal rights in trade and economic development in China.

At the time when the Government of the United States was informed by that of Germany that it had leased from His Majesty the Emperor of China the port of Kiao-chao and the adjacent territory in the province of Shantung, assurances were given to the ambassador of the United States at Berlin by the Imperial German minister for foreign affairs that the rights and privileges insured by treaties with China to citizens of the United States would not thereby suffer or be in anywise impaired within the area over which Germany had thus obtained control.

More recently, however, the British Government recognized by a formal agreement with Germany the exclusive right of the latter country to enjoy in said leased area and the contiguous "sphere of influence or interest" certain privileges, more especially those relating to railroads and mining enterprises; but as the exact nature and extent of the rights thus recognized have not been clearly defined, it is possible that serious conflicts of interest may at any time arise not only between British and German subjects within said area, but that the interests of our citizens may also be jeopardized thereby.

Earnestly desirous to remove any cause of irritation and to insure at the same time to the commerce of all nations in China the undoubted benefits which should accrue from a formal recognition by the various powers claiming "spheres of interest" that they shall enjoy perfect equality of treatment for their commerce and navigation within such "spheres," the Government of the United States would be pleased to see His German Majesty's Government give formal assurances, and lend its cooperation in securing like assurances from the other interested powers, that each, within its respective sphere of whatever influence—

First. Will in no way interfere with any treaty port or any vested interest within any so-called "sphere of interest" or leased territory it may have in China.

Second. That the Chinese treaty tariff of the time being shall apply to all merchandise landed or shipped to all such ports as are within said "sphere of interest" (unless they be "free ports"), no matter to what nationality it may belong, and that duties so leviable shall be collected by the Chinese Government.

Third. That it will levy no higher harbor dues on vessels of another nationality frequenting any port in such "sphere" than shall be levied on vessels of its own nationality, and no higher railroad charges over lines built, controlled, or operated within its "sphere" on merchandise belonging to citizens or subjects of other nationalities transported through such "sphere" than shall be levied on similar merchandise belonging to its own nationals transported over equal distances.

The liberal policy pursued by His Imperial German Majesty in declaring Kiao-chao a free port and in aiding the Chinese Government in the establishment there of a custom-house are so clearly in line with the proposition which this Government is anxious to see recognized that it entertains the strongest hope that Germany will give its acceptance and hearty support.

The recent ukase of His Majesty the Emperor of Russia declaring the port of Ta-lien-wan open during the whole of the lease under which it is held from China to the merchant ships of all nations, coupled with the categorical assurances made to this Government by His Imperial Majesty's representative at this capital at the time and since repeated to me by the present Russian ambassador, seem to insure the support of the Emperor to the proposed measure. Our ambassador at the Court of St. Petersburg has in consequence been instructed to submit it to the Russian Government and to request their early consideration of it. A copy of my instruction on the subject to Mr. Tower is herewith inclosed for your confidential information.

The commercial interests of Great Britain and Japan will be so clearly served by the desired declaration of intentions, and the views of the Governments of these countries as to the desirability of the adoption of measures insuring the benefits of equality of treatment of all foreign trade throughout China are so similar to those entertained by the United States, that their acceptance of the propositions herein outlined and their cooperation in advocating their adoption by the other powers can be confidently expected. I inclose herewith copy of the instruction which I have sent to Mr. Choate on the subject.

In view of the present favorable conditions, you are instructed to submit the above considerations to His Imperial German Majesty's Minister for Foreign Affairs, and to request his early consideration of the subject.

Copy of this instruction is sent to our ambassadors at London and at St. Petersburg for their information.
Source: United States Department of State, Papers Relating to Foreign Affairs

HOW WELL DID YOU UNDERSTAND THIS SELECTION?

16. What are the basic demands of the Open Door note?

17. Why is access to China so important to the United States?

18. How would expect the other nations to respond?

THE WHITE MAN'S BURDEN, by Rudyard Kipling, 1899

British poet and novelist Rudyard Kipling composed this poem in 1899 in response to the American acquisition of the Philippines. In "The White Man's Burden: The United States and The Philippine Islands," Kipling encouraged Americans to emulate Britain and in assuming the "burden" of empire.

Take up the White Man's burden—
Send forth the best ye breed—
Go bind your sons to exile
To serve your captives' need;
To wait in heavy harness,
On fluttered folk and wild—
Your new-caught, sullen peoples,
Half-devil and half-child.

Take up the White Man's burden—
In patience to abide,

To veil the threat of terror
And check the show of pride;
By open speech and simple,
An hundred times made plain
To seek another's profit,
And work another's gain.
Take up the White Man's burden—
The savage wars of peace—
Fill full the mouth of Famine
And bid the sickness cease;
And when your goal is nearest
The end for others sought,
Watch sloth and heathen Folly
Bring all your hopes to nought.

Take up the White Man's burden—
No tawdry rule of kings,
But toil of serf and sweeper—
The tale of common things.
The ports ye shall not enter,
The roads ye shall not tread,
Go mark them with your living,
And mark them with your dead.

Take up the White Man's burden—
And reap his old reward:
The blame of those ye better,
The hate of those ye guard—
The cry of hosts ye humour
(Ah, slowly!) toward the light:—
"Why brought he us from bondage,
Our loved Egyptian night?"

Take up the White Man's burden—
Ye dare not stoop to less—
Nor call too loud on Freedom
To cloke your weariness;
By all ye cry or whisper,
By all ye leave or do,
The silent, sullen peoples
Shall weigh your gods and you.

Take up the White Man's burden—
Have done with childish days—
The lightly proferred laurel,
The easy, ungrudged praise.
Comes now, to search your manhood
Through all the thankless years
Cold, edged with dear-bought wisdom,
The judgment of your peers!

HOW WELL DID YOU UNDERSTAND THIS SELECTION?

1. What does Kipling mean by the term "White Man's Burden"?

2. Is he supporting or objecting to the American actions in the Philippines?

3. How well do his ideas reflect the views of Americans at that time?

Self Test:
Multiple Choice Questions:

1. According to Frederick Jackson Turner's "Frontier Thesis,"
    a. the frontier was not an uninhabited wilderness; it had thousands of Native American inhabitants.
    b. the frontier had fostered rugged individualism, egalitarianism and a democratic faith.
    c. the West was a still undeveloped region.
    d. the frontier had simply reinforced European democratic traditions.

2. The theory of Social Darwinism
    a. supported the claim of Anglo-Saxon racially superiority.
    b. was proven false by imperialists like Josiah Strong.
    c. was employed to support the position of the Anti-Imperialist League.
    d. was based on racial equality among all people.

3. The revolution in Hawaii was instigated by
    a. President Grover Cleveland to gain a naval base at Pearl Harbor.
    b. Queen Liliuokalani so she could claim the crown held by king Kalakaua.
    c. American planters who wanted the U.S. to make Hawaii a protectorate.
    d. native Hawaiians who wanted to drive out the American sugar planters.

4. The Open Door Policy
    a. was designed to protect American economic interests in China.
    b. was designed to give the U.S. exclusive control in China.
    c. led the U.S. to support the "Boxers" in their rebellion against the Manchu dynasty.
    d. was welcomed by Europe, Russia and Japan.

5. The term "yellow-journalism" was applied to the newspapers owned by Hearst and Pulitzer because of
    a. reports about the rebellion in China.
    b. accounts of the yellow-fever epidemic in Cuba.
    c. exaggerated or fabricated reports about Spanish atrocities in Cuba.
    d. their reluctance to get involved in reporting the war.

6. The explosion on board the U.S. battleship *Maine*
    a. was the result of an attack by Spanish loyalists.
    b. claimed the lives of more that 2000 sailors.
    c. led Congress to unanimously appropriate $50 million for military preparations.
    d. led the American public to demand an end to the war with Spain.

7. As a result of the Treaty of Paris, 1898, the United States
    a. gained control of Guam.
    b. paid Spain a sum of $100 million.
    c. granted independence to the Philippines.
    d. annexed Cuba.

8. A number of anti-imperialists resisted American acquisition of the Philippines because
    a. they felt the U.S. should not spread its democratic principles abroad.
    b. they feared racial "contamination" would result from contact with Filipinos immigrants.
    c. the felt the money and effort would be better spent addressing poverty in the U.S.
    d. they felt it was the duty of Americans to colonize the islands.

9. The Philippine-American war
    a. ended in easy victory for Aguinaldo's rebels.
    b. was supported by the American Anti-Imperialist League.
    c. was concluded by the Platt Amendment.
    d. was longer and more costly than the war with Spain

10. The Foraker Act involved annexation of
    a. Cuba.
    b. Hawaii.
    c. The Philippines.
    d. Puerto Rico.

Answers: 1-b; 2-a; 3-c; 4-a; 5-c; 6-c; 7-a; 8-b; 9-d; 10-d

Essays:

1. The United States fought a war with Spain to liberate Cuba. Explain why the United States did not grant independence to the Philippines following that conflict.

2. Examine the connection between concepts of Manifest Destiny, Social Darwinism and American imperialism.

3. Evaluate the impact of economic concerns on American imperialism. Support your position with specific examples.

Optional Activities:

1. Create a poster displaying and explaining political cartoons that illustrate the different positions in the debate over American imperialism.

2. The United States annexed Hawaii without consulting the native Hawaiians. Imagine you are a native of Hawaii; write a letter to President McKinley explaining your reaction to the news of annexation.

3. After reading through the primary sources, organize a classroom debate over annexation of the Philippines.

WEB SITE LISTINGS:

Imperialism - general
Internet Modern History Sourcebook: Imperialism
http://www.fordham.edu/halsall/mod/modsbook34.html
Professor Vincent Ferraro's Documents Relating to American Foreign Policy, 1898-1914
http://www.mtholyoke.edu/acad/intrel/to1914.htm
National History Day, National Archives & Records Administration, USA Freedom Corps,
"100 Milestone Documents": http://www.ourdocuments.gov
Small Planet Communications: "The Age of Imperialism"
http://www.smplanet.com/imperialism/toc.html
Anti-imperialism in the U.S., 1898-1935
http://www.boondocksnet.com/ai/
American Social History Project: Poetry Analysis: "The White Man's Burden"
http://historymatters.gmu.edu/d/6609/
Digital History: Imperialism and the Spanish American War
http://www.digitalhistory.uh.edu/historyonline/us27.cfm

Annexation of Hawaii
PBS: Hawaii's Last Queen
http://www.pbs.org/wgbh/amex/hawaii/

China
Small Planet Communications: "Boxer Rebellion":
http://www.smplanet.com/imperialism/fists.html

Spanish-American War
PBS: Crucible of Empire, The Spanish-American War
http://www.pbs.org/crucible/

William McKinley and the Spanish-American War
http://www.history.ohio-state.edu/projects/McKinley/SpanAmWar.htm
Library of Congress: The World of 1898, the Spanish American War
http://lcweb.loc.gov/rr/hispanic/1898/
Small Planet Communications: "Spanish-American War"
http://www.smplanet.com/imperialism/remember.html

Philippine-American War

Philippine Revolution & Philippine-American War
http://www.boondocksnet.com/centennial/
American Social History Project: Should the U.S. Annex the Philippines?
    http://historymatters.gmu.edu/d/6613/

Yellow Journalism & Political Cartoons

PBS: Crucible of Empire, The Spanish-American War, Yellow Journalism
http://www.pbs.org/crucible/frames/_journalism.html
Cartoons from the American Anti-Imperialist Movement
http://www.history.ohio-state.edu/projects/uscartoons/AntiImperialismCartoons.htm
Political Cartoons
http://www.boondocksnet.com/gallery/political_cartoons.html

Chapter Sixteen

PROGRESSIVISM

By the turn of the nineteenth century, America had become a nation fundamentally different from the place it had been just fifty years before. While continuities with the past were plainly evident, what was more striking about the nation in 1900 were its discontinuities with an earlier America. Change, both rapid and sweeping, marked the nation's social, economic, political, and cultural landscape. Its origins were unmistakable: the experiences of rapid industrialization in the post-Civil War era, massive immigration that brought tens of millions of foreigners to America's shores as a labor force, and the concomitant urbanization that would soon transform Americans into a nation of predominantly city-dwellers. While many moved upward into an enlarging middle class, they decried the negative consequences of industrialization, immigration, and urbanization. Economic consolidation produced monopoly; the periodic fall of the business cycle brought frequent periods of unemployment for masses of unskilled factory workers; poverty on a mass scale made an appearance in America. The industrial city was marked by haphazard, unplanned growth; tenement-filled slums bulged with unassimilated immigrants, many of them Catholics and Jews from southern and eastern Europe. The influx of so many New Wave immigrants provoked anxiety in an America whose dominant group was white, Anglo-Saxon, and Protestant; nativism increased. Municipal services failed to keep pace with the demands placed upon them by exploding populations; political machines operated by corrupt bosses rose to fill the vacuum, providing services in exchange for immigrants' votes. Urban public health declined as poor sanitation and high population density led to high rates of disease. Broken families, prostitution, and alcoholism became more commonplace. Change brought reaction from those who gloried in its benefits but sought to undo its undesirable effects. The Progressive era was born.

Spanning roughly the period from the turn of the century until World War I, the roots of Progressivism reached back into the late nineteenth century agrarian discontent that gave birth to Populism. Reformers who attacked monopoly, particularly the railroads, and called upon government to address the needs of farmers and industrial workers, the Populists developed a reform agenda that many Progressives would later embrace. Progressivism was not a single unified movement but rather a set of reform movements with three major areas of focus: economic, political, and social reform. Progressives' goal was to create a more orderly, stable, fair, and just society. To that end, they enlisted government as an agent of positive change.

Government would be called upon to institute reforms that would take power out of the hands of a few and give it back to the people. Progressives exhorted government to abandon its laissez-faire posture and intervene to put an end to the corrupt practices of big business that had distorted capitalism, leaving workers, farmers, and consumers vulnerable and unprotected. Finally, government would be called upon to address social injustice.

Deeply involved in the social justice movement, women reformers paid particular attention to the plight of working women and children and immigrant families. Settlement houses were established to provide a nurturing residential environment where hygiene, childcare, and middle class values could be taught. From these efforts, the profession of social work was born. As they struggled to improve opportunities and secure rights for others, women paid greater attention to their own rights, including the right to vote.

Who were the Progressives and what were their motivations? Primarily white, middle class, educated, and Protestant, Progressives were reformers, not radicals. They sought to clean up the excesses of capitalism, not to abandon and replace it. Deeply rooted in Christian morality and Protestant values, they strove to help the less fortunate, especially immigrants, by "Americanizing" them—in effect, making them over in their own image. And while many Progressives actively crusaded for social justice, most exhibited a blind spot when it came to recognizing and addressing the injustices suffered by African Americans. A product of the time in which they lived, very few were able to rise above contemporary prejudices. While motivated, then, by a sense of humanitarianism, idealism, and moral outrage, Progressives acted, as well, out of self-interest, anxiety, and fear, as undesirable change threatened to erode their economic well being, political power, and social status. Given Progressives' mixed motivations, social justice and social control were often simultaneous but contradictory objectives. Many Progressives supported legislation aimed at establishing social and moral control over the poor, the working class, and foreign-born, advocating prohibition, immigration restriction, and even sterilization laws.

Progressivism was grounded in optimism and animated by faith in humans' capacity to use reason, science, technology, and education to solve America's problems. To that end, Progressives championed investigative research to gather data and the creation of commissions and regulatory agencies that would rely on professional expertise.

Public interest in and support for reform was fueled by investigative journalism called "muckraking." Mass circulation magazines like *McClure's* made their appearance in the 1890s as higher literacy rates coupled with technological advances in printing and cheaper paper made it possible for more Americans to read and afford newspapers and magazines. Investigative reports that unearthed the corrupt practices of monopolies like Standard Oil, of the meat-packing and patent medicine industries, and of countless politicians invested with the peoples' trust roused the public's consciousness and stirred its conscience. The sail of Progressive reform was filled with the wind of public outrage.

Calls for political, economic, and social reform met with action first on the local and state level where legislation regulating monopolies, providing social services, strengthening existing housing and fire codes, regulating working hours of women and children, creating workman's compensation, and promoting workplace safety was passed. When Theodore Roosevelt ascended to the presidency in 1901, Progressivism was carried to the federal level. By promoting legislation that put teeth into the 1890 Sherman Anti-Trust Act, first Roosevelt, then his successors, Taft and Wilson, made the economy subject to federal government regulation. Along with anti-trust suits brought by the Justice Department to break up monopolies, economic competition was fostered by the creation of a Federal Trade Commission with the power to prevent unfair business practices. In addition, consumer protection laws, aid to farmers, and banking reform that created the Federal Reserve System and broke the power of the "money trust" were all instituted at the federal level. The principle that government should intervene to regulate the economy was now firmly established.

Among the most significant developments of the Progressive era would be the expansion of the power of the national government, a strengthening of the presidency, and the growth of the federal bureaucracy. Each of these tendencies would intensify through the course of the twentieth century.

Why did the Progressive Era end? The mood of the nation would change with the outbreak of World War I. As Americans mobilized for possible involvement in the war, their energy and focus shifted away from problems at home and toward problems abroad. In both the mobilization and, then, in waging war, the nation would rely heavily upon the expertise of Progressive reformers, many of whom entered government to serve their country.

While many reforms fell short of their intended result, by offering a vision of a more humane and just society and working toward its realization, Progressives had initiated a major transformation: the state had been forced to alter its relationship to the people, expanding its role to include taking responsibility for the well-being of its citizens.

IDENTIFICATION: Briefly describe each item.

Monopoly

Economic consolidation

Muckrakers

Henry Demarest Lloyd

Jacob Riis

Lincoln Steffens

Ida Tarbell

Upton Sinclair

Ida Wells Barnett

Women's Christian Temperance Union

Social Gospel

Settlement house movement

Jane Addams

Hull House

Florence Kelley

Woman suffrage

Carrie Chapman Catt

National American Woman Suffrage Association [NAWSA]

Alice Paul

Muller v Oregon

Triangle Shirtwaist Company Fire

Theodore Roosevelt

Hepburn Act

Pure Food and Drug Act

Meat Inspection Act

William Taft

Bull Moose Party

Woodrow Wilson

Underwood Tariff

Sixteenth Amendment

Seventeenth Amendment

Federal Reserve Act

Federal Trade Commission Act

Clayton Antitrust Act

Eighteenth Amendment

Nineteenth Amendment

Big stick diplomacy

Panama Canal

Roosevelt Corollary

Gentleman's Agreement

Dollar Diplomacy

THINK ABOUT:

1. What were the negative social, economic, and political consequences of America's rapid industrialization? Of massive immigration? Of urbanization?

2. What were the positive social, economic, and political consequences of America's rapid industrialization, urbanization, and massive immigration?

3. Could America have become an economic powerhouse without a virtually unlimited supply of cheap labor?

4. How did Progressive era reforms initiated at the national level alter the relationship between American government and American society?

HOW THE OTHER HALF LIVES: Studies Among the Tenements of New York, By Jacob Riis, 1890

---

*In the late nineteenth century, America's progress and prosperity were uneven and had come at the price of great poverty. Jacob Riis was a Danish immigrant whose work as a police reporter familiarized him with life in New York City's worst slums. His first-hand knowledge of tenement life led to the publication in 1890 of **How the Other Half Lives**, an effort to call attention to the evils of the slums in order to bring about reforms. While he sought to present to the American public the harsh social reality of America's cities, Riis embraced the prevailing ethnic stereotypes of the era and his work served to reinforce them.*

Introduction

Long ago it was said that "one half of the world does not know how the other half lives." That was true then. It did not know because it did not care. The half that was on top cared little for the struggles, and less for the fate of those who were underneath, so long as it was able to hold them there and keep its own seat. There came a time when the discomfort and crowding below were so great, and the consequent upheavals so violent, that it was no longer an easy thing to do, and then the upper half fell to inquiring what was the matter. Information on the subject has been accumulating rapidly since, and the whole world has had its hands full answering for its old ignorance.

In New York, the youngest of the world's great cities, that time came later than elsewhere, because the crowding had not been so great. There were those who believed it would never come; but their hopes were vain. Greed and reckless selfishness wrought like results here as in cities of older lands....

...To-day three-fourths of its [New York's—Ed.] people live in the tenements, and the nineteenth century drift of the population to the cities is sending ever-increasing multitudes to crowd them. The fifteen thousand tenant-houses that were the despair of the sanitarian in the past generation have swelled into thirty-seven thousand, and more than twelve hundred thousand persons call them home...We know now that there is no way out; that the "system" that was the evil offspring of public neglect and private greed has come to stay, a storm-centre forever of our civilization....

...If it shall appear that the sufferings and sins of the "other half," and the evil they breed, are but as a just punishment upon the community that gave it no other choice, it will be because that is the truth....in the tenements all the influences make for evil; because they are the hot-beds of the epidemics that carry death to rich and poor alike; that throw off a scum of forty thousand human wrecks to the asylums and workhouses year by year; that turned out in the last eight years a round half million beggars to prey upon our charities; that maintain a standing army of ten thousand tramps with all that that implies; because, above all, they touch the family life with deadly moral contagion. This is their worst crime, inseparable from the system.

Chapter 3: The Mixed Crowd

The Italian scavenger of our time is fast graduating into exclusive control of the corner fruit-stands, while his black-eyed boy monopolizes the boot-blacking industry in which a few years ago he was an intruder. The Irish hod-carrier in the second generation has become a brick-layer, if not the Alderman of his ward, while the Chinese coolie is in almost exclusive possession of the laundry business. The reason is obvious. The poorest immigrant comes here with the purpose and ambition to better himself and, given half a chance, might be reasonably expected to make the most of it. To the false plea that he prefers the squalid homes in which his kind are housed there could be no better answer. The truth is, his half chance has too long been wanting, and for the bad result he has been unjustly blamed....

The Irishman is the true cosmopolitan immigrant. All-pervading, he shares his lodging with perfect impartiality with the Italian, the Greek, and the "Dutchman," yielding only to sheer force of numbers, and objects equally to them all. A map of the city, colored to designate nationalities, would show more stripes than on the skin of a zebra, and more colors than a rainbow.

Hardly less aggressive than the Italian, the Russian and Polish Jew, having overrun the district between Rivington and Division Streets, east of the Bowery, to the point of suffocation, is filling the tenements of the old Seventh Ward to the river front, and disputing with the Italian every foot of available space in the back alleys of Mulberry Street. The two races, differing hopelessly in much, have this in common: they carry their slums with them wherever they go, if allowed to do it. Little Italy already rivals its parent, the "Bend," in foulness. Other nationalities that begin at the bottom make a fresh start when crowded up the ladder. Happily both are manageable, the one by rabbinical, the other by the civil law. Between the dull gray of the Jew, his favorite color, and the Italian red, would be seen squeezed in on the map a sharp streak of yellow, marking the narrow boundaries of Chinatown. Dovetailed in with the German population, the poor but thrifty Bohemian might be picked out by the sombre hue of his life as of his philosophy, struggling against heavy odds in the big human bee-hives of the East Side...The Bohemian is the only foreigner with any considerable representation in the city who counts no wealthy man of his race, none who has not to work hard for a living, or has got beyond the reach of the tenement.

Down near the Battery the West Side emerald would be soiled by a dirty stain, spreading rapidly like a splash of ink on a sheet of blotting paper, headquarters of the Arab tribe, that in a single year has swelled from the original dozen to the twelve hundred, intent, every mother's son, on trade and barter. Dots and dashes of color here and there would show where the Finnish sailors worship their djumala (God), the Greek pedlars the ancient name of their race, and the Swiss the goddess of thrift. And so on to the end of the long register, all toiling together in the galling fetters of the tenement. Were the question raised who makes the most of life thus mortgaged, who resists most stubbornly its levelling tendency—knows how to drag even the barracks upward a part of the ways at least toward the ideal plane of the home—the palm must be unhesitatingly awarded the Teuton. The Italian and the poor Jew rise only by compulsion. The Chinaman does not rise at all; here, as at home, he simply remains stationary. The Irishman's genius runs to public affairs rather than domestic life; wherever he is mustered in force the saloon is the gorgeous centre of political activity. The German struggles vainly to learn his trick; his Teutonic wit is too heavy, and the political ladder he raises from his saloon usually too short or too clumsy to reach the desired goal. The best part of his life is lived at home, and he makes himself a home independent of his surroundings, giving the lie to the saying, unhappily become a maxim of social truth, that pauperism and drunkenness naturally grow in the tenements. He makes the most of his tenement, and it should be added that whenever and as soon as he can save up money enough, he gets out and never crosses the threshold of one again.

Chapter V: The Italian in New York

…..The Italian comes in at the bottom, and in the generation that came over the sea he stays there. In the slums he is welcomed as a tenant who "makes less trouble" than the contentious Irishman or the order-loving German, that is to say: is content to live in a pig-sty and submits to robbery at the hands of the rent-collector without murmur. Yet this very tractability makes of him in good hands, when firmly and intelligently managed, a really desirable tenant. But it is not his good fortune often to fall in with other hospitality upon his coming than that which brought him here for its own profit, and has no idea of letting go its grip upon him as long as there is a cent to be made out of him....His ignorance and unconquerable suspicion of strangers dig the pit into which he falls. He not only knows no word of English, but he does not know enough to learn. Rarely only can he write his own language. Unlike the German, who begins learning English the day he lands as a matter of duty, or the Polish Jew, who takes it up as soon as he is able as an investment, the Italian learns slowly, if at all....

Did the Italian always adapt himself as readily to the operation of the civil law as to the manipulation of political "pull" on occasion, he would save himself a good deal of unnecessary trouble. Ordinarily he is easily enough governed by authority—always excepting Sunday, when he settles down to a game of cards and lets loose all his bad passions. Like the Chinese, the Italian is a born gambler. His soul is in the game the moment the cards are on the table, and very frequently his knife is in it too before the game is ended.....

With all his conspicuous faults, the swarthy Italian immigrant has his redeeming traits. He is as honest as he is hot-headed. There are no Italian burglars in the Rogues' Gallery; the ex-brigand toils peacefully with pickaxe and shovel on American ground....The women are faithful wives and devoted mothers....The Italian is gay, lighthearted and, if his fur is not stroked the wrong way, inoffensive as a child. His worst offence is that he keeps the stale-beer dives.....

Chapter IX: Chinatown

Between the tabernacles of Jewry and the shrines of the Bend, Joss has cheekily planted his pagan worship of idols, chief among which are the celestial worshipper's own gain and lusts. Whatever may be said about the Chinaman being a thousand years behind the age on his own shores, here he is distinctly abreast of it in his successful scheming to "make it pay." It is doubtful if there is anything he does not turn to a paying account, from his religion down, or up, as one prefers. At the risk of distressing some well-meaning, but, I fear, too trustful people, I state it in advance as my opinion, based on the steady observation of years, that all attempts to make an effective Christian of John Chinaman will remain abortive in this generation; of the next I have, if anything, less hope. Ages of senseless idolatry, a mere grub-worship, have left him without the essential qualities for appreciating the gentle teachings of a faith whose motive and unselfish spirit are alike beyond his grasp. He lacks the handle of a strong faith in something, anything, however wrong, to catch him by. There is nothing strong about him, except his passions when aroused. I am convinced that he adopts Christianity, when he adopts it at all, as he puts on American clothes, with what the politicians would call an ulterior motive, some sort of gain in the near prospect—washing, a Christian wife perhaps, anything he happens to rate for the moment above his cherished pigtail. It may be that I judge him too harshly. Exceptions may be found. Indeed, for the credit of the race, I hope there are such. But I am bound to say my hope is not backed by lively faith.

Chapter X: Jewtown

The tenements grow taller, and the gaps in their ranks close up rapidly as we cross the Bowery and, leaving Chinatown and the Italians behind, invade the Hebrew quarter....No need of asking here where we are. The jargon of the street, the signs of the sidewalk, the manner and the dress of the people, their unmistakable physiognomy, betray their race at every step. Men with queer skull-caps, elbow the ugliest and the handsomest women in the land....

Thrift is the watchword of Jewtown, as of its people the world over. It is at once its strength and its fatal weakness, its cardinal virtue and its foul disgrace. Become an over-mastering passion with these people who come here in droves from Eastern Europe to escape persecution, from which freedom could be bought only with gold, it has enslaved them in bondage worse than that from which they fled. Money is their God. Life itself is of little value compared with even the leanest bank account. In no other spot does life wear so intensely bald and materialistic an aspect as in Ludlow Street. Over and over again I have met with instances of these Polish or Russian Jews deliberately starving themselves to the point of physical exhaustion, while working night and day at a tremendous pressure to save a little money....

Source: Jacob Riis, *How the Other Half Lives*, Charles Scribner's, New York, 1890

HOW WELL DID YOU UNDERSTAND THIS SELECTION?

1. What racial and ethnic stereotypes does Riis employ?

2. What picture of immigrants does Riis paint with his use of animal imagery?

3. Compare the author's sympathy with and concern for the plight of the immigrant masses as displayed in the *Introduction* with his distaste for certain kinds of immigrants when he characterizes them in individual chapters. What role might Riis' own ethnic heritage and identity—Old Wave immigrant—have played in his stereotyping of Southern and Eastern European and Asian New Wave immigrants?

Woodrow Wilson was a professor of government and history and author of a five-volume history of America. In 1902 he became president of Princeton University; in 1910, progressive governor of NJ; and in 1912 was elected to his first of two presidential terms as a progressive.

The census of 1890 showed the population of the country increased to 62,622,250, an addition of 12,466,467 within the decade. Immigrants poured steadily in as before, but with an alteration of stock which students of affairs marked with uneasiness. Throughout the century men of the sturdy stocks of the north of Europe had made up the main strain of foreign blood which was every year added to the vital working force of the country, or else men of the Latin-Gallic stocks of France and Northern Italy; but now came multitudes of men of the lowest class from the south of Italy and men of the meaner sort out of Hungary and Poland, men out of the ranks where there was neither skill nor energy nor any initiative of quick intelligence; and they came in numbers which increased from year to year, as if the countries of the south of Europe were disburdening themselves of the more sordid and hapless elements of their population, the men whose standards of life and of work were such as American workmen had never dreamed of hitherto. The people of the Pacific coast had clamored these many years against the admission of immigrants out of China, and in May, 1892, got at last what they wanted, a federal statute which practically excluded from the United States all Chinese who had not already acquired the right of residence; and yet the Chinese were more to be desired, as workmen if not as citizens, than most of the coarse crew that came crowding in every year at the eastern ports. They had, no doubt, many an unsavory habit, bred unwholesome squalor in the crowded quarters where they most abounded in the western seaports, and seemed separated by their very nature from the people among whom they had come to live; but it was their skill, their intelligence, their hardy power of labor, their knack at succeeding and driving duller rivals out, rather than their alien habits, that made them feared and hated and led to their exclusion at the prayer of the men they were likely to displace should they multiply. The unlikely fellows who came in at the eastern ports were tolerated because they usurped no place but the very lowest in the scale of labor.

Source: Woodrow Wilson, *History of the American People*, Harper & Brothers, Vol. 5, 1902

HOW WELL DID YOU UNDERSTAND THIS SELECTION?

1. What is Wilson's appraisal of the new wave immigrant? What evidence does Wilson present to substantiate these views?

2. Why does he regard Chinese immigrants more favorably? Is his assessment of them devoid of prejudice?

3. Compare Riis's and Wilson's characterizations of Chinese immigrants.

This cartoon appeared in 1904 in **Life**, *a humor magazine. It depicts the prevailing racial stereotypes of the day and serves to reinforce them with its simian-like characterization of African Americans. The cartoon's creator, James Montgomery Flagg, would become one of America's foremost illustrators, best known for his World War I era "I Want You!" Uncle Sam poster. The following events provide a context for the cartoon's appearance: Harvard's acceptance of African-American students; the addition of an African American to Harvard's 1904 football team (William Clarence Matthews), the negative reaction of many white Americans, both northern and southern, to President Theodore Roosevelt's invitation to Booker T. Washington to dine at the White House in 1901, and the call by W.E.B. Du Bois for the creation of an African-American elite through higher education.*

HARVARD'S FOOTBALL ELEVEN OF 1909, UNDER PRESIDENT ROOSEVELT, OF HARVARD.

Source: *Life*, New York, vol. 44, December 15, 1904.

HOW WELL DID YOU UNDERSTAND THIS SELECTION?

1. What prevailing racial stereotypes does Flagg play on in his cartoon? What visual cliches does Flagg employ?

2. By captioning his cartoon "Harvard's Football Team of 1909, Under President Roosevelt, of Harvard," what is Flagg suggesting?

3. Who would have found this cartoon humorous?

Although Woodrow Wilson carried his reformist agenda to the White House, his progressivism, like that of so many other whites of his era, did not extend to African Americans. Raised in the South with that region's traditional attitudes toward blacks, Wilson permitted segregation of several departments of the federal government headed by Southerners. In November 1913, black leaders, including the anti-lynching crusader and journalist Ida Wells Barnett and the civil rights activist and journalist William Monroe Trotter, visited the president to address what they regarded as a step backward. In her autobiography, Wells Barnett recounted what transpired: "President Wilson received us standing, and seemingly gave careful attention to the appeal directed by Mr. Trotter. At its conclusion he said he was unaware of such discrimination, although Mr. Trotter left with him an order emanating from one of his heads of the department which forbade colored and white clerks to use the same restaurants or toilet rooms. The president promised to look into the matter and again expressed doubt as to the situation." One year later, after Wilson had neither responded to the delegation nor taken action, a delegation led by Trotter returned to meet with the president.

Mr. Monroe Trotter. Mr. President, we are here to renew our protest against the segregation of colored employees in the departments of our National Government. We [had] appealed to you to undo this race segregation in accord with your duty as President and with your pre-election pledges to colored American voters. We stated that such segregation was a public humiliation and degradation, and entirely unmerited and far-reaching in its injurious effects....

President Woodrow Wilson. The white people of the country, as well as I, wish to see the colored people progress, and admire the progress they have already made, and want to see them continue along independent lines. There is, however, a great prejudice against colored people....It will take one hundred years to eradicate this prejudice, and we must deal with it as practical men. Segregation is not humiliating but a benefit, and ought to be so regarded by you gentlemen. If your organization goes out and tells the colored people of the country that it is a humiliation, they will so regard it, but if you do not tell them so, and regard it as a benefit, they will regard it the same. The only harm that will come will be if you cause them to think it is a humiliation.

Mr. Monroe Trotter. It is not in accord with the known facts to claim that the segregation was started because of race friction of white and colored [federal] clerks. The indisputable facts of the situation will not permit of the claim that the segregation is due to the friction. It is untenable, in view of the established facts, to maintain that the segregation is simply to avoid race friction, for the simple reason that for fifty years white and colored clerks have been working together in peace and harmony and friendliness, doing so even through two [President Grover Cleveland] Democratic administrations. Soon after your inauguration began, segregation was drastically introduced in the Treasury and postal departments by your appointees.

President Woodrow Wilson. If this organization is ever to have another hearing before me it must have another spokesman. Your manner offends me....Your tone, with its background of passion.

Mr. Monroe Trotter. But I have no passion in me, Mr. President, you are entirely mistaken; you misinterpret my earnestness for passion.

Source: *The Crisis*, 9 (January 1915): 119-120, W.E.B. Du Bois, ed.

HOW WELL DID YOU UNDERSTAND THIS SELECTION?

1. What assumptions underlie President Wilson's claim that segregation is a benefit rather than a humiliation?

2. In your estimation, what angered President Wilson? Was it simply Trotter's tone?

3. Do you believe Wilson was justified in his anger?

"OF OUR SPIRITUAL STRIVINGS," *The Souls of Black Folk,* **By W.E.B. Du Bois, 1903**

A Harvard-educated sociologist and an historian, in this work W.E.B. Du Bois weaves together autobiography, scholarship, and a literary and poetic style to reveal the soul and strivings of African Americans. Du Bois seeks to pierce the veil that separates whites from blacks, enabling not only whites to peer into the souls of black folk, but blacks as well to more clearly recognize their history, culture, and spirituality. During the Progressive era, evidence of the absence of white America's comprehension of the strivings and humanity of black Americans can be found in Flagg's cartoon (previous article) and Woodrow Wilson's attitudes and behavior toward blacks when he was president.

Between me and the other world there is ever an unasked question: unasked by some through feelings of delicacy; by others through the difficulty of rightly framing it. All, nevertheless, flutter round it. They approach me in a half-hesitant sort of way, eye me curiously or compassionately, and then, instead of saying directly, How does it feel to be a problem? they say, I know an excellent colored man in my town; or, I fought at Mechanicsville; or, Do not these Southern outrages make your blood boil? At these I smile, or am interested, or reduce the boiling to a simmer, as the occasion may require. To the real question, How does it feel to be a problem? I answer seldom a word.

And yet, being a problem is a strange experience, - peculiar even for one who has never been anything else, save perhaps in babyhood and in Europe. It is in the early days of rollicking boyhood that the revelation first bursts upon one, all in a day, as it were. I remember well when the shadow swept across me. I was a little thing, away up in the hills of New England, where the dark Housatonic winds between Hoosac and Taghkanic to the sea. In a wee wooden schoolhouse, something put it into the boys' and girls' heads to buy gorgeous visiting-cards—ten cents a package—and exchange. The exchange was merry, till one girl, a tall newcomer, refused my card,—refused it peremptorily, with a glance. Then it dawned upon me with a certain suddenness that I was different from the others; or like, mayhap, in heart and life and longing, but shut out from their world by a vast veil. I had thereafter no desire to tear down that veil, to creep through; I held all beyond it in common contempt, and lived above it in a region of blue sky and great wandering shadows. That sky was bluest when I could beat my mates at examination-time, or beat them at a foot-race, or even beat their stringy heads. Alas, with the years all this fine contempt began to fade; for the worlds I longed for, and all their dazzling opportunities, were theirs, not mine. But they should not keep these prizes, I said; some, all, I would wrest from them. Just how I would do it I could never decide: by reading law, by healing the sick, by telling the wonderful tales that swam in my head,—some way. With other black boys the strife was not so fiercely sunny: their youth shrunk into tasteless sycophancy, or into silent hatred of the pale world about them and mocking distrust of everything white; or wasted itself in a bitter cry, Why did God make me an outcast and a stranger in mine own house? The shades of the prison-house closed round about us all: walls strait and stubborn to the whitest, but relentlessly narrow, tall, and unscalable to sons of night who must plod darkly on in resignation, or beat unavailing palms against the stone, or steadily, half hopelessly, watch the streak of blue above.

After the Egyptian and Indian, the Greek and Roman, the Teuton and Mongolian, the Negro is a sort of seventh son, born with a veil, and gifted with second-sight in this American world,—a world which yields him no true self-consciousness, but only lets him see himself through the revelation of the other world. It is a peculiar sensation, this double-consciousness, this sense of always looking at one's self through the eyes of others, of measuring one's soul by the tape of a world that looks on in amused contempt and pity. One ever feels his twoness,—an American, a Negro; two souls, two thoughts, two unreconciled strivings; two warring ideals in one dark body, whose dogged strength alone keeps it from being torn asunder.

The history of the American Negro is the history of this strife,—this longing to attain self-conscious manhood, to merge his double self into a better and truer self. In this merging he wishes neither of the older selves to be lost. He would not Africanize America, for America has too much to teach the world and Africa. He would not bleach his Negro soul in a flood of white Americanism, for he knows that Negro blood has a message for the world. He simply wishes to make it possible for a man to be both a Negro and an American, without being cursed and spit upon by his fellows, without having the doors of Opportunity closed roughly in his face.

This, then, is the end of his striving: to be a co-worker in the kingdom of culture, to escape both death and isolation, to husband and use his best powers and his latent genius. These powers of body and mind have in the past been strangely wasted, dispersed, or forgotten. The shadow of a mighty Negro past flits through the tale of Ethiopia the Shadowy and of Egypt the Sphinx. Throughout history, the powers of single black men flash here and there like falling stars, and die sometimes before the world has rightly gauged their brightness. Here in America, in the few days since Emancipation, the black man's turning hither and thither in hesitant and doubtful striving has often made his very strength to lose effectiveness, to seem like absence of power, like weakness. And yet it is not weakness,—it is the contradiction of double aims. The double-aimed struggle of the black artisan—on the one hand to escape white contempt for a nation of mere hewers of wood and drawers of water, and on the other hand to plough and nail and dig for a poverty-stricken horde—could only result in making him a poor craftsman, for he had but half a heart in either cause. By the poverty and ignorance of his people, the Negro minister or doctor was tempted toward quackery and demagogy; and by the criticism of the other world, toward ideals that made him ashamed of his lowly tasks. The would-be black *savant* was confronted by the paradox that the knowledge his people needed was a twice-told tale to his white neighbors, while the knowledge which would teach the white world was Greek to his own flesh and blood. The innate love of harmony and beauty that set the ruder souls of his people a-dancing and a-singing raised but confusion and doubt in the soul of the black artist; for the beauty revealed to him was the soul-beauty of a race his larger audience despised, and he could not articulate the message of another people. This waste of double aims, this seeking to satisfy two unreconciled ideals, has wrought sad havoc with the courage and faith and deeds of ten thousand thousand people, - has sent them often wooing false gods and invoking false means of salvation, and at times has even seemed about to make them ashamed of themselves.

Away back in the days of bondage they thought to see in one divine event the end of all doubt and disappointment; few men ever worshipped Freedom with half such unquestioning faith as did the American Negro for two centuries. To him, so far as he thought and dreamed, slavery was indeed the sum of all villainies, the cause of all sorrow, the root of all prejudice; Emancipation was the key to a promised land of sweeter beauty than ever stretched before the eyes of wearied Israelites. In song and exhortation swelled one refrain—Liberty; in his tears and curses the God he implored had Freedom in his right hand. At last it came,—suddenly, fearfully, like a dream. With one wild carnival of blood and passion came the message in his own plaintive cadences:

"Shout, O children!
Shout, you're free!
For God has bought your liberty!"

Years have passed away since then,—ten, twenty, forty; forty years of national life, forty years of renewal and development, and yet the swarthy spectre sits in its accustomed seat at the Nation's feast. In vain do we cry to this our vastest social problem:—

"Take any shape but that, and my firm nerves
Shall never tremble!"

The Nation has not yet found peace from its sins; the freedman has not yet found in freedom his promised land. Whatever of good may have come in these years of change, the shadow of a deep disappointment rests upon the Negro people,—a disappointment all the more bitter because the unattained ideal was unbounded save by the simple ignorance of a lowly people....

Up the new path the advance guard toiled, slowly, heavily, doggedly; only those who have watched and guided the faltering feet, the misty minds, the dull understandings, of the dark pupils of these schools know how faithfully, how piteously, this people strove to learn. It was weary work....To the tired climbers, the horizon was ever dark, the mists were often cold, the Canaan was always dim and far away. If however, the vistas disclosed as yet no goal, no resting-place, little but flattery and criticism, the journey at least gave leisure for reflection and self-examination; it changed the child of Emancipation to the youth with dawning self-consciousness, self-realization, self-respect. In those sombre forests of his striving his own soul rose before him, and he saw himself,—darkly as through a veil; and yet he saw in himself some faint revelation of his power, of his mission. He began to have a dim feeling that, to attain his place in the world, he must be himself, and not another. For the first time he sought to analyze the burden he bore upon his back, that dead-weight of social degradation partially masked behind a half-named Negro problem. He felt his poverty; without a cent, without a home, without land, tools, or savings, he had entered into competition with rich, landed, skilled neighbors. To be a poor man is hard, but to be a poor race in a land of dollars is the very bottom of hardships. He felt the weight of his ignorance,—not simply of letters, but of life, of business, of the humanities; the accumulated sloth and shirking and awkwardness of decades and centuries shackled his hands and feet. Nor was his burden all poverty and ignorance. The red stain of bastardy, which two centuries of systematic legal defilement of Negro women had stamped upon his race, meant not only the loss of ancient African chastity, but also the hereditary weight of a mass of corruption from white adulterers, threatening almost the obliteration of the Negro home.

A people thus handicapped ought not to be asked to race with the world, but rather allowed to give all its time and thought to its own social problems. But alas! while sociologists gleefully count his bastards and his prostitutes, the very soul of the toiling, sweating black man is darkened by the shadow of a vast despair. Men call the shadow prejudice, and learnedly explain it as the natural defence of culture against barbarism, learning against ignorance, purity against crime, the "higher" against the "lower" races. To which the Negro cries Amen! and swears that to so much of this strange prejudice as is founded on just homage to civilization, culture, righteousness, and progress, he humbly bows and meekly does obeisance. But before that nameless prejudice that leaps beyond all this he stands helpless, dismayed, and well-nigh speechless; before that personal disrespect and mockery, the ridicule and systematic humiliation, the distortion of fact and wanton license of fancy, the cynical ignoring of the better and the boisterous welcoming of the worse, the all-pervading desire to inculcate disdain for everything black, from Toussaint to the devil, - before this there rises a sickening despair that would disarm and discourage any nation save that black host to whom "discouragement" is an unwritten word.

But the facing of so vast a prejudice could not but bring the inevitable self-questioning, self-disparagement, and lowering of ideals which ever accompany repression and breed in an atmosphere of contempt and hate. Whisperings and portents came borne upon the four winds: Lo! we are diseased and dying, cried the dark hosts; we cannot write, our voting is vain; what need of education, since we must always cook and serve? And the Nation echoed and enforced this self-criticism, saying: Be content to be servants, and nothing more; what need of higher culture for half-men? Away with the black man's ballot, by force or fraud,—and behold the suicide of a race! Nevertheless, out of the evil came something of good,—the more careful adjustment of education to real life, the clearer perception of the Negroes' social responsibilities, and the sobering realization of the meaning of progress.

So dawned the time of *Sturm und Drang:* storm and stress to-day rocks our little boat on the mad waters of the worldsea; there is within and without the sound of conflict, the burning of body and rending of soul; inspiration strives with doubt, and faith with vain questionings. The bright ideals of the past,—physical freedom, political power, the training of brains and the training of hands, - all these in turn have waxed and waned, until even the last grows dim and overcast. Are they all wrong,—all false? No, not that, but each alone was over-simple and incomplete,—the dreams of a credulous race-childhood, or the fond imaginings of the other world which does not know and does not want to know our power. To be really true, all these ideals must be melted and welded into one. The training of the schools we need to-day more than ever,—the training of deft hands, quick eyes and ears, and above all the broader, deeper, higher culture of gifted minds and pure hearts. The power of the ballot we need in sheer self-defence,—else what shall save us from a second slavery? Freedom, too, the long-sought, we still seek,—the freedom of life and limb, the freedom to work and think, the freedom to love and aspire. Work, culture, liberty,— all these we need, not singly but together, not successively but together, each growing and aiding each, and all striving toward that vaster ideal that swims before the Negro people, the ideal of human brotherhood, gained through the unifying ideal of Race; the ideal of fostering and developing the traits and talents of the Negro, not in opposition to or contempt for other races, but rather in large conformity to the greater ideals of the American

Republic in order that some day on American soil two world-races may give each to each those characteristics both so sadly lack. We the darker ones come even now not altogether empty-handed: there are to-day no truer exponents of the pure human spirit of the Declaration of Independence than the American Negroes; there is no true American music but the wild sweet melodies of the Negro slave; the American fairy tales and folk-lore are Indian and African; and, all in all, we black men seem the sole oasis of simple faith and reverence in a dusty desert of dollars and smartness. Will America be poorer if she replace her brutal dyspeptic blundering with light-hearted but determined Negro humility? or her coarse and cruel wit with loving jovial good-humor? or her vulgar music with the soul of the Sorrow Songs?

Merely a concrete test of the underlying principles of the great republic is the Negro Problem, and the spiritual striving of the freedmen's sons is the travail of souls whose burden is almost beyond the measure of their strength, but who bear it in the name of an historic race, in the name of this the land of their fathers' fathers, and in the name of human opportunity.

Source: W.E.B. Du Bois, *The Souls of Black Folk*, A.C. McClurg, Chicago, 1903

HOW WELL DID YOU UNDERSTAND THIS SELECTION?

1. What does Du Bois mean by the "veil"? Why does he believe the veil must be pierced by the Negro as well as by the white?

2. Explain what Du Bois means by the "twoness" or "doubleself" that the Negro feels.

3. What has made it impossible for a man to be "both a Negro and an American"?

4. Has Du Bois given up on "the greater ideals of the American Republic"?

5. Why does Du Bois suggest that the denial of full human rights to American Negroes has left American whites less than fully human?

*Upton Sinclair's **The Jungle** was one of muckraking's foremost triumphs. His depiction of Chicago's meatpacking industry was influential in stirring a public outcry for legislation to protect American consumers. Although a novel, **The Jungle** drew no less than did the work of other muckrakers upon investigative research. Sinclair wrote in 1906: "I went out there and lived among the people for seven weeks…I would sit in their homes at night, and talked with them, and then in the daytime they would lay off their work, and take me around, and show me whatever I wished to see. I studied every detail of their lives…I talked, not merely with workingmen and their families, but with bosses and superintendents, with night-watchmen and saloonkeepers and policemen, with doctors and lawyers and merchants, with politicians and clergymen and settlement-workers…**The Jungle** is as authoritative as if it were a statistical compilation."*

With one member trimming beef in a cannery, and another working in a sausage factory, the family had a firsthand knowledge of the great majority of Packingtown swindles. For it was the custom, as they found, whenever meat was so spoiled that it could not be used for anything else, either to can it or else to chop it up into sausage. With what had been told them by Jonas, who had worked in the pickle rooms, they could now study the whole of the spoiled-meat industry on the inside, and read a new and grim meaning into that old Packingtown jest—that they use everything of the pig except the squeal.

Jonas had told them how the meat that was taken out of pickle would often be found sour, and how they would rub it up with soda to take away the smell, and sell it to be eaten on free-lunch counters; also of all the miracles of chemistry which they performed, giving to any sort of meat, fresh or salted, whole or chopped, any color and any flavor and any odor they chose. In the pickling of hams they had an ingenious apparatus, by which they saved time and increased the capacity of the plant—a machine consisting of a hollow needle attached to a pump; by plunging this needle into the meat and working with his foot a man could fill a ham with pickle in a few seconds. And yet, in spite of this, there would be hams found spoiled, some of them with an odor so bad that a man could hardly bear to be in the room with them. To pump into these the packers had a second and much stronger pickle which destroyed the odor—a process known to the workers as "giving them thirty per cent." Also, after the hams had been smoked, there would be found some that had gone to the bad. Formerly these had been sold as "Number Three Grade," but later on some ingenious person had hit upon a new device, and now they would extract the bone, about which the bad part generally lay, and insert in the hole a white-hot iron. After this invention there was no longer Number One, Two, and Three Grade—there was only Number One Grade. The packers were always originating such schemes—they had what they called "boneless hams," which were all the odds and ends of pork stuffed into casings, and "California hams" which were the shoulders, with big knuckle joints, and nearly all the meat cut out; and fancy "skinned hams," which were made of the oldest hogs, whose skins were so heavy and coarse that no one would buy them—that is until they had been cooked and chopped fine and labelled "head cheese"!

It was only when the whole ham was spoiled that it came into the department of Elzbieta. Cut up by the two-thousand-revolutions-a-minute flyers, and mixed with half a ton of other meat, no odor that ever was in a ham could make any difference. There was never the least attention paid to what was cut up for sausage; there would come all the way back from Europe old sausage that had been rejected, and that was mouldy and white—it would be dosed with borax and glycerine, and dumped into the hoppers, and made over again for home consumption. There would be meat that had tumbled out on the floor, in the dirt and sawdust, where the workers had tramped and spit uncounted billions of consumption germs. There would be meat stored in great piles in rooms; and the water from leaky roofs would drip over it, and thousands of rats would race about on it. It was too dark in these storage places to see well, but a man could run his hand over these piles of meat and sweep off handfuls of the dried dung of rats. These rats were nuisances, and the packers would put poisoned bread out for them, they would die, and then rats, bread, and meat would go into the hoppers together. This is no fairy story and no joke; the meat would be shovelled into carts, and the man who did the shovelling would not trouble to lift out a rat even when he saw one—there were things that went into the sausage in comparison with which a poisoned rat was a tidbit.

Source: Upton Sinclair, *The Jungle,* Doubleday, Page & Company: New York, 1906

HOW WELL DID YOU UNDERSTAND THIS SELECTION?

1. Why did passages such as this from *The Jungle* arouse such a strong public reaction and lead to governmental action?

2. In response to accounts such as this, what federal legislation was passed to promote consumer protection?

TRIANGLE MEMORIAL SPEECH, By Rose Schneiderman, 1911

On March 25, 1911, a fire extinguished the lives of 146 people—all but three of them young women—mostly Italian and Jewish immigrants who worked at the Triangle Shirtwaist Company located on the Lower East Side of New York. Doors from which workers could have escaped had been locked to prevent their leaving work early and stealing company equipment. There was only one fire escape, and it quickly gave way under the weight of so many fleeing victims. Fire department ladders failed to reach high enough to provide a safe avenue of descent. Women leapt to their deaths as the fire nets they jumped into tore; broken bodies lay in piles on the pavement. In general, the dress company was operating in compliance with the existing regulations of the era. In the fire's aftermath, a wave of regulations governing factory fire safety, working conditions, and child labor were effected across the nation. Rose Schneiderman, a Jewish immigrant from Russian Poland and an organizer and leader in the trade union movement (Women's Trade Union League), addressed a memorial meeting held in the Metropolitan Opera House on April 2, 1911.

I would be traitor to these poor burned bodies if I came here to talk good fellowship. We have tried you good people of the public, and we have found you wanting. The old Inquisition had its rack and its thumbscrews and its instruments of torture with iron teeth. We know what these things are today: the iron teeth are our necessities, the thumbscrews are the high-powered and swift machinery close to which we must work, and the rack is here in the firetrap structures that will destroy us the minute they catch on fire.

This is not the first time girls have been burned alive in the city. Every week I must learn of the untimely death of one of my sister workers. Every year thousands of us are maimed. The life of men and women is so cheap and property is so sacred. There are so many of us for one job it matters little if 146 of us are burned to death.

We have tried, you citizens; we are trying you now, and you have a couple of dollars for the sorrowing mothers and daughters and sisters by way of a charity gift. But every time the workers come out in the only way they know to protest against conditions which are unbearable, the strong hand of the law is allowed to press down heavily upon us.

Public officials have only words of warning to us—warning that we must be intensely orderly and must be intensely peaceable, and they have the workhouse just back of all their warnings. The strong hand of the law beats us back, when we rise, into the conditions that make life bearable.

I can't talk fellowship to you who are gathered here. Too much blood has been spilled. I know from my experience it is up to the working people to save themselves. The only way they can save themselves is by a strong working-class movement.

Source: *The Survey*, April 8, 1911

HOW WELL DID YOU UNDERSTAND THIS SELECTION?

1.   What was the important lesson that Schneiderman drew from the fire?

2.   Why does Schneiderman renounce "good fellowship" with the "good citizens" she addresses? What tone does she take?

3.   In effect, Schneiderman claims public officials value law and order more than justice. Half a century later, in his *Letter from a Birmingham Jail*, Martin Luther King would make this very same point. How comparable are these two struggles for social justice—the struggle of workers for rights and of black Americans for civil rights?

A NEW CONSCIENCE AND AN ANCIENT EVIL, **By Jane Addams, 1911**

In her 1911 work, **A New Conscience and an Ancient Evil,** *Jane Addams, a leader in the settlement house movement in America, addressed the growing problem of prostitution and "the white slave trade." Of considerable concern to many Americans were the rising rates of alcoholism, crime, disease, and prostitution in America's cities. Small town, rural America was linked in the minds of many Americans with virtue, and the city, with vice. While the response of many would be to simply attack women working outside the home, Addams called for government to take action to improve the wages and working and living conditions of women as an important step toward improving workers' lives and eradicating vice. The information upon which Addams based her book was drawn from documents compiled in the course of a series of special investigations made by the Juvenile Protective Association of Chicago.*

Chapter III: Amelioration of Economic Conditions

....It is as yet difficult to distinguish between the results of long hours and the results of overstrain. Certainly the constant sense of haste is one of the most nerve-racking and exhausting tests to which the human system can be subjected. Those girls in the sewing industry whose mothers thread needles for them far into the night that they may sew without a moment's interruption during the next day; those girls who insert eyelets into shoes, for which they are paid two cents a case, each case containing twenty-four pairs of shoes, are striking victims of the over-speeding which is so characteristic of our entire factory system....
  Yet factory girls who are subjected to this overstrain and overtime often find their greatest discouragement in the fact that after all their efforts they earn too little to support themselves. One girl said that she had first yielded to temptation when she had become utterly discouraged because she had tried in vain for seven months to save enough money for a pair of shoes. She habitually spent two dollars a week for her room, three dollars for her board, and sixty

cents a week for carfare, and she had found the forty cents remaining from her weekly wage of six dollars inadequate to do more than re-sole her old shoes twice. When the shoes became too worn to endure a third soling and she possessed but ninety cents towards a new pair, she gave up her struggle; to use her own contemptuous phrase, she "sold out for a pair of shoes."

Usually the phrases are less graphic but after all they contain the same dreary meaning: "Couldn't make both ends meet," "I had always been used to having nice things," "Couldn't make enough money to live on," "I got sick and ran behind," "Needed more money," "Impossible to feed and clothe myself," "Out of work, hadn't been able to save." Of course a girl in such a strait does not go out deliberately to find illicit methods of earning money, she simply yields in a moment of utter weariness and discouragement to the temptations she has been able to withstand up to that moment. The long hours, the lack of comforts, the low pay, the absence of recreation, the sense of "good times" all about her which she cannot share, the conviction that she is rapidly losing health and charm, rouse the molten forces within her. A swelling tide of self-pity suddenly storms the banks which have hitherto held her and finally overcomes her instincts for decency and righteousness, as well as the habit of clean living, established by generations of her forebears.

The aphorism that "morals fluctuate with trade" was long considered cynical, but it has been demonstrated in Berlin, in London, in Japan, as well as in several American cities, that there is a distinct increase in the number of registered prostitutes during periods of financial depression and even during the dull season of leading industries. Out of my own experience I am ready to assert that very often all that is necessary to effectively help the girl who is on the edge of wrong-doing is to lend her money for her board until she finds work, provide the necessary clothing for which she is in such desperate need, persuade her relatives that she should have more money for her own expenditures, or find her another place at higher wages. Upon such simple economic needs does the tried virtue of a good girl sometimes depend....

Another experience during which a girl faces a peculiar danger is when she has lost one "job" and is looking for another. Naturally she loses her place in the slack season and pursues her search at the very moment when positions are hardest to find, and her unemployment is therefore most prolonged. Perhaps nothing in our social order is so unorganized and inchoate as our method, or rather lack of method, of placing young people in industry. This is obvious from the point of view of their first positions when they leave school at the unstable age of fourteen, often as high as ten a year, then they are dismissed or change voluntarily through sheer restlessness....

Difficult as is the position of the girl out of work when her family is exigent and uncomprehending, she has incomparably more protection than the girl who is living in the city without home ties. Such girls form sixteen per cent of the working women of Chicago. With absolutely every penny of their meagre wages consumed in their inadequate living, they are totally unable to save money. That loneliness and detachment which the city tends to breed in its inhabitants is easily intensified in such a girl into isolation and a desolating feeling of belonging no-where. As youth resents the sense of the enormity of the universe in relation to the insignificance of the individual life, and youth, with that intense self-consciousness which makes each young person the very centre of all emotional experience, broods over this as no older person can possibly do. At such moments of black oppression, the instinctive fear of solitude, will send a lonely girl restlessly to walk the streets even when she is "too tired to stand," and when her desire for companionship in itself constitutes a grave danger. Such a girl living in a rented room is usually without any place in which to properly receive callers....Many girls quite innocently permit young men to call upon them in their bedrooms, pitifully disguised as "sitting-rooms," but the danger is obvious, and the standards of the girl gradually become lowered.

Certainly during the trying times when a girl is out of work she should have much more intelligent help than is at present extended to her; she should be able to avail herself of the state employment agencies much more than is now possible, and the work of the newly established vocational bureaus should be enormously extended.

When once we are in earnest about the abolition of the social evil, society will find that it must study industry from the point of view of the producer in a sense which has never been done before. Such a study with reference to industrial legislation will ally itself on one hand with the trades-union movement, which insists upon a living wage and shorter hours for the workers, and also upon an opportunity for self-direction, and on the other hand with the efficiency movement, which would refrain from over-fatiguing an operator as it would from over-speeding a machine....

As working women enter fresh fields of labor which ever open up anew as the old fields are submerged behind them, society must endeavor to speedily protect them by an amelioration of the economic conditions which are now so unnecessarily harsh and dangerous to health and morals. The world-wide movement for establishing governmental control of industrial conditions is especially concerned for working women....

Although amelioration comes about so slowly that many young girls are sacrificed each year under conditions which could so easily and reasonably be changed, nevertheless it is apparently better to overcome the dangers in this new and freer life, which modern industry has opened to women, than it is to attempt to retreat into the domestic industry of the past; for all statistics of prostitution give the largest number of recruits for this life as coming from domestic service and the second largest number from girls who live at home with no definite occupation whatever. Therefore, although in the economic aspect of the social evil more than in any other, do we find ground for despair, at the same time we discern, as nowhere else, the young girl's stubborn power of resistance. Nevertheless, the most superficial survey of her surroundings shows the necessity for ameliorating, as rapidly as possible, the harsh economic conditions which now environ her.

That steadily increasing function of the state by which it seeks to protect its workers from their own weakness and degradation, and insists that the livelihood of the manual laborer shall not be beaten down below the level of efficient citizenship, assumes new forms almost daily. From the human as well as the economic standpoint there is an obligation resting upon the state to discover how many victims of the white slave traffic are the result of social neglect, remedial incapacity, and the lack of industrial safeguards, and how far discontinuous employment and non-employment are factors in the breeding of discouragement and despair.

Is it because our modern industrialism is so new that we have been slow to connect it with the poverty and vice all about us? The socialists talk constantly of the relation of economic law to destitution and point out the connection between industrial maladjustment and individual wrong-doing, but certainly the study of social conditions, the obligation to eradicate vice, cannot belong to one political party or to one economic school. It must be recognized as a solemn obligation of existing governments, and society must realize that economic conditions can only be made more righteous and more human by the unceasing devotion of generations of men.

Source: Jane Addams, *A New Conscience and an Ancient Evil*, Macmillan, New York, 1911

HOW WELL DID YOU UNDERSTAND THIS SELECTION?

1. What connection does Addams establish between industrialization and urbanization, on the one hand, and the breakdown of moral order, on the other?

2. Where does Addams place the responsibility for a young working woman's loss of "virtue"?

3. What kinds of changes does Addams advocate to insure the well being of young working women?

NAWSA CONVENTION SPEECH, *Remarks on Emotionalism in Politics,*
By Anna Howard Shaw, 1913

A medical doctor and Protestant minister, Anna Howard Shaw served as president of NAWSA, National American Woman Suffrage Association, from 1904 to 1915.

By some objectors women are supposed to be unfit to vote because they are hysterical and emotional, and of course men would not like to have emotion enter into a political campaign. They want to cut out all emotion and so they would like to cut us out. I had heard so much about our emotionalism that I went to the last Democratic National Convention, held at Baltimore, to observe the calm repose of male politicians. I saw some men take a picture of one gentleman whom they wanted elected, and it was so big they had to walk sidewise as they carried it forward; they were followed by hundreds of other men screaming and yelling, shouting and singing the "Houn' Dawg;" then, when there was a lull, another set of men would start forward under another man's picture, not to be outdone by the "Houn' Dawg" melody, whooping and howling still louder. I saw men jump up on the seats and throw their hats in the air and shout: "What's the matter with Champ Clark?" Then when those hats came down, other men would kick them back in the air, shouting at the top of their voices: "He's all right!!" Then I heard others howling for "Underwood Underwood, first, last and all the time!!" No hysteria about it—just patriotic loyalty, splendid manly devotion to principle. And so they went on and on until 5 o'clock in the morning—the whole night long. I saw men jump up on their seats and jump down again and run around in a ring. I saw two men turn towards another man to hug him both at once, and they split his coat up the middle of his back and sent him spinning around like a wheel. All this with the perfect poise of the legal male mind in politics!

I have been to many women's conventions in my day, but I never saw a woman leap up on a chair and take off her bonnet and toss it up in the air and shout : "What's the matter with" some-body. I never saw a woman knock another woman's bonnet off her head as she screamed: "She's all right!" I never heard a body of women whooping and yelling for five minutes when somebody's name was mentioned in the convention. But we are willing to admit that we are emotional. I have actually seen women stand up and wave their handkerchiefs. I have even seen them take hold of hands and sing "Blest be the tie that binds." Nobody denies that women are excitable. Still, when I hear how emotional and how excitable we are, I cannot help seeing in my mind's eye the fine repose and dignity of this Baltimore and other political conventions I have attended!

Source: *History of Woman Suffrage,* Susan B. Anthony, ed., vol. 5, Fowler & Wells, New York, 1922

HOW WELL DID YOU UNDERSTAND THIS SELECTION?

1. How does Shaw dismiss the anti-suffragists' argument that women were too emotional and too irrational to vote?

2. In what ways does Shaw's speech itself undermine the anti-suffragists assertions?

In addition to working to improve the wages and working conditions of women, Rose Schneiderman campaigned in support of women's right to vote. The occasion of the following speech is a mass meeting at Cooper Union on April 22, 1912 that brought together middle class and working class women. Schneiderman was one of a number of working women who responded to quotations from speeches of NY legislators who argued against woman suffrage.

Rose Schneiderman, Cap Maker, answers the New York Senator who says:

"Get women into the arena of politics with its alliances and distressing contests—the delicacy is gone, the charm is gone, and you emasculize women."

Fellow-workers, it already has been whispered to you that there is a possibility that our New York Senators don't know what they are talking about. I am here to voice the same sentiment. It seems to me that if our Senators really represented the people of New York State, they ought to know the conditions under which the majority of the people live. Perhaps, working women are not regarded as women, because it seems to me, when they talk all this trash of theirs about finer qualities and "man's admiration and devotion to the sex"—"Cornelia's Jewels" "Preserving Motherhood"—"Woman's duty to minister to man in the home"—"The delicacy and charm of women being gone," they cannot mean the working women. We have 800,000 women in New York State who go out into the industrial world, not through any choice of their own, but because necessity forces them out to earn their daily bread.

I am inclined to think if we were sent home now we would not go home.

We want to work, that is the thing. We are not afraid of work, and we are not ashamed to work, but we do decline to be driven; we want to work like human beings; we want to work for the welfare of the community and not for the welfare of a few....

We have women working in the foundries, stripped to the waist, if you please, because of the heat. *Yet the Senator says nothing about these women losing their charm.* They have got to retain their charm and delicacy and work in foundries. Of course, you know the reason they are employed in foundries is that they are cheaper and work longer hours than men.

Women in the laundries, for instance, stand for 13 or 14 hours in the terrible steam and heat with their hands in hot starch. Surely these women won't lose any more of their beauty and charm by putting a ballot in a ballot box once a year than they are likely to lose standing in foundries or laundries all year round.

There is no harder contest than the contest for bread, let me tell you that. Women have got to meet it and in a good many instances they contest for the job with their brother workman. When the woman is preferred, it is because of her weakness, because she is frail, because she will sell her labor for less money than man will sell his.

When our Senators acknowledge that our political life has *alliances and distressing contests* which would take the charm away from women if she got into them, let me reassure the gentlemen that women's great charm has always been that when she found things going she has set to work to make them go right. Do our Senators fear that when women get the vote they will demand clean polling places, etc.? It seems to me that this rather gives them away....

What about the delicacy and charm of women who have to live with men in the condition of a good many male voters on election day? Perhaps the Senators would like them to keep that condition all year round; they would not demand much of their political bosses and he could be sure that they would cast their votes for the man who gave them the most booze....

We hear our anti-suffragettes saying, "Why, when you get the vote it will hinder you from doing welfare work, doing uplift work." Who are they going to uplift? Is it you and I they want to uplift? I think if they would lift themselves off our shoulders they would be doing a better bit of useful work. I think you know by now that if the workers got what they earn there would be no need of uplift work and welfare work or anything of that kind.

We want to tell our Senators that the working women of our State demand the votes as an economic necessity. We need it because we are workers and because the workers are the ones that have to carry civilization on their backs.

What does all this talk about becoming mannish signify? I wonder if it will add to my height when I get the vote. I might work for it all the harder if it did. It is too ridiculous, this talk of becoming less womanly, just as if a woman could be anything else except a woman.

This vote that she is going to cast is going to work this marvellous change in her all of a sudden. Just by beginning to think of how the laws are made and using such intelligence as she has to put good men in office with her vote she will be made over into a creature without delicacy or charm...

I honestly believe that it is fear of the enfranchisement of working-women that prompts the Senators to oppose us. They do not want the working-women enfranchised because politicians know that a woman who works will use her ballot intelligently; she will make the politicians do things which he may not find so profitable; therefore, they come out with all these subterfuges....

Source: *Senators vs. Working Women, Miss Rose Scheiderman, CapMaker replies to New York Senator on Delicacy and Charm of Women*, Wage Earners' Suffrage League: New York, 1912
online at: www.binghamton.edu/womhist/law/doc19.htm

HOW WELL DID YOU UNDERSTAND THIS SELECTION?

1. Why were so many advocates of improved working conditions for women also proponents of woman suffrage?

2. What imagery does Schneiderman employ as she calls into question the traditional and widely held conception of who functions as civilization's uplifters?

3. On what grounds does Schneiderman attack the claim that giving women the vote will degrade their charm and femininity?

4. According to the author, what is the real reason why many politicians are opposed to giving women the vote?

SELF TEST

MULTIPLE CHOICE: Circle the correct response. The correct answers are given at the end.

1. Progressives believed:
    a. the unequal distribution of wealth in America was beneficial
    b. government was becoming more democratic
    c. poverty in America needed to be addressed
    d. economic consolidation benefited workers and consumers

2. Muckraking refers to:
    a. digging up of dirt by farmers to promote higher crop yields
    b. investigative journalism that exposed societal ills
    c. the practice of employing child laborers
    d. a business practice used to drive out competitors

3. The primary objective of settlement houses was:
    a. to offer an alternative to the courts in settling labor disputes
    b. to provide halfway houses to victims of alcoholism
    c. to aid poverty-stricken slum dwellers by providing a nurturing environment
    d. to demonstrate alternative means of constructing high-density housing

4. Progressivism championed all of the following *except*:
    a. extension of the right to vote to eighteen-year-olds
    b. reliance upon a commission of administrators to run cities
    c. government regulation of big business
    d. the redistribution of wealth in America

5. The amendment to the U.S. Constitution that gave women the vote was:
    a. the Seventeenth Amendment
    b. the Eighteenth Amendment
    c. the Nineteenth Amendment
    d. the Twentieth Amendment

6. Each of the following were major concerns of Progressive reformers *except* :
    a. safety in the workplace
    b. long hours of factory work by women and children
    c. high rates of crime, prostitution, and disease
    d. discrimination suffered by African Americans

7. The progressive who first carried progressive reform to the federal level was:
    a. William McKinley
    b. Theodore Roosevelt
    c. William Taft
    d. Woodrow Wilson

8. In the election of 1912, all of the following events took place *except*:
    a. a third-party candidate garnered a sizable portion of the popular vote
    b. a split occurred in the Republican ranks
    c. a Democrat was elected president
    d. the election marked the end of the Progressive era

9. Progressive era foreign policy was marked by:
   a. a reluctance to extend America's involvement beyond her domestic borders
   b. the conviction that American interests did not extend into the Caribbean
   c. a "gentleman's agreement" barring Latin American workers from the U.S.
   d. an effort to link the Atlantic and Pacific Oceans by constructing a canal

10. Progressive era reforms that have become entrenched aspects of American government and American life include all of the following *except* the:
   a. Federal Reserve system
   b. Eighteenth Amendment
   c. Federal Trade Commission
   d. Sixteenth Amendment

Answers: 1-c; 2-b; 3-c; 4-a; 5-c; 6-d; 7-b; 8-d; 9-d; 10-b

ESSAYS:

1. Rejecting the Social Darwinists' claim that poverty was the product of character, Progressives asserted poverty was a product of environment. It would no longer be absurd, then, to attempt to make the world over. Explain, citing specific historical examples of the Progressive conviction that social engineering would lead to social progress.

2. What were Progressivism's strengths and weaknesses? Consider the effectiveness of government regulation of large corporations, of efforts to redistribute wealth and power, of reforms directed at improving working and living conditions, as well as the overall quality of life in urban America.

3. Ethnocentrism is the belief in the superiority of one's own group. It results when one group uses its values, beliefs, and attitudes as the standard to judge another group or groups. Cite specific examples of ethnocentrism displayed by Progressives.

OPTIONAL ACTIVITIES: (Use your knowledge **and** imagination.)

1. Presentism is the practice of taking the values of one historical era and using them to evaluate another period of history. Are we guilty of presentism and therefore unfair when we label many Progressive reformers prejudiced?

2. In your estimation, what were Progressivism's greatest accomplishments and failures?

3. Find an article in a current newspaper or periodical that is an example of present-day muckraking. What evil, injustice, or corruption does it expose?

WEB SITE LISTINGS:

Cartoons of the Gilded Age and Progressive Era
http://www.history.ohio-state.edu/projects/
uscartoons/GAPECartoons.htm

On the Lower East Side: Observations of Life in Lower Manhattan at the Turn of the Century
http://tenant.net:80/Community/LES/contents.html

Immigration History Research Center
http://www1.umn.edu/ihrc

The Triangle Shirtwaist Factory Fire
http://www.ilr.cornell.edu/trianglefire

The Gilded Age and Progressive Era
http://www.uccs.edu/~history/index/shgape.html

Online Texts of the Gilded Age and Progressive Era
http://www.library.csi.cuny.edu/dept/history/lavender/gilded.html

Walter Rauschenbusch: The Social Gospel
http://www.fordham.edu/halsall/mod/rausch-socialgospel.html

Woman Suffrage and the Nineteenth Amendment
http://www.nara.gov/education/teaching/woman/home.html

Margaret Sanger Papers Project
http://www.nyu.edu/projects/sanger

Votes for Women
http://henry.huntington.org/vfw/main.html

Chapter Seventeen

THE "GREAT" WAR:
World War I

European national rivalries in the early years of the twentieth century were fueled by rising militarism, nationalism, and imperialism. The assassination of the heir to the throne of the Austro-Hungarian Empire in Sarajevo, Bosnia by a Serbian nationalist in June, 1914 ignited a conflagration between rival European camps that would rage for four and one-half years, involve nations around the globe, and leave a record of death and destruction unprecedented in world history.

When war erupted in Europe, the reaction of Americans was generally one of shock. Many believed that western civilization had moved beyond the barbarism of war. The most advanced nations, it was argued, would no longer need to resort to large-scale warfare; reason, technological and scientific advances, and a balance of power would insure peace and progress. Most Americans viewed events in Europe as a war far away; the Wilson Administration proclaimed American neutrality. The war's belligerents expected the conflict would be shortlived.

However, years of bloody carnage marked by the introduction of new technologies and techniques of warfare followed. The war soon stripped its participants of the notion that battle was a romantic adventure, a manly rite of passage. The illusion that war was a noble and honorable enterprise quickly evaporated when the Germans introduced poison gas and the Allies responded in kind. Improved machine guns and artillery produced high casualties. On land, troops dug in; trench warfare created a conflict marked by stalemate and attrition. During one day alone in the three-and-a-half month Battle of the Somme, the British toll was 60,000 casualties. Yet little ground was gained or lost. On the seas, each side used its navy to blockade the other, seeking to diminish its opponent's capacity to wage war. In this effort, both would run afoul of America's demand it be accorded freedom of the seas and freedom of trade. However, Wilson would react differently to infractions by the British and Germans—a product of an "unneutral" neutrality that tipped in favor of the Allies. A shared ethnicity, religion, language, history, and democratic institutions bound many Americans to Britain. Further, the autocracy of the Central Powers was considered "unAmerican." Trained as a political scientist and a champion of constitutional government, Wilson was an anglophile and many of his close advisers were pro-British.

As the war raged, American merchant vessels engaged in brisk trade with the Allies. American passengers on British and French ships entered the waters around the British Isles, which Germany had declared a war zone. A reluctant Wilson would find himself drawn into war as a result of the conflict between his demand America be granted the traditional rights of neutral nations and Germany's use of the submarine. This new guerrilla weapon's advantage lay in the element of surprise; it could not succeed in strangling Britain's capacity to wage war if it followed the established rules of stopping and searching ships and insuring the safety of passengers. Doing so required U-boats to surface and risk destruction. After the sinking of the British passenger liners *Lusitania* and *Arabic* with the loss of American lives in 1915, Wilson threatened to break diplomatic relations if Germany did not pledge to stop unrestricted submarine warfare against unarmed passenger ships. Germany promised modifications in her behavior. But a U-Boat attack in 1916 that injured American passengers traveling aboard the French channel-crossing vessel, the *Sussex*, renewed Wilson's demand for an end to unrestricted submarine warfare; Germany complied rather than risk America's entrance into the war at this time. Wilson embarked on a preparedness campaign, should war come, while at the same time continuing his efforts to mediate peace. They would prove unsuccessful. In February, 1917 Germany would revoke her pledge not to engage in unwarned submarine warfare. Renewed U-boat attacks on American ships coupled with Britain's interception, decoding, and revelation of the Zimmermann Telegram convinced Wilson of the peril Germany posed to the nation. A solemn president went to the U.S. Capitol on April 2, 1917 to ask Congress for a declaration of war. Wilson explained America's entry into war as a fight to preserve democracy and freedom. Just months before, he had outlined his vision of a new world order—a community of cooperating rather than competing nations guided by legal and moral principles rather than by power and self-interest. The president hoped by going to war America could influence the peace and reshape international relations in conformity with his idealistic, progressive principles.

Both American manpower and war materiel would eventually prove decisive in the Allied victory. America's economic might and fresh troops would help turn the tide against the Central Powers when Germany mounted a powerful offensive on the Western Front in the spring of 1918. Germany agreed to an armistice on November 11, 1918, believing peace negotiations would be based on the framework outlined in Woodrow Wilson's Fourteen Points. Personally leading the U.S. peace delegation in Paris, the president would sacrifice many of these points in negotiations with the other Allied Powers to get what he most wanted, a permanent association or league of nations. Wilson's compromises on the principles of open diplomacy, an end to colonialism, and a reduction of armaments by all would contribute to growing disillusionment at home with both the war and the peace. Framing both the nation's war and peace objectives in idealistic terms, Wilson created high expectations that would go unmet by reality. His insistence on incorporating the charter of the League of Nations into the treaty bound the United States to the principle of collective security. It would be primarily this issue, along with the president's unwillingness to compromise and accept any changes to the treaty, that led the Senate to reject the Treaty of Versailles and refuse to join the League.

World War I would bring significant change to America. President Wilson used the broad powers granted him by Congress to mobilize the economy and society for war. In the process, the size and reach of American government greatly expanded. Five hundred federal agencies were created as government extended its authority into the everyday lives of its citizens. A planned economy replaced a competitive free enterprise system. Seeking to enlist the cooperation of both business and labor, the Wilson Administration suspended anti-trust laws and instituted cost-plus contracts; it offered labor collective bargaining and an eight-hour work day in defense industries.

As men went off to fight, women found new employment opportunities. Nearly eight million working women moved into higher paying factory jobs while another million entered the workforce for the first time. Women also shouldered the nation's war effort more directly, serving abroad as nurses, YWCA canteen workers, and in the Army Signal Corps. The war also increased economic opportunity for black and Mexican Americans. Spurred by the availability of jobs in northern factories, the war initiated the migration of more than 400,000 blacks from the rural south into northern cities where they hoped to escape poverty and discrimination. More often than not, migrating blacks found they left neither behind. As the racial landscape of northern neighborhoods and workplaces was altered, racial violence in the form of riots soon followed. Hundreds of thousands of black men entered the nation's armed forces, hoping their service and sacrifice would lead to winning greater equality. They would be sorely disappointed.

The Committee on Public Information was established to mobilize public support for the war. Seeking to rouse Americans' patriotism, the CPI mounted a propaganda campaign that led some individuals and vigilante groups to engage in violent and even murderous excesses. Patriotic propaganda along with widespread rumors and often unsubstantiated media reports of German-Americans engaged in subversive activities generated hatred, fear, and intolerance. Intense patriotism fueled an unofficial crusade to root out suspected subversives. An official crusade was waged, as well. Congress passed the Espionage and Sedition Acts that criminalized behavior and activities deemed harmful to the war effort. Civil liberties were severely abridged. Dissent was suppressed as free speech became a casualty in the name of a war fought to preserve democracy, expand freedom, and promote justice.

Internment camps were established to incarcerate "enemy aliens"—people of German and Austro-Hungarian birth who were not naturalized—as well as conscientious objectors and dissidents. Change also came to America during the war years in the form of reform. Linked to patriotism and labeled "war measures," both the cause of prohibition and of woman suffrage would be advanced by the war. As progressives became bureaucrats directing and staffing wartime agencies, they brought with them their expertise and principles of management, professionalizing government.

At the war's end, Americans looked forward to returning to a 'normal' life after enduring so many hardships, sacrifices, and uncertainties. However, war's immediate aftermath would prove anything but normal. Just when the German threat to democracy had been defeated, a new enemy, bolshevism, appeared to replace it. Racial violence flared in northern cities as returning white soldiers discovered large numbers of black Americans had moved into the factories and cities where they lived and worked. In the South, a campaign of terror and lynchings was employed to keep blacks in "their place." When their expectations for improved treatment went unmet, many returning black soldiers responded by refusing to accept the status quo. During the war, although workers suffered the effects of wartime inflation, they had generally deferred higher wages. But when management was not forthcoming with pay increases, labor unrest exploded across America in 1919. Many Americans blamed these upheavals on Bolsheviks and anarchists. A Red Scare swept the nation and set a tone of fear and intolerance that would cast a long shadow over the decade of the Twenties.

IDENTIFICATION: Briefly describe each term.

Missionary diplomacy

Triple Entente

Triple Alliance

Neutrality

Contraband

U-boat

Unrestricted submarine warfare

Lusitania

Sussex Pledge

Zimmermann Telegram

Trench warfare

Poison gas

Selective Service Act

Conscientious objector

American Expeditionary Force

German western offensive, 1918

Allied offensive, 1918

War Industries Board

Cost-plus contracts

Food Administration

National War Labor Board

Industrial Workers of the World

Liberty Loans

Committee on Public Information

Propaganda

Espionage and Sedition Acts

Eugene Debs

Schenck v. United States, 1919

Nineteenth Amendment

Race riots

Fourteen Points

League of Nations

Treaty of Versailles

Reparations

War guilt clause

Article X

Principle of collective security

Red Scare and Palmer Raids

A. Mitchell Palmer

J. Edgar Hoover

THINK ABOUT:

1. What important changes did America's mobilization for war and prosecution of the war initiate in American government? In American society? In the American economy?

2. What was the war's impact upon civil liberties on the homefront?

3. How did the war serve to both reinforce and harden racial prejudices as well as to undermine them?

PRESIDENT WOODROW WILSON'S WAR MESSAGE TO THE U. S. CONGRESS, April 2, 1917

On April 2, 1917, in a special session of Congress, President Wilson asked Congress to declare our nation at war against Germany. On April 6, a war resolution was passed.

Gentlemen of the Congress:

I have called the Congress into extraordinary session because there are serious, very serious, choices of policy to be made, and made immediately, which it was neither right nor constitutionally permissible that I should assume the responsibility of making.

On the 3d of February last I officially laid before you the extraordinary announcement of the Imperial German Government that on and after the 1st day of February it was its purpose to put aside all restraints of law or of humanity and use its submarines to sink every vessel that sought to approach either the ports of Great Britain and Ireland or the western coasts of Europe or any of the ports controlled by the enemies of Germany within the Mediterranean. That had seemed to be the object of the German submarine warfare earlier in the war, but since April of last year the Imperial Government had somewhat restrained the commanders of its undersea craft in conformity with its promise then given to us that passenger boats should not be sunk and that due warning would be given to all other vessels which its submarines might seek to destroy, when no resistance was offered or escape attempted, and care taken that their crews were given at least a fair chance to save their lives in their open boats. The precautions taken were meagre and haphazard enough, as was proved in distressing instance after instance in the progress of the cruel and unmanly business, but a certain degree of restraint was observed The new policy has swept every restriction aside. Vessels of every kind, whatever their flag, their character, their cargo, their destination, their errand, have been ruthlessly sent to the bottom without warning and without thought of help or mercy for those on board, the vessels of friendly neutrals along with those of belligerents. Even hospital ships and ships carrying relief to the sorely bereaved and stricken people of Belgium, though the latter were provided with safe-conduct through the proscribed areas by the German Government itself and were distinguished by unmistakable marks of identity, have been sunk with the same reckless lack of compassion or of principle.

I was for a little while unable to believe that such things would in fact be done by any government that had hitherto subscribed to the humane practices of civilized nations. International law had its origin in the attempt to set up some law which would be respected and observed upon the seas, where no nation had right of dominion and where lay the free highways of the world. By painful stage after stage has that law been built up, with meagre enough results, indeed, after all was accomplished that could be accomplished, but always with a clear view, at least, of what the heart and conscience of mankind demanded. This minimum of right the German Government has swept aside under the plea of retaliation and necessity and because it had no weapons which it could use at sea except these which it is impossible to employ as it is employing them without throwing to the winds all scruples of humanity or of respect for the understandings that were supposed to underlie the intercourse of the world. I am not now thinking of the loss of property involved, immense and serious as that is, but only of the wanton and wholesale destruction of the lives of noncombatants, men, women, and children, engaged in pursuits which have always, even in the darkest periods of modern history, been deemed innocent and legitimate. Property can be paid for; the lives of peaceful and innocent people can not be. The present German submarine warfare against commerce is a warfare against mankind.

It is a war against all nations. American ships have been sunk, American lives taken, in ways which it has stirred us very deeply to learn of, but the ships and people of other neutral and friendly nations have been sunk and overwhelmed in the waters in the same way. There has been no discrimination. The challenge is to all mankind. Each nation must decide for itself how it will meet it. The choice we make for ourselves must be made with a moderation of counsel and a temperateness of judgment befitting our character and our motives as a nation. We must put excited feeling away. Our motive will not be revenge or the victorious assertion of the physical might of the nation, but only the vindication of right, of human right, of which we are only a single champion....

With a profound sense of the solemn and even tragical character of the step I am taking and of the grave responsibilities which it involves, but in unhesitating obedience to what I deem my constitutional duty, I advise that the Congress declare the recent course of the Imperial German Government to be in fact nothing less than war against the Government and people of the United States; that it formally accept the status of belligerent which has thus been thrust upon it, and that it take immediate steps not only to put the country in a more thorough state of defense but also to exert all its power and employ all its resources to bring the Government of the German Empire to terms and end the war....

While we do these things, these deeply momentous things, let us be very clear, and make very clear to all the world what our motives and our objects are....Our object....is to vindicate the principles of peace and justice in the life of the world as against selfish and autocratic power and to set up amongst the really free and self-governed peoples of the world such a concert of purpose and of action as will henceforth ensure the observance of those principles. Neutrality is no longer feasible or desirable where the peace of the world is involved and the freedom of its peoples, and the menace to that peace and freedom lies in the existence of autocratic governments backed by organized force which is controlled wholly by their will, not by the will of their people. We have seen the last of neutrality in such circumstances. We are at the beginning of an age in which it will be insisted that the same standards of conduct and of responsibility for wrong done shall be observed among nations and their governments that are observed among the individual citizens of civilized states....

We are accepting this challenge of hostile purpose because we know that in such a government, following such methods, we can never have a friend; and that in the presence of its organized power, always lying in wait to accomplish we know not what purpose, there can be no assured security for the democratic governments of the world. We are now about to accept gage of battle with this natural foe to liberty and shall, if necessary, spend the whole force of the nation to check and nullify its pretensions and its power. We are glad, now that we see the facts with no veil of false pretense about them, to fight thus for the ultimate peace of the world and for the liberation of its peoples, the German peoples included: for the rights of nations great and small and the privilege of men every-where to choose their way of life and of obedience. The world must be made safe for democracy. Its peace must be planted upon the tested foundations of political liberty. We have no selfish ends to serve. We desire no conquest, no dominion. We seek no indemnities for ourselves, no material compensation for the sacrifices we shall freely make. We are but one of the champions of the rights of mankind. We shall be satisfied when those rights have been made as secure as the faith and the freedom of nations can make them.

Just because we fight without rancor and without selfish object, seeking nothing for ourselves but what we shall wish to share with all free peoples, we shall, I feel confident, conduct our operations as belligerents without passion and ourselves observe with proud punctilio the principles of right and of fair play we profess to be fighting for....

It is a distressing and oppressive duty, gentlemen of the Congress, which I have performed in thus addressing you. There are, it may be, many months of fiery trial and sacrifice ahead of us. It is a fearful thing to lead this great peaceful people into war, into the most terrible and disastrous of all wars, civilization itself seeming to be in the balance. But the right is more precious than peace, and we shall fight for the things which we have always carried nearest our hearts,—for democracy, for the right of those who submit to authority to have a voice in their own governments, for the rights and liberties of small nations, for a universal dominion of right by such a concert of free peoples as shall bring peace and safety to all nations and make the world itself at last free. To such a task we can dedicate our lives and our fortunes, everything that we are and everything that we have, with the pride of those who know that the day has come when America is privileged to spend her blood and her might for the principles that gave her birth and happiness and the peace which she has treasured. God helping her, she can do no other.

Source: 65th Congress, 1st Session Senate Document No. 5, Serial No. 7264, Washington, D.C., 1917

HOW WELL DID YOU UNDERSTAND THIS SELECTION?

1. What reasons does Wilson present for the decision to go to war?

2. In Wilson's view, precisely what is at stake in this war?

When war broke out in Europe, many young Americans were eager to aid the Allied cause. Alan Seeger joined the French Foreign Legion in 1914 and saw action in France. He would meet his death there at the Battle of the Somme. Seeger's letters and diaries chronicle his experience of war. A volume of his poetry was published posthumously in 1916. He is one of a group of writers called the "Lost Poets," so named because they died fighting in World War I.

TO THE "NEW YORK SUN" AT THE FRENCH FRONT, May 22, 1915.

Night of violent attacks. All yesterday we listened to the hum of aeroplanes overhead and watched them cruising about amid their little satellites of shrapnel puffs as the vertical batteries bombarded them. About an hour after nightfall the firing began on a sector a few miles to our right, at first the abrupt fusillade, then the rumble of grenades, then the cannon entered into the medley, and the rattle of rifle and machine gun was completely drowned in the steady thunder of high explosives. At regular intervals a terrific explosion as a heavy piece bombarded a village behind our lines to embarrass re-enforcements coming up....

Today was the sixth and last at second line *petit poste*. Fine weather, warm and sunny. Some of the men, careless after a week without bombardment were up on top of the turf-covered bombproof playing cards. Suddenly the distant boom of a cannon, and then, half a second later—whang! A shrapnel had burst twenty yards away in the branches of the grove that screened us from the enemy.

The sudden stampede into the dugout, then a heart-rending cry, and the frantic voices: "Pick up-! pick up-!" Two men go out, braving the momentary recurrence of the danger with that unassuming courage which is a matter of course in the trenches. They bring in the poor comrade, cruelly, mortally wounded. Another, less badly, has had his shoulder torn. We wait till the next shell bursts immediately overhead with a deafening crash. A man has been waiting for it, crouching in the doorway like a sprinter waiting for the signal. By the time the third shell comes he is far away in his race for the litter-bearers half a mile back. Until they arrive we who are not necessary to tend the wounded sit with downcast eyes and shaken nerves, trying not to look or listen, while six other shells in regular succession burst outside, the fragments pattering on the roof of the dugout and the acrid smell of the powder drifting inside.

This is the most distressing thing about the kind of warfare we are up against here. Never a sight of the enemy, and them some fine day when a man is almost tempted to forget that he is on the front—when he is reading cards or writing home that he is in the best of health—bang! And he is carried off or mangled by a cannon fired five kilometers away. It is not glorious. The gunner has not the satisfaction of knowing that he has hit, nor the wounded at least of hitting back. You cannot understand how after months of this one longs for the day when this miserable trench warfare will cease and when in the *elan* of open action he can return blow for blow.

How is it that the enemy know so well our positions, for we are well hidden and they probably see no more of us than we of them? One principal way was explained to me by a friend who had visited the aviation fields a few days ago. While we take pains to keep concealed from the enemy's lines opposite, the aeroplanes are so much a matter of course that one scarcely takes the trouble to look up when the hum of a motor is heard, much less of ducking underground.

But here is a very real danger. It is not so much from the bombs that occasionally drop on the lines and on the villages in the rear, but the observer up there with a camera of powerful telescopic lens is photographing all the time the country underneath. The film is developed that night and the prints scrutinized under a microscope. Details show up in this way that would escape the naked eye. It is thus that batteries and camps, posts and all kinds of military works are located.

In billets again. Was out on guard early this morning. Suppressed excitement in the little village as the streets begin to fill with officers and soldiers. Then a friend passes. "*Eh bien! On y met,*" he calls out.......means that we are going to clear out. The rumor is soon confirmed. Yes, after just seven months in this more or less tranquil sector we are actually going to get the change we have all been longing for, and on twelve hours notice too. We leave tonight. Where? Nobody knows; but nobody doubts that it is to be into the thick of it.

I should like to give you some impressions of the state of mind before going into action, but unfortunately there is no time. The sacks must be made right away. Let me only say that I am heartily glad, and this feeling is increased when the news comes that poor little ——, who was wounded the other day, has died in hospital. Poor boy! It was the best thing for him.

It is good to get away from the constant danger here of dying thus ingloriously. If it must be, let it come in the heat of action. Why flinch? It is by far the noblest form in which death can come. It is in a sense almost a privilege to be allowed to meet it in this way. The cause is worth fighting for. If one goes it is in company with the elite of the world. *Ave atque vale!* If I write again it will no doubt be to tell you of wonderful things.

We are all in fine form, fit and eager for the assault. I think it will come soon. *Le jour de gloire est arrive!*

From: Letters and Diary of Alan Seeger, Charles Scribner's Sons, NY: 1917
Source- ukans.edu lib website: www.ukans.edu/~libsite/wwi-www/Seeger/Alan1.htm

HOW WELL DID YOU UNDERSTAND THIS SELECTION?

1. What are the new technologies and techniques of warfare introduced in World War I that Seeger discusses? What were their effects upon soldiers?

2. What is Seeger's reaction when he learns he will be leaving the trenches?

3. What is Seeger's attitude about the cause for which he is fighting? How does it affect his feelings about the fact that he might soon meet his death on the field of battle?

4. According to Seeger, in what lay the difference between an inglorious and a glorious death?

5. Do you think that Seeger's attitudes toward war and death were widely shared?

THE BACKWASH OF WAR: *The Human Wreckage of the Battlefield as Witnessed by an American Hospital Nurse*, 1916, By Ellen N. LaMott

In 1915, Ellen N. La Motte, an American woman, went to Belgium to nurse the casualties of war in a French field hospital. La Motte's wartime experiences were published in 1916 as **The Backwash of War.** *In 1918, in an America at war and inhospitable to so starkly vivid and negative an account of the war, her publisher refused to produce further printings of her volume. The work would not be republished until 1934.*

Pour la Patrie [For the fatherland]

THIS is how it was. It is pretty much always like this in a field hospital. Just ambulances rolling in, and dirty, dying men, and the guns off there in the distance! Very monotonous, and the same, day after day, till one gets so tired and bored. Big things may be going on over there, on the other side of the captive balloons that we can see from a distance, but we are always here, on this side of them, and here, on this side of them, it is always the same. The weariness of it—the sameness of it! The same ambulances, and dirty men, and groans, or silence. The same hot operating rooms, the same beds, always full, in the wards. This is war. But it goes on and on, over and over, day after day, till it seems like life. Life in peace time. It might be life in a big city hospital, so alike is the routine. Only the city hospitals are bigger, and better equipped, and the ambulances are smarter, and the patients don't always come in ambulances—they walk in sometimes, or come in street cars, or in limousines, and they are of both sexes, men and women, and have ever so many things the matter with them—the hospitals of peace time are not nearly so stupid, so monotonous, as the hospitals of war. Bah! War's humane compared to peace! More spectacular, I grant you, more acute,—that's what interests us,—but for the sheer agony of life—oh, peace is way ahead!

War is so clean. Peace is so dirty. There are so many foul diseases in peace times. They drag on over so many years, too. No, war's clean! I'd rather see a man die in prime of life, in war time, than see him doddering along in peace time, broken hearted, broken spirited, life broken, and very weary, having suffered many things,—to die at last, at a good, ripe age! How they have suffered, those who drive up to our city hospitals in limousines, in peace-time. What's been saved them, those who die young, and clean and swiftly, here behind the guns. In the long run it dots up just the same. Only war's spectacular, that's all.

Well, he came in like the rest, only older than most of them. A shock of iron-gray hair, a mane of it, above heavy, black brows, and the brows were contracted in pain. Shot, as usual, in the abdomen. He spent three hours on the table after admission—the operating table—and when he came over to the ward, they said, not a dog's chance for him. No more had he. When he came out of ether, he said he didn't want to die. He said he wanted to live. Very much. He said he wanted to see his wife again and his children. Over and over he insisted on this, insisted on getting well. He caught hold of the doctor's hand and said he must get well, that the doctor must get him well. Then the doctor drew away his slim fingers from the rough, imploring grasp, and told him to be good and patient.

"Be good! Be patient!" said the doctor, and that was all he could say, for he was honest. What else could he say, knowing that there were eighteen little holes, cut by the bullet, leaking poison into that gashed, distended abdomen? When these little holes, that the doctor could not stop, had leaked enough poison into his system, he would die. Not today, no, but day after tomorrow. Three days more.

So all that first day, the man talked of getting well. He was insistent on that. He was confident. Next day, the second of the three days the doctor gave him, very much pain laid hold of him. His black brows bent with pain and he grew puzzled. How could one live with such pain as that? That afternoon, about five o'clock, came the General. The one who decorates the men. He had no sword, just a riding whip, so he tossed the whip on the bed, for you can't do an accolade with anything but a sword. Just the *Médaille Militaire*. Not the other one. But the *Médaille Militaire* carries a pension of a hundred francs a year, so that's something. So the General said, very briefly: "In the name of the Republic of France, I confer upon you the *Médaille Militaire*." Then he bent over and kissed the man on his forehead, pinned the medal to the bedspread, and departed.

There you are! Just a brief little ceremony, and perfunctory. We all got that impression. The General has decorated so many dying men. And this one seemed so nearly dead. He seemed half-conscious. Yet the General might have put a little more feeling into it, not made it quite so perfunctory. Yet he's done this thing so many, many times before. It's all right, he does it differently when there are people about, but this time there was no one present—just the doctor, the dying man, and me. And so we four knew what it meant—just a widow's pension. Therefore there wasn't any reason for the accolade, for the sonorous, ringing phrases of a dress parade—We all knew what it meant. So did the man. When he got the medal, he knew too. He knew there wasn't any hope. I held the medal before him, after the General had gone, in its red plush case. It looked cheap, somehow. The exchange didn't seem even. He pushed it aside with a contemptuous hand sweep, a disgusted shrug.

"I've seen these things before!" he exclaimed. We all had seen them too. We all knew about them too, he and the doctor, and the General and I. He knew and understood, most of all. And his tone was bitter.

After that, he knew the doctor couldn't save him, and that he could not see his wife and children again. Where upon he became angry with the treatment, and protested against it. The piqûres [injections] hurt—they hurt very much, and he did not want them. Moreover, they did no good, for his pain was now very intense, and he tossed and tossed to get away from it. So the third day dawned, and he was alive, and dying, and knew that he was dying. Which is unusual and disconcerting. He turned over and over, and black fluid vomited from his mouth into the white enamel basin. From time to time, the orderly emptied the basin, but always there was more, and always he choked and gasped and knit his brows in pain. Once his face broke up as a child's breaks up when it cries. So he cried in pain and loneliness and resentment. He struggled hard to hold on. He wanted very much to live, but he could not do it. He said, "Je ne tiens plus."

Which was true. He couldn't hold on. The pain was too great. He clenched his hands and writhed, and cried out for mercy. But what mercy had we? We gave him morphia, but it did not help. So he continued to cry to us for mercy, he cried to us and to God. Between us, we let him suffer eight hours more like that, us and God.

Then I called the priest. We have three priests on the ward, as orderlies, and I got one of them to give him the Sacrament. I thought it would quiet him. We could not help him with drugs, and he had not got it quite in his head that he must die, and when he said, "I am dying," he expected to be contradicted. So I asked Capolarde to give him the Sacrament, and he said yes, and put a red screen around the bed, to screen him from the ward. Then Capolarde turned to me and asked me to leave. It was summer time. The window at the head of the bed was open, the hay outside was new cut and piled into little haycocks. Over in the distance the guns rolled. As I turned to go, I saw Capolarde holding a tray of Holy Oils in one hand, while with the other he emptied the basin containing black vomitus out the window.

No, it did not bring him comfort, or resignation. He fought against it. He wanted to live, and he resented Death, very bitterly. Down at my end of the ward—it was a silent, summer afternoon—I heard them very clearly. I heard the low words from behind the screen.

"Dites: Dieu je vous donne ma vie librement pour ma patrie" (God, I give you my life freely for my country). The priests usually say that to them, for death has more dignity that way. It is not in the ritual, but it makes a soldier's death more noble. So I suppose Capolarde said it. I could only judge by the response. I could hear the heavy, labored breath, the choking, wailing cry.

"Oui! Oui!" Gasped out at intervals. "Ah mon Dieu! Oui!"

Again the mumbling, guiding whisper.

"Oui—oui!" came sobbing, gasping, in response.

So I heard the whispers, the priest's whispers, and the stentorous choke, the feeble, wailing, rebellious wailing in response. He was being forced into it. Forced into acceptance. Beaten into submission, beaten into resignation.

"Oui—oui!" came the protesting moans. "Ah, oui!"

It must be dawning upon him now. Capolarde is making him see.

"Oui! Oui!" The choking sobs reach me. "Ah, mon Dieu, oui!" Then very deep, panting, crying breaths: "Dieu je vous donne ma vie librement pour ma patrie!"

"Librement! Librement! Au, oui! Oui!" He was beaten at last. The choking, dying, bewildered man had said the noble words.

"God, I give you my life freely for my country!"

After which came a volley of low toned Latin phrases, rattling in the stillness like the popping of a mitrailleuse [machine-gun].

145

Two hours later he was still alive, restless, but no longer resentful. "It is difficult to go," he murmured, and then: "Tonight, I shall sleep well." A long pause followed, and he opened his eyes.

"Without doubt, the next world is more chic than this," he remarked smiling, and then: "I was mobilized against my inclination. Now I have won the *Médaille Militaire*. My Captain won it for me. He made me brave. He had a revolver in his hand."

Source: Ellen N. La Motte, *The Backwash of War*, G.P. Putnam's Sons, New York, 1916

HOW WELL DID YOU UNDERSTAND THIS SELECTION?

1. Why do you think La Motte chose "the backwash of war" for her title?

2. Compare Alan Seeger's portrait of war to the one presented here by La Motte. How do you account for their different views?

3. What was it about LaMotte's account of war that led to its not being reprinted during World War I?

SECRET INFORMATION CONCERNING BLACK AMERICAN TROOPS,
French Military Mission, Stationed with the American Army, August 7, 1918

In 1919 W.E.B. Du Bois, editor of the NAACP journal, **The Crisis,** *compiled and published a set of documents that provide evidence of the widespread discrimination to which black American soldiers were subjected while in the service of their nation. One in particular reveals in unambiguous terms the concerns that were secretly expressed by many white American officials in the Wilson Administration as well as by many Army officials: that allowing blacks to serve with whites in the armed services would jeopardize maintaining their subservience to whites upon their reentry into American society. Of the almost 400,000 black Americans who served in the armed forces during World War I, about 100,000 were sent to France as part of the American Expeditionary Force. The vast majority were placed in noncombat roles as laborers, since prevailing white racist attitudes considered the arming of "inferior" blacks a dangerous enterprise. In the summer of 1918 U.S. Army officials requested that the French Military Mission liaison, Linard, issue instructions to French army personnel regarding "appropriate" treatment of black American troops. The following directive was issued to French officers; however, when the French Ministry of War learned of it, it issued orders for copies to be destroyed. Du Bois acquired a copy.*

1. It is important for French officers who have been called upon to exercise command over black American troops, or to live in close contact with them, to have an exact idea of the position occupied by Negroes in the United States. The information set forth in the following communication ought to be given to these officers and it is to their interest to have these matters known and widely disseminated. It will devolve likewise on the French Military Authorities, through the medium of the Civil Authorities, to give information on this subject to the French population residing in the cantonments occupied by American colored troops.

2. The American attitude upon the Negro question may seem a matter for discussion to many French minds. But we French are not in our province if we undertake to discuss what some call "prejudice." American opinion is unanimous on the "color question" and does not admit of any discussion.

The increasing number of Negroes in the United States (about 15,000,000) would create for the white race in the Republic a menace of degeneracy were it not that an impassable gulf has been made between them.

As this danger does not exist for the French race, the French public has become accustomed to treating the Negro with familiarity and indulgence. This indulgence and this familiarity are matters of grievous concern to the Americans. They consider them an affront to their national policy. They are afraid that contact with the French will inspire in black Americans aspirations which to them [the whites] appear intolerable. It is of the utmost importance that every effort be made to avoid profoundly estranging American opinion.

Although a citizen of the United States, the black man is regarded by the white American as an inferior being with whom relations of business or service only are possible. The black is constantly being censured for his want of intelligence and discretion, his lack of civic and professional conscience and for his tendency toward undue familiarity.

The vices of the Negro are a constant menace to the American who has to repress them sternly. For instance, the black American troops in France have, by themselves, given rise to as many complaints for attempted rape as all the rest of the army. And yet the [black American] soldiers sent to us have been the choicest with respect to physique and morals, for the number disqualified at the time of mobilization was enormous.

CONCLUSION

1. We must prevent the rise of any pronounced degree of intimacy between French officers and black officers. We may be courteous and amiable with these last, but we cannot deal with them on the same plane as with the white American officers without deeply wounding the latter. We must not eat with them, must not shake hands or seek to talk or meet with them outside of the requirements of military service.

2. We must not commend too highly the black American troops, particularly in the presence of [white] Americans. It is all right to recognize their good qualities and their services, but only in moderate terms, strictly in keeping with the truth.

3. Make a point of keeping the native cantonment population from "spoiling" the Negroes. [White] Americans become greatly incensed at any public expression of intimacy between white women with black men. They have recently uttered violent protests against a picture in the "Vie Parisienne" entitled "The Child of the Desert" which shows a [white] woman in a "cabinet particulier" with a Negro. Familiarity on the part of white women with black men is furthermore a source of profound regret to our experienced colonials who see in it an over-weening menace to the prestige of the white race.

Military authority cannot intervene directly in this question, but it can through the civil authorities exercise some influence on the population.

(Signed)   LINARD.

Source: "Documents of the War," *The Crisis*, (May, 1919) vol.18: 1, pp. 16-18, W.E.B. Du Bois, ed

HOW WELL DID YOU UNDERSTAND THIS SELECTION?

1. Precisely what do American officials fear?

2. What difficulties might equal treatment of black Americans by the French present for white Americans?

3. What traditional charge of uncivilized behavior is leveled against the Negro in France to justify white America's repression of the Negro?

4. What do you think might be a more appropriate title for this document?

During World War I, the U.S. Congress enacted laws giving the federal government vastly expanded powers for the purpose of mobilizing the American people and the nation's resources to win the war. Government would reach into the daily lives of Americans in an unprecedented way. In August 1917, Congress passed the Food and Fuel Control Act [Lever Act]. With the authority granted the president under this law, Wilson created the U.S. Food Administration, headed by Herbert Hoover. Like the CPI, the Food Administration recognized the value of advertising. An advertising section was central to the Food Administration's success in promoting the supply, distribution, and conservation of food during the war, enabling the nation to feed American and Allied soldiers, our war-torn European Allies' populations, and the American people.

HOW WELL DID YOU UNDERSTAND THIS SELECTION?

1. The artist who created the "Sow the Seeds of Victory" poster was James Montgomery Flagg. What visual imagery does Flagg employ to shape public sentiment and action?

2. What emotions and convictions does this poster seek to evoke?

3. What is meant by the caption "every garden a munition plant"?

4. Compare the Flagg poster with his cartoon in the chapter on the Progressive Era (Chapter 4). How effective is each in accomplishing its respective objective?

5. How does the "Food Will Win the War" poster use visual images to shape public sentiment and action?

6. What emotions and convictions does the poster seek to evoke?

CONSCRIPTION, By H. J. Glintenkamp, 1917

*When America went to war in 1917, the U.S. government began to crack down on periodicals publishing articles and illustrations critical of America's involvement in the war. Under the Espionage Act of 1917, a group of writers and cartoonists who published their work in the socialist magazine, **The Masses**, were charged with undermining the war effort. They were indicted in July 1917 when the August edition of **The Masses** was delivered to a U.S. Post Office. One of the items in the August 1917 edition of the journal that was considered particularly offensive was the following illustration by H.J. Glintenkamp. Glintenkamp fled the country rather than stand trial. In the first of two trials in April 1918, the jury could not agree on the guilt or innocence of the defendants. They were retried in January 1919. Once again there was a hung jury. With the war over, the defendants were not put on trial again.*

*In 1918, as part of its continuing effort to mobilize public support for the war, the U.S. government created a Bureau of Cartoons within the Committee on Public Information. It published a weekly **Bulletin for Cartoonists**, which suggested appropriate topics for cartoonists. The August 31, 1918 edition of the **Bulletin** stated: "You, the cartoonists of the country, have here an opportunity to be of immeasurable aid to the Government.... Through your cartoons you can inspire in every man a keen sense of his obligation to the cause of democracy and stimulate public opinion on this vital issue as few other forces in this country can." Clearly, the U.S. government recognized the power of images to shape public sentiment both for and against the war.*

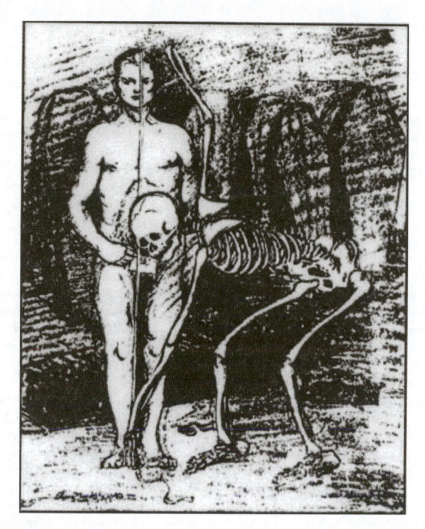

Source: *The Masses*, New York, August, 1917

HOW WELL DID YOU UNDERSTAND THIS SELECTION?

1. Why did Glintenkamp entitle his drawing "Conscription"?

2. What message did he seek to convey through this drawing?

3. What powerful images does Glintenkamp use to present his message?

A war President Wilson described as a "fight to make the world safe for democracy" would, ironically, test the limits of democracy and freedom within America. Historically, when the nation's security had been threatened during national emergencies or wars, civil liberties had been abridged. The Alien and Sedition Acts of 1798 and Lincoln's suspension of the writ of habeas corpus are two notable examples. World War I would prove no exception.

In June 1917 Congress passed, and President Wilson signed, the Espionage Act, which declared numerous activities illegal, including the effort to impede the draft or military training. It banned treasonous materials from the U.S. mails. The law, however, gave no clear definition of precisely what constituted treason. This was left to postal authorities to decide. With the Sedition Act of the following year, which made it a federal crime to use profane or abusive language against the U.S. government, flag, or uniform of the armed services, these loosely worded laws gave the Wilson Administration broad latitude to crack down on anyone who differed with the government's position. Nearly 2000 Americans were arrested under these laws; 1000 would be convicted. Those arrested and prosecuted included publishers and contributors to journals like The Masses, *pacifists, and socialists like Eugene Debs and Charles Schenck. Schenck, the general secretary of the Socialist Party, appealed his conviction under the Espionage Act to the U.S. Supreme Court. Ironically, the author of the unanimous decision was Justice Oliver Wendell Holmes, a jurist known for his strong advocacy of civil liberties.*

MR. JUSTICE HOLMES delivered the opinion of the Court:
This is an indictment in three counts. The first charges a conspiracy to violate the Espionage Act of June 15, 1917, by causing and attempting to cause insubordination, in the military and naval forces of the United States, and to obstruct the recruiting and enlistment service of the United States, when the United States was at war with the German Empire, to-wit, that the defendants wilfully conspired to have printed and circulated to men who had been called and accepted for military service under the Act of May 18, 1917, a document set forth and alleged to be calculated to cause such insubordination and obstruction. The count alleges overt acts in pursuance of the conspiracy, ending in the distribution of the document set forth. The second count alleges a conspiracy to commit an offense against the United States, to-wit, to use the mails for the transmission of . . . the above mentioned document.... The third count charges an unlawful use of the mails for the transmission of the same matter and otherwise as above. The defendants were found guilty on all the counts. They set up the First Amendment to the Constitution forbidding Congress to make any law abridging the freedom of speech, or of the press, and bringing the case here on that ground have argued some other points also of which we must dispose.... The document in question upon its first printed side recited the first section of the Thirteenth Amendment, said that the idea embodied in it was violated by the Conscription Act and that a conscript is little better than a convict. In impassioned language it intimated that conscription was despotism in its worst form and a monstrous wrong against humanity in the interest of Wall Street's chosen few. It said "Do not submit to intimidation," but in form at least confined itself to peaceful measures such as a petition for the repeal of the act. The other and later printed side of the sheet was headed "Assert Your Rights." . . . it denied the power to send our citizens away to foreign shores to shoot up the people of other lands, and added that words could not express the condemnation such coldblooded ruthlessness deserves, &c., &c., winding up "You must do your share to maintain, support and uphold the rights of the people of this country." Of course the document would not have been sent unless it had been intended to have some effect, and we do not see what effect it could be expected to have upon persons subject to the draft except to influence them to obstruct the carrying of it out. The defendants do not deny that the jury might find against them on this point. But it is said, suppose that that was the tendency of this circular, it is protected by the First Amendment to the Constitution....We admit that in many places and in ordinary times the defendants in saying all that was said in the circular would have been within their constitutional rights. But the character of every act depends upon the circumstances in which it is done. The most stringent protection of free speech would not protect a man in falsely shouting fire in a theatre and causing a panic. It does not even protect a man from an injunction against uttering words that may have all the effect of force. The question in every case is whether the words used are used in such circumstances and are of such a nature as to create clear and present danger that they will bring about the substantive evils that Congress has a right

to prevent. It is a question of proximity and degree. When a nation is at war many things that might be said in time of peace are such a hindrance to its effort that their utterance will not be endured so long as men fight and that no Court could regard them as protected by any constitutional right. It seems to be admitted that if an actual obstruction of the recruiting service were proved, liability for words that produced that effect might be enforced. The statute of 1917 in section …4 punishes conspiracies to obstruct as well as actual obstruction. If the act, (speaking, or circulating a paper), its tendency and the intent with which it is done are the same, we perceive no ground for saying that success alone warrants making the act a crime....

Judgments affirmed.

Source: www.thisnation.com/library/schenck.html

HOW WELL DID YOU UNDERSTAND THIS SELECTION?

1. What two competing interests is the Court wrestling with in the *Schenck* case?

2. What criterion does the Court employ to determine when free speech can be suppressed?

3. Are there any dangers to the nation in the silencing of dissent? Does the Court address these dangers?

THE LYNCHING OF ROBERT PRAGER AND THE ACQUITTAL OF HIS MURDERERS

Wartime propaganda focused attention on "enemies within." With the patriotism of many Americans whipped up to a fever pitch, vigilante groups often meted out "justice." One of the worst examples of such wartime vigilantism is the case of Robert Prager, a German coal miner. Two press reports follow: an account of Prager's fate at the hands of an angry mob, and a report on the acquittal of his murderers.

The St. Louis Globe-Democrat (April 5, 1918)

GERMAN ENEMY OF U.S. HANGED BY MOB
ST. LOUIS COLLINSVILLE MAN KILLED FOR ABUSING WILSON

Robert P. Prager Taken from Jail and Strung Up to Tree by 300 Men and Boys After Officers are Overpowered
    Robert P. Prager, 45 years old, of Collinsville, Ill., a coalminer, charged with making disloyal utterances against the United States and President Wilson, was hanged to a tree on Mauer Heights, one mile west of Collinsville on the St. Louis road, by a mob of 300 men and boys after he had twice escaped mob violence, at 12:15 o'clock this

morning. Collinsville is ten miles northeast of East St. Louis. Prager was taken from the Collinsville Jail by the mob, which battered down the doors. The prisoner was found hidden under a pile of rubbish in the basement of the Jail, where he had been placed by the police when they had learned that the mob was on the way to the Jail. The police were overpowered, there being only four on the night force, and the prisoner was carried down the street, the mob cheering and waving flags. The police were not allowed to follow the mob by a guard which had been placed over them. When led to the tree upon which he was hanged Prager was asked if he had anything to say. "Yes," he replied in broken English. "I would like to pray." He then fell to his knees, clasped his hands to his breast and prayed for three minutes in German. Without another word the noose was placed about his neck and the body pulled 10 feet into the air by a hundred or more hands which grasped the rope. Before praying, Prager wrote a letter to his parents, Mr. and Mrs. Carl Henry Prager, Preston, Germany. It follows: "Dear Parents - I must this day, the 5th of April, 1918, die. Please pray for me, my dear parents. This is my last letter. Your dear son. ROBERT PAUL PRAGER." Prager was an enemy alien and registered in East St. Louis.

Prager Attended Socialist Meeting Short Time Before He was Lynched

After the mob had returned to Collinsville, several residents at Collinsville who had heard of the hanging went to the scene. Two unidentified persons were found guarding the body. They would let no one approach and warned whoever came close that they would meet the same fate if they attempted to cut down the body. The mob took their prisoner from the jail about 10 o'clock last night. Prager earlier in the evening had attended a Socialist meeting in Maryville, where it is alleged he made a speech in which he uttered remarks which were termed disloyal. After word had been passed around Maryville, a mob collected there and started a search for the miner. Prager had been informed about that the mob was after him and he escaped to Collinsville. They told of the remarks of Prager and finally a mob of 300 was assembled. Prager was found on the street in front of his home, 208 Vandalia Avenue. He was marched to the main street, where his shoes were removed and a large American flag was wrapped about his body. Prager was made to kiss the flag many times and march up and down the street waving two small flags which he carried in his hands. For fear that violence would result from the mob, the police took Prager from them and placed him in jail.

Mayor Induces Mob to Go Home, but It Reassembles Later

Mayor J. H. Siegel pleaded with the mob and asked them to go to their homes. He had previously closed all the saloons. "We do not want a stigma marking Collinsville," said Mayor Siegel, "and I implore you to go to your homes and discontinue this demonstration." The mob disbanded and the mayor, thinking that everything had quieted down, went to his home. But a short time later the mob again formed and stormed the jail, taking the prisoner from the police. This is the first killing for disloyalty in the United States, although many persons have been mobbed and tarred and feathered. Prager begged for mercy. He said that he was a loyal citizen, and in a signed statement, which he had previously made to the police, he said that his heart and soul were for the United States. He admitted being a native of Germany. He said that he had applied for naturalization papers and that his second papers were waiting for him. Prager had been in Maryville looking for work. He was a coal miner. He found he could not obtain employment because the union had rejected his application. On March 22, four men, including a Polish Catholic priest, were tarred and feathered at Christopher, Ill., a mining town eighty miles from St. Louis. Previous to that time two other men were tarred and feathered in the same mining district. For the past three months many loyalty demonstrations have occurred in an effort to drive disloyal persons from Southern Illinois.

Edwardsville Intelligencer (June 8, 1918)

JURY FINDS PRAGER DEFENDANTS NOT GUILTY AND OTHERS ARE FREE

Edwardsville—Eleven residents of Collinsville walked from the court house Saturday afternoon, exonerated for the death of Robert P. Prager, German alien enemy, who was lynched in that city during the early morning hours of April 5. On the second ballot and with deliberations of only a few minutes the jury reached its verdict.… On the first vote the jurors stood 11 to 1 for acquittal, the discussions, it is understood, lasted but a few minutes and then the second vote was taken. It found the defendants not guilty.…. The court room was filled with spectators when the defendants were taken back to the court room Saturday afternoon to hear their fate. A few minutes later the court was ready to receive the jury and the twelve men filed into the court room and took their places in the jury box....There was wild applauding and cheers from most everyone present. Relatives, friends and acquaintances rushed toward the bar to shake hands with the defendants. In a few minutes the crowd was quieted and the jury was discharged by Judge Bernreuter. Afterwards the defendants shook hands with the members of the jury.

There was a peculiar coincidence at the trial Saturday. The Jackie Band was in Edwardsville for a patriotic demonstration. When a shower of rain came up the musicians were sent to the court house where it had been arranged to give a program. At 2:40 o'clock Judge Bernreuter ordered a recess after the completion of arguments and before reading the instructions. Then word was sent that the band might play until court re-convened. The first number of all concerts is the Star Spangled Banner and it was played Saturday. The strains from the Jackie Band caused tears to flow down the cheeks of Riegel [a defendant-Ed.]. He was still crying when he returned to the court room. As the jury came in with its verdict the band was at the head of a procession of draft boys and in passing the court house played "Over There." The acquittal of most of the prisoners was no great surprise to most of those who heard the evidence. After returning the verdict, several of the jurors told reporters that the state had failed to connect up the charges and remove the reasonable doubts, even to those charged with being most prominently connected with the death....

State's Attorney Streuber made the following statement today: "Since the trial of the eleven defendants charged with the murder of Robert Paul Prager, there have been intimations and expressions that the acquittal of the defendants was, in substance, an approval of mob law. With this view I do not concur...."

Sources: *The St. Louis Globe-Democrat*, April 5, 1918; *Edwardsville Intelligencer*, June 8, 1918

HOW WELL DID YOU UNDERSTAND THIS SELECTION?

1. Why was Robert Prager lynched?

2. Does the Prager verdict represent the rule of law or rule of men?

3. Having read the *St. Louis Globe-Democrat* account of the murder of Prager, how does the verdict reinforce the importance of the rule of law?

World War I would prove to be a singularly important event in bringing about woman suffrage in America. Carrie Chapman Catt, president of the National American Woman Suffrage Association, promoted the Nineteenth Amendment as a "war measure." Catt argued, if America was fighting a war for democracy, where was democracy for half of the American population long denied it? Women's war work would help to convince many in Congress that women deserved the vote. For many, a vote on behalf of woman suffrage was justified as a reward for women's patriotic service. The Nineteenth Amendment to the Constitution was passed in the Senate in 1919 and ratified by three-fourths of the states in 1920. But just as the war would reshape pro-suffrage arguments, it would lead anti-suffrage forces to refashion their arguments. This petition was forwarded to the U.S. Congress in 1917 after America went to war.

PETITION
From the Women Voters Anti-suffrage Party of New York
TO THE
United States Senate

Whereas, This country is now engaged in the greatest war in history, and

Whereas, The advocates of the Federal Amendment, though urging it as a war measure, through their president, Mrs. Catt, that its passage "means a simultaneous campaign in 48 States. It demands organization in every precinct; activity, agitation, education in every corner. Nothing less than this nation-wide vigilant, unceasing campaign will win the ratification," therefore be it

Resolved, That our country, in this hour of peril should be spared the harassing of its public men and the distracting of its people from work for the war, and further

Resolved, That the United States Senate be respectfully urged to pass no measure involving such a radical change in our government while the attention of the patriotic portion of the people is concentrated on the all-important task of winning the war, and during the absence of over a million men abroad.

[Signatures]

Source: National Archives and Records Administration, Woman Suffrage and the Nineteenth Amendment, Primary Documents. website: http://www.nara.gov/education/teaching/woman/ww1pet.html

HOW WELL DID YOU UNDERSTAND THIS SELECTION?

1. What is your assessment of the anti-suffrage party's claim that the proposed amendment is a distraction from war work?

2. What is the natural conclusion one would draw from the statement that "the attention of the patriotic portion of the American people is concentrated on the all-important task of winning the war"?

3. Are being patriotic and pro-suffrage mutually exclusive positions?

In 1919 major race riots erupted in Charleston, Chicago, Knoxville, Long View, Texas, Omaha, and the nation's capital. As whites entered the armed services during the war, job opportunities in northern cities offered southern blacks an escape from the discrimination and poverty they experienced in the South. However, black migration northward generated increased racial tensions. The black population of many cities rose rapidly, doubling in Chicago between 1916 and 1919. Black and white neighborhoods inched closer. Once exclusively white jobs were now filled by black men and women. White soldiers returned home to altered living and working arrangements. Having been treated as equals by European whites and anticipating improved treatment by American whites for having served their country, many returning black soldiers displayed a new militancy. Intensifying racial tensions were exacerbated by the government's rapid, haphazard demobilization of American troops as well as by the dislocations and hardships generated by the shift from a wartime to a peacetime economy. The result was increased competition for declining jobs.

A week-long race riot swept Chicago in the summer of 1919 that took the lives of thirty-eight people and left 537 injured. At the urging of black and white Chicago civic leaders just days after the riot, the governor of Illinois appointed a biracial commission to study the event. The result was published in 1922 as **The Negro in Chicago: A Study of Race Relations and a Race Riot.**

Background

In July, 1919, a race riot involving whites and Negroes occurred in Chicago. For some time thoughtful citizens, white and Negro, had sensed increased tension, but having no local precedent of riot and wholesale bloodshed, had neither prepared themselves for it nor taken steps to prevent it. The collecting of arms by members of both races was known to the authorities, and it was evident that this was in preparation for aggression as well as for self-defense.

Several minor clashes preceded the riot. On July 3, 1917, a white saloon-keeper who, according to the coroner's physician, died of heart trouble, was incorrectly reported in the press to have been killed by a Negro. That evening a party of young white men riding in an automobile fired upon a group of Negroes at Fifty-third and Federal Streets. In July and August of the same year recruits from the Great Lakes Naval Training Station clashed frequently with Negroes, each side accusing the other of being the aggressor.

Gangs of white "toughs," made up largely of the membership of so-called "athletic clubs"....were a constant menace to Negroes who traversed sections of the territory going to and returning from work. The activities of these gangs and "athletic clubs" became bolder in the spring of 1919, and on the night of June 21, five weeks before the riot, two wanton murders of Negroes occurred, those of Sanford Harris and Joseph Robinson. Harris, returning to his home....about 11:30 at night, passed a group of young white men. They threatened him and he ran. He had gone but a short distance when one of the group shot him. He died soon afterward. Policemen who came on the scene made no arrests, even when the assailant was pointed out by a white woman witness of the murder. On the same evening Robinson, a Negro laborer....was attacked while returning from work by a gang of white "roughs"....apparently without provocation, and stabbed to death.

Negroes were greatly incensed over these murders, but their leaders, joined by many friendly whites, tried to allay their fears and counseled patience.

After the killing of Harris and Robinson notices were conspicuously posted on the South Side that an effort would be made to "get all the niggers on July 4th." The notices called for help from sympathizers. Negroes in turn whispered around the warning to prepare for a riot; and they did prepare....

Aside from general lawlessness and disastrous riots that preceded the riot here discussed, there were other factors which may be mentioned briefly here. In Chicago considerable unrest had been occasioned in industry by increasing competition between white and Negro laborers following a sudden increase in the Negro population due to the migration of Negroes from the South. This increase developed a housing crisis. The Negroes overran the hitherto recognized area of Negro residence, and when they took houses in adjoining neighborhoods, friction ensued. In the two years just preceding the riot, twenty-seven Negro dwellings were wrecked by bombs thrown by unidentified persons.

Story of the Riot

Sunday afternoon, July 27, 1919, hundreds of white and Negro bathers crowded the lake-front beaches at Twenty-sixth and Twenty-ninth Streets. This is the eastern boundary of the thickest Negro residence area. At Twenty-sixth Street Negroes were in great majority; at Twenty-ninth Street there were more whites. An imaginary line in the water separating the two beaches had been generally observed by the two races. Under the prevailing relations, aided by wild rumors and reports, this line served virtually as a challenge to either side to cross. Four Negroes who attempted to enter the water from the "white" side were driven away by the whites. They returned with more Negroes, and then there followed a series of attacks with stones, first one side gaining the advantage, then the other.

Eugene Williams, a Negro boy of seventeen, entered the water from the side used by Negroes and drifted across the line supported by a railroad tie. He was observed by the crowd on the beach and promptly became a target for stones. He suddenly released the tie, and went down and was drowned. Guilt was immediately placed on Stauber, a young white man, by Negro witnesses who declared that he threw the fatal stone.

White and Negro dived for the boy without result. Negroes demanded that the policeman arrest Stauber. He refused, and at this crucial moment arrested a Negro on a white man's complaint. Negroes then attacked the officer. These two facts, the drowning and the refusal of the policeman to arrest Stauber, together marked the beginning of the riot.

Two hours after the drowning, a Negro, James Crawford, fired into a group of officers summoned by the policeman at the beach and was killed by a Negro policeman. Reports and rumors circulated rapidly, and new crowds began to gather. Five white men were injured in clashes near the beach. As darkness came Negroes in white districts to the west suffered severely. Between 9:00PM and 3:00AM twenty-seven Negroes were beaten, seven stabbed, and four shot. Monday morning was quite, and Negroes went to work as usual.

Returning from work in the afternoon many Negroes were attacked by white ruffians. Street-car routes, especially at transfer points, were the centers of lawlessness. Trolleys were pulled from the wires, and Negro passengers were dragged into the street, beaten, stabbed, and shot. The police were powerless to cope with these numerous assaults. During Monday, four Negro men and one white assailant were killed, and thirty Negroes were severely beaten in street-car clashes. Four white men were killed, six stabbed, five shot, and nine severely beaten. It was rumored that the white occupants of the Angelus Building....had shot a Negro. Negroes gathered about the building. The white tenants sought police protection, and one hundred policemen, mounted and on foot responded. In a clash with the mob the police killed four Negroes and injured many.

Raids into the Negro residence area then began. Automobiles sped through the streets, the occupants shooting at random. Negroes retaliated by "sniping" from ambush. At midnight, surface and elevated car service was discontinued because of a strike for wage increases, and thousands of employees were cut off from work.

On Tuesday, July 29, Negro men enroute on foot to their jobs through hostile territory were killed. White soldiers and sailors in uniform, aided by civilians, raided the "Loop" business section, killing two Negroes and beating and robbing several others. Negroes living among white neighbors in Englewood, far to the south, were driven from their homes, their household goods were stolen, and their houses were burned or wrecked. On the West Side an Italian mob, excited by a false rumor that an Italian girl had been shot by a Negro, killed Joseph Lovings, a Negro.

Wednesday night at 10:30 Mayor Thompson yielded to pressure and asked the help of three regiments of militia which had been stationed in nearby armories during the most severe rioting, awaiting the call. They immediately took up positions throughout the South Side. A rainfall Wednesday night and Thursday kept many people in their homes, and by Friday the rioting had abated. On Saturday incendiary fires burned forty-nine houses in the immigrant neighborhood west of the Stock Yards. Nine hundred and forty-eight people, mostly Lithuanians, were made homeless, and the property loss was about $250,000. Responsibility for the fires was never fixed.

The total casualties of this reign of terror were thirty-eight deaths—fifteen white, twenty-three Negro—and 537 people injured. Forty-one per cent of the reported clashes occurred in the white neighborhood....and 34 per cent in the "Black Belt"....Others were scattered....

Source: *The Negro in Chicago; A Study of Race Relations and a Race Riot,* Chicago Commission on Race Relations: Chicago, 1922

HOW WELL DID YOU UNDERSTAND THIS SELECTION?

1. What are the factors the report singles out as causes of the riot?

2. What role did rumor play in promoting racial violence?

3. Does this account of the riot reveal a bias against any of the participants, or is its tone fairly balanced?

THE NEW MENACE, 1918

---

*On November 11, 1918, German and Allied representatives signed an armistice ending the war. This cartoon appeared in the **Chicago Tribune** just three days later, suggesting, in the midst of joy over the war's end, that all was not well.*

THE NEW MENACE

Source: *Chicago Tribune*, November, 14, 1918

HOW WELL DID YOU UNDERSTAND THIS SELECTION?

1. What do each of the three figures—militarism, freedom, and bolshevism—represent?

2. Compare the cartoonist's depiction of freedom and bolshevism. What visual cues reveal the cartoonist's attitude toward each?

3. What is the cartoon's message?

SELF TEST

MULTIPLE CHOICE: Circle the correct response. The correct answers are given at the end.

1. The event that ignited World War I was:
    a. the interception and publication of a telegram
    b. a dispute involving overseas colonies in Africa
    c. the assassination of the heir to the Austro-Hungarian throne
    d. a perceived slight to the honor of the Russian Czar

2. When war broke out in Europe:
    a. most Americans had expected it
    b. President Wilson declared American neutrality
    c. most Americans favored America's entering the war
    d. United States trade with the Central Powers increased

3. All of the following statements regarding Woodrow Wilson are true *except*:
    a. he hoped that by staying out of the war he could broker peace
    b. he hoped by entering the war he could shape the terms of the peace
    c. he sought to create a new world order
    d. he believed the self-interest of nations must guide international relations

4. In the effort to mobilize America for war, all of the following occurred *except:*
    a. government and business entered an era of cooperation
    b. government acted to protect the rights of enemy aliens
    c. government adopted a more favorable attitude toward labor
    d. the American economy was placed under government control

160

5. The government's primary means of financing the cost of the war was:
    a. raising taxes
    b. profits earned through trade
    c. borrowing
    d. inflating the currency

6. All of the following statements are true *except*: During World War I,
    a. government price controls prevented inflation
    b. a competitive, free enterprise economy was replaced by a planned economy
    c. America experienced great prosperity
    d. the nation's railroads were nationalized

7. The Committee on Public Information did all of the following *except*:
    a. mobilize public opinion in support of the war effort
    b. intercept and publish the Zimmermann Telegram
    c. whip up a patriotism that some Americans took to extremes
    d. produce films that portrayed Germany in a negative way

8. Which of the following is NOT the case: In America, the war contributed to:
    a. increased tolerance toward "hyphenated" Americans
    b. heightened racial tensions and violence
    c. restrictions on free speech
    d. expanded economic opportunities for minorities

9. In *Schenck v. U.S.,* the Supreme Court established the following principle: It is constitutional for the government:
    a. to nationalize private companies during wartime
    b. to establish a draft to recruit men for the armed service
    c. to set limits to free speech when the national interest is threatened
    d. to engage in collective bargaining during wartime to prevent strikes

10. The U.S. Senate rejected the Treaty of Versailles because:
    a. of a desire to exact harsher terms on the Germans
    b. of the principle of collective security
    c. the Senate wanted greater territorial gains for the U.S. than were negotiated
    d. many Senators regarded it as too isolationist

Answers: 1-c; 2-b; 3-d; 4-b; 5-c; 6-a; 7-b; 8-a; 9-c; 10-b

ESSAYS:

1. America went to war in 1917 with the goal of making the world safe for democracy and preserving liberty. Discuss the effect that going to war would have on American democracy and the civil liberties of the American people.

2. "It was inevitable that America would enter World War I." Do you agree or disagree with this statement? Explain.

3. Discuss the war's impact on black Americans and the effect it would have on race relations.

OPTIONAL ACTIVITIES: (Use your knowledge **and** imagination.)

1.   Imagine you are a black American soldier in France, serving in a segregated unit, and subject to daily occurrences of discrimination both large and small. Now read Woodrow Wilson's War Message to Congress and write a letter to the president detailing the extent to which his lofty ideals and principles have been realized in your own personal reality.

2.   Could a race riot like the one that took place in Chicago in 1919 occur in America today? Why or why not?

3.   Read Ernest Hemingway's *A Farewell to Arms* and Erich Maria Remarque's *All Quiet on the Western Front*. Compare the experiences and attitudes of men fighting on opposite sides during the war.

WEB SITE LISTINGS:

Trenches on the Web
   http://www.worldwar1.com

The Soldier's Experience in World War I
   http://www.people.virginia.edu/~egl2r/wwi.html

The Great War Society
   http://www.mcs.net/~mikei/tgws

The First World War
   http://www.spartacus.schoolnet.co.uk/FWW.htm

The World War I Document Archive
   http://www.lib.byu.edu/~rdh/wwi

Posters from the Food Administration During World War I
   http://www.nara.gov/education/cc/foodww1.html

The Lost Poets of World War I
   http://www.emory.edu/ENGLISH/LostPoets

Great War Primary Documents Archive
   http://www.ukans.edu/~kansite/ww_one

World War I Internet Links
   http://www.fordham.edu/halsall/mod/modsbook38.html

Photos of the Great War
   http://www.ukans.edu/~kansite/ww_one/photos/greatwar.htm

Chapter Eighteen

THE ROARING TWENTIES

The Twenties was a decade marked by sharp contrasts and contradictions. On the surface, good times and prosperity were underpinned by a far less rosy reality. Amidst affluence there was considerable poverty; optimism coexisted with disillusionment, contentment with anxiety. After years of wartime sacrifice, Americans looked forward to returning to the normal rhythms of life and indulging themselves in material comforts. These expectations, however, would not be immediately met by post-war realities. The conversion of the economy back to peacetime production did not go smoothly. Rapid demobilization of millions of servicemen, a drop in demand for farm goods, government's lifting of wartime price controls and ending of its wartime contracts with defense industries—all these developments contributed to high unemployment, runaway inflation, and an economic recession in the decade's initial years. In addition, a wave of more than 3,600 strikes in 1919 spread across America. Subjected to discomforts and uncertainties at a time when they were eager to get on with their lives, millions of Americans had little sympathy for workers seeking higher wages. Following the lead of the Justice Department, most blamed the strikes on "alien" radicals, especially after bombs were sent to prominent businessmen and public officials. The Red Scare set a tone for the Twenties, rekindling the nativism and intolerance that were never far below the surface of American society. Intense patriotic feelings that had been whipped up during the war were now attached to new objects—suspicion, fear, and hatred shifted from the "enemy without" to the "enemy within." As immigration that had slowed to a trickle during the war years resumed, many Americans now supported a movement to restrict immigration, targeting especially Jewish and Catholic "new wave" immigrants from southern and eastern Europe. For many conservative Americans who embraced traditional values, change was threatening, as it eroded and menaced the traditional certainties they embraced.

During the Twenties, change made itself felt in abundant ways and took various shapes. Freudianism, birth control, and "petting" were perceived as threats to conventional Christian morality. Modern science, in the form of biological evolutionary theory, undermined the literal truth of the Bible that anchored religious fundamentalists. Change appeared as the new woman who abandoned traditional roles, appearances, and behaviors, imperiling a male-dominated society that preferred its women to be dependent and subservient to fathers, husbands, and brothers; it surfaced in the guise of a new demeanor on the part of many black Americans, reflected in their unwillingness to simply accept white violence directed against them without retaliating in kind. The reaction of various groups to change stirred numerous social and cultural controversies throughout the decade, revealing a host of fault lines and cleavages within American society. The KKK, immigration restrictionists, prohibitionists, and religious fundamentalists shared a common goal: to save America from what was unAmerican. Each demanded conformity and targeted a perceived offender. The Red Scare, the Sacco and Vanzetti case, Immigration Acts, revived KKK activity, the Scopes Trial and religious fundamentalism, Prohibition, and anti-black riots alike represented efforts to remove, exclude, or contain what was alien, whether in the form of individuals or ideas.

The social and cultural controversies that marked the Twenties unfolded in a period of general prosperity. Many of the changes that provoked anxiety were the byproduct of a booming economy. Prosperity both fostered change and accelerated its pace. Tens of millions of Americans acquired automobiles that promoted freedom and mobility and radios that carried newer, more modern ideas and values associated with the city into small town, rural America. As the work day and work week shortened and leisure time activities expanded, Americans regularly flocked to the movies. Mass communications contributed to the creation of a national culture. Mass entertainments like broadcast radio shows, movies, and organized sports shaped that culture and, in the process, often reinforced existing prejudices.

Central to the prosperity of the Twenties was the increased productivity of the economy. That productivity was fueled by the impact of new technology, like the moving assembly line, by the electrification of American industry, and by corporations' growing reliance upon professional managers. It was fostered, as well, by a new, positive attitude toward big business, given the public's perception that business had done its part to win the war. Additionally, the reemergence of laissez-faire and the pro-business policies of the Republican administrations of Harding, Coolidge and Hoover contributed to a booming economy. The automobile was also central to America's prosperity. Like railroads in the nineteenth century, auto manufacturing was a multiplier industry. Demand for automobiles stimulated the growth of the steel, rubber, glass, and petroleum industries.

A mass production economy required mass consumption and during the Twenties advertising was pivotal in promoting that consumption. While not new, advertising now came of age. Having so successfully sold the war to the American people, advertising dramatically proved its worth to American business. Business utilized it to both create demand for its goods and to shape consumer tastes. Advertising executives focused on selling products by selling the benefits of consuming them. Selling soap meant selling sex appeal; cars were marketed not simply as a mode of transport, but as a status symbol.

Mass consumption in the Twenties was facilitated, as well, by the introduction of a new form of consumer credit, the installment buying plan. Large ticket items like automobiles, refrigerators, vacuum cleaners, and radios could be consumed by virtually anyone who could put a little money down now and pay the rest later. One no longer had to save money to make purchases. The traditional American value of saving was replaced by a new value—spending and consuming. During the 1920s consumption became an end in itself.

In their novels and short stories in the Twenties, some of America's most important writers focused on the shallowness, narrowness, and materialism of American culture and society. Sinclair Lewis and F. Scott Fitzgerald questioned equating happiness with material success and attacked the conformity of Americans. Other members of the "lost generation," like Ernest Hemingway, dealt with their alienation and disillusionment by physically removing themselves from American culture and society, choosing instead to live abroad. The Twenties was a particularly creative period in American literature and arts. New York's Harlem witnessed a flowering of black American culture, as black writers, painters, and musicians drew upon their African heritage and used various media to explore the black American experience. Black racial pride was stirred, too, by Marcus Garvey's focus on black's contributions to world civilizations. His rejection of black integration into a white America was coupled with a call for black separatism and a return to Africa.

The Twenties was a transitional decade between the old and the new, the traditional and the modern. As such, it was marked by a clash of attitudes and values that sparked conflicts and tensions, on the one hand, and considerable creativity, on the other. Cultural and social dynamism together with enormous economic growth contributed to the formation of a modern American society in the 1920s.

IDENTIFICATION: Briefly describe each term.

Religious fundamentalism

Scopes Trial

Clarence Darrow

William Jennings Bryan

Aimee Semple McPherson

Eighteenth Amendment

Al Capone

Ku Klux Klan

Birth of a Nation

William Simmons

Immigration restriction

National Origins Act

Sacco and Vanzetti

Warren Harding

Teapot Dome Scandal

Calvin Coolidge

Washington Naval Conference

Kellogg-Briand Pact

Consumerism

Installment buying

Advertising

Bruce Barton

Automobile culture

Farm crisis

Welfare capitalism

Great Migration

A. Philip Randolph

Marcus Garvey

United Negro Improvement Association

Harlem Renaissance

Langston Hughes

Anti-Semitism

Flapper

Freudianism

Margaret Sanger

Birth control movement

Herbert Hoover

Bull market

Margin buying

Stock market crash

THINK ABOUT:

1.   After women acquired the vote, did their voting patterns differ markedly from those of men? Why or why not?

2.   No decade of the twentieth century was more riddled with conflicts and tensions than the Twenties. What role did its being a "transitional" decade play in generating the conflicts, tensions, and contradictions that marked the era?

3.   To what do you attribute the enormous creativity that marked the arts in the Twenties?

THE RISING TIDE OF COLOR AGAINST WHITE WORLD SUPREMACY,
By Lothrop Stoddard, 1920

A crusade to restrict immigration drew support from the eugenics movement in America. The goal of eugenics was to use knowledge of human genetics to improve the human genetic stock and breed better people. It flourished in America during the first decades of the new century when science was highly valued and efforts were made to bring scientific knowledge to bear on solving social problems. Many educated Americans, including progressives, viewed eugenics as another tool to use to improve society. During the 1920s, eugenics courses were widely taught in American colleges. In reality, eugenics was a pseudo-science devoid of reliable scientific evidence or scientific method. It was rooted in the racism and ethnic prejudice of its proponents.

The eugenics movement gained support at a time when many Americans expressed concern about the negative impact immigrants and their "alien" ideas were having on the nation. Advocates of eugenics adopted a social and political program that included efforts to restrict immigration, promote state sterilization laws, and racial segregation (especially, anti-miscegenation laws). Lothrop Stoddard was a leading member of the eugenics movement in America and a supporter of immigration restriction.

....since the various human stocks differ widely in genetic worth, nothing should be more carefully studied than the relative values of the different strains in a population, and nothing should be more rigidly scrutinized than new strains seeking to add themselves to a population, because such new strains may hold simply incalculable potentialities for good or for evil. The potential reproductive powers of any stock are almost unlimited. Therefore the introduction of even a small group of prolific and adaptable but racially undesirable aliens may result in their subsequent prodigious multiplication, thereby either replacing better native stocks or degrading these by the injection of inferior blood.

The admission of aliens should, indeed, be regarded just as solemnly as the begetting of children, for the racial effect is essentially the same. There is no more damning indictment of our lopsided, materialistic civilization than the way in which, throughout the nineteenth century, immigration was almost universally regarded, not from the racial, but from the material point of view, the immigrant being viewed not as a creator of race-values but as a mere vocal tool for the production of material wealth.

Immigration is thus, from the racial standpoint, a form of procreation, and like the more immediate form of procreation it may be either the greatest blessing or the greatest curse. Human history is largely the story of migrations, making now for good and now for ill. Migration peopled Europe with superior white stocks displacing ape-like aborigines, and settled North America with Nordics instead of nomad redskins. But migration also bastardized the Roman world with Levantine mongrels, drowned the West Indies under a black tide, and is filling our own land with the sweepings of the European east and south.

Migration, like other natural movements, is of itself a blind force. It is man's divine privilege as well as duty, having been vouchsafed knowledge of the laws of life, to direct these blind forces, rejecting the bad and selecting the good for the evolution of higher and nobler destinies....

Probably few persons fully appreciate what magnificent racial treasures America possessed at the beginning of the nineteenth century. The colonial stock was perhaps the finest that nature had evolved since the classic Greeks. It was the very pick of the Nordics of the British Isles and adjacent regions of the European continent—picked at a time when those countries were more Nordic than now, since the industrial revolution had not yet begun and the consequent resurgence of the Mediterranean and Alpine elements had not taken place.

The immigrants of colonial times were largely exiles for conscience's sake, while the very process of migration was so difficult and hazardous that only persons of courage, initiative, and strong will-power would voluntarily face the long voyage overseas to a life of struggle in an untamed wilderness haunted by ferocious savages.

Thus the entire process of colonial settlement was one continuous, drastic cycle of eugenic selection. Only the racially fit ordinarily came, while the few unfit who did come were mostly weeded out by the exacting requirements of early American life.

The eugenic results were magnificent. As Madison Grant well says: "Nature had vouchsafed to the Americans of a century ago the greatest opportunity in recorded history to produce in the isolation of a continent a powerful and racially homogeneous people, and had provided for the experiment a pure race of one of the most gifted and vigorous stocks on earth, a stock free from the diseases, physical and moral, which have again and again sapped the vigor of the older lands. Our grandfathers threw away this opportunity in the blissful ignorance of national childhood and inexperience." (Madison Grant, *The Passing of the Great Race*....) The number of great names which America produced at the beginning of its national life shows the high level of ability possessed by this relatively small people (only about 3,000,000 whites in 1790). With our hundred-odd millions we have no such output of genius to-day.

The opening decades of the nineteenth century seemed to portend for America the most glorious of futures. For nearly seventy years after the Revolution, immigration was small, and during that long period of ethnic isolation the colonial stock, unperturbed by alien influences, adjusted its cultural differences and began to display the traits of a genuine new type, harmonious in basic homogeneity and incalculably rich in racial promise. The general level of ability continued high and the output of talent remained extraordinarily large. Perhaps the best feature of the nascent "native American" race was its strong idealism....It was a wonderful time and it was only the dawn!

But the full day of that wondrous dawning never came. In the late forties of the nineteenth century the first waves of the modern immigrant tide began breaking on our shores, and the tide swelled to a veritable deluge which never slackened till temporarily restrained by the late war. This immigration, to be sure, first came mainly from northern Europe, was thus largely composed of kindred stocks, and contributed many valuable elements. Only during the last thirty years have we been deluged by the truly alien hordes of the European east and south. But, even at its best, the immigrant tide could not measure up to the colonial stock which it displaced, not reinforced, while latterly it became a menace to the very existence of our race, ideals, and institutions. All our slowly acquired balance—physical, mental, and spiritual—has been upset, and we to-day flounder in a veritable Serbonian bog, painfully trying to regain the solid ground on which our grandsires confidently stood....

The perturbing influence of recent immigration must vex American life for many decades. Even if laws are passed tomorrow so drastic as to shut out permanently the influx of undesirable elements, it will yet take several generations before the combined action of assimilation and elimination shall have restabilized our population and evolved a new type-norm approaching in fixity that which was on the point of crystallizing three-quarters of a century ago....

Thus, under even the most favorable circumstances, we are in for generations of racial readjustment—an immense travail, essentially needless, since the final product will probably not measure up to the colonial standard. We will probably never (unless we adopt positive eugenic measures) be the race we might have been if America had been reserved for the descendants of the picked Nordics of colonial times.

But that is no reason for folding our hands in despairing inaction. On the contrary, we should be up and doing, for though some of our race-heritage has been lost, more yet remains. We can still be a very great people—if we will it so. Heaven be praised, the colonial stock was immensely prolific before the alien tide wrought its sterilizing havoc. Even to-day nearly one-half of our population is of the old blood, while many millions of the immigrant stock are sound in quality and assimilable in kind. Only the immigrant tide must at all costs be stopped and America given a chance to stabilize her ethnic being. It is the old story of the sibylline books. Some, to be sure, are ashes of the dead past; all the more should we conserve the precious volumes which remain.

One fact should be clearly understood: If America is not true to her own race-soul, she will inevitably lose it, and the brightest star that has appeared since Hellas will fall like a meteor from the human sky, its brilliant radiance fading into the night. "We Americans," says Madison Grant, "must realize that the altruistic ideals which have controlled our social development during the past century and the maudlin sentimentalism that has made America 'an asylum for the oppressed,' are sweeping the nation toward a racial abyss. If the melting-pot is allowed to boil without control and we continue to follow our national motto and deliberately blind ourselves to 'all distinctions of race, creed, or color,' the type of native American of colonial descent will become as extinct as the Athenian of the age of Pericles and the Viking of the days of Rollo."....

And let us not lay any sacrificial unction to our souls. If we cheat our country and the world of the splendid promise of American life, we shall have no one to blame but ourselves, and we shall deserve, not pity, but contempt.....

Source: Lothrop Stoddard, *The Rising Tide of Color Against White World Supremacy*, Scribner, New York, 1920

HOW WELL DID YOU UNDERSTAND THIS SELECTION?

1. By what yardstick does Stoddard assess the course of both American and world history?

2. What, according to Stoddard, have been the racial effects of immigration upon America?

3. Stoddard employs the terms "genetic worth," "race-values," "race heritage," "race soul," "racial promise," "racially fit," and "racial abyss." Do you believe most Americans reading Stoddard at the time would have questioned his use of this terminology? Why?

4. Does Stoddard develop an effective argument for restricting immigration to America?

In a 1924 speech before the Senate, Senator David Walsh of Massachusetts (Dem.) made an impassioned plea against passage of a proposed immigration act [National Origins Act] that would discriminate against southern and eastern European immigrants. During five terms in the United States Senate beginning in 1918, Walsh also spoke out against the segregation of black Americans and in favor of labor unions, supporting the rights of American workers.

Mr. President, the proposal to make the census of 1890, instead of that of 1910, the basis for the quota hereafter to be admitted, as advocated by many, is objectionable on many grounds.

A few facts regarding the population census of 1890, as compared with the census of 1910, give practical assurance that a great American principle would be violated by the change proposed.

Two per cent of the alien inhabitants in 1890 would total about 160,000, whereas the same percentage in 1910 would number about 238,000. This represents a material reduction in the number of aliens to be admitted and indicates a tendency to further restrict the number of admissible immigrants.

The most important aspect of this question, however, is that such a change would inject into the law a very apparent discrimination against immigrants of certain nationalities. The census of 1890 shows that a large majority of our alien inhabitants were then natives of northern and western Europe, while the census of 1910 shows more nearly equal proportions from southern and eastern Europe. In 1890 about 87 per cent of our alien population were people from northern and western Europe, as compared with 56 per cent in 1910. Who can say that it would be fair to abandon a basis of calculation that is very close to an equal division between the races of northern and western Europe and the races of southern and eastern Europe and adopt a basis that will give the peoples of northern and western Europe 87 per cent of our immigration during the coming years?

Since we have said to the people of all nations, "We are going to admit only a certain percentage of your future immigrants," can we go further and add that to certain nationalities we shall extend preference? That is what the suggestion of the 1890 census basis means. It simply amounts to reducing and practically eliminating all emigration from southern and eastern Europe.

Whatever may be the surface reason for the change in date, it must be insisted that the true reason is social discrimination. An attempt is being made to slip by this proposal, which is aimed clearly and mercilessly at the Slav, the Latin, and the Jew, under the harmless guise of a change in the date of the census....

Mr. President, what is the real driving force behind the movement of basing the quota on the census of 1890? The peoples of the world will attribute it to our belief that the "Nordic" is a superior race. The world will assume that our Government considers the Italians, Greeks, Jews, Poles, and the Slavs inferior to the Nordics, congenitally as well as culturally. It is a dangerous assumption. Millions of people here in America will resent this slur upon their racial character....

What are the nationalities whose coming to America is chiefly curtailed by this arbitrary resort to the 1890 census? The Greeks, to whom civilization owes so much in the fields of literature, science, art, and government. The Italians, who from the day of early Roman history have contributed immensely to civilization along the lines of government, literature, art, music, and navigation, including the gift of the discoverer of America. The liberty-loving Poles, whose sacrifices and struggles for freedom have arrested the admiration of mankind and who saved all Europe from the Turks at Vienna scarcely two centuries ago, and who were once in the van of culture. The Jews, who contributed to the world literature, religion, standards of righteous conduct that can not be overvalued....

Have we learned nothing from the earlier generations' mistaken notions about the Dutch, the French, the Irish, the Germans, and the Scandinavians, now an essential element in our assumed racial superiority? They were condemned and criticized by the earlier settlers, just as we are now undertaking to condemn the races from southern Europe. Have we forgotten that at the time of the Revolution one-fifth of the population of America could not speak the English language? Have we forgotten that more than one-half of the population of America at the time of the Revolution was not Anglo-Saxon?

Factors of all sorts enter into play in determining race values, and often an alien most desirable from one point of view is least so from another. But is not the whole concept in variance with fundamental American principles and policies?....

Attempt to grade our aliens! Which race is to be rated "100 per cent American"? It is a shortsighted view which measures the desirability or undesirability of any group of aliens only by the rapidity or tardiness with which they forget their past spiritual connections and allow themselves to be rapidly molded into an undeterminate type which is vaguely termed a "100 percent American." . . .

"Keep America American." Yes; but do not keep out of America through discriminatory immigration laws any lover of liberty, whatever his accident of birth may be, if he is willing to live in America, accept its ideals, and die, if necessary, for the preservation of American institutions....

Source: Congressional Record, 68th Cong., Ist Sess., pp. 6355ff.

HOW WELL DID YOU UNDERSTAND THIS SELECTION?

1. According to Walsh, why does the proposed law use the 1890 rather than the 1910 census?

2. What arguments does Walsh present against immigration restriction?

3. What is Walsh's response to the claim of Stoddard and other immigration restrictionists that immigrants are of inferior racial stock?

4. What evidence does Walsh present to counter Stoddard's assertion that until the nineteenth century America was racially homogeneous?

Unlike the original Ku Klux Klan of the Reconstruction era, the KKK that was reborn in 1915 and that thrived in the 1920s targeted a diverse set of groups whose ethnicity, religion, and ideas it judged unAmerican. To the traditional anti-black racism of the former KKK was now added nativism, anti-Semitism, and anti-Catholicism. During the Twenties, the membership of the Klan grew to between two to four million, including prominent politicians. No longer confined like the Klan of old to the south, the KKK drew widespread support from discontented workers in southern, midwestern, and western cities where "native American" whites found themselves competing for jobs with black and immigrant Americans. Championing 100 percent Americanism, the Klan assumed the role of the nation's moral protector. Ironically, its downfall would commence with the arrest of a high Klan official for sexual crimes. On the occasion of the Klan's tenth anniversary, the KKK's Imperial Wizard and Emperor, Hiram Evans, set forth its objectives and achievements.

The greatest achievement so far has been to formulate, focus, and gain recognition for an idea—the idea of preserving and developing America first and chiefly for the benefit of the children of the pioneers who made America....we have won the leadership in the movement for Americanism. Except for a few lonesome voices, almost drowned by the claim of the alien and the alien-minded "Liberal," the Klan alone faces the invader....

Other achievements of these ten years have been the education of the millions of our own membership in citizenship, the suppression of much lawlessness and increase of good government wherever we have become strong, the restriction of immigration, and the defeat of the Catholic attempt to seize the Democratic party. All these we have helped; and all are important.

The outstanding proof of both our influence and our service, however, has been in creating, outside our ranks as well as in them, not merely the growing concentration on the problem of Americanism, but also a growing sentiment against radicalism, cosmopolitanism, and alienism of all kinds....We have enlisted our racial instincts for the work of preserving and developing our American traditions and customs....

The Klan....has now come to speak for the great mass of Americans of the old pioneer stock. We believe that it does fairly and faithfully represent them, and our proof lies in their support. To understand the Klan, then, it is necessary to understand the character and present mind of the mass of old-stock Americans. The mass, it must be remembered, as distinguished from the intellectually mongrelized "Liberals."

These are....a blend of various peoples of the so-called Nordic race, the race which, with all its faults, has given the world almost the whole of modern civilization. The Klan does not try to represent any people but these.

There is no need to recount the virtues of the American pioneers; but it is too often forgotten that in the pioneer period a selective process of intense rigor went on. From the first only hardy, adventurous and strong men and women dared the pioneer dangers; from among these all but the best died swiftly, so that the new Nordic blend which became the American race was bred up to a point probably the highest in history. This remarkable race character, along with the new-won continent and the new-created nation, made the inheritance of the old-stock Americans the richest ever given to a generation of men.

In spite of it, however, these Nordic Americans for the last generation have found themselves increasingly uncomfortable, and finally deeply distressed. There appeared first confusion in thought and opinion, a groping and hesitancy about national affairs and private life alike, in sharp contrast to the clear, straightforward purposes of our earlier years. There was futility in religion, too, which was in many ways even more distressing. Presently we began to find that we were dealing with strange ideas; policies that always sounded well, but somehow always made us still more uncomfortable.

Finally came the moral breakdown that has been going on for two decades. One by one all our traditional moral standards went by the boards, or were so disregarded that they ceased to be binding. The sacredness of our Sabbath, of our homes, of chastity, and finally even of our right to teach our own children in our own schools fundamental facts and truths were torn away from us. Those who maintained the old standards did so only in the face of constant ridicule.

Along with this went economic distress. The assurance for the future of our children dwindled. We found our great cities and the control of much of our industry and commerce taken over by strangers, who stacked the cards of success and prosperity against us. Shortly they came to dominate our government....Every kind of inhabitant except the Americans gathered in groups which operated as units in politics, under orders of corrupt, self-seeking and un-American leaders, who both by purchase and threat enforced their demands on politicians. Thus it came about that the interests of Americans were always the last to be considered by either national or city governments, and that the native Americans were constantly discriminated against, in business, in legislation and in administrative government.

So the Nordic American today is a stranger in large parts of the land his fathers gave him....

All this has been true for you years, but it was the World War that gave us our first hint of the real cause of our troubles, and began to crystallize our ideas. The war revealed that millions whom we had allowed to share our heritage and prosperity, and whom we had assumed had become part of us, were in fact not wholly so. They had other loyalties....the excitement caused by the discovery of disloyalty subsided rapidly after the war ended. But it was not forgotten by the Nordic Americans. They had been awakened and alarmed; they began to suspect that the hyphenism which had been shown was only a part of what existed; their quiet was not that of renewed sleep, but of strong men waiting very watchfully....

They decided that even the crossing of salt-water did not dim a single spot on a leopard; that an alien usually remains an alien no matter what is done to him, what veneer of education he gets, what oaths he takes, nor what public attitudes he adopts. They decided that the melting pot was a ghastly failure, and remembered that the very name was coined by a member of one of the races—the Jews—that most determinedly refuses to melt....They decided that in character, instincts, thought, and purposes—in his whole soul—an alien remains fixedly alien to American and all it means......

They learned, though more slowly, that alien ideas are just as dangerous to us as the alien themselves, no matter how plausible such ideas may sound....

One more point about the present attitudes of the old stock American: he has revived and increased his distrust of the Roman Catholic Church....The fact is, of course, that our quarrel with the Catholics is not religious but political....

The real indictment against the Roman Church is that it is fundamentally and irredeemably, in its leadership, in politics, in thought, and largely in membership, actually and actively alien, un-American and usually anti-American. The old stock Americans, with the exception of the few such of Catholic faith—who are in a class by themselves, standing tragically torn between their faith and their racial and national patriotism—see in the Roman Church today the chief leader of alienism, and the most dangerous alien power with a foothold inside our boundaries....

Thus the Klan goes back to the American racial instincts, and to the common sense which is their first product, as the basis of its beliefs and methods. The fundamentals of our thought are convictions, not mere opinions. We are pleased that modern research is finding scientific backing for these convictions....

There are three of these great racial instincts, vital elements in both the historic and the present attempts to build an America which shall fulfill the aspirations and justify the heroism of the men who made the nation. These are the instincts of loyalty to the white race, to the traditions of America, and to the spirit of Protestantism, which has been an essential part of Americanism ever since the days of Roanoke and Plymouth Rock. They are condensed into the Klan slogan: "Native, white, Protestant supremacy."......

The Negro the Klan considers a special duty and the problem of the white American. He is among us through no wish of his; we owe it to him and to ourselves to give him full protection and opportunity. But his limitations are evident; we will not permit him to gain sufficient power to control our civilization. Neither will we delude him with promises of social equality which we know can never be realized. The Klan looks forward to the day when the Negro problem will have been solved on some much saner basis than miscegenation, and when every State will enforce laws making any sex relations between a white and a colored person a crime.....

The Jew is a more complex problem. His abilities are great, he contributes much to any country where he lives. This is particularly true of the Western Jew, those of the stocks we have known so long. Their separation from us is more religious than racial. When freed from persecution these Jews have shown a tendency to disintegrate and amalgamate. We may hope that shortly, in the free atmosphere of America, Jews of this class will cease to be a problem. Quite different are the Eastern Jews of recent immigration, the Jews known as the Askhenasim. It is interesting to note that anthropologists now tell us that these are not true Jews, but only Judaized Mongols—

Chazars. These, unlike the true Hebrew, show a divergence from the American type so great that there seems little hope of their assimilation.

The most menacing and most difficult problem facing America today is this of the permanently unassimilable alien.....This is a problem which must shortly engage the best American minds. We can neither expel, exterminate nor enslave these low-standard aliens, yet their continued presence on the present basis means our doom. Those who know the American character know that if the problem is not soon solved by wisdom, it will be solved by one of those cataclysmic outbursts which have so often disgraced—and saved!—the race. Our attempt to find a sane solution is one of the best justifications of the Klan's existence.....

The Klan today, because of the position it has come to fill, is by far the strongest movement recorded for the defense and fulfillment of Americanism. It has a membership of millions, the support of millions more. If there be any truth in the statement that the voice of the people is the voice of God, we hold a Divine commission....

Originally published in: North American Review, CCXXII (March 1926).
[Online Source]: American Radicalism Digital Collection; Michigan State Univ
www.lib.msu.edu/spc/digital/radicalism/hs2330.k63e.htm

HOW WELL DID YOU UNDERSTAND THIS SELECTION?

1. To what factors does Evans attribute the moral breakdown and economic distress he claims America has experienced?

2. What internal danger to America did World War I reveal?

3. To what "science" is Evans referring when he suggests the Klan's convictions have scientific support?

4. Of the groups that Evans has singled out as alien, which poses the greatest threat to Nordic Americans and "Americanism"? Why?

Under siege during the Progressive era for their excesses and subjected to government regulation, corporations emerged from the war with a new found respect. In partnership with government, business had done its part to win the war. In the eyes of many Americans, business had been transformed from evil incarnate to virtue personified. In 1925, advertising executive Bruce Barton's **The Man Nobody Knows** *became a bestseller. "The man" was Jesus. Every age reinterprets historical figures through the lens of its own concerns and interests. Tellingly, Barton reconceived Jesus as the greatest businessman in the history of the world and the founder of modern business. Why? "He picked up twelve men from the bottom ranks of business and forged them into an organization that conquered the world," wrote Barton. For many Americans, business became the new religion of the Twenties. Barton was not the first to wed business to Christianity. The author Edward Earl Purinton conceived of business not only in this way, but as much more. In Purinton's view, every important life-lesson and virtue could be gleaned from business.*

Among the nations of the earth today America stands for one idea: Business. National opprobrium? National opportunity. For in this fact lies, potentially, the salvation of the world.

Thru business, properly conceived, managed and conducted, the human race is finally to be redeemed. How and why a man works foretells what he will do, think, have, give and be. And real salvation is in doing, thinking, having, giving and being—not in sermonizing and theorizing. I shall base the facts of this article on the personal tours and minute examinations I have recently made of twelve of the world's largest business plants: U.S. Steel Corporation, International Harvester Company, Swift & Company, E. I. du Pont de Nemours & Company, National City Bank, National Cash Register Company, Western Electric Company, Sears, Roebuck & Company, H. J. Heinz Company, Peabody Coal Company, Statler Hotels, Wanamaker Stores.

These organizations are typical, foremost representatives of the commercial group of interests loosely termed "Big Business." A close view of these corporations would reveal to any trained, unprejudiced observer a new conception of modern business activities. Let me draw a few general conclusions regarding the best type of business house and business man.

What is the finest game? Business. The soundest science? Business. The truest art? Business. The fullest education? Business. The fairest opportunity? Business. The cleanest philanthropy? Business. The sanest religion? Business.

You may not agree. That is because you judge business by the crude, mean, stupid, false imitation of business that happens to be located near you.

The finest game is business. The rewards are for everybody, and all can win. There are no favorites-Providence always crowns the career of the man who is worthy. And in this game there is no "luck"—you have the fun of taking chances but the sobriety of guaranteeing certainties. The speed and size of your winnings are for you alone to determine; you needn't wait for the other fellow in the game—it is always your move. And your slogan is not "Down the Other Fellow!" but rather "Beat Your Own Record!" or "Do It Better Today!" or "Make Every job a Masterpiece!" The great sportsmen of the world are the great business men.

The soundest science is business. All investigation is reduced to action, and by action proved or disproved. The idealistic motive animates the materialistic method. Hearts as well as minds are open to the truth. Capital is furnished for the researches of "pure science"; yet pure science is not regarded pure until practical. Competent scientists are suitably rewarded—as they are not in the scientific schools.

The truest art is business. The art is so fine, so exquisite, that you do not think of it as art. Language, color, form, line, music, drama, discovery, adventure—all the components of art must be used in business to make it of superior character.

The fullest education is business. A proper blend of study, work and life is essential to advancement. The whole man is educated. Human nature itself is the open book that all business men study; and the mastery of a page of this educates you more than the memorizing of a dusty tome from a library shelf. In the school of business, moreover, you teach yourself and learn most from your own mistakes. What you learn here you live out, the only real test.

The fairest opportunity is business. You can find more, better, quicker chances to get ahead in a large business house than anywhere else on earth. The biographies of champion business men show how they climbed, and how you can climb. Recognition of better work, of keener and quicker thought, of deeper and finer feeling, is gladly offered by the men higher up, with early promotion the rule for the man who justifies it. There is, and can be, no such thing as buried talent in a modern business organization.

The cleanest philanthropy is business. By "clean" philanthropy I mean that devoid of graft, inefficiency and professionalism, also of condolence, hysterics and paternalism. Nearly everything that goes by the name of Charity was born a triplet, the other two members of the trio being Frailty and Cruelty. Not so in the welfare departments of leading corporations. Savings and loan funds; pension and insurance provisions; health precautions, instructions and safeguards; medical attention and hospital care; libraries, lectures and classes; musical, athletic and social features of all kinds; recreational facilities and financial opportunities—these types of "charitable institutions" for employees add to the worker's self-respect, self-knowledge and self-improvement, by making him an active partner in the welfare program, a producer of benefits for his employer and associates quite as much as a recipient of bounty from the company. I wish every "charity" organization would send its officials to school to the heads of the welfare departments of the big corporations; the charity would mostly be transformed into capability, and the minimum of irreducible charity left would not be called by that name.

The sanest religion is business. Any relationship that forces a man to follow the Golden Rule rightfully belongs amid the ceremonials of the church. A great business enterprise includes and presupposes this relationship. I have seen more Christianity to the square inch as a regular part of the office equipment of famous corporation presidents than may ordinarily be found on Sunday in a verbalized but not vitalized church congregation. A man is not wholly religious until he is better on weekdays than he is on Sunday. The only ripened fruits of creeds are deeds. You can fool your preacher with a sickly sprout or a wormy semblance of character, but you can't your employer. I would make every business house a consultation bureau for the guidance of the church whose members were employees of the house.

I am aware that some of the preceding statements will be challenged by many readers. I should not myself had made them, or believed them, twenty years ago, when I was a pitiful specimen of a callow youth and cocksure professional man combined. A thorough knowledge of business has implanted a deep respect for business and real business men.

The future work of the business man is to teach the teacher, preach to the preacher, admonish the parent, advise the doctor, justify the lawyer, superintend the statesman, fructify the farmer, stabilize the banker, harness the dreamer, and reform the reformer.

Source: Edward Earle Purinton, "Big Ideas from Big Business, *The Independent,* (April 16, 1921)

HOW WELL DID YOU UNDERSTAND THIS SELECTION?

1. What are the great virtues and life-lessons Purinton finds in business?

2. Why does Purinton need to distinguish between business in its pure and crude forms?

3. What reversal of values enables Purinton to claim that business can teach the church rather than the church teach business?

4. Has Purinton's claim that "there...can be...no such thing as buried talent in a modern business organization" been born out by American corporate history in the decades of the twentieth century since the Twenties?

In the 1880s, Listerine was marketed by St. Louis druggist J.W. Lambert as an antiseptic. With sales lagging due to a recession in 1921 and 1922, Lambert's son searched for new product uses to boost declining revenues. A meeting with advertising executives hit upon the idea of promoting Listerine as a cure for bad breath and a company chemist provided the medical terminology "halitosis" as a way of avoiding an objectionable reference. Drawing a connection between "good breath," on the one hand, and social acceptance and success, on the other, company advertisements sold the product by selling its social benefits.

In his discreet way he told her

It had never occurred to her before. But in his discreet, professional way he was able to tell her. And she was sensible enough to be grateful instead of resentful.

In fact, the suggestion he made came to mean a great deal to her.

It brought her greater poise—that feeling of self-assurance that adds to a woman's charm—and, moreover, a new sense of daintiness that she had never been quite so sure of in the past.

.　.　.　.　.　.　.　.

Many people suffer in the same way. Halitosis (the scientific term for unpleasant breath) creeps upon you unawares. Usually you are not able to detect it yourself. And, naturally enough, even your best friends will not tell you.

Fortunately, however, halitosis is usually due to some local condition—often food fermentation in the mouth; something you have eaten; too much smoking. And it may be corrected by the systematic use of Listerine as a mouth wash and gargle.

Dentists know that this well-known antiseptic they have used for half a century, possesses these remarkable properties as a breath deodorant.

Your druggist will supply you. He sells lots of Listerine. It has dozens of other uses as a safe antiseptic. It is particularly valuable, too, at this time of year in combating sore throat. Read the circular that comes with each bottle.—*Lambert Pharmacal Company, Saint Louis, U. S. A.*

For **HALITOSIS** use **LISTERINE**

Source: *The Literary Digest*, November 17, 1923 Used with the permission of Warner-Lambert Company

HOW WELL DID YOU UNDERSTAND THIS SELECTION?

1. What reasons are presented for using Listerine?

2. What visual gender stereotyping is employed?

3. What gender stereotyping is present in the ad's copy?

4. Would this advertisement be effective today? Why or why not?

"PETTING AND THE CAMPUS," Eleanor Rowland Wembridge, 1925

The new woman was typified by her new behaviors as well as her new appearance. Young women emulated their idols on the silver screen and began to curl their hair, wear rouge and lipstick, and even smoke and drink. One behavior that provoked considerable concern in the Twenties was increased sexual permissiveness. An older generation regarded it as the reflection of a growing sexual immorality.

...Last summer I was at a student conference of young women comprised of about eight hundred college girls from the middle western states. The subject of petting was very much on their minds, both as to what attitude they should take toward it with the younger girls (being upperclassmen themselves), and also how much renunciation of this pleasurable pastime was required of them. If I recall correctly, two entire mornings were devoted to discussing the matter, two evenings, and another overflow meeting.

So far as I could judge from their discussion groups, the girls did not advise younger classmen not to pet-they merely advised them to be moderate about it, not lose their heads, not go too far—in fact the same line of conduct which is advised for moderate drinking. Learn temperance in petting, not abstinence. . . .

Just what does petting consist in? What ages take it most seriously? Is it a factor in every party? Do "nice" girls do it, as well as those who are not so "nice"? Are they "stringing" their elders, by exaggerating the prevalence of petting, or is there more of it than they admit? . . .

One fact is evident, that whether or not they pet, they hesitate to have anyone believe that they do not. It is distinctly the mores of the time to be considered as ardently sought after, and as not too priggish to respond. As one girl said—"I don't particularly care to be kissed by some of the fellows I know, but I'd let them do it any time rather than think I wouldn't dare. As a matter of fact, there are lots of fellows I don't kiss. It's the very young kids that never miss a chance."

That petting should lead to actual illicit relations between the petters was not advised nor countenanced among the girls with whom I discussed it. They drew the line quite sharply. That it often did so lead, they admitted, but they were not ready to allow that there were any more of such affairs than there had always been. School and college scandals, with their sudden departures and hasty marriages, have always existed to some extent, and they still do. But only accurate statistics, hard to arrive at, can prove whether or not the sex carelessness of the present day extends to an increase of sex immorality, or whether since so many more people go to college, there is an actual decrease in the amount of it, in proportion to the number of students. The girls seemed to feel that those who went too far were more fools than knaves, and that in most cases they married. They thought that hasty and secret marriages, of which most of them could report several, were foolish, but after all about as likely to turn out well as any others. Their attitude toward such contingencies was disapproval, but it was expressed with a slightly amused shrug, a shrug which one can imagine might have sat well on the shoulders of Voltaire. In fact the writer was torn, in her efforts to sum up their attitude, between classifying them as eighteenth century realists and as Greek nymphs existing before the dawn of history!

I sat with one pleasant college Amazon, a total stranger, beside a fountain in the park, while she asked if I saw any harm in her kissing a young man whom she liked, but whom she did not want to marry. "It's terribly exciting. We get such a thrill. I think it is natural to want nice men to kiss you, so why not do what is natural?" There was no embarrassment in her manner. Her eyes and her conscience were equally untroubled. I felt as if a girl from the Parthenon frieze had stepped down to ask if she might not sport in the glade with a handsome faun. Why not indeed? Only an equally direct forcing of twentieth century science on primitive simplicity could bring us even to the same level in our conversation, and at that, the stigma of impropriety seemed to fall on me, rather than on her. It was hard to tell whether her infantilism were real, or half-consciously assumed in order to have a child's license and excuse to do as she pleased. I am inclined to think that both with her and with many others, it is assumed. One girl said, "When I have had a few nights without dates I nearly go crazy. I tell my mother she must expect me to go out on a fearful necking party." In different parts of the country, petting and necking have opposite meanings. One locality calls necking (I quote their definition) "petting only from the neck up." Petting involves anything else you please. Another section reverses the distinction, and the girl in question was from the latter area. In what manner she announces to her mother her plans to neck, and in what manner her mother accepts the announcement, I cannot be sure.

But I imagine that the assumed childish attitude of the daughter is reflected by her mother, who longs to have her daughter popular, and get her full share of masculine attention. And if the daughter takes for granted that what her mother does not know will not hurt her, so does her mother's habit of blind and deaf supervision indicate that she too does not want to know any more than she has to. The college student is no longer preeminently from a selected class. One has only to look at the names and family status in the college registers to see that. If petting is felt to be poor taste in some families, there are many more families of poor taste than there used to be, whose children go to college. Their daughters are pretty and their sons have money to spend, and they seem prodigies of learning and accomplishment, especially to their unlettered mothers, who glow with pride over their popularity. The pleasant side of the picture is that anybody's daughter may go to college and pass on her own merits. The less agreeable side is that more refined, but timid and less numerous stocks feel obliged to model their social behavior on the crude amorousness and doubtful pleasantries which prevail at peasant parties. If anyone charges the daughters with being vulgar, the chances are that the mothers, though more shy, are essentially just as vulgar. The mothers have no accomplishments in which the daughters cannot surpass them, or no alternate social grace or cultivated recreation to suggest, if petting is denied them. Indeed the daughters are really at war with their mothers in point of view, I do not believe. On the contrary, thousands of mothers live all their emotional life in the gaiety of their daughters—having nothing else to live it in, and they suffer quite as deeply as their daughters if maternal strictness threatens to make wallflowers of them. Do not listen to what their mothers *say*, but *watch* them, if you want to know how they feel about their daughter's petting! Their protests are about as genuine, as the daughter's, "Aren't you terrible?" when a young man starts to pet.

The sex manners of the large majority of uncultivated and uncritical people have become the manners for all, because they have prospered, they are getting educated, and there are so many of them. They are not squeamish, and they have never been. But their children can set a social standard as the parents could not. The prudent lawyer's child has no idea of letting the gay daughter of the broad-joking workman get the dates away from her. If petting is the weapon Miss Workman uses, then petting it must be, and in nine cases out of ten, not only Mrs. Workman, but also Mrs. Lawyer agree not to see too much. At heart both women are alike. Neither one can bear to see her daughter take a back seat in the struggle for popularity, and neither woman has any other ambition for her daughter but a successful husband. If by any chance, petting led *away* from popularity and possible husbands instead of to them, the mothers would be whole-heartedly against it, and if they were—petting, as a recognized recreation, would stop.

Source: *Survey*, LIV, (July 1, 1925)

HOW WELL DID YOU UNDERSTAND THIS SELECTION?

1. What does Wembridge's attitude toward the behavior of college girls in the Twenties reveal about the response of the older generation to what they perceived as changing sexual morality?

2. To what factors does she attribute their "sex carelessness"?

3. In Wembridge's view, what role does class play in college girls' behavior?

4. What is the author's assessment of the parenting of these girls?

5. Ironically, what was the conservative objective of the increased sexuality of college girls?

6. In the Twenties, sexuality was a more openly discussed topic than in the past. What role do you think this may have played in giving rise to the perception that sexual immorality was on the rise?

DEBATE ON BIRTH CONTROL, Margaret Sanger and Winter Russell, c. 1921

Margaret Sanger led a crusade to promote birth control for women. As a visiting nurse in the poor neighborhoods of New York's Lower East Side, she had direct experience with the problems women and families faced because birth control was unavailable. Sanger challenged the 1873 Comstock Law and state statutes that made it a crime to distribute information on contraception. In 1914 she was indicted for violating obscenity laws by making information available on birth control. In 1916 she opened America's first birth control clinic in Brooklyn, N.Y. where women were provided with information on the female reproductive system along with instructions on the use of contraceptives. The clinic was raided and Sanger was arrested. In 1921 Sanger formed the American Birth Control League (a forerunner of Planned Parenthood Federation) to promote education, reform, and research on birth control.

....By birth control, I mean a voluntary, conscious control of the birth rate by means that prevent conception—scientific means that prevent conception. I don't mean birth control by abstinence or by continence or anything except the thing that agrees with most of us, and as we will develop later on, most of us are glad that there are means of science at the present time that are not injurious, not harmful, and all conception can be avoided.

Now let us look upon life as it really is, and we see society today is divided distinctly into two groups: those who use the means of birth control and those who do not.

On the one side we find those who do use means in controlling birth. What have they? They are the people who bring to birth few children. They are the people who have all the happiness, who have the wealth and the leisure for culture and mental and spiritual development. They are people who rear their children to manhood and womanhood and who fill the universities and the colleges with their progeny. Nature has seemed to be very kind to that group of people....

On the other hand we have the group who have large families and have for generations perpetuated large families, and I know from my work among them that the great percentage of these people that are brought into the world in poverty and misery have been unwanted. I know that most of these women are just as desirous to have means to control birth as the women of wealth. I know she tries desperately to obtain the information, not for selfish purposes, but for her own benefit and for that of her children. In this group, what do we have? We have poverty, misery, disease, overcrowding, congestion, child labor, infant mortality, maternal mortality, all the evils which today are grouped in the crowd where there are large families of unwanted and undesired children.

Take the first one and let us see how these mothers feel. I claim that a woman, whether she is rich or poor, has a right to be a mother or not when she feels herself fit to be so. She has just as much right not to be a mother as she has to be a mother. It is just as right and as moral for people to talk of small families and to demand them as to want large families. It is just as moral.

If we let, as we are supposed to do, Nature take her course, we know that any woman from the age of puberty until the age of the period of menopause could have anywhere from 15 to 20 children in her lifetime, and it will only take one relationship between man and woman to give her one a year, to give her that large family. Let us not forget that.

Are we today, as women who wish to develop, who wish to advance in life, are we willing to spend all of our time through those years of development in bringing forth children that the world does not appreciate? Certainly, anyone who looks into that will find that there is very little place in the world for children. And besides, if a woman does spend all her time in child-bearing, do you know that, even with healthy women, one out of ten who have children as often as Nature sends them, dies from child bearing? One out of every ten women who lets Nature take her course and has from 12 to 16 children dies from child bearing. Furthermore, there are many cases where it is absolutely indispensable for a woman's health, for her life, in fact, to have means to control birth. There are cases....of syphilis, cases of tuberculosis; do you realize that out of every seven women who have tuberculosis today four of them die, not from tuberculosis, my friends, but from pregnancy. They die because they have not that knowledge of birth control, because physicians and all the others who should be disseminating information and safeguarding these women's lives are not giving them the fundamental things to cure their disease, but allowing them to become pregnant. They keep them in ignorance of this particular knowledge that should assist them in recovering their health. Not only tuberculosis, but there are other diseases that are inimical to woman's health and happiness. Heart disease is another thing that pregnancy absolutely stimulates and it means a woman's death....

The only weapon that women have, and the most uncivilized weapon that they must use, if they will not submit to having children every year and a half, is abortion. We know how detrimental abortion is to the physical side as well as to the psychic side of woman's life. Yet there are in this nation, because of these generalities and opinions that are here before us, and that are stopping the tide of progress, more than one million women who have abortions performed on them each year.

What does this mean? It is a very bad sign when women indulge in it, and it means they are absolutely determined that they cannot continue bringing children into the world that they cannot clothe, feed, and shelter. It is a woman's instinct, and she knows herself when she should and should not give birth to children, and it is much more natural to trust this instinct and to let her be the judge than it is to let her judge herself by some unknown God. I claim it is a woman's duty and right to have for herself the power to say when she shall and shall not have children.

We know that the death rate, maternal death rate, has not been falling in the United States of America, although the death rate from diseases has been falling. That shows woman is given little consideration in scientific and medical lines. But then woman will never get her own freedom until she fights for it, and she has to fight hard to hold and keep it. We know too that when the children that come to these mothers against their will and against their desires, are born into the world, we have the appalling number of 300,000 if you please, and it is safe to say, as anyone knows who has gone among these mothers and these children—it is safe to say that the great percentage of these children that are born have been unwanted. The mother knows that the child should not come to birth, when the five or six or seven that she has have not enough to eat. That takes common sense and every working woman has that common sense.

We have these 300,000 babies, this oppression of little coffins, and we shake our heads sadly and say something must be done to reduce the number; but nevertheless we go right on allowing 600,000 parents to remain in ignorance of how to prevent 300,000 more babies coming to birth the next year only to die from poverty and sickness.

We speak of the rights of the unborn. I say that it is time to speak of those who are already born. I also say and know that the infant death rate is affected tremendously by those who arrive last. The first child that comes—the first or second or third child which arrives in a family, has a far better chance than those that arrive later.

We know that out of a thousand children born 200 of them die when they are either the second or third child. When the seventh arrives there are 300 that die out of that thousand, and by the time that the twelfth child arrives, 600 of this thousand pass away, and so we can see that the man or woman who brings to birth two or three children has a far better chance of bringing them to maturity than if they continued to have nine or ten or twelve children.

Those are facts. They are not generalities or opinions. The United States Government stands behind these facts....

Haldeman-Julius, Girard, Kansas, c. 1921
Source: electronic text, in Radicalism Collection, Birth Control Movement, www.msu.edu/spc/digital/radicalism/hq766.s281921.htm

HOW WELL DID YOU UNDERSTAND THIS SELECTION?

1. What reasons does Sanger present for supporting birth control?

2. What individual and social problems does Sanger link to an absence of birth control?

3. How does Sanger's view of a woman's rights conflict with the more traditional and widely held view that it was a woman's role and duty to bring children into the world?

4. What conclusion does Sanger draw from the high number of abortions performed each year?

5. According to Sanger, who should have the right to determine when a woman should and should not have children?

*Novelist Sinclair Lewis wrote of the Midwest he was born in and knew. In satirical works like **Main Street** and **Babbitt**, he revealed the complacency and conformity of the Americans who lived there. George Babbitt typifies the shallowness of middle class American culture; he is a man who defines himself through his material possessions. In Babbitt's universe, acquisition becomes an end in itself and external appearances become the measure of a man. Babbitt is the quintessence of form over substance, the book that wants to be judged by its cover. In 1930 Lewis would become the first American to win the Nobel Prize for Literature.*

The Towers of Zenith aspired above the morning mist; austere towers of steel and cement and limestone, sturdy as cliffs and delicate as silver rods. They were neither citadels nor churches, but frankly and beautifully office-buildings.....

In one of the skyscrapers the wires of the Associated Press were closing down....The dawn mist spun away. Cues of men with lunch boxes clumped toward the immensity of new factories, sheets of glass and hollow tile, glittering shops where five thousand men worked beneath one roof, pouring out the honest wares that would be sold up the Euphrates and across the veldt. The whistles rolled out in greeting a chorus cheerful as the April dawn; the song of labor in a city built—it seemed—for giants.

There was nothing of the giant in the aspect of the man who was beginning to awaken on the sleeping-porch of a Dutch Colonial house in that residential district of Zenith known as Floral Heights.

His name was George F. Babbitt. He was forty-six years old now, in April, 1920, and he made nothing in particular, neither butter nor shoes nor poetry, but he was nimble in the calling of selling houses for more than people could afford to pay....

Rumble and bang of the milk-truck.

Babbitt moaned, turned over, struggled back toward his dream....

He escaped from reality till the alarm-clock rang, at seven-twenty.

It was the best of nationally advertised and quantitatively produced alarm-clocks, with all modern attachments, including cathedral chime, intermittent alarm, and a phosphorescent dial. Babbitt was proud of being awakened by such a rich device. Socially it was almost as creditable as buying expensive cord tires. He sulkily admitted no that there was no more escape, but he lay and detested the grind of the real-estate business, and disliked his family, and disliked himself for disliking them.... From the bedroom beside the sleeping-porch, his wife's detestably cherful "Time to get up, Georgie boy," and the itchy sound, the brisk and scratchy sound, of combing hairs out of a stiff brush....

He creaked to his feet....he looked blurrily out at the yard. It delighted him, as always; it was the neat yard of a successful business man of Zenith, that is, it was perfection, and made him also perfect. He regarded the corrugated iron garage. For the three-hundred-and-sixty-fifth time in a year he reflected,

"No class to that tin shack. Have to build me a frame garage. But by golly it's the only thing on the place that isn't up-to-date!" While he stared he thought of a community garage for his acreage development, Glen Oriole. He stopped puffing and jiggling. His arms were akimbo. His petulant, sleep-swollen face was set in harder lines. He suddenly seemed capable, an official, a man to contrive, to direct, to get things done.

On the vigor of his idea he was carried down the hard, clean, unused-looking hall into the bathroom.

Though the house was not large it had, like all houses on Floral Heights, an altogether royal bathroom of porcelain and glazed tile and metal sleek as silver. The towel-rack was a rod of clear glass set in nickel. The tub was long enough for a Prussian Guard, and above the set bowl was a sensational exhibit of tooth-brush holder, shaving-brush holder, soap-dish, sponge-dish, and medicine cabinet, so glittering and so ingenious that they resembled an electrical instrument-board. But the Babbitt whose god was Modern Appliances was not pleased. The air of the bathroom was thick with the smell of a heathen toothpaste....He finished his shaving......When he was done, his round face smooth and steamy and his eyes stinging from soapy water, he reached for a towel. The family towels were wet, he found, as he blindly snatched them......Then George F. Babbitt did a dismaying thing. He wiped his face on the guest-towel! It was a pansy-embroidered trifle which always hung there to indicate that the Babbitts were in the best Floral Heights society. No one had ever used it. No guest had ever dared to. Guests secretively took a corner of the nearest regular towel.....

Myra Babbitt—Mrs. George F. Babbitt—was definitely mature...........She had become so dully habituated to married life that in her full matronliness she was as sexless as an anemic nun. She was a good woman, a kind woman, a diligent woman, but no one, save perhaps Tinka her ten-year-old, was at all interested in her or entirely aware that she was alive...

He was fairly amiable in the conference on the brown suit.

"What do you think, Myra?.......How about it? Shall I wear the brown suit another day?"

"Well, it looks awfully nice on you."

"I know, but gosh, it needs pressing."

"That's so. Perhaps it does."

"It certainly could stand being pressed, all right."

"Yes, perhaps it wouldn't hurt it to be pressed."

"But gee, the coat doesn't need pressing. No sense in having the whole darn suit pressed, when the coat doesn't need it."

That's so."...............

"Well, why don't you put on the dark gray suit to-day, and stop in at the tailor and leave the brown trousers?".......

He was able to get through the other crises of dressing with comparative resoluteness and calm.

His first adornment was the sleeveless dimity B.V.D. undershirt.....His second embellishment was combing and slicking back his hair.....But most wonder-working of all was the donning of his spectacles.

There is character in spectacles—the pretentious tortoise-shell, the meek pince-nez of the school teacher, the twisted silver-framed glasses of the old villager. Babbitt's spectacles had huge, circular, frameless lenses of the very best glass; the ear-pieces were thin bars of gold. In them he was the modern business man; one who gave orders to clerks and drove a car and played occasional golf and was scholarly in regard to Salesmanship. His head suddenly appeared not babyish but weighty, and you noted his heavy, blunt nose, his straight mouth and thick, long upper lip, his chin over-fleshy but strong; with respect you beheld him put on the rest of his uniform as a Solid Citizen...............

A sensational event was changing from the brown suit to the gray the contents of his pockets. He was earnest about these objects. They were of eternal importance, like baseball or the Republican Party. They included a fountain pen and silver pencil (always lacking a supply of new leads) which belonged in the righthand upper vest pocket. Without them he would have felt naked. On his watch-chain were a gold pen-knife, silver cigar-cutter, seven keys (the use of two of which he had forgotten), and incidentally a good watch. Depending from the chain was a large, yellowish elk's-tooth-proclamation of his membership in the Benevolent and Protective Order of Elks. Most significant of all was his loose-leaf pocket note-book, that modern and efficient note-book which contained the addresses of people whom he had forgotten, prudent memoranda of postal money-orders which had reached their destinations months ago, stamps which had lost their mucilage, clippings of verses by T. Cholmondeley Frink and of the newspaper editorials from which Babbitt got his opinions and his polysyllables, notes to be sure and do things which he did not intend to do............

Last, he stuck in his lapel the Boosters' Club button. With the conciseness of great art the button displayed two words: "Boosters-Pep!" It made Babbitt feel loyal and important. It associated him with Good Fellows, with men who were nice and human, and in important business circles. It was his V.C., his Legion of Honor ribbon, his Phi Beta Kappa key......

Before he followed his wife, Babbitt stood at the western-most window of their room. This residential settlement, Floral Heights, was on a rise; and though the center of the city was three miles away—Zenith had between three and four hundred thousand inhabitants now—he could see the top of the Second National Tower, an Indiana limestone building of thirty-five stories.

Its shining walls rose against April sky to a simple cornice like a streak of white fire. Integrity was in the tower, and decision. It bore its strength lightly as a tall soldier. As Babbitt stared, the nervousness was soothed from his face, his slack chin lifted in reverence. All he articulated was "That's one lovely sight!" but he was inspired by the rhythm of the city; his love of it renewed. He beheld the tower as a temple-spire of the religion of business, a faith passionate, exalted, surpassing common men; and as he clumped down to breakfast he whistled the ballad "Oh, by gee, by gosh, by jingo" as though it were a hymn melancholy and noble.

Source: Sinclair Lewis, *Babbitt*, Harcourt Brace: New York, 1922

HOW WELL DID YOU UNDERSTAND THIS SELECTION?

1.   What is the significance of the opening lines of the novel, in which Lewis states: "The Towers of Zenith...were neither citadels nor churches, but frankly and beautifully office-buildings"?

2.   Why are certain nouns capitalized?

3.   What is the narrator's tone?

4.   What is the significance of Babbitt's living in "Floral Heights" within the city of "Zenith"?

5.   How would you characterize Babbitt's values?

Langston Hughes was a central figure in the Harlem Renaissance, a black literary and artistic movement born in Harlem, New York in the Twenties. His poems and essays bear witness to the black American's struggle for identity. In 1926 Hughes wrote a seminal essay, The Negro Artist and the Racial Mountain, *which both defined the daunting problem confronting the Negro artist in white America and proposed a solution. The "mountain" or problem "standing in the way of any true Negro art in America" was "this urge within the race toward whiteness, the desire to pour racial individuality into the mold of American standardization, and to be as little Negro and as much American as possible." Hughes' solution was to urge black artists to be black: "it is the duty of the younger Negro artist...to change through the force of his art that old whispering "I want to be white," hidden in the aspirations of his people, to "Why should I want to be white? I am a Negro—and beautiful!" Rather than fear "the strange unwhiteness of his own features," Hughes proclaimed, an "artist must be free to choose what he does, certainly, but he must also never be afraid to do what he must choose...We younger Negro artists who create now intend to express our individual dark-skinned selves without fear or shame." In his poetry, Hughes would draw upon his own experience, the Negro's African heritage, and upon the rhythms of black music.*

The Negro Speaks Of Rivers

I've known rivers;
I've known rivers ancient as the world and older than the
flow of human blood in human veins.

My soul has grown deep like the rivers.

I bathed in the Euphrates when dawns were young.
I built my hut near the Congo and it lulled me to sleep.
I looked upon the Nile and raised the pyramids above it.
I heard the singing of the Mississippi when Abe Lincoln
went down to New Orleans, and I've seen its muddy
bosom turn all golden in the sunset.

I've known rivers;
Ancient, dusky rivers.

My soul has grown deep like the rivers.

Source: *The Crisis*, June, 1921 (vol. 22), W.E.B. DuBois, ed.

HOW WELL DID YOU UNDERSTAND THIS SELECTION?

1. In linking the Negro to the Euphrates, Congo, Nile, and Mississippi Rivers, what is Hughes claiming about the Negro?

2. What is Hughes suggesting about the Negro in the line "My soul has grown deep like the rivers"?

BLACK SEPARATISM AND THE BACK TO AFRICA MOVEMENT OF MARCUS GARVEY

*Born in Jamaica in 1887, Marcus Garvey came to Harlem in 1916 preaching a message of black racial pride and black nationalism. Rejecting the goal of integration—the objective of the mainstream black leadership of DuBois and the NAACP—Garvey embraced a radical position. He called instead for separation of the races (a goal he ironically shared with the KKK) and sought, through the Universal Negro Improvement Association, to promote the colonization of Africa by black Americans. Garvey's solution to America's race problem lay in championing a Back to Africa movement. To promote this end, he founded a newspaper, **The Negro World**, to carry his message to black Americans. While Marcus Garvey would draw support from working class urban black Americans, his message also drew the attention of white government officials. Garvey was placed under FBI surveillance, convicted of mail fraud, and sent to jail. Deported to Jamaica, he eventually went to live in London where he died in 1940.*

MARCUS GARVEY, Editorial, 1925

Fellow Men of the Negro Race, Greeting:

The time has come for the Negro to forget and cast behind him his hero worship and adoration of other races, and to start out immediately, to create and emulate heroes of his own.

We must canonize our own saints, create our own martyrs, and elevate to positions of fame and honor black men and women who have made their distinct contributions to our racial history. Sojourner Truth is worthy of the place of sainthood alongside of Joan of Arc; Crispus Attucks and George William Gordon are entitled to the halo of martyrdom with no less glory than that of the martyrs of any other race. Toussaint L'Ouverture's brilliancy as a soldier and statesman outshone that of a Cromwell, Napoleon and Washington; hence, he is entitled to the highest place as a hero among men. Africa has produced countless numbers of men and women, in war and in peace, whose lustre and bravery outshine that of any other people. Then why not see good and perfection in ourselves?

We must inspire a literature and promulgate a doctrine of our own without any apologies to the powers that be. The right is ours and God's. Let contrary sentiment and cross opinions go to the winds. Opposition to race independence is the weapon of the enemy to defeat the hopes of an unfortunate people. We are entitled to our own opinions and not obligated to or bound by the opinions of others....

The world today is indebted to us for the benefits of civilization. They stole our arts and sciences from Africa. Then why should we be ashamed of ourselves?....

As the Jew is held together by his religion, the white races by the assumption and the unwritten law of superiority, and the Mongolian by the precious tie of blood, so likewise the African must be united in one grand racial hierarchy. Our union must know no clime, boundary, or nationality. Like the great Church of Rome, Negroes the world over must practice one faith, that of Confidence in themselves, with One God! One Aim! One Destiny! Let no religious scruples, no political machination divide us, but let us hold together under all climes and in every country, making among ourselves a Racial Empire upon which "the sun shall never set."....

Source: Editorial, *Negro World*, June 6, 1925

Marcus Garvey, An Appeal to the Soul of White America: The Solution to the Problem of Competition Between Two Opposite Races: Negro Leader Appeals to the Conscience of White Race to Save His Own, 1923

Surely, the soul of liberal, philanthropic, liberty-loving white America is not dead....

It is to that feeling that I appeal at this time for four hundred million Negroes of the world, and fifteen million of America in particular.

There is no real white man in America, who does not desire a solution of the Negro problem. Each thoughtful citizen has probably his own idea of how the vexed question of the races should be settled. To some the Negro could be gotten rid of by wholesale butchery, by lynching, economic starvation, by a return to slavery and legalized oppression; while others would have the problem solved by seeing the race all herded together and kept somewhere among themselves, but a few—those in whom they have an interest should be allowed to live around as the wards of a mistaken philanthropy; yet, none so generous as to desire to see the Negro elevated to a standard of real progress, and prosperity, welded into a homogeneous whole, creating of themselves a mighty nation with proper systems of government, civilization, and culture, to mark them admissible to the fraternities of nations and races without any disadvantage....

Let white and black stop deceiving themselves. Let the white race stop thinking that all black men are dogs and not be considered as human beings. Let foolish Negro agitators and so-called reformers, encouraged by deceptive and unthinking white associates, stop preaching and advocating the doctrine of "social equality," meaning thereby the social intermingling of both races, intermarriages, and general social co-relationship....

There is but one solution, and that is to provide an outlet for Negro energy, ambition, and passion, away from the attraction of white opportunity and surround the race with opportunities of its own. If this is not done, and if the foundation for same is not laid now, then the consequences will be sorrowful for the weaker race, and be disgraceful to white ideals of justice, and shocking to white civilization.

The Negro must have a country, and a nation of his own....We have found a place, it is Africa and as black men for three centuries have helped white men build America, surely generous and grateful white men and women will help black men build Africa.

And why shouldn't Africa and America travel down the ages as protectors of human rights and guardians of democracy? Why shouldn't black men help white men secure and establish universal peace? We can only have peace when we are just to all mankind; and for that peace, and for the reign of universal love I now appeal to the soul of white America. Let the Negroes have a Government of their own account proving to the world that they are capable of evolving a civilization of their own....

I appeal to the considerate and thoughtful conscience of white America not to condemn the cry of the Universal Negro Improvement Association for a nation in Africa for Negroes, but to give us a chance to explain ourselves to the world. White America is too big and when informed and touched, too liberal to turn down the cry of the awakened Negro for "a place in the sun."

Source: *Philosophy and Opinions of Marcus Garvey*, Amy Jacques-Garvey, ed., The Universal Publishing House, New York, 1923-1925

HOW WELL DID YOU UNDERSTAND THIS SELECTION?

1. What historical experiences does Garvey draw upon to foster racial pride?

2. Compare Garvey's solution to the "Negro problem" to the solution proposed by the American Colonization Society during the 1830s.

3. What reactions do you suppose white Americans of the time might have had to Garvey's message of black racial pride and his Back to Africa movement?

MULTIPLE CHOICE: Circle the correct response. The correct answers are given at the end.

1. During the Twenties, America was characterized by all of the following except:
   a. the development of a national culture
   b. the general prosperity of the American people
   c. the reduced indebtedness of the American people
   d. the increased mobility of the American people

2. In the view of the Republican Administrations of the 1920s, the appropriate relationship between government and business was:
   a. a laissez-faire attitude toward business
   b. government regulation of business
   c. a mutual mistrust and wariness
   d. none of the above

3. The *primary* reason why American business instituted welfare capitalism was:
   a. out of humanitarian concern for the plight of workers
   b. because of a Supreme Court decision that required it
   c. to prevent the formation of labor unions
   d. to increase the productivity of workers

4. Regarding advertising in the Twenties, all of the following are true *except*:
   a. it helped to promote mass consumption
   b. it was an invention of the Twenties
   c. it appeared in both print media and on radio
   d. it created a desire for products that were not necessities

5. American writers who were critics of the lifestyles and values of Americans in the Twenties include all of the following *except*:
   a. Ernest Hemingway
   b. Sinclair Lewis
   c. F. Scott Fitzgerald
   d. Bruce Barton

6. Factors that contributed to a growing sense on the part of many Americans that immorality was increasing include all of the following *except*:
   a. the popularization of Freudian psychology
   b. immigration restriction
   c. new fashions in women's clothing
   d. the automobile

7. The primary target of religious fundamentalists in the Twenties was:
   a. the candidacy of Al Smith for the presidency
   b. the vast number of immigrants flooding America's shores
   c. the theory of biological evolution of Charles Darwin
   d. the theory of Sigmund Freud

8. During the 1920s, the KKK:
    a. exerted only limited political influence
    b. was largely confined to the southern states
    c. abandoned the vigilante tactics of the original KKK
    d. was anti-black, anti-Jewish, and anti-Catholic

9. During the 1920s, immigration quotas:
    a. favored southern and eastern Europeans
    b. were based on national origin
    c. were opposed by labor unions
    d. were raised to increase the labor pool in America

10. The stock market crash did all of the following *except*:
    a. it brought down unstable financial institutions
    b. it exposed an economy riddled with excessive debt
    c. it enabled working class Americans to invest in stocks
    d. it shook public confidence in America's financial institutions

Answers: 1-c; 2-a; 3-c; 4-b; 5-d; 6-b; 7-c; 8-d; 9-b; 10-c

ESSAYS:

1. During the Twenties, advertising would have a profound effect on the values and lifestyles of Americans. Explain, citing specific examples.

2. The decade of the Twenties was marked by contrasts and contradictions. Prosperity coexisted with poverty. Contentment coexisted with anxiety. Old, traditional values coexisted with newer, modern values. Explain, citing specific historical evidence.

3. Discuss the appeal of Marcus Garvey's philosophy for urban black Americans during the Twenties.

4. Discuss the weaknesses in the American economy during the Twenties that contributed to the Great Depression.

OPTIONAL ACTIVITIES: (Use your knowledge **and** imagination.)

1. Compare the social and cultural controversies of the 1920s to those that characterized America in the 1990s. How are they alike? How do they differ?

2. Imagine it is 1923 and you are in your sixties. You reside in a small town in middle America. Write a series of letters to the editor of your local newspaper that address some of your pressing concerns.

3. Read F. Scott's Fitzgerald's *The Great Gatsby* and describe how Fitzgerald uses Jay Gatsby to attack the American success myth that equates success with wealth.

WEB SITE LISTINGS:

Woman Suffrage and the Nineteenth Amendment
http://www.nara.gov/education/teaching/woman/home.html

The Volstead Act and Related Prohibition Documents
http://www.nara.gov/education/cc/prohib.html

The Red Scare
http://newman.baruch.cuny.edu/digital/redscare

Prosperity and Thrift: The Coolidge Era and the Consumer Economy, 1921-1929.
http://memory.loc.gov/ammem/coolhtml/coolhome.html

The 1920s
http://www.louisville.edu/~kprayb01/1920s.html

F. Scott Fitzgerald
http://www.sc.edu/fitzgerald/index.html

Ku Klux Klan
http://www.lib.msu.edu/coll/main/spec_col/radicalism/klan.htm

The Scopes Trial
http://www.law.umkc.edu/faculty/projects/ftrials/scopes/scopes.htm

Harlem Renaissance: New York in the Twenties
http://www.humanitieswest.org/Harlem.html

Marcus Garvey and the Universal Negro Improvement Association
http://www.isop.ucla.edu/mgpp

Chapter Nineteen

THE DEPRESSION

Black Thursday, October 24, 1929 saw the stock market crash. Thousands of investors tried to sell but it was difficult to find buyers. Financiers raised enough money to buy millions of dollars worth of stocks to stem the downturn. For a few days this seemed to work but the bottom dropped out of the market on Black Tuesday, October 29, wiping out $30 billion in stock values and signaling the beginning of the Great Depression. Fundamental weaknesses in the economy of the 1920s produced the crash and the ensuing depression. Farmers, textile workers, and coal miners were depressed even in the prosperous twenties. Wages of workers were far less than needed to consume what the economy produced. The Mellon Tax Plan favored the rich who used their income to finance luxurious living and speculation. American workers became more productive, which created a need for increasing consumption, but greedy business owners refused to increase wages that would have enabled employees to buy more products. When demand for consumer goods fell in 1929, factories laid off workers. The layoffs caused a further decline in consumer purchases, which produced more layoffs. The nation found itself in a vicious cycle of declining consumption and joblessness that seemed to have no end. About one year after the Great Depression began four million Americans (9 percent of the work force) had lost their jobs. Two years later twenty-one million (one quarter of the work force) were unemployed. Perhaps another 25 to 30 percent were under employed, working only one or two days per week. The unemployment and under employment produced hunger and homelessness. Thousands of Americans were evicted from their residences and lived outside in tents and cardboard boxes, which they called Hoover Homes in honor of President Herbert Hoover, blamed by many for causing the Great Depression. Others roamed the streets and rode the rails as Hobos, looking for work. Hunger was widespread. Countless Americans stood in soup lines operated by churches and other charities in cities waiting for food. These lines sometimes stretched several blocks in length. By 1933, over nine thousand banks had failed as a result of the banking crisis that gripped the nation. Panicked depositors tried to withdraw their money before the bank closed its doors. Millions of Americans lost their life savings when the bank they had trusted did not have enough cash to cover deposits.

The Great Depression did more than create unemployment, poverty, hunger, homelessness, and bankruptcy. It deprived Americans of the belief that they were somehow special in the world. People lost faith in the idea of history as progress. No longer did they believe that history inevitably moved forward in an unending line of progress. It also changed American government and its relationship to the larger society. The executive branch was strengthened, and the government began to regulate the economy much more heavily than ever before.

Most of the changes in government came with Franklin Delano Roosevelt's New Deal. Its goals were three fold—relief, reform, and recovery. Numerous government programs, such as the National Bank Holiday and the Works Progress Administration (WPA), were initiated to ease the suffering of Americans. Some, like the Federal Deposit Insurance Corporation, sought to bring fundamental reform to the economy to prevent future depressions while others, like the National Industrial Recovery Act, attempted to restore the economy to it pre-depression status. The New Deal caused much debate within American society about government involvement in shaping social and economic policy and represented the single largest legislative program in American history up to that time. The New Deal did not end the Great Depression, but it forever changed America.

IDENTIFICATION: Briefly describe each item.

Bonus Army

Herbert Hoover

FDIC

New Deal

Franklin D. Roosevelt

Stock Market Crash

Okies

CIO

A. Philip Randolph

Cesar Chavez

RFC

Frances Perkins

Bank Holiday

Brain Trust

The Hundred Days

Homeowners Loan Corporation

TVA

AAA

National Industrial Recovery Act

NRA

FERA

PWA

CWA

CCC

Harry Hopkins

Harold Ickes

Securities and Exchange Commission

Francis Townsend

Charles Coughlin

Huey Long

Share the Wealth Plan

Scottsboro case

Social Security Act

Schecter v. United States

National Labor Relations Act

Emergency Relief Appropriations Act

Alf Landon

Court Packing Plan

National Housing Act

THINK ABOUT:

1. How did the Great Depression change the outlook of Americans about the future? How do views of people who survived the Great Depression compare with views of contemporary Americans?

2. What caused the Great Depression? Could an event similar to the Great Depression happen again? Why or why not?

3. How did the Great Depression change the nature of the American government and economy?

4. How did critics of the New Deal attack the program? Do politicians today use these same tactics to sway public opinion in their favor?

FRANKLIN D. ROOSEVELT'S FIRST INAUGURAL ADDRESS

Franklin Delano Roosevelt was elected president in 1932. When he took office in March 1933, the nation was at its lowest point in the Great Depression. The government faced problems with unemployment, hunger, and homelessness. Capitalism, the economic system that had sustained Americans for decades, was near collapse. Roosevelt perceived that his primary job was restoring confidence in the American people that things would get better. He used his first inaugural address to do just that. Speaking over the radio to countless millions of Americans he uttered the famous phrase "the only thing we have to fear is fear itself...." He also used this speech to outline his plans for bringing the country out of the Great Depression.

I am certain that my fellow Americans expect that on my induction into the Presidency I will address them with a candor and a decision which the present situation of our nation impels. This is preeminently the time to speak the truth, the whole truth, frankly and boldly nor need we shrink from honestly facing conditions in our country today. This great Nation will endure as it has endured, will revive and will prosper. So, first of all, let me assert my firm belief that the only thing we have to fear is fear itself-nameless, unreasoning, unjustified terror which paralyzes needed efforts to convert retreat into advance. In every dark hour of our national life a leadership of frankness and vigor has met with that understanding and support of the people themselves, which is essential to victory. I am convinced that you will again give that support to leadership in these critical days.

In such a spirit on my part and on yours we face our common difficulties. They concern, thank God, only material things. Values have shrunken to fantastic levels, taxes have risen, our ability to pay has fallen, government of all kinds is faced by serious curtailment of income, the means of exchange are frozen in the currents of trade, the withered leaves of industrial enterprise lie on every side, farmers find no markets for their produce, the savings of many years in thousands of families are gone.

More important, a host of unemployed citizens face the grim problem of existence, and an equally great number toil with little return. Only a foolish optimist can deny the dark realities of the moment.

Yet our distress comes from no failure of substance. We are stricken by no plague of locusts. Compared with the perils which our forefathers conquered because they believed and were not afraid, we have still much to be thankful for. Nature still offers her bounty and human efforts have multiplied it. Plenty is at our doorstep, but a generous use of it languishes in the very sight of the supply. Primarily this is because the rulers of the exchange of mankind's goods have failed, through their own stubbornness and their own incompetence, have admitted their failure, and abdicated. Practices of the unscrupulous money changers stand indicted in the court of public opinion, rejected by the hearts and minds of men.

True they have tried, but their efforts have been cast in the pattern of an outworn tradition. Faced by failure of credit they have proposed only the lending of more money. Stripped of the lure of profit by which to induce our people to follow their false leadership, they have resorted to exhortations, pleading tearfully for restored confidence. They know only the rules of a generation of self-seekers. They have no vision, and when there is no vision the people perish.

The money changers have fled from their high seats in the temple of our civilization. We may now restore that temple to the ancient truths. The measure of the restoration lies in the extent to which we apply social values more noble than mere monetary profit.

Happiness lies not in the mere possession of money, it lies in the joy of achievement, in the thrill of creative effort. The joy and moral stimulation of work no longer must be forgotten in the mad chase of evanescent profits. These dark days will be worth all they cost us if they teach us that our true destiny is not to be ministered unto but to minister to ourselves and to our fellow men.

Recognition of the falsity of material wealth as the standard of success goes hand in hand with the abandonment of the false belief that public office and high political position are to be valued only by the standards of pride of place and personal profit, and there must be an end to a conduct in banking and in business which too often has given to a sacred trust the likeness of callous and selfish wrongdoing. Small wonder that confidence languishes, for it thrives only on honesty, on honor, on the sacredness of obligations, on faithful protection, on unselfish performance, without them it cannot live.

Restoration calls, however, not for changes in ethics alone. This Nation asks for action, and action now.

Our greatest primary task is to put people to work. This is no unsolvable problem if we face it wisely and courageously. It can be accomplished in part by direct recruiting by the Government itself, treating the task as we would treat the emergency of a war, but at the same time, through this employment, accomplishing greatly needed projects to stimulate and reorganize the use of our natural resources.

Hand in hand with this we must frankly recognize the overbalance of population in our industrial centers and, by engaging on a national scale in a redistribution, endeavor to provide a better use of the land for those best fitted for the land. The task can be helped by definite efforts to raise the values of agricultural products and with this the power to purchase the output of our cities. It can be helped by preventing realistically the tragedy of the growing loss through foreclosure of our small homes and our farms. It can be helped by insistence that the Federal, State, and local governments act forthwith on the demand that their cost be drastically reduced. It can be helped by the unifying of relief activities which today are often scattered, uneconomical, and unequal. It can be helped by national planning for and supervision of all forms of transportation and of communications and other utilities which have a definitely public character. There are many ways in which it can be helped, but it can never be helped merely by talking about it. We must act and act quickly.

Finally, in our progress toward a resumption of work we require two safeguards against a return of the evils of the old order, there must be a strict supervision of all banking and credits and investments, there must be an end to speculation with other people's money, and there must be provision for an adequate but sound currency.

There are the lines of attack I shall presently urge upon a new Congress in special session detailed measures for their fulfillment, and I shall seek the immediate assistance of the several States.

Through this program of action we address ourselves to putting our own national house in order and making income balance outgo. Our international trade relations, though vastly important, are in point of time and necessity secondary to the establishment of a sound national economy. I favor as a practical policy the putting of first things first. I shall spare no effort to restore world trade by international economic readjustment, but the emergency at home cannot wait on that accomplishment.

The basic thought that guides these specific means of national recovery is not narrowly nationalistic. It is the insistence, as a first consideration, upon the interdependence of the various elements in all parts of the United States-a recognition of the old and permanently important manifestation of the American spirit of the pioneer. It is the way to recovery. It is the immediate way. It is the strongest assurance that the recovery will endure.

In the field of world policy I would dedicate this nation to the policy of the good neighbor-the neighbor who resolutely respects himself and, because he does so, respects the rights of others-the neighbor who respects his obligations and respects the sanctity of his agreements in and with a world of neighbors.

If I read the temper of our people correctly, we now realize as we have never realized before our interdependence on each other, that we can not merely take but we must give as well, that if we are to go forward, we must move as a trained and loyal army willing to sacrifice for the good of a common discipline, because without such discipline no progress is made, no leadership becomes effective. We are, I know, ready and willing to submit our lives and property to such discipline, because it makes possible a leadership which aims at a larger good. This I propose to offer, pledging that the larger purposes will bind upon us all as a sacred obligation with a unity of duty hitherto evoked only in time of armed strife.

With this pledge taken, I assume unhesitatingly the leadership of this great army of our people dedicated to a disciplined attack upon our common problems.

Action in this image and to this end is feasible under the form of government which we have inherited from our ancestors. Our Constitution is so simple and practical that it is possible always to meet extraordinary needs by changes in emphasis and arrangement without loss of essential form. That is why our constitutional system has proved itself the most superbly enduring political mechanism the modern world has produced. It has met every stress of vast expansion of territory, of foreign wars, of bitter internal strife, of world relations.

It is to be hoped that the normal balance of executive and legislative authority may be wholly adequate to meet the unprecedented task before us. But it may be that an unprecedented demand and need for undelayed action may call for temporary departure from that normal balance of public procedure.

I am prepared under my constitutional duty to recommend the measures that a stricken nation in the midst of a stricken world may require. These measures, or such other measures as the Congress may build out of its experience and wisdom, I shall seek, within my constitutional authority, to bring to speedy adoption.

But in the event that the Congress shall fail to take one of these two courses, and in the event that the national emergency is still critical, I shall not evade the clear course of duty that will then confront me. I shall ask the Congress for the one remaining instrument to meet the crisis-broad executive power to wage a war against the emergency, as great as the power that would be given to me if we were in fact invaded by a foreign foe. For the trust reposed in me I will return the courage and the devotion that befit the time I can do no less. We face the arduous days that lie before us in the warm courage of the national unity, with the clear consciousness of seeking old and precious moral values, with the clean satisfaction that comes from the stern performance of duty by old and young alike. We aim at the assurance of a rounded and permanent national life. We do not distrust the fixture of essential democracy. The people of the United States have not failed. In their need they have registered a mandate that they want direct, vigorous action. They have asked for discipline and direction under leadership. They have made me the present instrument of their wishes. In the spirit of the gift I take it. In this dedication of a nation we humbly ask the blessing of God. May he protect each and every one of us. May he guide me in the days to come.

Source: Public Papers and Address of Franklin D. Roosevelt

HOW WELL DID YOU UNDERSTAND THIS SELECTION?

1. How does Roosevelt describe the condition America is in?

2. What does Roosevelt say he will do to end the Great Depression?

3. Does Roosevelt's speech give hope to the millions of Americans listening on the radio? Why or Why not?

4. What does Roosevelt ask ordinary Americans to do?

5. Does Roosevelt's speech give any hint of the changing relationship between American government and the economy? Why or why not? Support your answer with evidence from the speech.

FRANKLIN D. ROOSEVELT'S SECOND INAUGURAL ADDRESS

Roosevelt's second inaugural was on January 20, 1937, the first presidential inauguration to occur in January. States had amended the Constitution (Twentieth Amendment) to move the president's inauguration from March back to January so that the time in which a president was a lame duck would be lessened. Roosevelt, having been elected by a wide margin over his Republican opponent, Alf Landon, in November 1936, outlined plans in his Second Inaugural Address to continue programs of the New Deal Americans apparently liked.

When four years ago we met to inaugurate a President, the Republic, single-minded in anxiety, stood in spirit here. We dedicated ourselves to the fulfillment of a vision-to speed the time when there would be for all the people that security and peace essential to the pursuit of happiness. We of the Republic pledged ourselves to drive from the temple of our ancient faith those who had profaned it, to end by action, tireless and unafraid, the stagnation and despair of that day. We did those first things first.

Our covenant with ourselves did not stop there. Instinctively we recognized a deeper need—the need to find through government the instrument of our united purpose to solve for the individual the ever-rising problems of a complex civilization. Repeated attempts at their solution without the aid of government had left us baffled and bewildered. For, without that aid, we had been unable to create those moral controls over the services of science which are necessary to make science a useful servant instead of a ruthless master of mankind. To do this we knew that we must find practical controls over blind economic forces and blindly selfish men.

We of the Republic sensed the truth that democratic government has innate capacity to protect its people against disasters once considered inevitable, to solve problems once considered unsolvable. We would not admit that we could not find a way to master economic epidemics just as, after centuries of fatalistic suffering we had found a way to master epidemics of disease. We refused to leave the problems of our common welfare to be solved by the winds of chance and the hurricanes of disaster.

In this we Americans were discovering no wholly new truth, we were writing a new chapter in our book of self-government.

This year marks the one hundred and fiftieth anniversary of the Constitutional Convention which made us a nation. At that convention our forefathers found the way out of the chaos which followed the Revolutionary War, they created a strong government with powers of united action sufficient then and now to solve problems utterly beyond individual or local solution. A century and a half ago they established the Federal Government in order to promote the general welfare and secure the blessings of liberty to the American people.

Today we invoke those same powers of government to achieve the same objectives.

Four years of new experience have not belied our historic instinct. They hold out the clear hope that government within communities, government within the separate States, and government of the United States can do the things the times require, without yielding its democracy. Our tasks in the last four years did not force democracy to take a holiday.

Nearly all of us recognize that as intricacies of human relationships increase, so power to govern them also must increase—power to stop evil, power to do good. The essential democracy of our Nation and the safety of our people depend not upon the absence of power, but upon lodging it with those whom the people can change or continue at stated intervals through an honest and free system of elections. The Constitution of 1787 did not make our democracy impotent.

In fact, in these last four years, we have made the exercise of all power more democratic, for we have begun to bring private autocratic powers into their proper subordination to the public's government. The legend that they were invincible—above and beyond the processes of a democracy—has been shattered. They have been challenged and beaten.

Our progress out of the depression is obvious But that is not all that you and I mean by the new order of things. Our pledge was not merely to do a patchwork job with secondhand materials. By using the new materials of social justice we have undertaken to erect on the old foundations a more enduring structure for the better use of future generations.

In that purpose we have been helped by achievements of mind and spirit. Old truths have been relearned, untruths have been unlearned. We have always known that heedless self-interest was bad morals; we know now that it is bad economics. Out of the collapse of a prosperity whose builders boasted their practicality has come the conviction that in the long run economic morality pays. We are beginning to wipe out the line that divides the practical from the ideal, and in so doing we are fashioning an instrument of unimagined power for the establishment of a morally better world.

This new understanding undermines the old admiration of worldly success as such. We are beginning to abandon our tolerance of the abuse of power by those who betray for profit the elementary decencies of life.

In this process evil things formerly accepted will not be so easily condoned. Hardheadedness will not so easily excuse hardheartedness. We are moving toward an era of good feeling. But we realize that there can be no era of good feeling save among men of good will.

For these reasons I am justified in believing that the greatest change we have witnessed has been the change in the moral climate of America.

Among men of good will, science and democracy together offer an ever-richer life and ever-larger satisfaction to the individual. With this change in our moral climate and our rediscovered ability to improve our economic order, we have set our feet upon the road of enduring progress.

Shall we pause now and turn our back upon the road that lies ahead? Shall we call this the promised land? Or, shall we continue on our way? For each age is a dream that is dying, or one that is coming to birth.

Many voices are heard as we face a great decision. Comfort says, tarry a while. Opportunism says, this is a good spot. Timidity asks, how difficult is the road ahead?

True, we have come far from the days of stagnation and despair. Vitality has been preserved. Courage and confidence have been restored. Mental and moral horizons have been extended.

But our present gains were won under the pressure of more than ordinary circumstances. Advance became imperative under the goad of fear and suffering. The times were on the side of progress.

To hold to progress today, however, is more difficult. Dulled conscience, irresponsibility, and ruthless self-interest already reappear Such symptoms of prosperity may become portents of disaster. Prosperity already tests the persistence of our progressive purpose.

Let us ask again, have we reached the goal of our vision of that fourth day of March, 1937? Have we found our happy valley?

I see a great nation, upon a great continent, blessed with a great wealth of natural resources. Its hundred and thirty million people are at peace among themselves, they are making their country a good neighbor among the nations. I see a United States which can demonstrate that, under democratic methods of government, national wealth can be translated into a spreading volume of human comforts hitherto unknown, and the lowest standard of living can be raised far above the level of mere subsistence.

But here is the challenge to our democracy. In this nation I see tens of millions of its citizens—a substantial part of its whole population—who at this very moment are denied the greater part of what the very lowest standards of today call the necessities of life.

I see millions of families trying to live on incomes so meager that the pall of family disaster hangs over them day by day.

I see millions whose daily lives in city and on farm continue under conditions labeled indecent by a so-called polite society half a century ago.

I see millions denied education, recreation, and the opportunity to better their lot and the lot of their children.

I see millions lacking the means to buy the products of farm and factory and by their poverty denying work and productiveness to many other millions.

I see one-third of a nation ill-housed, ill-clad, ill-nourished.

It is not in despair that I paint you that picture. I paint it for you in hope—because the nation, seeing and understanding the injustice in it, proposes to paint it out. We are determined to make every American citizen the subject of his country's interest and concern, and we will never regard any faithful law-abiding group within our borders as superfluous. The test of our progress is not whether we add more to the abundance of those who have much, it is whether we provide enough for those who have too little.

If I know aught of the spirit and purpose of our Nation, we will not listen to comfort, opportunism, and timidity. We will carry on.

Overwhelmingly, we of the Republic are men and women of good will, men and women who have more than warm hearts of dedication, men and women who have cool heads and willing hands of practical purpose as well. They will insist that every agency of popular government use effective instruments to carry out their will. Government is competent when all who compose it work as trustees for the whole people. It can make constant progress when it keeps abreast of all the facts. It can obtain justified support and legitimate criticism when the people receive true information of all that government does.

If I know aught of the will of our people, they will demand that these conditions of effective government shall be created and maintained. They will demand a nation uncorrupted by cancers of injustice and, therefore, strong among the nations in its example of the will to peace.

Today we reconsecrate our country to long-cherished ideals in a suddenly changed civilization. In every land there are always at work forces that drive men apart and forces that draw men together. In our personal ambitions we are individualists. But in our seeking for economic and political progress as a nation, we all go up, or else we all go down, as one people.

To maintain a democracy of effort requires a vast amount of patience in dealing with differing methods, a vast amount of humility. But out of the confusion of many voices rises an understanding of dominant public need. Then political leadership can voice common ideals, and aid in their realization.

In taking again the oath of office as President of the United States, I assume the solemn obligation of leading the American people forward along the road over which they have chosen to advance.

While this duty rests upon me I shall do my utmost to speak their purpose and to do their will, seeking Divine guidance to help us each and every one to give light to them that sit in darkness and to guide our feet into the way of peace.

Source: Public Papers and Address of Franklin D. Roosevelt

HOW WELL DID YOU UNDERSTAND THIS SELECTION?

1. Compare Roosevelt's first inaugural address with his second. How are they different? How are they similar?

2. Does Roosevelt think his New Deal has been successful? Why or why not?

3. How does Roosevelt refer to America's past to refute charges that his New Deal destroyed democracy?

4. What does Roosevelt say the greatest change in America has been? Explain what he means.

5. Does Roosevelt outline what he will do over the next four years? Explain.

SHARE OUR WEALTH PLAN By Huey Long

Huey Long was a prominent politician in Louisiana. He represented Louisiana as both governor and United States Senator. At first, he supported Roosevelt's New Deal but eventually decided it was too conservative. Long decided to challenge Roosevelt for the Democratic presidential nomination in 1936. He campaigned largely on a program he devised called the Share Our Wealth Plan. This plan was designed to appeal to people unemployed, hungry, and homeless from the Great Depression. Like Roosevelt, Long was a master of radio and exploited its political possibilities. He most likely would have run for president had an assassins' bullet not have taken his life before the election was underway. The following is Long's Share Our Wealth Plan.

Here is the whole sum and substance of the Share Our Wealth movement:

1.   Every family to be furnished by the government a homestead allowance, free of debt, of not less than one-third the average family wealth of the country, which means, at the lowest that every family shall have the

reasonable comforts of life up to a value of from $5,000 to $6,000: No person to have a fortune of more than 100 to 300 times the average family fortune, which means that the limit to fortune is between $1,500.000 and 5,000,000, with annual capital levy taxes imposed on all above $1,000,000.

2. The yearly income of every family shall be not less than one-third of the average family income, which means that, according to the estimates of the statisticians of the U. S. Government and Wall Street, no family's annual income would be less than from $2,000 to $2,500.

3. No yearly income shall be allowed to any person larger than from 100 to 300 times the size of the average family income, which means that no person would be allowed to earn in any year more than $600,000 to $1,800,000, all to be subject to present income tax laws.

4. To limit or regulate the hours of work to such an extent as to prevent over-production; the most modern and efficient machinery would be encouraged so that as much would be produced as possible so as to satisfy all demands of the people, but also to allow the maximum time to the workers for recreation, convenience, education, and luxuries of life.

5. An old age pension to the persons over 60.

6. To balance agricultural production with what can be consumed according to the laws of God, which includes the preserving and storing of surplus commodities to be paid for and held by the Government for emergencies when such are needed. Please bear in mind, however, that when the people of America have had money to buy things they needed, we have never had a surplus of any commodity. This plan of God does not call for destroying any of the things raised to eat or wear, nor does it countenance whole destruction of hogs, cattle or milk.

7. To pay the veterans of our wars what we owe them and to care for their disabled.

8. Education and training for all children to be equal in opportunity in all schools, colleges, universities and other institutions for training in the professions and vocations of life; to be regulated on the capacity of children to learn, and not on the ability of parents to pay the costs. Training for life's work to be as much universal and thorough for all walks in life as has been the training in the arts of killing.

9. The raising of revenues and taxes for the support of this program to come from the reduction of swollen fortunes from the top, as well as for the support of public works.

10. Give employment whenever there may be any slackening necessary in private enterprise.

Source: Congressional Record, 73rd Congress, 2nd Session, 1934

HOW WELL DID YOU UNDERSTAND THIS SELECTION?

1. Summarize the Share Our Wealth Plan. What kind of income and housing did it promise Americans?

2. How did Long propose to finance the Share Our Wealth Plan?

3. What limits did Long place on income?

4. Could the Share Our Wealth Plan have worked? Why or Why not?

5. What weaknesses can you find in the Share Our Wealth Plan? Explain.

Roosevelt's New Deal struck a tremendous blow for organized labor in 1935 with passage of the National Labor Relations Act. This statute gave workers the right to join a labor union and gave the union the right to engage in collective bargaining for its members. With passage of the National Labor Relations Act, Congress also created the National Labor Relations Board to oversee union elections and contract negotiations. Workers now had the right to choose whether they wanted to join a union. Employers were forbidden from denying employees this right. The National Labor Relations Board was also empowered to investigate allegations of unfair labor practices by employers, employees, and unions. If unfair labor practices were proven, the National Labor Relations Board had the right to stop them and provide redress for all grievances. The National Labor Relations Act was one of the most popular New Deal laws and cemented the relationship between Roosevelt's Democratic Party and organized labor.

FINDINGS AND POLICY

SECTION I The denial by employers of the right of employees to organize and the refusal by employers to accept the procedure of collective bargaining lead to strikes and other forms of industrial strife or unrest, which have the intent or the necessary effect of burdening or obstructing commerce by (a) impairing the efficiency, safety, or operation of the instrumentalities of commerce, (b) occurring in the current of commerce, (c) materially affecting, restraining, or controlling the flow of raw materials or manufactured or processed goods from or into the channels of commerce, or the prices of such materials or goods in commerce, or (d) using diminution of employment and wages in such volume as substantially to impair or disrupt the market for goods flowing from or into the channels of commerce. The inequality of bargaining power between employees who do not possess full freedom of association or actual liberty of contract, and employers who are organized in the corporate or other forms of ownership association substantially burdens and affects the flow of commerce, and tends to aggravate recurrent business depressions, by depressing wage rates and the purchasing power of wage earners in industry and by preventing the stabilization of competitive wage rates and working conditions within and between industries. Experience has proved that protection by law of the right of employees to organize and bargain collectively safeguards commerce from injury, impairment, or interruption, and promotes the flow of commerce by removing certain recognized sources of industrial strife and unrest, by encouraging practices fundamental to the friendly adjustment of industrial disputes arising out of differences as to wages, hours, or other working conditions, and by restoring equality of bargaining power between employers and employees. It is hereby declared to be the policy of the United States to eliminate the causes of certain substantial obstructions to the free flow of commerce and to mitigate and eliminate these obstructions when they have occurred by encouraging the practice and procedure of collective bargaining and by protecting the exercise by workers of full freedom of association, self-organization, and designation of representatives of their own choosing, for the purpose of negotiating the terms and conditions of their employment or other mutual aid or protection.

NATIONAL LABOR RELATIONS BOARD

SEC 3 (a) There is hereby created a board, to be known as the National Labor Relations Board, which shall be composed of three members, who shall be appointed by the President, by and with the advice and consent of the Senate. One of the original members shall be appointed for a term of one year, one for a term of three years, and one for a term of five years, but their successors shall be appointed for terms of five years each, except that any individual chosen to fill a vacancy shall be appointed only for the unexpired term of the member whom he shall succeed. The President shall designate one member to serve as chairman of the Board. Any member of the Board may be removed by the President, upon notice and hearing, for neglect of duty or malfeasance in office, but for no other cause.

RIGHTS OF EMPLOYEES

SEC 7 Employees shall have the right of self organization, to form, join, or assist labor organizations, to bargain collectively through representatives of their own choosing, and to engage in concerted activities, for the purpose of collective bargaining or other mutual aid or protection.

SEC 8 It shall be an unfair labor practice for an employer (1) To interfere with, restrain, or coerce employees in the exercise of the rights guaranteed in section 7 (2) To dominate or interfere with the formation or administration of any labor organization or contribute financial or other support to it. Provided, that subject to rules and regulations made and published by the Board pursuant to section 6 (a), an employer shall not be prohibited from permitting employees to confer with him during working hours without loss of time or pay. (3) By discrimination in regard to hire or tenure of employment or any term or condition of employment to encourage or discourage membership in any labor organization provided, that nothing in this Act, or in the National Industrial Recovery Act, as amended from time to time, or in any code or agreement approved or prescribed thereunder, or in any other statute of the United States, shall preclude an employer from making an agreement with a labor organization (not established, maintained or assisted by any action defined in this Act as an unfair labor practice) to require as a condition of employment membership therein, if such labor organization is the representative of the employees as provided in section 9 (a), in the appropriate collective bargaining unit covered by such agreement when made (4) To discharge or otherwise discriminate against an employee because he has filed charges or given testimony under this Act (5) To refuse to bargain collectively with the representatives of his employees....

Source: U.S. Statutes at Large, Vol. XLIX

HOW WELL DID YOU UNDERSTAND THIS SELECTION?

1. What problems led to passage of the National Labor Relations Act?

2. What rights does the National Labor Relations Act guarantee workers? Employers? Unions?

3. How are labor disputes to be resolved?

OKIES: TESTIMONY OF CAREY MCWILLIAMS IN CONGRESS

Okie was the term given to migrant farmers who moved to California from Oklahoma and other areas in the Midwest and Southwest during the 1930s. It was generally considered to be a derogatory term. Countless thousands of these migrants, victimized by the Dust Bowl and the Great Depression, drove rickety old jalopies along Route 66 to California in search of a better life. They had heard that work was available in California. Once there, however, most faced poor living conditions and limited opportunities for employment or land ownership. Some found seasonal work on vegetable and fruit farms. Like people across the nation, they settled in cardboard and tent colonies. Carey McWilliams, a journalist, visited and wrote about living conditions in migrant communities. He provided the following testimony to a committee in the House of Representatives investigating the problems Okies faced in California.

The most characteristic of all housing in California in which migrants reside at the moment is the shacktown or cheap subdivision. Most of these settlements have come into existence since 1933 and the pattern which obtains is somewhat similar throughout the State. Finding it impossible to rent housing in incorporated communities on their meager incomes, migrants have created a market for a very cheap type of subdivision of which the following may be taken as being representative. In Monterey County, according to a report of Dr. D. M. Bissell, county health officer, under date of November 28, 1939, there are approximately three well established migrant settlements. One of these, the development around the environs of Salinas, is perhaps the oldest migrant settlement of its type in California. In connection with this development I quote a paragraph of the report of Dr. Bissell: "This area is composed of all manners and forms of housing without a public sewer system. Roughly 10,000 persons are renting or have established homes there. A chief element in this area is that of refugees from the Dust Bowl who inhabit a part of Alisal called Little Oklahoma. Work in lettuce harvesting and packing and sugar beet processing have attracted these people who, seeking homes in Salinas without success because they aren't available, have resorted to makeshift adobes outside the city limits. Complicating the picture is the impermeable substrata which makes septic tanks with leaching fields impractical. Sewer wells have resulted with the corresponding danger to adjacent water wells and to the water wells serving the Salinas public. Certain districts, for example, the Airport Tract and parts of Alisal have grown into communities with quite satisfactory housing but others as exemplified by the Graves district are characterized by shacks and lean-tos which are unfit for human habitation. Typical of the shacktown problem are two such areas near the city limits of Sacramento, one on the eastside of B Street, extending from Twelfth Street to the Sacramento city dump and incinerator; and the other so-called Hoovertown, adjacent to the Sacramento River and the city filtration plant. In these two areas there were on September 17, 1939, approximately 650 inhabitants living in structures that, with scarcely a single exception, were rated by the inspectors of this division as unfit for human occupancy. The majority of the inhabitants were white Americans, with the exception of 50 or 60 Mexican families, a few single Mexican men, and a sprinkling of Negroes. For the most part they are seasonally employed in the canneries, the fruit ranches, and the hop fields of Sacramento County. Most of the occupants are at one time or another upon relief, and there are a large number of occupants in these shacktowns from the Dust

205

Bowl area." Describing the housing, an inspector of this division reports: The dwellings are built of brush, rags, sacks, boxboard, odd bits of tin and galvanized iron, pieces of canvas and whatever other material was at hand at the time of construction. Wood floors, where they exist, are placed directly upon the ground, which because of the location of the camps with respect to the Sacramento River, is damp most of the time. To quote again from the report: entire families, men, women, and children, are crowded into hovels, cooking and eating in the same room. The majority of the shacks have no sinks or cesspools for the disposal of kitchen drainage, and this, together with garbage and other refuse, is thrown on the surface of the ground. Because of the high-water table, cesspools, where they exist, do not function properly; there is a large overflow of drainage and sewage to the surface of the ground. Many filthy shack latrines are located within a few feet of living quarters. Rents for the houses in these shacktowns range from $3 to $20 a month. In one instance a landlord rents ground space for $1.50 to $5 a month, on which tenants are permitted to erect their own dugouts. The Hooverville section is composed primarily of tents and trailers, there being approximately 125 tent structures in this area on September 17, 1939. Both areas are located in unincorporated territory. They are not subject at the present time to any State or county building regulation. In Hooverville, at the date of the inspection, many families were found that did not have even a semblance of tents or shelters. They were cooking and sleeping on the ground in the open and one water tap at an adjoining industrial plant was found to be the source of the domestic water supply for the camp....

Source: U.S. Congress, House Select Committee to Investigate the Interstate Migration of Destitute Citizens, Hearings, 76th Cong., 3rd Sess., 1941.

HOW WELL DID YOU UNDERSTAND THIS SELECTION?

1. Describe the living conditions of migrant workers. How do they compare to living conditions elsewhere in the nation during the Great Depression?

2. What problems do migrant workers face in California? Are they similar to problems faced by other workers across the nation?

3. If you were a New Dealer, how would you solve the problems of migrant workers?

President Roosevelt was a master at radio. He had a well modulated voice that reassured the American public during the Great Depression. Roosevelt made use of his ability to communicate by radio through what he called "fireside chats." Periodically, he addressed the public in an informal setting, outlining accomplishments of the New Deal and informing Americans about future programs. One such fireside chat was delivered on June 28, 1934. Not only did Roosevelt talk about what the New Deal had done but he seemed to foreshadow Social Security, a program he later enacted.

It has been several months since I have talked with you concerning the problems of government. Since January, those of us in whom you have vested responsibility have been engaged in the fulfillment of plans and policies which had been widely discussed in previous months. It seems to us our duty not only to make the right path clear but also to tread that path.

As we review the achievement of the session of the Seventy-third Congress, it is made increasingly clear that its task was essentially that of completing and fortifying the work it had begun in March, 1933. That was no easy task, but the congress was equal to it. It has been well said that while there were a few exceptions, this Congress displayed a greater freedom from mere partisanship than any other peace-time Congress since the Administration of President Washington himself. The session was distinguished by the extent and variety of legislation enacted and by the intelligence and good will of debate upon these measures.

I mention only a few of the major enactments. It provided for the readjustment of the debt burden through the corporate and municipal bankruptcy acts and the farm relief act. It lent a hand to industry by encouraging loans to solvent industries unable to secure adequate help from banking institutions. It strengthened the integrity of finance through the regulation of securities exchanges. It provided a rational method of increasing our volume of foreign trade through reciprocal trading agreements. It strengthened our naval forces to conform with the intentions and permission of existing treaty rights. It made further advances toward peace in industry through the labor adjustment. It supplemented our agricultural policy through measures widely demanded by farmers themselves and intended to avert price destroying surpluses. It strengthened the hand of the Federal Government in its attempts to suppress gangster crime. It took definite steps toward a national housing program through an act which I signed today designed to encourage private capital in the rebuilding of the homes of the Nation. It created a permanent Federal body for the just regulation of all forms of communication, including the telephone, the telegraph and the radio. Finally, and I believe most important, it reorganized, simplified and made more fair and just our monetary system, setting up standards and policies adequate to meet the necessities of modern economic life, doing justive to both gold and silver as the metal bases behind the currency of the United States. In the consistent development of our previous efforts toward the saving and safeguarding of our national life, I have continued to recognize three related steps. The first was relief, because the primary concern of any Government dominated by the humane ideals of democracy is the simple principle that in a land of vast resources no one should be permitted to starve. Relief was and continues to be our first consideration. It calls for large expenditures and will continue in modified form to do so for a long time to come. We may as well recognize that fact. It comes from the paralysis that arose as the after-effect of that unfortunate decade characterized by a mad chase for unearned riches and an unwillingness of leaders in almost every walk of life to look beyond their own schemes and speculations. In our administration of relief we follow two principles: First, that direct giving shall, whenever possible, be supplemented by provision for useful and remunerative work and, second, that where families in their existing surroundings will in all human probability never find an opportunity for full self-maintenance, happiness and enjoyment, we will try to give them a new chance in new surroundings.

The second step was recovery, and it is sufficient for me to ask each and every one of you to compare the situation in agriculture and in industry today with what it was fifteen months ago.

At the same time we have recognized the necessity of reform and reconstruction-reform because much of our trouble today and in the past few years has been due to a lack of understanding of the elementary principles of justice and fairness by those in whom leadership in business and finance was placed-reconstruction because new conditions in our economic life as well as old but neglected conditions had to be corrected. Substantial gains well known to all of you have justified our course. I could cite statistics to you as unanswerable measures of our national progress-statistics to show the gain in the average weekly pay envelope of workers in the great majority of industries-statistics to show hundreds of thousands reemployed in private industries and other hundreds of thousands given new employment through the expansion of direct and indirect government assistance of many kinds, although, of course, there are those exceptions in professional pursuits whose economic improvement, of necessity, will be delayed. I also could cite statistics to show the great rise in the value of farm products-statistics to prove the demand for consumers' goods, ranging all the way from food and clothing to automobiles and of late to prove the rise in the demand for durable goods-statistics to cover the great increase in bank deposits and to show the scores of thousands of homes and of farms which have been saved from foreclosure.

But the simplest way for each of you to judge recovery lies in the plain facts of your own individual situation. Are you better off than you were last year? Are you debts less burdensome? Is your bank account more secure? Are your working conditions better? Is your faith in your own individual future more firmly grounded?

Also, let me put to you another simple question: Have you as an individual paid too high a price for these gains? Plausible self-seekers and theoretical die-hards will tell you of the loss if individual of liberty. Answer this question also out of the fact of your own life. Have you lost any of your rights or liberty or constitutional freedom of action and choice? Turn to the Bill of rights of the Constitution, which I have solemnly sworn to maintain and under which your freedom rests secure. Read each provision of that Bill of rights and ask yourself whether you personally have suffered the impairment of a single jot of these great assurances. I have no question in my mind as to what your answer will be. The record is written in the experiences of your own personal lives.

In other words, it is not the overwhelming majority of the farmers or manufacturers or workers who deny the substantial gains of the past year. The most vociferous of the doubting Thomases may be divided roughly into two groups: First, those who seek special political privilege and, second, those who seek special financial privilege. About a year ago I used as an illustration the 90% of the cotton manufacturers of the United States who wanted to do the right thing by their employees and by the public but were prevented from doing so by the 10% who undercut them by unfair practices and un-American standards. It is well for us to remember that humanity is a long way from being perfect and that a selfish minority in every walk of life-farming, business, finance and even Government service itself-will always continue to think of themselves first and their fellow-being second.

In the working out of a great national program which seeks the primary good of the greater number, it is true that the toes of some people are being stepped on are going to be stepped on. But these toes belong to the comparative few who seek to retain or to gain position or riches or both by some short cut which is harmful to the greater good. In the execution of the powers conferred on it by Congress, the Administration needs and will tirelessly seek the best ability that the country affords. Public service offers better rewards in the opportunity for service than ever before in our history-not great salaries, but enough to live on. In the building of this service there are coming to us men and women with ability and courage from every part of the Union. The days of the seeking of mere party advantage through the misuse of public power are drawing to a close. We are increasingly demanding and getting devotion to the public service on the part of every member of the Administration, high and low.

The program of the past year is definitely in operation and that operation month by month is being made to fit into the web of old and new conditions. This process of evolution is well illustrated by the constant changes in detailed and organization and method going on in the National Recovery Administration. With every passing month we are making strides in the orderly handling of the relationship between employees and employers. Conditions differ, of course, in almost every part of the country and in almost every industry. Temporary methods of adjustment are being replaced by more permanent machinery and, I am glad to say, by a growing recognition on the part of employers and employees of the desirability of maintaining fair relationships all around.

So also, while almost everybody has recognized the tremendous strides in the elimination of child labor, in the payment of not less than fair minimum wages and in the shortening of hours, we are still feeling our way in solving problems which relate to self-government in industry, especially where such self-government tends to eliminate the fair operation of competition.

In this same process of evolution we are keeping before us the objectives of protecting on the one hand industry against chiselers within its own ranks, and on the other hand the consumer through the maintenance of reasonable competition for the prevention of the unfair sky-rocketing of retail prices. But in addition to this our immediate task, we must still look to the larger future. I have pointed out to the Congress that we are seeking to find the way once more to well-known, long-established but to some degree forgotten ideals and values. We seek the security of the men, women and children of the Nation. That security involves added means of providing better homes for the people of the Nation. That is the first principle of our future program.

The second is to plan the use of land and water resources of this country to the end that the means of livelihood of our citizens may be more adequate to meet their daily needs. And, finally, the third principle is to use the agencies of government to assist in the establishment of means to provide sound and adequate protection against the vicissitudes of modern life-in other words, social insurance.

Later in the year I hope to talk with you more fully about these plans. A few timid people, who fear progress, will try to give you new and strange names for what we are doing. Sometimes they will call it "Fascism," sometimes "Communism," sometimes "Regimentation," sometimes "Socialism." But in so doing, they are trying to make very complex and theoretical something that is really very simple and very practical. I believe in practical explanations and in practical policies. I believe that what we are doing today is a necessary fulfillment of what Americans have always been doing-a fulfillment of old and tested American ideals.

Let me give you a simple illustration: While I am away from Washington this summer, a long needed renovation of and addition to our White House office building is to be started. The architects have planned a few new rooms built into the present all too small one-story structure. We are going to include in this addition and in this renovation modern electric wiring and modern plumbing and modern means of keeping the offices cool in the hot Washington summers. But the structural lines of the old Executive Office Building will remain. The artistic lines of the White House buildings were the creation of master builders when our Republic was young. The simplicity and the strength of the structure remain in the face of every modern test. But within this magnificent pattern, the necessities of modern government business require constant reorganization and rebuilding. If I were to listen to the arguments of some prophets of calamity who are talking these days, I should hesitate to make these alterations. I should fear that while I am away for a few weeks the architects might build some strange new Gothic tower or a factory building or perhaps a replica of the Kremlin or of the Potsdam Palace. But I have no such fears. The architects and builders are men of common sense and of artistic American tastes. They know that the principles of harmony and of necessity itself require that the building of the new structure shall blend with the essential lines of the old. It is this combination of the old and the new that marks orderly peaceful progress-not only in building buildings but in building government itself. Our new structure is part of and a fulfillment of the old.

All that we do seeks to fulfill the historic traditions of the American people. Other nations may sacrifice democracy for the transitory stimulation of old and discredited autocracies. We are restoring confidence and well-being under the rule of the people themselves. We remain, as John Marshall said a century ago, "emphatically and truly, a government of the people." Our government "in form and in substance ... emanates from them. Its powers are granted by them, and are to be exercised directly on them, and for their benefits." Before I close, I want to tell you of the interest and pleasure with which I look forward to the trip on which I hope to start in a few days. It is a good thing for everyone who can possibly do so to get away at least once a year for a change of scene. I do not want to get into the position of not being able to see the forest because of the thickness of the trees.

I hope to visit our fellow Americans in Puerto Rico, in the Virgin Islands, in the Canal Zone and in Hawaii. And, incidentally, it will give me an opportunity to exchange a friendly word of greeting to the Presidents of our sister Republics: Haiti, Columbia and Panama.

After four weeks on board ship, I plan to land in our Pacific northwest, and then will come the best part of the whole trip, for I am hoping to inspect a number of our new great national projects on the Columbia, Missouri and Mississippi Rivers, to see some of our national parks and, incidentally, to learn much of the actual conditions during the trip across the continent back to Washington.

While I was in France during the War our boys used to call the United States "God's country." Let us make it and keep it "God's country."

Source: Social Security Administration Web Site http://www.ssa.gov/history/history6.html

HOW WELL DID YOU UNDERSTAND THIS SELECTION?

1. What does Roosevelt say the Seventy-third Congress accomplished?

2. What three principles of the New Deal does Roosevelt identify? Explain what each means.

3. How does Roosevelt refute the charge that the New Deal has destroyed American liberty?

4. Does Roosevelt identify what future course the New Deal will take? If so, what is he planning to do?

5. What does Roosevelt compare the New Deal to? Why does he do this?

REPUBLICAN PARTY PLATFORM, ELECTION OF 1936

Not everyone agreed with the New Deal. People seemed either to love or hate Roosevelt and the New Deal. Republicans believed the New Deal had destroyed individual liberty in the United States. The 1936 election was viewed as a popular referendum on the New Deal. The Republican Party nominated Alf Landon to oppose Roosevelt. The platform Landon and Republicans ran on in 1936 discusses the conservative complaints about the New Deal. The election was marked by bitter, personal attacks on Roosevelt and negative campaigning, which did not work. Roosevelt and the Democratic Party won landslides. Republicans were thoroughly trounced. The outcome of this election is viewed as a strong endorsement of the New Deal by the American public.

America is in peril. The welfare of American men and women and the future of our youth are at stake. We dedicate ourselves to the preservation of their political liberty, their individual opportunity and their character as free citizens, which today for the first time are threatened by Government itself.

For three long years the New Deal Administration has dishonored American traditions and flagrantly betrayed the pledges upon which the Democratic Party sought and received public support.

The powers of Congress have been usurped by the President.

The integrity and authority of the Supreme Court have been flouted.

The rights and liberties of American citizens have been violated.

Regulated monopoly has displaced free enterprise.

The New Deal Administration constantly seeks to usurp the rights reserved to the States and to the people.

It has insisted on the passage of laws contrary to the Constitution.

It has intimidated witnesses and interfered with the right of petition.

It has dishonored our country by repudiating its most sacred obligations.

It has been guilty of frightful waste and extravagance, using public funds for partisan political purposes.

It has promoted investigations to harass and intimidate American citizens, at the same time denying investigations into its own improper expenditures.

It has created a vast multitude of new offices, filled them with its favorites, set up a centralized bureaucracy, and sent out swarms of inspectors to harass our people.

It has bred fear and hesitation in commerce and industry, thus discouraging new enterprises, preventing employment and prolonging the depression.

It secretly has made tariff agreements with our foreign competitors, flooding our markets with foreign commodities.

It has coerced and intimidated voters by withholding relief from those opposing its tyrannical policies.

It has destroyed the morale of many of our people and made them dependent upon Government.

Appeals to passion and class prejudice have replaced reason and tolerance.

To a free people these actions are insufferable. This campaign cannot be waged on the traditional differences between the Republican and Democratic parties. The responsibility of this election transcends all previous political divisions. We invite all Americans, irrespective of party, to join us in defense of American institutions.

CONSTITUTIONAL GOVERNMENT AND FREE ENTERPRISE

WE PLEDGE OURSELVES:

1. To maintain the American system of constitutional and local self government, and to resist all attempts to impair the authority of the Supreme Court of the United States, the final protector of the rights of our citizens against the arbitrary encroachments of the legislative and executive branches of Government. There can be no individual liberty without an independent judiciary.

2. To preserve the American system of free enterprise, private competition, and equality of opportunity, and to seek its constant betterment in the interests of all.

REEMPLOYMENT

The only permanent solution of the unemployment problem is the absorption of the unemployed by industry and agriculture. To that end, we advocate:

Removal of restrictions on production.

Abandonment of all New Deal policies that raise production costs, increase the cost of living, and thereby restrict buying, reduce volume and prevent reemployment.

Encouragement instead of hindrance to legitimate business.

Withdrawal of Government from competition with private payrolls.

Elimination of unnecessary and hampering regulations.

Adoption of such policies as will furnish a chance for individual enterprise, industrial expansion, and the restoration of jobs.

RELIEF

The necessities of life must be provided for the needy, and hope must be restored pending recovery. The administration of relief is a major failure of the New Deal. It has been faithless to those who most deserve our sympathy. To end confusion, partisanship, waste and incompetence,

WE PLEDGE:

1. The return of responsibility for relief administration to non-political local agencies familiar with community problems.

2. Federal grants-in-aid to the States and Territories while the need exists, upon compliance with these conditions: (a) a fair proportion of the total relief burden to be provided from the revenues of States and local governments; (b) all engaged in relief administration to be selected on the basis of merit and fitness; (c) adequate provisions to be made for the encouragement of those persons who are trying to become self-supporting.
3. Undertaking of Federal public works only on their merits and separate from the administration of relief.
4. A prompt determination of the facts concerning relief and unemployment.

SECURITY

Real security will be possible only when our productive capacity is sufficient to furnish a decent standard of living for all American families and to provide a surplus for future needs and contingencies. For the attainment of that ultimate objective, we look to the energy, self-reliance and character of our people, and to our system of free enterprise.

Society has an obligation to promote the security of the people, by affording some measure of protection against involuntary unemployment and dependency in old age. The New Deal policies, while purporting to provide social security, have, in fact, endangered it....

We propose to encourage adoption by the States and Territories of honest and practical measures for meeting the problems of unemployment insurance.

The unemployment insurance and old age annuity sections of the present Social Security Act are unworkable and deny benefits to about two-thirds of our adult population, including professional men and women and all those engaged in agriculture and domestic service, and the self employed, while imposing heavy tax burdens upon al. The so-called reserve fund estimated at forty-seven billion dollars for old age insurance is not reserve at all, because the fund will contain nothing but the Government's promise to pay, while the taxes collected in the guise of premiums will be wasted by the Government in reckless and extravagant political schemes.

LABOR

The welfare of labor rests upon increased production and the prevention of exploitation. We pledge ourselves to:

Protect the right of labor to organize and to bargain collectively though representatives of its own choosing without interference from any source.

Prevent governmental job holders from exercising autocratic power over labor.

Support the adoption of State laws and interstate compacts to abolish sweatshops and child labor, and to protect women and children with respect to maximum hours, minimum wages and working conditions. We believe that this can be done within the Constitution as it now stands.

AGRICULTURE

The farm problem is an economic and social, not a partisan problem....

Our paramount object is to protect and foster the family type of farm, traditional in American life, and to promote policies which will bring about an adjustment of agriculture to meet the needs of domestic and foreign markets. As an emergency measure, during the agricultural depression, Federal benefit payments or grants-in-aid when administered within the means of the Federal Government are consistent with a balanced budged.

WE PROPOSE:

1. To facilitate economical production and increased consumption on a basis of abundance instead of scarcity.
2. A national land-use program, including the acquisition of abandoned and non-productive farm lands by voluntary sale or lease, subject to approval of the legislative and executive branches of the States concerned, and the devotion of such land to appropriate public use, such as watershed protection and flood prevention, reforestation, recreation, and conservation of wild life.
3. That an agricultural policy be pursued for the protection and restoration of the land resources designed to bring

about such a balance between soil-building and soil-depleting crops as will permanently insure productivity, with reasonable benefits to cooperating farmers on family-type farms, but so regulated as to eliminate the New Deal's destructive policy toward the dairy and live-stock industries.

4. To extent experimental aid to farmers developing new crops....

REGULATION OF BUSINESS

We recognize the existence of a field within which governmental regulation is desirable and salutary. The authority to regulate should be vested in an independent tribunal acting under clear and specific laws establishing definite standards. Their determinations on law and facts should be subject to review by the Courts. We favor Federal regulation, within the Constitution, of the marketing of securities to protect investors. We also favor Federal regulation of the interstate activities of public utilities....

GOVERNMENT FINANCE

The New Deal Administration has been characterized by shameful waste and general financial irresponsibility. It has piled deficit upon deficit. It threatens national bankruptcy and the destruction through inflation of insurance policies and savings bank deposits.

WE PLEDGE OURSELVES TO:

Stop the folly of uncontrolled spending.
> Balance the budget-not by increasing taxes but by cutting expenditures, drastically and immediately.
> Revise the Federal tax system and coordinate it with State and local tax systems.
> Use the taxing power for raising revenue and not for punitive or political purposes.

MONEY AND BANKING

We advocate a sound currency to be preserved at all hazards. The first requisite to a sound and stable currency is a balanced budget.
> We oppose further devaluation of the dollar.
> We will restore to the Congress the authority lodged with it by the Constitution to coin money and regulate the value thereof by repealing all the laws delegating this authority to the Executive.
> We will cooperate with other countries toward stabilization of currencies as soon as we can do so with due regard for our national interests and as soon as other nations have sufficient stability to justify such action.

CONCLUSION

We assume the obligations and duties imposed upon Government by modern conditions. We affirm our unalterable conviction that, in the future as in the past, the fate of the nation will depend, not so much on the wisdom and power of Government, as on the character and virtue, self-reliance, industry and thrift of the people and on their willingness to meet the responsibilities essential to the preservation of a free society.

Finally, as our party affirmed in its first Platform in 1856: "Believing that the spirit of our institutions as well as the Constitution of our country guarantees liberty of conscience and equality of rights among our citizens, we oppose all legislation tending to impair them," and "we invite the affiliation and cooperation of the men of all parties, however differing from us in other respects, in support of the principles herein declared."

The acceptance of the nomination tendered by this Convention carries with it, as a matter of private honor and public faith, an undertaking by each candidate to be true to the principles and program herein set forth.

Source: Proceedings, 21st Republican National Convention

HOW WELL DID YOU UNDERSTAND THIS SELECTION?

1. Why do Republicans disagree with the New Deal?

2. How do Republicans attack the New Deal?

3. What do Republicans propose to replace the New Deal with?

4. Identify the major planks of the Republican Party Platform of 1936.

5. Has the New Deal changed the Republican position on any issues since the 1920s? If so, explain.

6. What do Republicans propose to do regarding labor? Agriculture? Relief? Old age security? Regulation of business? Government finances? Currency?

FOLK SONGS FROM THE GREAT DEPRESSION

Poor people affected by the Great Depression often sang songs that reflected the suffering they had to endure. There were literally thousands of these songs that were heard at work, in Hoovervilles, on the road, and on radio. Most of these songs have no known author but were passed down from person to person. Others have their origins in ballads and legends American immigrants brought with them from Ireland, England, Germany, Italy, and other countries. The following songs were collected during the Great Depression by government workers and housed in the Library of Congress.

EVERY MAN A KING

Huey Long, the dominant politician in Louisiana who served as governor and United States Senator, like Franklin D. Roosevelt, was a master at radio. He understood the political uses of radio and employed it to advance his Share Our Wealth Plan. In 1935 he hired Castro Carrazo, the band director at Louisiana State University, to write a song depicting ideas found in the Share Our Wealth Plan. When Long was contemplating a run for the presidency in 1936, he declared that "Every Man a King" would be his campaign slogan and song. He even had it recorded on a national news reel by Ina Ray Hutton and her All Girl Orchestra.

214

Why weep or slumber America
Land of brave and true
With castles and clothing and food
for all
All belongs to you
Ev'ry man a King, ev'ry man a King
For you can be a millionaire
But there's something belonging to others
There's enough for all people to share
When its sunny June and December too
or in the Winter time or Spring
There'll be peace without end
Ev'ry neighbor a friend
With ev'ry man a King.

SOME MORE GREENBACK DOLLAR
(Unknown Author)

I don't want your little rag houses
I don't want your navy beans
All I want is a greenback dollar
For to buy some gasoline.

The scenery here is getting rusty
I'll go further up the line
Where the fields are green and purty
It will satisfy my mind.

We don't want to be a burden
On the people of this land
We just want to earn our money
And you people know we can.

So goodby my friends and neighbors
We are on the tramp
Many thanks to all officials
Of this migratory camp.

SUNNY CAL
(Unknown Author)

You all have heard the story
Of old Sunny Cal
The place where it never rains
They say it don't know how.

They say, Come on, you Okies,
Work is easy found
Bring along your cotton pack
You can pick the whole year round.

215

Get your money every night
Spread your blanket on the ground
It is always bright and warm
You can sleer right on the ground.

But listen to me Okies
I came out here one day
Spent all my money getting here
Now I can't get away.

THREE CROWS
(Unknown Author)

There were three crows that sat on a tree
They were as black as could be.

Said one crow unto his mate
What shall we do for meat to eat?

There is a horse in yonder field
Was by some cruel butcher slain.

We'll sit upon him in the sun
And pick his eyes out one by one.

Source: Library of Congress

HOW WELL DID YOU UNDERSTAND THIS SELECTION?

1. Why did Huey Long have "Every Man a King" written? What idea is he trying to convey with the song?

2. Who might have been the composer of "Some More Greenback Dollar" and "Sunny Cal"? What ideas do these songs reflect?

3. What problem from the Great Depression does the "Three Crows" address?

4. Do these songs have any common thread that connects them? If so, explain what it is.

The Federal Writers Project of the Works Progress Administration of the New Deal put unemployed writers to work doing various things. They wrote community histories, individual histories, and documented conditions during the Great Depression. Overall, the Federal Writers Project collected information that spans the years 1889 to 1942. The manuscripts below are part of a larger project entitled The American Memory Collection, which was itself part of the Folklore Project of the Federal Writers Project of the WPA. Both provide information on life for poor people during the Great Depression.

BEGGING
by Anne Winn Stevens

BEGGING REDUCED TO A SYSTEM

Four Garrett children, the oldest a girl of fifteen, huddled at the door of the principle's office in the public school. When asked why they had been absent from school for five weeks, the children could give no intelligible answer. The idea uppermost in their minds was that their mother had told them to ask for free lunches. They were scantily clad for a November day. Their clothers were clean, but they seemed to hae on little underclothing and to possess neither coats nor sweaters. Their shoes were full of holes. The group was obviously under-nourished, thin, pasty of complexion, anemic. One of the teachers said, "They look just like poor little rats."

The principle reached for the telephone. He called the State Aid worker assigned to the school. "Mrs. Holt look up the Garrett children; you know the address," he said. "Find out whay they have been absent from school for five weeks, and why they wish to be put on the free lunch list. They are always asking for something."

A few minutes later the worker parked her car near a large, yellow house on a sparsely settled street inhabited mostly by negroes. A muddy road led to it. On its door, a fly-specked, weather beaten, yellow card, hanging aslant, announced, "Quarantine, Measles." The small boy who stuck his head out at Mrs. Holt's knock was thickly broken out with a rash.

After a few minutes, Mrs. Garrett came out and stood with her visitor on the windy porch. She was a thin woman, about thirty-five years old, with a pasty complexion, and projecting teeth. Her hair was much too yellow-drug store gold. Although the morning was raw and cold she wore a thin, sleeveless summer dress and no wrap.

"Yes, I live here," she said, hugging herself to keep warm; "me and my husband and our six children live in three rooms, upstairs."

The Henson's, who are her parents, ant their youngest daughter and orphaned grandchildren occupy the lower floor.

She explained the children's absences. No they have had measles long ago; it was the children under school age who had it now. "My husband had been out of work for nine weeks," she declared. "When we was asked to leve the cabin whar we wuz living;" pointing to a tiny, log house in a hollow across the street, "we tuk the children and went to my brother's at Emma looking for work." That was five weeks ago.

"No'm, we didn't find no work. But my husband and me tuck in washin'. He'd go out and get the clothes, help me do them. Then he got back on WPA and we come back to Asheville." She explained that her husband had been on the WPA for some time. The project on which he was working "run out," as she put it. So he had been suspended until work could be found for him elsewhere.

"He has always been a hard worker," she maintained. He had worked in the mills. He had been a clerk in a grocery store at $12 a week. He had been a truck driver for the city, and for various transfer companies. Before the depression, he had made $20 a week.

"We lived real well then," she said. "But there wasn't as many of us."

But for the past few years he had worked mainly as an unskilled laborer on the WPA.

"He goes back to work tomorrow," she said. "After he gets his first pay check, we can get along. But we haven't had anything in the house to eat for a week now but two messes of flour and a peck of meal. The children has nothin' for breakfast but a biscuit or a slice of corn bread. They come home after school begging for food. But I can't give them but two meals a day. That's why I want to get free lunches."

So the family was given commodities by the welfare department; beans, flour, and dried milk. The school agreed to give them lunches, and a member of the parent-teacher association offered to find clothers and shoes for them.

Several weeks later, Mrs. Garrett, head tied up in a white cloth, was found trying to divert a fretful two-year old. The room was clean, but rather bare, with shappby linoleum on the floor. The bed was without sheets or pillow cases. But the mattress was covered by an unbleached coverslip. The blankets were clean, but mostly cotton.

"That's my baby," she said, indicating the two-year old. "He shore has had a hard time." She enumerted the illnesses of his two short years; diptheria, pneumonia, measles, and now an abscess in his ear. He had a bad cikd also, and a sore on his upper lip, which his mother wiped every now and then with a not-too-clean cotton cloth. Like the other children, he had too waxen a look.

"The doctor says as how he should have orange juice every day, and tomatoes and onions mashed with potatoes, but I don't have no money to buy them things for him. I ain't nothing to give him but cereal." However, she admitted some one was sending him milk every day. But she didn't know who.

She was still feeding the older children on biscuits, cornbread and now "white beans," but not bread and beans at the same meal. Christmas had been a great help to the family. "Nine dollars a week for eight people," she maintained nevertheless, "doesn't go far, after rent and coal has been paid for."

But they had "gotten" a bag of coal from a dealer, whose trucks her husband loaded on his way from work. Still, "It was mostly dust," she complained. "When it was poured into the stove it flew all over the room, until we was all sneezing."

The Christmas basket from a civic organization had helped. But again she said, "How long could five dollars worth of groceries last for eight people?"

However, she had profited by various Christman charities.

"I stood in line before Pender's Shoe Store two or three hours Christman morning. You know he allus gives away shoes on Christmas. I got three good pair for the children. And I got two of the boys into the dinner given by the Y.M.C.A. While I was waiting for them I went by the doctor's office and asked the nurse for a sample bottle of cod-liver oil for the baby. She gives me three bottles of it." she narrated.

It is easy to see where the Garrett children get their habit of always asking for something. As far as charitable organizations are concerned, their mother knows all the answers.

She enumerated her further needs. "You know," she said plaintively, "I ain't got but one sheet, no pillow cases, and only one towel, and I asked the Red Cross, and the welfare department both, for some. It looks like someone might give me a few towels; they are so cheap!"

Finally she admitted that she was seven months advanced in pregnancy, and as yet had no layette. "The Red Cross," she declared, "used to give lovely ones, all put up in a nice basket. "But," in an aggrieved tone, "they told me as how they didn't have any more.""

But Mrs. Garrett, who says she completed only the third grade in school, and never learned "to figger," has found a neighbor who is quite sympathetic. "Mrs. Garrett, my husband has a good steady job," said the neighbor, "I guess I'm just plum licky; so I'll find you some of my baby's things that he don't need, or has outgrowed."

However, there is a shoemaker in the neighborhood who is wondering: "Where do you suppose Garrett got those six new shirts he sold me last week?" Can it be that the Garretts are making money off charitable organizations, or off sympathetic individuals?

When Mr. Garrett came in, he was asked about his WPA job, his wages, and his situation in general.

"I used to be a foreman, but now I'm just doing common labor, getting a little over $18 every pay period, whenever the weather is good enough to put in full time. Weather like this-we'll lose some time this month. That ain't much for eight people to live on, is it? A little over $9 a week. They used to give us Government food, but they won't give us anything now. One fellow down there is the cause of it all. When they get it in for you, there ain't nothing you can do. Who'd you say you was with?"

"The Federal Writer's Project."

"Well, the WPA and the welfare department ought to be cleaned up. You can't get a thing now. My wife is going to have another baby soon, and I can't get any clothers for it, or anything. They won't do a thing. They've just got it in for me, that's all. Why right over on the next street is a WPA foreman who gets Government food every week-and clothes-and he only has four children. They won't give me a thing. Tht boy there, now, has got a sore throat, and I can't get a thing for him."

"Don't the chidren get medical attention from the city authorities, or the county?"

"No. They won't do nothing for anybody that ain't on relief. I have to just get whatever doctor I can."

"How is the house rented?"

"I rent the house for $15 a month, and the people downstirs pay $7.50 for their half."

"Do they pay regularly?"

"Yes; but they are going to move out next week, and I reckon we'll hae to move, too-then. The Wood Reality Company has got this house, and they're awful strict."

"Couldn't you rent the downstairs part to someone else?"

"Naw."

But Mrs. Garret, in the kitchen, at the same moment said, "Sure; there's somebody by here almost every day wants to rent a place." Mr. Garrett ignored this.

"They's only one bathroom in this house, and it's up here. I don't want strangers running in and out of my bathrom. They ain't no locks on none of the doors, either."

Indeed, ther are neither locks nor knobs, but each door has a string by which it is pulled open, or shut. However the radio, which was turned off to facilitate the conversation, is the very latest in design, and quite new. It came from one of the large mail-order houses that now maintain retail stores in principal cities, and it has the automatic features characteristic of the modern sets. The furniture, too, is of recent design, and not very old, but there is not much of it. Chairs are scarce, and there is no rug on the floor.

"Is your furniture paid for?"

"No, it ain't. They'll be taking that back, next."

"What will you do then?"

"Well, I don't know. Maybe I can get some more, somewhere."

"On credit?"

"Sure. I can't pay for no furniture."

"Do you buy other things on credit, too-that radio, for example?"

"Of course, I had to make a down payment on that, same as furniture, but you can't hardly get nop credit anywhere else."

It was apparent from further conversation that he must have sought credit everywhere, practically, and, failing to obtain credit, asked for gifts, although he would not acknowledge this. All efforts to draw him out further were in vain. He would not admit receiving gifts, money, or help from private individuals or organization. He always returned to the complaint that the public agencies seemed to have it in for him, and would not give him anything, would not help him; while others, already more fortunate, were getting free food, clothes, medicine, etc. He said it was not easy, on his wages, to keep the electric power turned on, but they had oil lamps to use whenever the power was off. However, he missed the radio during those times.

AFTERNOON IN A PUSHCART PEDDLERS' COLONY
by Frank Byrd

It was snowing and, shortly after noontime, the snow changed to sleet and beat a tattoo against the rocks and board shacks that had been carelessly thrown together on the west bank of the Harlem. It was windy too and the cold blasts that came in from the river sent the men shivering for cover behind their shacks where some of them had built huge bonfires to ward off the icy chills that swept down from the hills above.

Some of them, unable to stand it any linger, went below into the crudely furnished cabins that were located in the holds of some old abandoned barges that lay half in, half our of the water. But the men did not seem to mind. Even the rotting barges afforded them some kind of shelter. It was certainly better than nothing, not to mention the fact that it was their home; address, the foot of 133rd Street at Park Avenue on the west bank of the Harlem River; depression residence of a little band of part-time pushcart peddlers whose cooperative colony is one of the most unique in the history of New York City.

These men earn their living by cruising the streets long before daylight, collecting old automobile parts, pasteboard, paper, rags, rubber, magazines, brass, iron, steel, old clother or anything they can find that is saleable as junk. They wheel their little pushcarts around exploring cellars, garbage cans and refuse heaps. When they have a load, they turn their footsteps in the direction of the American Junk Dealers, Inc., whose site of wholesale and retail operations is locted directly opposite the pushcart colony at 134th Street and Park Avenue. Of the fifty odd colonists, many are ex-carpenters, painters, brick-masons, auto-mechanics, upholsters, plumbers and even an artist or two.

Most of the things the men collect they sell, but once in a while they run across something useful to themselves, like auto parts, pieces of wire, or any electrical equipment, especially in view of the fact that there are two or three electrical engineers in the group.

Joe Elder, a tall, serious minded Negro, was the founder of the group that is officially known as the National Negro Civil Association. Under his supervision, electrically inclined members of the group set up a complete power plant that supplied all the barges and shacks with electric light. It was constructed with an old automobile engine and an electrical generator brought from the City of New York.

For a long time it worked perfectly. After awhile, when a city inspector came around, he condemned it and the shacks were temporarily without light. It was just as well, perhaps, since part of the colony was forced to vacate the site in order to make room for a mooring spot for a coal company that rented a section of the waterfront.

A rather modern and up-to-date community hall remains on the site, however. One section of it is known as the gymnasium and many pieces of apparatus are to be found there. There are also original oil paintings in the other sections known as the library and recreation room. Here, one is amazed (to say the least) by the comfortable divans, lounges, bookshelves and, of all things, a drinking fountain. The water is purchased from the City and pumped directly to the hall and barges by a homemade, electrically motored pump. In the recreation room there are also three pianos. On cold nights when the men want companionship and relaxation, they bring the women there and dance to the accompaniment of typical Harlem jazz...jazz that is also supplied by fellow colonists....

After being introduced to some of the boys, we went down into Oliver's barage. It was shaky, weather-beaten and sprawling, like the other half-dozen that surrounded it. Inside, he had set up an old iron range and attached a pipe to it that carried the smoke out and above the upper deck. On top of the iron grating that had been laid across the open hole on the back of the stove were some spare-ribs that had been generously seasoned with salt, pepper, sage and hot-sauce. Later I discovered a faint flavor of mace in them. The smell and pungency os spices filled the low ceilinged room with an appetizing aroma. The faces of the men were alight and hopeful with anticipation.

There was no real cause for worry, however, since Oliver had more than enough for everybody. Soon he began passing out tin plates for everyone. It makes my mouth water just to think of it. When we had gobbled up everything in sight, all of us sat back in restful contemplation puffing on our freshly lighted cigarettes. Afterwards there was conversation, things the men elected to talk about of their own accord.

"You know one thing," Oliver began, "ain't nothin' like a man being his own boss. Now take today, here we is wit' plenty to eat, ha'f a jug of co'n between us and nairy a woman to fuss aroun' wantin' to wash up dishes or mess aroun' befo' duh grub gits a chance to settle good."

"Dat sho is right," Evans Drake agreed. He was Oliver's helper when there were trucks to be repaired. "A 'oman ain't good fuh nuthin' but one thing."

The conversation drifted along until I was finally able to ease in a query or two. "Boys," I ventured, "how is it that none of you ever got on Home Relief? You can get a little grub out of it, at least, and that would take a little of the load off you, wouldn't it?"

At this they all rose up in unanimous protest.

"Lis'en," one of them said, "befo' I'd take Home Relief I'd go out in duh street an' hit some bastard oveh de haid an' take myse'f some'n'. I know one uv duh boys who tried to git it an' one of dem uppity little college boys ovah der talked tuh him lak he was some damn jailbird or some'n'. If it had been me, I'd a busted hell outn' him an' walked outa duh place. What duh hell do we wants wid relief anynow? We is all able-bodied mens an' can take it. We can make our own livin's."

This, apparently, was the attitude of every man there. They seemed to take fierce pride in the fact that every member of Joe Elder's National Negro Civil Association (it used to be called the National Negro Boat Terminal) was entirely self-supporting. They even had their own unemployment insurance fund that provided an income for any member of the group who was ill and unable to work. Each week the men give a small part of their earnings toward this common fund and automatically agree to allow a certain amount to any temporarily incapacitated member. In addition to that, they divide among themselves their ill brother's work and provide a day and night attendant near his shack if his illness is at all serious.

After chatting awhile longer with them, I finally decided to leave.

"Well boys," I said getting up, "I guess I'll have to be shoving off. Thanks, a lot, for the ribs. See you again sometime."

Before leaving, however, I gave them a couple of packs of cigarettes I had on me in part payment for my dinner.

"O. K." they said. "Come ovah ag'in some time. Some Sat'd'y. Maybe we'll have a few broads (women) and a little co'n."

"Thanks."

Outside the snow and sleet had turned to rain and the snow that had been feathery and white was running down the river bank in brown rivulets of slush and mud. It was a little warmer but the damp air still had a penetrating sharpness to it. I shuddered, wrapped my muffler a little tighter and turned my coat collar up about my ears.

There was wind in the rain, and behind me lay the jagged outline of the ramshackle dwelling. I hated to think of what it would be like, living in them when there was a scarcity of wood or when the fires went out.

Source: Library of Congress Web Page http://rs6.loc.gov/wpaintro/wpahome.html

HOW WELL DID YOU UNDERSTAND THIS SELECTION?

1. Compare life in urban and rural America during the Great Depression. How is it similar? How is it different?

2. Compare the attitudes of the characters in "Beggin" with those in the Harlem pushcart colony? How are they similar? How are they different?

3. Do you think the experiences of the Garrett family are typical of people in the rural South during the Great Depression? Why or why not?

4. Are the experiences of urban dwellers similar to those detailed in "Afternoon in a Pushcart Peddlers' Colony"? Why or why not?

5. How did the Garrett family survive?

6. How did people in the pushcart peddlers' colony survive?

THE TOWNSEND PLAN

Dr. Charles Townsend was a critic of the New Deal. He believed Roosevelt's program did not do enough to address the problems of old age and unemployment. He devised a plan to provide every elderly American with a pension upon retirement contingent upon their spending the money within thirty days. Townsend believed that the retirement of elderly citizens would make room for younger people in the workforce and the pension they received would stimulate the economy through consumer spending, thus creating full employment. Most historians believe Townsend's criticism of the New Deal played a role in the creation of Social Security.

THE TOWNSEND PLAN IN BRIEF

Have the National Government enact legislation to the effect that all citizens of the United States-man or woman-over the age of 60 years may retire on a pension of $200 per month on the following conditions:

1. That they engage in no further labor, business or profession for gain.
2. That their past life is free from habitual criminality.
3. That they take oath to, and actually do spend, within the confines of the United States, the entire amount of their pension within thirty days after receiving same.

Have the National Government create the revolving fund by levying a general sales tax; have the rate just high enough to produce the amount necessary to keep the Old Age Revolving Pensions Fund adequate to pay the monthly pensions.

Have the act so drawn that such sales tax can only be used for the Old Age Revolving Pensions Fund.

ANALYSIS OF THE TOWNSEND PLAN

Insurance statistics show that only 8% of people reaching that age have achieved financial success to such a degree that they may live comfortably thereafter without depending upon further earnings. Eighty-five percent of the 92% of all people sixty years of age and over are still employed or are endeavoring in some manner to earn all or a part of their livelihood and the remainder are dependent upon public or private charity for their keep. Those of the 85% who are still earning are capable of producing only enough to partially pay for their living. A very small percentage actually earn enough for their total needs and but vary few earn any surplus for their declining years.

Approximately 8,000,000 people will be eligible to apply for the pension. Economists estimate that each person spending $200.00 per month creates a job for one additional worker. The retirement of all citizens of 60 years and over from all productive industry and gainful occupation, will thereby create jobs for 8,000,000 workers which will solve our national labor problem.

RETIREMENT ON A MONTHLY PENSION OF $200

The spending of $200 per month is for a constructive purpose. First, to place an adequate amount of buying power in the hands of these citizens which will permit them to satisfy their wants that have been so restricted for the past four years. Second, to create such a demand for new goods of all descriptions that all manufacturing plants in the country will be called upon to start their wheels of production at full speed and provide jobs for all workers.

This money made suddenly available to the channels of trade will immediately start a tremendous flood of buying, since the country has been on short commodity rations for the past four years, and since all sections of the country will be affected alike (the old are everywhere) and the poorest sections will at once become important buying centers.

All factories and avenues of production may be expected to start producing at full capacity and all workers called into activity at high wages, since there will be infinitely more jobs available and many less workers to fill the jobs, the old folks having retired from competition for places as producers.

HOW WILL THIS MONEY BE SPENT

It will go into the regular channels of trade for food, clothing, homes, rent, furniture, automobiles-all manner and description of things dear to the human heart. It will go for travel, the pleasure of riding hobbies, theatre tickets, professional and servant employment and the thousand and one things which modern man demands.

HOW WILL THIS EFFECT THE OWNERS OF PROPERTY OR BUSINESS

Those of 60 years and over owning income property, whose income is greater than the pension, would not need or possibly care to apply for this pension, as it is not designed to be compulsory. Those whose income is less than the pension, undoubtedly would dispose of their interests in income investment to younger people and receive the pension for their declining years. Thus performing the two-fold function that the plan provides, that of relieving industry of their productiveness and increasing industry through their consumption of goods and farm products.

Establishment of homes by those now living with relatives or in institutions, either through ownership or rental, or the holding of homes, now occupied, are encouraged under this plan. Each new home established simply means greater consumption of goods and use of labor.

This plan will effect a marked reduction in the tax burden which they are now compelled to carry and make more secure the profits that should accrue from business and property investment, since it will be less expensive to collect and spend two billions of money monthly than it is to maintain the monthly present-day costs of organized charity in its multiple forms, plus much of the cost of crime and disease due to overcrowding and undernourishment. It will add immensely to the volume of business done and thereby make possible profits in greater amount without increasing the cost of goods.

PENSIONERS TO RETIRE WITHOUT FURTHER GAIN FROM LABOR OR PROFESSION

This is an important feature of the plan since the idea is to create jobs for the young and able, eliminating competition for such jobs and positions on the part of elderly people.

Consumption of the products of farm and factory is the vital problem now facing our nation. The success of this plan is based entirely on the creation of jobs of production and by retiring all those pensioned, with adequate spending power, that they may consume for all their needs in comforts, necessities and pleasure.

RECORDS FREE FROM CRIME

This clause is designed to have a strong effect in restraining the young and impatient from taking the short cut of criminal activity to obtain money. They will hesitate to jeopardize their future welfare for the sake of getting money now by criminal activities.

The desire to honestly earn is uppermost in the minds of American people. The records of our law enforcement departments show that crime is largely the result of lack of opportunity to provide necessities of life through the sale of labor. Provide these opportunities for our younger generations and the crime problem will be greatly lessened.

SAVING FOR OLD AGE

We have been taught in the past that saving was essential in planning for security in old age. But recent experience has taught us that no one has yet been able to devise a sure method of saving. Statistical records show that ninety-two percent of all people reaching the age of sixty-five have, in spite of their best efforts, been unable to save enough to guard them from the humiliation of accepting charity in some form, either from relatives or from the state. Experience proves that no form of investment is infallible that human mind can devise which is based upon the small group or individual financing. The Townsend plan proposes that all who serve society to the best of their ability in whatever capacity shall not be denied that security in their declining years to which their services in active years have entitled them.

COSTS OF MAINTAINING THE HUGH REVOLVING FUND

The unthinking see a great increase in the cost of living due to the necessity for the retailer to raise his prices to meet the government tax for maintaining the pension roll. He fails to take into consideration the fact that the elimination of poor houses, organized state and county relief agencies, public and private pension systems, community chests, etc., are not costing the country the many millions of dollars per month that the Townsend plan would eliminate. And, too, would not the cost of crime and insane asylums be greatly reduced after the public became assured of the permanency of our prosperity? Further, the tremendous increase in the volume of retail business which this hugh revolving fund would insure makes certain that bigger profits would be possible to the retailer through his old rates than ever before and make unnecessary the advance in prices on any articles except those classed as luxuries. Estimated from the sources available a tax of 10% will be ample to raise this fund and the tax can be materially lowered as the volume of trade increases. Competition will still continue to operate and the profit hog will still find competitors who will hold him to a fair price rate. It is the logical foundation for our worthy President's NRA-National Recovery Act.

No one will object to paying the slight advance in price for commodities for the purpose of re-establishing prosperity and, in so doing, making it possible for the elderly people to retire and live comfortably the remainder of their days, since everyone in making his purchases will be providing for his own security when he reaches the age of sixty.

SALES TAX TO BE USED EXCLUSIVELY FOR THE PENSIONS

It is the intent of the plan to apply the sales tax solely to the one purpose of maintaining the pensions roll until such time as the public becomes fully assured of the beneficent and fair system of taxation for all that can be devised. Every individual who enjoys the benefits of the numerous social agencies maintained for his benefit, such as schools, police protection, sanitation, public health supervision and the thousand and one functions of government, should be compelled to carry his share of the costs just in proportion to his ability to do so; that is, in proportion to his ability to spend money. This compels the child to become a taxpayer at an early age and accustoms him to the idea that he must do his share throughout his life.

NO CHANGE IN FORM OF GOVERNMENT

This plan of Old Age Revolving Pensions interferes in no way with our present form of government, profit system of business or change of specie in our economic setup. It is a simple American plan dedicated to the cause of prosperity and the abolition of poverty. It retains the rights of freedom of speech and of press and of religious belief and insures us the right to perpetuate and make glorious the liberty we so cherish and enjoy.

THE MEANING OF SECURITY TO HUMANITY

Here lies the true value in the Townsend Plan. Humanity will be forever relieved from the fear of destitution and want. The seeming need for sharp practices and greedy accumulation will disappear. Benevolence and kindly consideration for others will displace suspicion and avarice, brotherly love and tolerance will blossom into full flower and the genial sun of human happiness will dissipate the dark clouds of distrust and gloom and despair.

CARTOONS THAT APPEARED IN THE TOWNSEND WEEKLY ON MAY 25, 1940

This cartoon, from the Townsend Plan's "Weekly" newspaper, expresses the group's continuing dissatisfaction with the Social Security program. In their view, the Social Security Act was an obstacle to passage of their own plan.

This cartoon, from the Townsend Plan's "Weekly" newspaper, expresses the group's main objection to Social Security—that it was not generous enough in the benefits it offered. The Townsend Plan promised every senior citizen $200 per month, regardless of past earnings. Under the social insurance program of the Social Security Act a worker whose earnings averaged $100 month for 40 years would collect a Social Security retirement benefit of only $35 month. This gave the Townsend Plan an immediate appeal, which is reflected in the cartoon. (Keep in mind, however, that economists estimated it would require one-half of the nation's total income to fund the level of benefits promised by Townsend!)

Source: Web Pages of Social Security Administration
http://www.ssa.gov/history/townbrief.html (http://www.ssa.gov/history/towns46.html)

HOW WELL DID YOU UNDERSTAND THIS SELECTION?

1. What are Dr. Townsend's objectives?

2. How does he propose to fund his pensions?

3. What effect does Dr. Townsend think his plan will have on crime?

4. Why does Dr. Townsend want to require elderly citizens to spend their pension within thirty days?

5. What problems do you find with the Townsend Plan?

MULTIPLE CHOICE: Circle the correct response. The correct answers are given at the end.

1. Roosevelt's plan to combat the Great Depression was called:
    a. The New Frontier.
    b. The Great Society.
    c. The New Freedom.
    d. The New Deal.

2. Huey Long's plan to have the government guarantee every American a basic income and ownership of property was called:
    a. The Townsend Plan.
    b. Share the Wealth Plan.
    c. The Income/Property Plan.
    d. Social Security.

3. The National Labor Relations Act provided:
    a. A minimum wage.
    b. That the government would enforce collective bargaining rights.
    c. The Open Shop.
    d. Time and a half.

4. People from the Midwest and Southwest who came to California in search of economic opportunity during the Great Depression were called:
    a. Texarkanas.
    b. Okies.
    c. Forty-niners.
    d. Middies.

5. What did Dr. Charles Townsend advocate?
    a. A return to pure capitalism.
    b. An end to the New Deal.
    c. Prenatal care for pregnant women.
    d. A retirement pension for elderly Americans.

6. How did Townsend propose to pay for his plan?
    a. By taxing the wealthy.
    b. By imposing a sales tax.
    c. By redistributing the nation's wealth.
    d. By printing paper money not backed by gold.

7. Which of the following statements best describes President Hoover's attitude about the Great Depression?
    a. Government should not help with relief and suffering.
    b. Government should establish social programs to provide jobs for unemployed Americans.
    c. Congress should issue food stamps to help those who can't help themselves.
    d. Congress should tax the wealthy to pay for social programs to combat the Great Depression.

8. What effect did Eleanor Roosevelt have on the position of First Lady?
   a. She had little effect.
   b. She continued the tradition of past First Ladies, making no changes.
   c. She broke with tradition and exerted a strong influence on the President and the nation.
   d. She made the position of First Lady one that stressed traditional feminine values of home and husband.

9. What did the Agricultural Adjustment Act do?
   a. Provide loans to farmers to prevent mortgage foreclosures.
   b. Gave cash allotments to farmers who cut production of tobacco, wheat, corn, cotton, hogs, rice and dairy products.
   c. Gave farmers the right to sell their products directly to food processors and raised incomes by cutting out the middleman.
   d. Forced landowners to rent to tenant farmers.

10. Who was the Republican candidate Franklin Roosevelt defeated in the 1936 election?
    a. Huey Long.
    b. Charles Townsend.
    c. Herbert Hoover.
    d. Alf Landon.

ANSWERS: 1-d; 2-b; 3-b; 4-b; 5-d; 6-a; 7-a; 8-c; 9-b; 10-d

ESSAYS:

1. How did the Great Depression and New Deal shape modern America?

2. Did Roosevelt and the New Deal save capitalism? Support your answer with historical evidence.

3. Compare and contrast the approach critics of the New Deal used to oppose Roosevelt's plan.

OPTIONAL ACTIVITIES: (Use your knowledge **and** imagination.)

1. Imagine that you are an Okie. Compose several entries in your journal in which you describe the difficulties you face as a result of the Great Depression.

2. Interview someone in the United States who lived through the Great Depression. How do his/her experiences compare with what you have learned in your history class.

3. Search newspapers during the Great Depression for political cartoons. Use them to show the view Americans had of the New Deal.

WEB SITE LISTINGS:

Federal Writer's Project Collection.
    A collection of the Library of Congress 2,900 life history manuscripts from the Folklore Project of the Federal Writer's Project, 1936-1940. http://memory.loc.gov/ammem/wpaintro/wpahome.html
Dear Mrs. Roosevelt.
    Information and statistics about the Great Depression. This site contains letters from children written to Eleanor Roosevelt and her responses. http://newdeal.feri.org/eleanor/index.htm

Federal Theatre Project Collection.
   This site contains original documents for the WPA Federal Theatre Project, an effort by the WPA to produce theater events. http://memory.loc.gov/ammem/fedtp/wpa.html

Songs of the Great Depression.
   Lyrics to popular Derpession era songs, including "We're in the Money" and "Brother, Can You Spare a Dime?" are found at this site. http://www.library.csi.cuny.edu/dept/history/lavender/cherries.html

Documenting America.
   Images from the Farm Security Administration taken by government photographers. http://rs6.loc.gov/ammem/fsowhome.html

WebQuest 1930s.
   Offers access to sites related to 1930s history and society. Features links to biographies, timelines, and events of the Great Depression. http://www.nde.state.ne.us/SS/1930.html

New Deal Network
   New Deal Network is a database of photographs, political cartoons, and texts (speeches, letters, and other historic documents) from the New Deal period. newdeal.feri.org

Great Depression & New Deal
   Provides links to various sources on the Great Depression and the New Deal americanhistory.about.com/cs/greatdepression

Great Depression of the 1930's History Guide
   Covers a variety of topics, including a Great Depression of the 1930's History Guide with top history re sources, timelines, FDR, Hoover and more! history.searchbeat.com/greatdepression.htm

New Deal/WPA Art Project
   Provides a look at the WPA Art Project. www.wpamurals.com

Franklin D. Roosevelt Library & Museum Photos of FDR
   Offers photographs of FDR and other people important in the New Deal. www.fdrlibrary.marist.edu/gdphotos.html

Depression and New Deal
   Provedes access to photographs of the Great Depression and New Deal housed by the Library of Congress. homepages.ius.edu/Special/OralHistory/GreatDepression2.htm

Picturing the Century : The Great Depression and the New Deal
   An exhibition of 20th century photographs from the holdings of the National Archives and Records Administration. www.archives.gov/exhibit_hall/picturing_the_century/galleries/greatdep...

Labor Unions During the Great Depression and New Deal
   The Library of Congress home Overview Documents relating to labor unions and strikes during the Great Depression. lcweb2.loc.gov/ammem/ndlpedu/features/timeline/depwwii/unions/unions.h...

Photographs of the Great Depression
   A large compilation of photos from the Great Depression, including photos of dust storms, farm foreclosures, migrant workers, women and children, unemployed, and breadlines and soup kitchens, Unemployed Workers Marching in New Jersey, etc. history1900s.about.com/library/photos/blyindexdepression.htm

Chapter Twenty

THE "GOOD" WAR:
World War II

As America was coping with the Depression by turning to the New Deal, other nations, particularly Germany, Italy, and Japan, embraced totalitarian government and military imperialism. Most Americans reacted to fascist aggression by supporting efforts to isolate the nation from growing world tensions. A series of neutrality acts sought to assure that the United States would not be dragged into the growing conflict as it had in World War I. The enemies of the 1930s, however, were far more dangerous, and the lessons of the First World War did not really apply to the changing world situation. Despite (or perhaps because of) attempts at appeasement by the democratic nations, the fascist powers were emboldened to escalate their aggressive actions from 1937-39. Although many Americans continued to advocate isolation, when full-scale war broke out in Europe in 1939, an increasing number came to the conclusion that the nation should support Britain against the rising power of Nazi Germany.

After winning a third term in 1940, President Roosevelt led the nation towards greater involvement in the world conflict through the Lend Lease Act, naval patrols, and widening collaboration with the British and their new Prime Minister, Winston Churchill. Tensions with Japan also increased until the Japanese bombed Pearl Harbor on December 7, 1941 (a day, according to FDR, "which will live in infamy"). This act propelled the United States into World War II.

America found itself involved in two wars: in Europe and in Asia. The war leaders decided to give greater priority to the destruction of Nazi Germany. This was accomplished as a result of America's massive industrial mobilization, making America the "arsenal of democracy," and the patience and sacrifices of the Soviet armies and people. The D-Day invasion by the Allies helped bring the European war to its inevitable conclusion, as the Allies advanced from the west and the Russians from the east. The slower and more difficult military progress in the Pacific finally culminated in the devastation of Hiroshima and Nagasaki by atomic bombs.

Millions of Americans were involved in the war effort in the armed forces or on the home front. Over fifteen million served in the armed forces, including women in their own newly formed branches. The struggle became a turning point in their lives, as well as in the international power balance. The economic mobilization finally brought an end to the depression. Government power and involvement in the economy greatly expanded. The power of the presidency was enhanced. Businesses, agriculture, and labor unions also grew bigger. New opportunities opened up for women and minorities in the flourishing wartime economy.

Even though the nation was crusading for the triumph of democracy in the world, violations of the rights of minority groups continued at home. The internment of Japanese-Americans who lived on the West Coast was, perhaps, the worst infringement of civil liberties. Although the wartime demand for labor undermined Jim Crow principles, it also heightened racial tensions between whites and blacks and led to race riots in 1943.

The war left unimaginable death and destruction. Millions of civilians died, including six million Jews who were systematically murdered in Nazi extermination centers. Despite all these horrors, however, Americans believed that they had fought a "good war" and defeated the forces of evil. The Big Three (Roosevelt, Stalin and Churchill) met at Yalta in February 1945. There, they made crucial decisions that would affect the world for years to come about the future of Eastern Europe, the establishment of the United Nations, and Soviet entry into the war against Japan. With the formation of the United Nations, Americans hoped that any future conflicts could be avoided.

Both the United States and the Soviet Union had emerged from the war as super powers. Although the two nations had cooperated to defeat the Germans, wariness of each other's actions and motives had continued through the war. The presence of atomic weapons of destruction added to the mistrust and ultimately led to the deadlock known as the Cold War. As a relatively unscathed United States towered above a world devastated by war, there was no longer the option of turning away from world leadership.

IDENTIFICATION: Briefly describe each term.

Fascism

Rome-Berlin-Tokyo Axis

Appeasement

Munich Conference

German invasion of Poland

Blitzkrieg

Nye Committee

Neutrality Acts of 1935-7

Voyage of the *St. Louis*

Selective Service

Lend Lease Act

Winston Churchill

"Four Freedoms"

Pearl Harbor

Tuskegee Airmen

WACs, WAVEs, and WASPs

Stalingrad

D-Day

War Production Board

Office of Price Administration

Office of War Information

Manhattan Project

Rosie the Riveter

Fair Employment Practices Commission

Detroit riot of 1943

"Zoot suit" riots

Internment of Japanese-Americans

Korematsu v. United States

Holocaust

Yalta Conference

Hiroshima and Nagasaki

THINK ABOUT:

1. If the democracies had not appeased Germany, Italy, and Japan when they committed aggression against other nations, would the history of events leading to World War II have been different? If so, how?

2. Could the United States and its Allies have prevented, or at least limited, the Holocaust? What could they have done? Would admitting more refugees have been helpful? Should they have bombed the extermination camps? What would have been the consequences of such an act?

3. Should the United States have dropped the atomic bomb on Hiroshima? Nagasaki? What other options existed? How effective would they have been?

4. Why were the Japanese-Americans picked for internment during the war? Why not German-Americans? What impact does war have on minority civil rights and liberties?

ROOSEVELT'S NEW INTERNATIONALISM

Franklin Roosevelt had arrived at the strong conviction that, in a rapidly changing world, the United States had a moral and political responsibility to oppose those totalitarian forces that had risen to power and pushed the world into war. He also understood that those forces posed a serious threat to American economic and political interests. His famous "Four Freedoms" speech reflects his increasingly global outlook. The Atlantic Charter, agreed to by Roosevelt and Churchill, is a further exposition of those ideals.

Roosevelt's "Four Freedoms" Speech, January 6, 1941

...Every realist knows that the democratic way of life is at this moment being directly assailed in every part of the world-assailed either by arms, or by secret spreading of poisonous propaganda by those who seek to destroy unity and promote discord in nations still at peace. During sixteen months this assault has blotted out the whole pattern of democratic life in an appalling number of independent nations, great and small. The assailants are still on the march, threatening other nations, great and small ....

As men do not live by bread alone, they do not fight by armaments alone. Those who man our defenses, and those behind them who build our defenses, must have the stamina and courage which come from an unshakable belief in the manner of life which they are defending. The mighty action which they are calling for cannot be based on a disregard of all things worth fighting for.

The Nation takes great satisfaction and much strength from the things which have been done to make its people conscious of their individual stake in the preservation of democratic life in America. Those things have toughened the fibre of our people, have renewed their faith and strengthened their devotion to the institutions we make ready to protect. Certainly this is no time to stop thinking about the social and economic problems which are the root cause of the social revolution which is today a supreme fact in the world.

There is nothing mysterious about the foundations of a healthy and strong democracy. The basic things expected by our people of their political and economic system are simple. They are: equality of opportunity for youth and for others: jobs for those who can work; security for those who need it; the ending of special privilege for the few, the preservation of civil liberties for all; the enjoyment of the fruits of scientific progress in a wider and constantly rising standard of living.

These are the simple and basic things that must never be lost sight of in the turmoil and unbelievable complexity of our modern world. The inner and abiding strength of our economic and political systems is dependent upon the degree to which they fulfill these expectations.

Many subjects connected with our social economy call for immediate improvement. As examples: We should bring more citizens under the coverage of old age pensions and unemployment insurance. We should widen the opportunities for adequate medical care. We should plan a better system by which persons deserving or needing gainful employment may obtain it.

I have called for personal sacrifice. I am assured of the willingness of almost all Americans to respond to that call ....

In the future days, which we seek to make secure, we look forward to a world founded upon four essential human freedoms.

The first is freedom of speech and expression-everywhere in the world.

The second is freedom of every person to worship God in his own way—everywhere in the world.

The third is freedom from want-which, translated into world terms, means economic understandings which will secure to every nation a healthy peace time life for its inhabitants—everywhere in the world.

The fourth is freedom from fear-which, translated into world terms, means a worldwide reduction of armaments to such a point and in such a thorough fashion that no nation will be in a position to commit an act of physical aggression against any neighbor-anywhere in the world.

That is no vision of a distant millennium. It is a definite basis for a kind of world attainable in our own time and generation. That kind of world is the very antithesis of the so-called new order of tyranny which the dictators seek to create with the crash of a bomb.

To that new order we oppose the greater conception—the moral order. A good society is able to face schemes of world domination and foreign revolutions alike without fear.

Since the beginning of our American history we have been engaged in change in a perpetual peaceful revolution-a revolution which goes on steadily, quietly adjusting itself to changing conditions-without the concentration camp or the quicklime in the ditch. The world order which we seek is the cooperation of free countries, working together in a friendly, civilized society.

This nation has placed its destiny in the hands and heads and hearts of its millions of free men and women; and its faith in freedom under the guidance of God. Freedom means the supremacy of human rights everywhere. Our support goes to those who struggle to gain those rights or keep them. Our strength is in our unity of purpose.

To that high concept there can be no end save victory.

Source: Franklin D. Roosevelt, Annual Message to Congress, January 6, 1941. Quoted from *The Public Papers of F. D. Roosevelt*, vol. 9, p. 663. Washington, D.C.: United States Government Printing Office.

The Atlantic Charter, August 14, 1941

The President of the United States of America and the Prime Minister, Mr. Churchill, representing His Majesty's Government in the United Kingdom, being met together, deem it right to make known certain common principles in the national policies of their respective countries on which they base their hopes for a better future for the world.

First, their countries seek no agrandizement, territorial or other;

Second, they desire to see no territorial changes that do not accord with the freely expressed wishes of the peoples concerned;

Third, they respect the right of all peoples to choose the form of government under which they will live; and they wish to see sovereign rights and self government restored to those who have been forcibly deprived of them;

Fourth, they will endeavor, with due respect for their existing obligations, to further the enjoyment by all States, great or small, victor or vanquished, of access, on equal terms, to the trade and to the raw materials of the world which are needed for their economic prosperity;

Fifth, they desire to bring about the fullest collaboration between all nations in the economic field with the object of securing, for all, improved labor standards, economic advancement and social security;

Sixth, after the final destruction of the Nazi tyranny, they hope to see established a peace which will afford to all nations the means of dwelling in safety within their own boundaries, and which will afford assurance that all the men in all the lands may live out their lives in freedom from fear and want;

Seventh, such a peace should enable all men to traverse the high seas and oceans without hindrance:

Eighth, they believe that all of the nations of the world, for realistic as well as spiritual reasons must come to the abandonment of the use of force. Since no future peace can be maintained if land, sea or air armaments continue to be employed by nations which threaten, or may threaten, aggression outside of their frontiers, they believe, pending the establishment of a wider and permanent system of general security, that the disarmament of such nations is essential. They will likewise aid and encourage all other practicable measures which will lighten for peace-loving peoples the crushing burden of armaments.

Franklin D. Roosevelt
Winston S. Churchill

Source: *The Public Papers of F. D. Roosevelt*, vol. 10, p. 314. Washington, D.C.: United States Government Printing Office.

HOW WELL DID YOU UNDERSTAND THIS SELECTION?

1. How does Roosevelt try to counter antiwar sentiments at the beginning of his "Four Freedoms" speech?

2. What did Roosevelt believe were the foundations of a "healthy and strong democracy"?

3. Of the four freedoms listed by Roosevelt, which do you think people of the 1940s would have considered most important? What about today?

4. How does the Atlantic Charter reflect some of the ideals of the "Four Freedoms"?

5. Why do you think the Atlantic Charter was so well received?

This is Roosevelt's famous message declaring war on Japan after the surprise attack on Pearl Harbor.

Address to Congress (1941)
Franklin D. Roosevelt

Yesterday, December 7, 1941—a date which will live in infamy—the United States of America was suddenly and deliberately attacked by naval and air forces of the Empire of Japan.

The United States was at peace with that nation and, at the solicitation of Japan, was still in conversation with its Government and its Emperor looking toward the maintenance of peace in the Pacific. Indeed, one hour after Japanese air squadrons had commenced bombing in Oahu, the Japanese Ambassador to the United States and his colleague delivered to the Secretary of State a formal reply to a recent American message. While this reply stated that it seemed useless to continue the existing diplomatic negotiations, it contained no threat or hint of war or armed attack.

It will be recorded that the distance of Hawaii from Japan makes it obvious that the attack was deliberately planned many days or even weeks ago. During the intervening time the Japanese Government has deliberately sought to deceive the United States by false statements and expressions of hope for continued peace.

The attack yesterday on the Hawaiian Islands has caused severe damage to American naval and military forces. Very many American lives have been lost. In addition American ships have been reported torpedoed on the high seas between San Francisco and Honolulu.

Yesterday the Japanese Government also launched an attack against Malaya. Last night Japanese forces attacked Hong Kong. Last night Japanese forces attacked Guam. Last night Japanese force's attacked the Philippine Islands. Last night the Japanese attacked Wake Island. This morning the Japanese attacked Midway Island.

Japan has, therefore, undertaken a surprise offensive extending throughout the Pacific area. The facts of yesterday speak for themselves. The people of the United States have already formed their opinions and well understand the implications to the very life and safety of our nation.

As Commander-in-Chief of the Army and Navy, I have directed that all measures be taken for our defense.

Always will we remember the character of the onslaught against us.

No matter how long it may take us to overcome this premeditated invasion, the American people in their righteous might will win through to absolute victory

I believe I interpret the will of the Congress and of the people when I assert that we will not only defend ourselves to the uttermost but will make very certain that this form of treachery shall never endanger us again.

Hostilities exist. There is no blinking at the fact that our people, our territory and our interests are in grave danger.

With confidence in our armed forces—with the unbounded determination of our people—we will gain the inevitable triumph-so help us God.

I ask that the Congress declare that since the unprovoked and dastardly attack by Japan on Sunday, December seventh, a state of war has existed between the United States and the Japanese Empire.

Source: The *New York Times*, December 9, 1941

HOW WELL DID YOU UNDERSTAND THIS SELECTION?

1. Why do you think Roosevelt issued such a brief declaration of war without the specific larger goals that Wilson had mentioned in his World War I declaration?

2. Why could the president confidently state that the American people had "already formed their opinion"?

3. How do American idealism and feelings of American uniqueness slip into the message?

INTERNMENT OF JAPANESE AMERICANS

After Pearl Harbor many Americans were alarmed by the large population of Japanese Americans in the West. Although there was never any evidence of any espionage or sabotage by these people, popular feelings rose to the level of hysteria. Roosevelt was persuaded to agree to an executive order allowing the roundup and relocation to camps of Japanese Americans on the West Coast. The first reading describes the conditions in the camps. The issue of the legality of putting American citizens in detention camps came before the Supreme Court in 1944. Justice Hugo Black wrote the majority opinion upholding the government's actions on the basis of military necessity. Three justices agreed with Frank Murphy's dissent.

Conditions in the Camps (1942-1945)

A visiting reporter from The San Francisco Chronicle described quarters at Tule Lake:

Room size—about 15 by 25, considered too big for two reporters.
  Condition—dirty.
  Contents—two Army cots, each with two Army blankets, one pillow, some sheets and pillow cases (these came as a courtesy from the management), and a coal-burning stove (no coal). There were no dishes, rugs, curtains, or housekeeping equipment of any kind. (We had in addition one sawhorse and three pieces of wood, which the management did not explain.)

The furnishings at other camps were similar. At Minidoka, arriving evacuees found two stacked canvas cots, a pot-bellied stove and a light bulb hanging from the ceiling; at Topaz, cots, two blankets, a pot-bellied stove and some cotton mattresses. Rooms had no running water, which had to be carried from community facilities. Running back and forth from the laundry room to rinse and launder soiled diapers was a particular inconvenience ....

Others, however, found not even the minimal comforts that had been planned for them. An unrealistic schedule combined with wartime shortages of labor and materials meant that the WRA (Wartime Relocation Administration) had difficulty meeting its construction schedule. In most cases, the barracks" were completed, but at some centers evacuees lived without electric light, adequate toilets or laundry facilities ....

Mess Halls planned for about 300 people had to handle 600 or 900 for short periods. Three months after the project opened, Manzanar still lacked equipment for 16 of 36 messhalls. At Gila:

There were 7,700 people crowded into space designed for 5,000. They were housed in messhalls, recreation halls, and even latrines. As many as 25 persons lived in a space intended for four.

As at the assembly centers, one result was that evacuees were often denied privacy in even the most intimate aspects of their lives .... Even when families had separate quarters, the partitions between rooms failed to give much privacy. Gladys Bell described the situation at Topaz:

[T]he evacuees . . . had only one room, unless there were around ten in the family. Their rooms had a pot-bellied stove, a single electric light hanging from the ceiling, an Army cot for each person and a blanket for the bed. Each barrack had six rooms with only three flues. This meant that a hole had to be cut through the wall of one room for the stovepipe to join the chimney of the next room. The hole was large so that the wall would not burn. As a result, everything said and some things whispered were easily heard by people living in the next room. Sometimes the family would be a couple with four children living next to an older couple, perhaps of a different religion, older ideas and with a difference in all ways of life—such as music.

Despite these wretched conditions the evacuees again began to rebuild their lives. Several evacuees recall "foraging for bits of wallboard and wood" and dodging guards to get materials from the scrap lumber piles to build shelves and furniture .... Eventually, rooms were partitioned and shelves, tables, chairs and other furniture appeared. Paint and cloth for curtains and spreads came from mail order houses at evacuee expense. Flowers bloomed and rock gardens emerged; trees and shrubs were planted. Many evacuees grew victory gardens. One described the change:

[W]hen we entered camp, it was a barren desert. When we left camp, it was a garden that had been built up without tools, it was green around the camp with vegetation, flowers, and also with artificial lakes, and that's how we left it.

The success of evacuees' efforts to improve their surroundings, however, was always tempered by the harsh climate. In the western camps, particularly Heart Mountain, Poston, Topaz and Minidoka, dust was a principal problem. Monica Sone described her first day at Minidoka:

[W]e were given a rousing welcome by a dust storm....We felt as if we were standing in a gigantic sand-mixing machine as the sixty mile gale lifted the loose earth up into the sky, obliterating everything. Sand filled our mouths and nostrils and stung our faces and hands like a thousand darting needles. Henry and Father pushed on ahead while Mother, Sumi and I followed, hanging onto their jackets, banging suitcases into each other. At last we staggered into our room, gasping and blinded. We sat on our suitcases to rest, peeling off our jackets and scarves. The window panels rattled madly, and the dust poured through the cracks like smoke. Now and then when the wind subsided, I saw other evacuees, hanging on to their suitcases, heads bent against the stinging dust. The wind whipped their scarves and towels from their heads and zipped them out of sight.

In desert camps, the evacuees met severe extremes of temperature as well. In winter it reached 35 degrees below zero and summers brought temperature as high as 115°. Because the desert did not cool off at night, evacuees would splash water on their cots to be cool enough to sleep. Rattlesnakes and desert wildlife added danger to discomfort.

The Arkansas camps had equally unpleasant weather. Winters were cold and snowy while summers were unbearably hot and humid, heavy with chiggers and clouds of mosquitos ....

Source: Commission on Wartime Relocation and Internment of Civilians, *Personal Justice Denied* (Washington, D.C. Government Printing Office, 1984), pp. 159-161.

Korematsu v. U.S.: The Majority Opinion

The petitioner, an American citizen of Japanese descent, was convicted in a federal district court for remaining in San Leandro, California, a "Military Area," contrary to Civil Exclusion Order No. 34, of the Commanding General of the Western Command, U.S. Army, which directed that after May 9, 1942, all persons of Japanese ancestry should be excluded from that area....

It should be noted, to begin with, that all legal restrictions which curtail the civil rights of a single racial group are immediately suspect. That is not to say that all such restrictions are unconstitutional. It is to say that courts must subject them to the most rigid scrutiny. Pressing public necessity may sometimes justify the existence of such restrictions; racial antagonism never can.

....Regardless of the true nature of the assembly and relocation centers—and we deem it unjustifiable to call them concentration camps with all the ugly connotations that term implies—we are dealing specifically with nothing but an exclusion order. To cast this case into outlines of racial prejudice, without reference to the real military dangers which were presented, merely confuses the issue.

Korematsu was not excluded from the Military Area be cause of hostility to him or his race. He was excluded because we are at war with the Japanese Empire, because the properly constituted military authorities feared an invasion of our West Coast . . . the military authorities considered that the need for action was great and time was short. We cannot—by availing ourselves of the calm perspective of hindsight—now say that at that time these actions were unjustified.

Dissent by Justice Frank Murphy

This exclusion of "all persons of Japanese ancestry, both alien and nonalien," from the Pacific Coast area on a plea of military necessity in the absence of martial law ought not to be approved. Such exclusion goes over "the very brink of constitutional power" and falls into the ugly abyss of racism . . . .

No adequate reason is given for the failure to treat these Japanese Americans on an individual basis by holding investigations and hearings to separate the loyal from the disloyal, as was done in the case of persons of German and Italian ancestry . . . .

Moreover, there was no adequate proof that the Federal Bureau of Investigation and the military and naval intelligence services did not have the espionage and sabotage situation well- in hand during this long period. Nor is there any denial of the fact that not one person of Japanese ancestry was accused or convicted of espionage or sabotage after Pearl Harbor- while they were still free . . . . It seems incredible that under these circumstances it would have been impossible to hold loyalty hearings for the mere 112,000 persons involved-or at least for the 70,000 American citizens especially when a large part of this number- represented children and elderly men and women. .

I dissent, therefore, from this legalization of racism . . . . All residents of this nation are kin is some way by blood or culture to a foreign land. Yet they are primarily and necessarily a part of the new and distinct civilization of the United States. They must accordingly be treated at all times as the heirs of the American experiment and as entitled to all the rights and freedoms guaranteed by the Constitution.

Source: U. S. Supreme Court, *Korematsu v. U. S.* (1944)

HOW WELL DID YOU UNDERSTAND THIS SELECTION?

1. What conditions in the detention camps would have bothered you the most had you been forced to go there?

2. What did the Japanese Americans do to make the most of their circumstances?

3. What were the grounds for the majority of the Supreme Court to uphold the government's detention of Japanese Americans in the *Korematsu* case? How convincing do find the Court's argument to be?

4. Why did Justice Murphy dissent? Whose argument do you feel has best stood the test of time?

"A LOYAL NEGRO SOLDIER"

African-American soldiers were drafted in World War II. Some one million black men and women served in the armed forces during the war. But, despite the slogans of liberty and tolerance that marked the propaganda for the war, they served in segregated regiments and continued to suffer from racial discrimination. Black leaders launched a "Double V" campaign for victory against racism at home, as well as victory in the war. This letter by an anonymous black soldier reflects these feelings.

November 5, 1943

Truman K Gibson, Jr.
Civilian Aide to the Secretary of War
Washington, D.C.

Dear Mr. Gibson:

And I fight—for Democracy?

Upon reading the title of this article the average reader would assume that I am a member of the armed forces in the U.S.A. In your assumption, reader, you are definitely correct. I was selected by the President and citizens, to fight for a "non-existing Democracy." I am one soldier who waited to be drafted. I didn't volunteer out. I am learning to fight to protect whatever cause for which the Allies are fighting. I am forced to learn to be ready to kill or be killed-for "Democracy." When fighting time arrives I will fight for it.

I learned early in life that for the Negro there is no Democracy. Of course I know the principles set forth in the Amendments and the Bill of Rights. I learned that I knew nothing of the operation of a true democratic form of government. I found that a Negro in civilian life has [a] very tough time with segregation in public places and discrimination in industry. I knew this and I thought that white people would react differently toward a colored soldier.

I had heard and read of the cruel treatment given colored soldiers and somehow, even among existing conditions of civilian life, I couldn't understand how white people could be so down on one who wears the uniform of the fighting forces of their country. From civilian life I was drafted and now I prepare to fight for the continuation of discriminatory practices against me and my people.

I have long known that the fighting forces are composed of two divisions. Namely, a white division composed of Germans, Jews, Italians, Dutch and all white people of the remaining countries (The question is: Are they loyal?). A Negro division composed of American Negroes and all dark skin people. The American Negro has fought in every war since the Revolutionary War. There can be no question as to his loyalty. He is put into a division composed of the members of his race not because of his educational qualities, his fighting abilities or his inability to live with others, but he's put into a separate division because of the color of his skin.

This is serious since the Negroes are trained to a large extent in Southern States whose white civilians are more drastic in showing their dislike than in Northern white people.

I prayed that I'd be sent to a camp in my home state or that I'd be sent to some camp in a Northern State. My prayers weren't answered and I find myself at this outpost of civilization. I never wanted to be within twenty hundred miles of Alexandria, Louisiana. I am here and I can do nothing to improve my condition. Nevertheless, I prepare to fight for a country where I am denied the rights of being a full-fledged citizen.

A few weeks after my arrival at this camp, I went to a post exchange on my regimental area. I knew that each area has an exchange but I thought that I could make my purchase at any of them. Upon entering I could feel the place grow cold. All conversation ceased. It was then that I noticed that all the soldiers and the saleswomen were white. Not to be outdone I approached the counter and was told (even before asking for the article) that, "Negroes are not served here. This post exchange is for white soldiers. You have one near your regiment. Buy what you want there."

My answer to these abrupt and rudely made statements was in the form of a question—"I thought that post exchanges are for soldiers regardless of color, am I right?"

I left this post exchange and returned to my regimental area. I know that these saleswomen knew not the way of a true democracy.

As long as I am a soldier I fight for a mock Democracy. I was called to report to the camp hospital for an eye examination last week. I was surprised to find the waiting room full of Negro and white soldiers who were sharing the same seats and reading the same newspapers. I was shocked. I didn't believe that the camp hospital could be so free from segregation while the camp itself was built on prejudice.

My second surprise came when registering. Each person filled out a blank and all blanks were placed in the same basket in order of the entrance regardless of the race of the entree. I was just beginning to feel proud of the hospital when a list of names were called off and my name was last on the list. I found myself in line of sixteen (16) men, seven of whom were white. The white men gradually fell out of line and the Negroes found themselves continually waiting . . . waiting for the white soldiers to finish their examinations.

It wouldn't have been noticed had not the sergeant in charge been contented to carry only those white soldiers in the line, but he proceeded to bring more from the waiting room. When I could stand this no longer I protested.

Result: We were immediately examined and allowed to return to our regimental area. I was asked a few days later, "Don't you want to fight for the U.S.A. and its policies?"

I am a soldier; I made no answer, but deep down inside I knew when I faced America's enemies I will fight for the protection of my loved ones at home.

Listen, Negro America, I am writing this article believing that it will act as a stimulant. You need awakening. Many of you have come to realize that your race is fighting on the battlefields of the world, but do you know why they fight? I can answer this question.

The right on the battlefield is for your existence, not for Democracy. It is upon you that each soldier depends. In my fight my thoughts will invariably return to you who can fight for Democracy. You must do this for the soldiers because Democracy will be, and Democracy must, must be won at home—not on battlefields but through your bringing pressure to bear on Congress.

A Loyal Negro Soldier

HOW WELL DID YOU UNDERSTAND THIS SELECTION?

1. Why was the "Loyal Negro Soldier" not anxious to serve in the army?

2. Why does he object to where he is sent for training camp?

3. Why does he ask about the "white division," "the question is are they loyal"?

4. Why wasn't he served at the post exchange?

5. How would you have reacted if you were asked to fight for democracy in a segregated regiment?

6. Do you think his anger is justified during wartime? Why or why not?

During World War II, the female work force grew by 50 percent. These women workers were needed and welcomed, in striking contrast to the disapproval encountered by working women during the Depression. The public assumed that these jobs would be temporary, to be ended when wartime necessities ended. The experience of one such "Rosie the Riveter" is shown in the following document.

Sunday

I am back from my first day on the Ways [staging on which ships are built], and I feel as if I had seen some giant phenomenon. It's incredible! It's inhuman! It's horrible! And it's marvelous! I don't believe a blitz could be noisier—I didn't dream that there could be so much noise, anywhere. My ears are still ringing like high-tension wires, and my head buzzes. When you first see it, when you look down Way after Way, when you see the thousands each going about his own business and seeming to know what to do, you're so bewildered you can't see anything or make sense out of it.

First came the bus ride to the Yard. Crowded as usual. I was intrigued by knowing that this time I was going to Mart's Marsh. The name has always fascinated me. I gather that it refers to bottom or marshy land once owned by a family named Mart. From the [welding] school our road led along the water where I could see several of the ships already launched and now lying at the outfitting dock to receive the finishing touches. It was easy to spot the various stages of completion; each ship gets moved up one when a new ship arrives for outfitting.

When the bus came to a stop, I followed the crowd across a pontoon bridge between rails at which stood guards checking for badges. The far side of the bridge brought us to the part of the Yard where the prefabricated parts are stored, right in the open, pile upon pile. I saw a huge building marked "Assembly Shop," another "Marine Shop," and still another "Pipe Assembly." There were lots of little houses marked with numbers. Most of them seemed to be in the sixties. And I was looking for check-in station No. 1.

I hunted and hunted without success, and finally asked someone where "new hires" check in. He immediately directed me. I showed my badge, told my number, and was given another badge to be picked up and turned in daily as we did at school. It was marked "New Hire." About then who should come along but Red-headed Marie and the Big Swede! We went together to the Welders' Office where our off days were assigned to us. I was given "C" day and told that it was the only day available. This means that I get Tuesday off this week, Wednesday next, and so on. The Big Swede said she had to have "D" day to get a ride to work and to have the same day as her husband. Although "C" day was "the only one available," strangely enough she was given "D" day. One has to learn to insist on what one wants even when told it is impossible.

The Big Swede is a real pal. She had not forgotten the patch for my overall trouser leg. She had cut a piece from an old pair of her husband's, scrubbed it to get the oil out, and brought it to me with a needle stuck in the center and a coil of black thread ready for action. "Here," she said, "I knew you wouldn't have things handy in a hotel room. Now you mend that hole before you catch your foot in it and fall." . . .

Today my book on welding came from the Washington office. I read that a welder's qualifications are "physical fitness which insures a reasonable degree of endurance during a full day of work; steady nerves and considerable muscular strength." For a shipyard welder I'd amend that to read: "An unreasonable degree of endurance during a full day of strain, plus muscular strength, plus no nerves." If you haven't the muscular strength before you start, you will have it afterward. If you haven't the nerves before, you may have them afterward, though I doubt it. By tomorrow I shall be "reasonably" acclimated, but tonight I quite frankly "ain't."

I, who hate heights, climbed stair after stair after stair till I thought I must be close to the sun. I stopped on the top deck. I, who hate confined spaces, went through narrow corridors, stumbling my way over rubbercoats leads—dozens of them, scores of them, even hundreds of them. I went into a room about four feet by ten where two shipfitters, a shipfitter's helper, a chipper, and I all worked. I welded in the poop deck lying on the floor while another welder spattered sparks from the ceiling and chippers like giant woodpeckers shattered our eardrums. I, who've taken welding, and have sat at a bench welding flat and vertical plates, was told to weld braces along a baseboard below a door opening. On these a heavy steel door was braced while it was hung to a fine degree of accuracy. I welded more braces along the side, and along the top. I did overhead welding, horizontal, flat, vertical. I welded around curved hinges which were placed so close to the side wall that I had to bend my rod in a curve to get it in. I made some good welds and some frightful ones. But now a door in the poop deck of an oil tanker is hanging, four feet by six of solid steel, by my welds. Pretty exciting!

The men in the poop deck were nice to me. The shipfitter was toothless. The grinder had palsy, I guess, for his hands shook pitifully and yet he managed to handle that thirty-pound grinder. The welder was doing "pickup" work, which meant touching up spots that had been missed. An inspector came through and marked places to chip, and the ship's superintendent stopped and woke the shipfitter's helper....

As a result of all this, I feel very strongly that we'd go to the Yard better prepared if in the school we did more welding in varied positions. Even a fillet weld of two plates could be placed on the floor, and one could get down and do it there and so learn something of what will later be required in the Yard. I don't see why, too, the butterflies, the clips, and even the bolts couldn't be welded at various angles in school. We could practice some   one-handed welding instead of always using two hands while sitting at a bench with plates conveniently placed. There are times when you have to use one hand to cling to a ladder or a beam while you weld with the other. I notice that the most experienced welders I have watched seldom use two hands. One large, fine-looking woman (Norwegian, I think) who has been there three months told me: "They don't teach us enough at school. Why don't they let us weld there the same things we'll do here?" I countered with, "Oh, they do teach a lot or we'd be no good here at all; but what you say would certainly help." I think she "has something," however. We do need more experience in setting our machines and recognizing when they are too hot or too cold. Struggling with an inaccurate setting and the wrong amount of heat makes a harder day than doing a lot of actual work. Yet it's hardly the fault of the training that we lack adequate experience. More and more I marvel at training that in eight days can give enough to make us worth anything on the job. And we are worth something. We're building ships.

Source: *Augusta Clawson*, Diary of a Woman Welder, 1945

HOW WELL DID YOU UNDERSTAND THIS SELECTION?

1. Why is the woman welder so amazed by what she sees on her first day on the job?

2. What things does she do on the job that she had never expected herself to be able to do?

3. How do the women workers react to each other?

4. Why is she proud of the work she is doing?

5. What does her experience tell you about women workers in World War II?

6. What do you think the permanent results would be from women's experiences in the war?

IWO JIMA
Edgar L. Jones, *Atlantic Monthly*, **February 1945**

On February 19, 1945, thousands of marines landed on Iwo Jima. It was part of the dangerous "island hopping" operations that characterized the last months of the war in the Pacific. Four days after they landed, the famous flag raising on Mt. Suribachi took place. Jones, reporting for the **Atlantic Monthly***, accompanied the troops.*

I went in with a large group of Fourth Division Marines.... The Japanese were lobbing shells into supply dumps, ammunition depots, communication centers, and every other place where they saw men or machinery concentrated. No man on the beach felt secure. The Americans held about one square mile of low ground at that point, most of which I toured. Everywhere men were struggling: to keep landing craft from submerging, to dig roads in the deep sand, to push mired trucks onto solid ground, to haul equipment to sheltered locations, and to fight nature for the chance to get on with the battle. And all the time the Japanese shells whined down and tore into sand and flesh with indiscriminate fury.

No one who was at Iwo can analyze the battle objectively. The carnage was so horrifying that the blood and agony of the struggle saturated one's mind, dismally coloring all thought. Iwo was unlike any war I had ever seen. It was a fight to the finish, with no man asking for quarter until he was dead. Of the nearly 20,000 American casualties, approximately two thirds were wounded, but all except a few score of the 20,000 Japanese died where they fell. There is such a thing as dying decently, but not on Iwo. I do not believe anything practical can be achieved by describing men blown apart. Veterans of two and three years of war in the Pacific were sickened. An estimated 26,000 men died in eight square miles of fighting. There were 3,000 dead and wounded American and Japanese soldiers for every square mile.

I returned to Iwo on D Day (a standard military term, not referring to events in Europe) plus six, seven and eight. By that time the Marines had captured territory where Japanese had lain dead in the hot sun for more than a week. I crawled into pillboxes burned out by flamethrowers, and into deep caves where the Japanese had been burning their own dead to conceal the extent of their losses. I was torturing myself to look at the results of war, because I think it is essential for civilians occasionally to hold their noses and see what is going on.

The sight on Iwo which I could not force myself to see again was the section of the beach allotted for an American cemetery.... On the afternoon I walked by, there was half an acre of dead Marines stretched out so close together that they blanketed the beach for two hundred yards. The stench was overpowering.... The smell of one's countrymen rotting in the sun is a lasting impression.

Source: "To the Finish; A Letter from Iwo Jima," *The Atlantic Monthly*, 1945

HOW WELL DID YOU UNDERSTAND THIS SELECTION?

1. What was so horrifying about the battle of Iwo Jima, according to Jones?

2. Why did the Japanese burn their dead?

3. How do you think an American reader would have reacted to this story?

4. What did the combat at Iwo Jima show about the continuation of the war in the Pacific?

U.S. GOVERNMENT ACQUIESCENCE IN THE MURDER OF JEWS

On January 13, 1944, Secretary of the Treasury Henry Morgenthau presented President Roosevelt with an eighteen-page memorandum entitled "Report to the Secretary on the Acquiescence of This Government in the Murder of Jews." It was a powerful document, charging that State Department officials had completely failed to prevent the mass annihilation of Jews. It began with a direct attack:

One of the greatest crimes in history, the slaughter of the Jewish people in Europe, is continuing unabated.

This Government has for a long time maintained that its policy is to work out programs to save those Jews of Europe who could be saved.

I am convinced on the basis of the information which is available to me that certain officials in our State Department, which is charged with carrying out this policy, have been guilty not only of gross procrastination and willful failure to act, but even of willful attempts to prevent action from being taken to rescue Jews from Hitler.

I fully recognize the graveness of this statement and I make it only after having most carefully weighed the shocking facts which have come to my attention during the last several months.

Unless remedial steps of a drastic nature are taken, and taken immediately, I am certain that no effective action will be taken by this Government to prevent the complete extermination of the Jews in German controlled Europe, and that this Government will have to share for all time responsibility for this extermination.

The tragic history of this Government's handling of this matter reveals that certain State Department officials are guilty of the following:

(1) They have not only failed to use the *Governmental machinery* at their disposal to rescue Jews from Hitler, but have even gone so far as to use this Government machinery to prevent the rescue of these Jews.

(2) They have not only failed to cooperate with *private organizations* in the efforts of these organizations to work out individual programs of their own, but have taken steps designed to prevent these programs from being put into effect.

(3) They not only have failed to facilitate the obtaining of information concerning Hitler's plans to exterminate the Jews of Europe but in their official capacity have gone so far as to surreptitiously attempt to stop the obtaining of information concerning the murder of the Jewish population of Europe.

(4) They have tried to cover up their guilt by:
    (a) concealment and misrepresentation;
    (b) the giving of false and misleading explanations for their failures to act and their attempts to prevent action; and
    (c) the issuance of false and misleading statements concerning the "action" which they have taken to date.

Source: *Diaries of Henry Morgenthau Jr.*—available at Franklin D. Roosevelt Library, Hyde Park, N.Y.

HOW WELL DID YOU UNDERSTAND THIS SELECTION?

1. Why do you think Morgenthau sent this document to President Roosevelt?

2. How do think Roosevelt reacted to the charges?

3. Who does Morgenthau blame for the failure of American government policy?

4. Could the American government have taken any actions to stop or lessen the Holocaust? What could it have done?

Franklin Delano Roosevelt had been president during the most difficult times in modern American history—the Great Depression and World War II, a period of more than twelve years. There were many Americans who could not recall another president. The sudden news of his death, just as victory in the war seemed within reach, shocked the nation. Merriman Smith was a United Press reporter on the funeral train on April 13, the day after Roosevelt died.

EN ROUTE TO WASHINGTON

Franklin Delano Roosevelt was borne across the hushed Southern countryside today on the long, last journey to the White House and Hyde Park. The eleven-coach funeral train made a slow trip northward from Warm Springs, Ga., where he died Thursday afternoon...

The funeral procession from the "Little White House," where the President died, was a pageant of grief. Mr. Roosevelt made his last trip through the grounds he loved so well in a black hearse. An Army honor guard of 2,000 troops marched before it, kicking up red clay dust on the winding country road to the village. Behind the hearse rode Mrs. Roosevelt, sitting stiffly upright. Fala, the President's Scottie, sat quietly at her feet, as if aware that something was wrong. At the end of the thirty-five minute procession from the cottage to the terminal, Mrs. Roosevelt's eyes were misty. She was fighting hard to retain composure.

...The patients [of the Warm Springs Foundation] with whom the President shared such a deep bond were not forgotten. It was Mr. Roosevelt's custom, when he ended each Warm Springs visit, to give a brief call and wave of the hand to those gathered before the foundation's main dormitory. Today, the hearse came to a full stop before the crowded porch. In mute grief, the patients watched. Two hours before the faint beat of drums signaled its approach, some had hobbled out to wait. Some were wheeled out. To them, the President was a magnificent inspiration.

A thirteen-year-old, Jay Fribourg, said: "I loved him so much." He clenched his teeth as he held back the tears. Chief Petty Officer Graham Jackson, a Georgia Negro, a favorite of Mr. Roosevelt, stepped out from the circle with the accordion which he had played often for the President. As the procession approached he began the plaintive strains of "Going Home." Then he played "Nearer My God to Thee." There was scarcely a dry eye.

...Farther down the road, troops--overseas veterans-wept openly as [the hearse] passed. When it reached the tiny station, the troops moved into company front and presented arms. The townspeople bared their heads and watched the funeral party board the train. They stood silently as the train gathered speed and rumbled northward. Then it rounded a bend, and all that could be seen was a thin trail of black smoke. Still they stood, with the scorching sun beating down on the row of modest stores that lined the street. Then, finally, they began to leave.

Source: *New York Herald Tribune*, April 14, 1945

HOW WELL DID YOU UNDERSTAND THIS SELECTION?

1. How did the American public react to the death of Roosevelt?

2. Do you think the grief was greater than might have been the case for another president dying under the same circumstances? Why or why not?

3. How do you think the reaction to Roosevelt's death would compare to that of Kennedy?

4. What do you think the consequences of Roosevelt's death were to American government, foreign policy, and the conclusion of the war?

The death of Roosevelt brought Vice President Harry Truman into office. Truman, who had not been told about the Manhattan Project, developing the atomic bomb, was now faced with the difficult decision of whether to use the bomb against Japan. He relied on his military advisors and rejected other suggested alternatives.

Harry S Truman (from his *Memoirs*).
My own knowledge of these developments had come about only after I became President, when Secretary Stimson had given me the full story. He had told me at that time that the project was nearing completion and that a bomb could be expected within another four months. It was at his suggestion, too, that I had then set up a committee of top men and had asked them to study with great care the implications the new weapon might have for us...

[Here Truman identifies the eight-man Interim Committee, composed of leading figures in government, business, and education, and reports that the Interim Committee's recommendations were brought to him by Stimson on June 1, 1945.]

It was their recommendation that the bomb be used against the enemy as soon as it could be done. They recommended further that it should be used without specific warning and against a target that would clearly show its devastating strength. I had realized, of course, that an atomic bomb explosion would inflict damage and casualties beyond imagination. On the other hand, the scientific advisers of the committee reported, "We can propose no technical demonstration likely to bring an end to the war; we see no acceptable alternative to direct military use." It was their conclusion that no technical demonstration they might propose, such as over a deserted island, would be likely to bring the war to an end. It had to be used against an enemy target.

The final decision of where and when to use the atomic bomb was up to me. Let there be no mistake about it. I regarded the bomb as a military weapon and never had any doubt that it should be used. The top military advisers to the President recommended its use, and when I talked to Churchill he unhesitatingly told me that he favored the use of the atomic bomb if it might aid to end the war.

In deciding to use this bomb I wanted to make sure that it would be used as a weapon of war in the manner prescribed by the laws of war. That meant that I wanted it dropped on a military target. I had told Stimson that the bomb should be dropped as nearly as possible upon a war production center of prime military importance....

Source: Harry S. Truman, *Memoirs: Year of Decisions* (New York, 1955), pp. 10-11

HOW WELL DID YOU UNDERSTAND THIS SELECTION?

1. What was unusual about the way Truman learned about the atomic bomb?

2. What was the basis for his decision to use it?

3. Were there any alternatives to using the atomic bomb? If so, why didn't President Truman choose one of them?

4. Do you think the decision President Truman made to drop the atomic bomb on Hiroshima was the proper one?

SELF TEST

MULTIPLE CHOICE: Circle the correct response. The correct answers are given at the end.

1. The response of the British and French to Hitler's aggression from 1935 to 1938 was to
    a. pursue a defense treaty with the Soviet Union
    b. convince the League of Nations to send troops to stop aggression.
    c. follow a policy of appeasing the Nazis.
    d. try to get the United States involved in stopping Hitler.

2. From 1935 to 1939 congressional thinking on foreign policy issues favored the idea of
    a. building up American defenses.
    b. world balance of power.
    c. international action by the League of Nations.
    d. strict neutrality of the United States.

3. After Franklin Roosevelt won re-election in 1940, he reacted to events in the war in Europe by
    a. continuing to maintain the strictest neutrality.
    b. supporting the Lend Lease Act to help the British war effort.
    c. telling the American people that U.S. entrance into the war was inevitable.
    d. doing all he could to aid Germany, short of actually entering the war.

4. The Japanese bombing of Pearl Harbor
    a. was the result of a conspiracy by Roosevelt and his aides.
    b. led to the immediate passage of the "Cash and Carry" act.
    c. totally destroyed any chance Roosevelt would have to be re-elected.
    d. united all Americans, regardless of ethnic group, behind the war effort.

5. The strategy of the Allies in World War II stressed
    a. defeating Germany first and then Japan.
    b. uniting Latin America behind the war effort.
    c. Britain and Russia fighting in Europe while the U.S. concentrated on defeating Japan.
    d. keeping the Soviet Union out of the war in the Pacific.

6. The internment of Japanese-Americans during the war was mostly based on
    a. their consistent support for their homeland, Japan.
    b. their widespread espionage and sabotage.
    c. their racial and ethnic origin.
    d. well-documented individual arrests for spying.

7. Black soldiers serving during World War II
    a. faced almost no prejudice from white soldiers serving alongside them.
    b. felt that while they fought for freedom abroad, their own rights were severely limited.
    c. were always sent to the worst conflict and suffered greater casualties than whites.
    d. served in integrated units as a result of a presidential order.

8. During the war the public's feeling about women in the work force was that
    a. there was no way women had the physical strength to do men's work.
    b. women were better workers than men because they were more highly motivated.
    c. any woman who got a job proved that she would never be able to find a husband.
    d. women should work to help win the war, but return to the home when the war ended.

9. The United States response to news about Nazi persecution of the Jews in Europe was to
    a. take little direct action of any real significance until very late in the war.
    b. ease immigration restrictions to allow Jewish refugees to come to America.
    c. conduct bombing raids to destroy concentration camps where Jews were being murdered.
    d. assist the victims by sending supplies through the International Red Cross.

10. Which of the following was NOT an immediate domestic consequence of World War II?
    a. growth of the power of the national government.
    b. expansion of the proportion of women in the work force.
    c. abolition of racial segregation in America.
    d. stimulation of the economy.

Answers: 1-c; 2-d; 3-b; 4-d; 5-a; 6-c; 7-b; 8-d; 9-a; 10-c.

ESSAYS:

1. Explain the major foreign policy decisions made by the American government and other democratic nations from the 1930s until the Japanese attacked Pearl Harbor. Why did these actions fail to stop fascist aggression? Why was the United States unable to avoid another war?

2. What was the impact of World War II upon American life and society? What changes were made in the lives of women, blacks, and workers? How did the war affect the American economy and the role of government?

3. What decisions made by the Allied leaders during the war do you feel had the greatest impact on the future? (You might want to consider such issues as how to deal with the Holocaust, where and when to launch an invasion of Europe, whether or not to drop the atomic bombs, and setting up the United Nations.)

OPTIONAL ACTIVITIES : (Use your knowledge **and** imagination when appropriate.)

1. Write a series of letters home as a soldier (white, black, male, or female) describing your experiences in World War II.

2. Write a diary about your experiences at home during World War II. You might be a woman in a defense factory, a Japanese internee, or any other American of the era.

3. Interview your grandparent or any other older member of your family or friend who served in World War II. Summarize his or her experience and the ways in which it affected his or her life. How does this experience compare to what you have learned about World War II?

WEB SITE LISTINGS:

Oral history
   http://www.tankbooks.com/dayone.htm
Battles and American Experiences
   http://www.historyplace.com/worldwar2
   http://www.historyplace.com/worldwar2/pacificwar/index.html
   http://www.thehistorynet.com/WorldWarII
   http://www.thehistorynet.com/WorldWarII/THNarchives/eyewitnessaccounts (Bataan Death March)
The National Archives site includes Advertisements, Posters, Speeches
   http://www.nara.gov/education/teaching/fdr/infamy.html
   http://www.nara.gov/powers/stampem.html
   http://www.nara.gov/exhall/powers/powers.html
   http://www.nara.gov/exhall/powers/manguns.html
   http://www.nara.gov/people/people/html
   http://www.nara.gov/people/newroles.html
   http://www.nara.gov/originals/fdr.html
Afroam.org includes sections on Tuskegee Airmen & other black units
   http://www.afroam.org/history/history.html
Pictures of Women At War
   http://lcweb.loc.gov/exhibits/wcf/wcf0001.html
   http://www.u.arizona.edu/~kari/rosie.htm
   http://www.nara.gov/exhall/powers/women.html
   http://userpages.aug.com/captbarb/
Japanese American Internment
   http://www.geocities.com/Athens/8420/main.html

Chapter Twenty-one

THE COLD WAR:
The Truman-Eisenhower Years

After the death of Franklin Delano Roosevelt in April 1945, Harry S Truman led the United States into the post-war era. Truman faced a number of challenges in both domestic and foreign affairs. No longer an American ally as it had been during the war, the Soviet Union was now a major source of concern. Truman's efforts to contain the expansion of Soviet communism shaped U.S. foreign policy throughout the Cold War. Dwight D. Eisenhower continued Truman's foreign and domestic agenda when he succeeded Truman as president in the 1952 election.

Unfortunately, the end of World War II did not mean the end of international conflict. To help ensure peace, the United Nations (U.N.) and the Security Council were created in 1945. The Council worked in conjunction with the International Court to mediate disputes. To promote the economic recovery of Europe and secure American interests there, Truman implemented the Marshall Plan designed to rebuild Western Europe and promote U.S. economic interests. To safeguard American strategic interests in the region, Truman worked to establish the North Atlantic Treaty Organization designed to protect Europe from Soviet expansion.

In 1947, State Department official George Kennan recommended a policy of "containment," concerning Soviet expansion. Truman incorporated this idea in the Truman Doctrine, which was intended to assist free people in their efforts to resist internal and outside threats to their governments. With the aid of U.S. economic and military support, the Greek government defeated communist insurgents in 1949, and Turkey became a staunch American ally along the Soviet border. In order to protect American interests throughout the world, and prevent another catastrophe like the one that occurred at Pearl Harbor in 1941, the U.S. passed the National Security Act of 1947. This act created a National Military Establishment, the Joint Chiefs of Staff, and the Central Intelligence Agency.

Europe and the Middle East were not the only areas of concern. Asia also commanded American attention. Communist forces led by Mao Zedong succeeded in ousting Chiang Kai-Shek's nationalist government and established the Peoples Republic of China in 1949. The U.S. supported French efforts to resist Ho Chi Minh and the communist, nationalist Vietnamese forces fighting to liberate Vietnam from French control. When communist North Korean troops invaded South Korea in 1950, the U.S. found itself at war in an effort to contain the expansion of communism. With unanimous support from the U.N. Security Council, the U.S. led a multinational force to drive the communist forces out of South Korea. Under the leadership of General Douglas MacArthur U.N. forces pushed the North Koreans back to the 38th parallel that had divided the country. MacArthur, with Truman's support, continued to push until the North Koreans retreated all the way to the border with China. This action drew Chinese troops into the conflict and enlarged the war. The conflict ended in 1953 during the Eisenhower administration, not with the liberation of Korea, but with a return to the pre-war division of Korea. Although the war fostered economic prosperity in the U.S., it also brought inflation and increased defense spending at the expense of the Truman's domestic programs.

Truman's concerns about communism affected his domestic policies as well. He instituted a program to oust disloyal federal employees, particularly those suspected of being communists or communist sympathizers. The

House Committee on Un-American Activities (HUAC) conducted a series of hearings, the most notorious of which focused on alleged communist subversion within the entertainment industry. Wisconsin Senator Joseph McCarthy brought this "red scare" to a climax in the early 1950s. His campaign to eradicate alleged communists from the State Department went to such far-fetched extremes that the term "McCarthyism" was coined to mean the act of making unfounded charges of disloyalty or subversion. Although unsubstantiated, McCarthy's charges and the actions of the Truman administrations doomed the Democratic Party in 1952.

Dwight D. Eisenhower, a Republican war hero, was elected to lead the American people into a new era of prosperity while simultaneously cutting back on government expenditures. Eisenhower continued Truman's containment policy. In an effort to avoid prolonged and expensive conventional military action, Eisenhower expanded the authority of the Central Intelligence Agency (CIA), authorizing them to move beyond the collection and interpretation of intelligence data, into the area of covert action—even to the point of subverting legitimate governments if their positions proved to be contrary to American interests. The CIA overthrew popularly elected governments in Iran and Guatemala, bribed foreign officials, fixed elections, and led military coups throughout the Third World. The CIA began efforts to oust the Cuban leader Fidel Castro who had led a successful coup against pro-American dictator Fulgencio Batista in 1959. Under Eisenhower's direction, the U.S. also began to take a much more active role in the Vietnamese situation after the fall of French control.

Although the Eisenhower years are associated with tremendous economic growth and prosperity, with 25 percent of the general population living in poverty, no federal programs to offer assistance, and widespread racism and discrimination, the mid-to late 1950s was also a period of social upheaval. Civil rights activists mobilized to push for racial equality and won support from the Supreme Court. The 1954 decision in Brown v. Board of Education of Topeka declared segregated schools unconstitutional; a decision Eisenhower was reluctant to enforce. Two years later the court ruled that Montgomery, Alabama's segregated seating on the city bus system was unconstitutional. These decisions signaled that social change was coming, but it was not without tremendous white resistance.

During Eisenhower's tenure in office the United States witnessed the growth of its economic and military power. The middle class expanded and technological innovations improved the quality of life for many Americans. This prosperity, however, was not uniform. As the decade came to an end, minority groups increased their demands for equal rights, and the Eisenhower era of conformity and consensus was coming to an end.

IDENTIFICATION: Briefly describe each term.

The Truman Doctrine

Domino Theory

Containment

The "Iron Curtain" Speech

North Atlantic Treaty Organization

United Nations

The Marshall Plan

The Berlin Airlift

CORE

Insurgents

38th parallel

Demilitarized zone

Loyalty Order

HUAC

The Hollywood Ten

McCarthyism

Gen. Douglas MacArthur

Brown v. Board of Education

WPC

Little Rock Central High School, Little Rock, AR

Orval Faubus

Emmett Till

Montgomery Bus Boycott

Sit-In

SCLC

Interstate Highway Act

Alger Hiss

The GI Bill of Rights

Suburbia

The Suez Crisis

John Foster Dulles

Gamal Abdul Nasser

The Eisenhower Doctrine

CIA

Brinkmanship

U-2 Spy Plane

SNCC

The military-industrial complex

THINK ABOUT:

1. Evaluate Truman's doctrine of containment.

2. Examine the impact of McCarthyism on American politics. In what ways did Truman and Eisenhower respond to McCarthy's tactics?

3. Evaluate American official reactions when leaders in Iran, Guatemala, and Cuba nationalized foreign owned property.

4. Explain Eisenhower's reluctance to enforce the *Brown* decision.

In 1946, communist insurgents threatened to overthrow the corrupt, British-backed government in Greece. Not yet recovered from World War II, Britain lacked the resources to put down the rebellion. In one of the first applications of containment, President Truman requested congressional approval and public support for the United States to intervene in Greece. Although the communists received support from Yugoslavia rather than the Soviet Union, Truman was anxious to prevent the spread of communism into Eastern Europe.

March 12, 1947
Washington, D.C.

PRESIDENT HARRY TRUMAN

The peoples of a number of countries of the world have recently had totalitarian regimes forced upon them against their will. The Government of the United States has made frequent protests against coercion and intimidation in violation of the Yalta agreement, in Poland, Rumania, and Bulgaria. I must also state that in a number of other countries there have been similar developments.

At the present moment in world history nearly every nation must choose between alternative ways of life. The choice is too often not a free one.

One way of life is based upon the will of the majority, is distinguished by free institutions, representative government, free elections, guarantees of individual liberty, freedom of speech and religion, and freedom from political oppression.

The second way of life is based on upon the will of a minority forcibly imposed upon the majority. It relies upon terror and oppression, a controlled press and radio, fixed elections, and the suppression of personal freedom.

I believe that it must be the policy of the United States to support free peoples who are resisting attempted subjugation by armed minorities or by outside pressure.

I believe that we must assist free peoples to work out their own destinies in their own way.

I believe that our help should be primarily through economic stability and orderly political processes.

The world is not static, and the *status quo* is not sacred. But we cannot allow changes in the *status quo* in violation of the Charter of the United Nations by such methods as coercion, or by such subterfuges as political infiltration. In helping free and independent nations to maintain their freedom, the United States will be giving effect to the principles of the Charter of the United Nations.

It is necessary only to glance at a map to realize that the survival and integrity of the Greek nation are of grace importance in a much wider situation. If Greece should fall under the control of an armed minority, the effect upon its neighbor, Turkey, would be immediate and serious. Confusion and disorder might be well spread throughout the entire Middle East.

Moreover, the disappearance of Greece as an independent state would have a profound effect upon those countries in Europe whose peoples are struggling against great difficulties to maintain their freedoms and their independence while they repair the damages of war.

It would be an unspeakable tragedy if these countries, which have struggled so long against overwhelming odds, should lose that victory for which they sacrificed so much. Collapse of free institutions and loss of independence would be disastrous not only for them but for the world. Discouragement and possibly failure would quickly be the lot of neighboring peoples striving to maintain their freedom and independence...

We must take immediate and resolute action.

I therefore ask the Congress to provide authority for assistance to Greece and Turkey in the amount of $400,000,000 for the period ending June 30, 1948. In requesting these funds, I have taken into consideration the maximum amount of relief assistance which would be furnished to Greece out of the $350,000,000 which I recently requested that the Congress authorize for the prevention of starvation and suffering in countries devastated by the war.

In addition to funds, I ask the Congress to authorize the detail of American civilian and military personnel to Greece and Turkey, at the request of those countries, to assist in the tasks of reconstruction, and for the purpose of supervising the use of such financial and material assistance as may be furnished. I recommend that authority also be provided for the instruction and training of selected Greek and Turkish personnel.

Source: Harry S. Truman Speech 3/12/47
Public Papers of the Presidents, Harry S. Truman, 1947 (Washington: Government Printing Office, 1963) 176-180

HOW WELL DID YOU UNDERSTAND THIS SELECTION?

1. What would be the result if the communist insurgents succeeded in ousting the monarchy?

2. What does Truman propose to do to aid the Greek government?

3. How does Truman use the Charter of the United Nations to justify his desire to intervene?

As Cold War tensions escalated in late 1940s and early 1950s, some Americans concluded that the roots of America's difficulties abroad were domestic treason and subversion. The House Committee on Un-American Activities, created in 1938, had originally served as a platform for conservatives to attack the alleged communism of the New Deal. After World War II, increasing numbers of moderates supported the Committee's efforts to investigate allegations of disloyalty within the government. In 1946, the Committee began hearings to expose the communist influence in American life. When a number of prominent film directors, actors, and screenwriters refused to cooperate, some were cited for contempt and sent to federal prison; others were simply blacklisted, which effectively barred them from employment in the entertainment industry.

October 27, 1947
House of Representatives, Washington, D.C.
John Howard Lawson, Hollywood screenwriter, testifying before HUAC

John Howard Lawson, Screenwriter
Mr. Stripling, the first witness.

MR. CRUM. Mr. Chairman————
MR. STRIPLING. Mr. John Howard Lawson.
MR. CRUM. Mr. Chairman————
THE CHAIRMAN. I am sorry————
MR. CRUM. May I request the right of cross-examination? I ask you to bring back and permit us to cross-examination the witness, Adolph Menjou, Fred Niblo, John Charles Moffitt, Richard Macauley, Rupert Hughes, Sam Wood, Ayn Rand, James McGuinness————
THE CHAIRMAN. The request————
MR. CRUM. Howard Rushmore————
(The chairman pounding gavel.)
MR. CRUM. Morrie Ryskind, Oliver Carlson————
THE CHAIRMAN. That request is denied.
MR. CRUM. In order to show that these witnesses lied.
THE CHAIRMAN. That request is denied. Mr. Stripling, the first witness.
MR. STRIPLING. John Howard Lawson.
(John Howard Lawson, accompanied by Robert W. Kenny and Barley Crum takes places at witness table.)
THE CHAIRMAN. Stand and please raise your right hand. Do you solemnly swear the testimony you are about to give is the truth, the whole truth, and nothing but the truth, so help you God?
MR. LAWSON. I do.
THE CHAIRMAN. Sit down, please.
MR. LAWSON. Mr. Chairman, I have a statement here which I wish to make————
THE CHAIRMAN. Well, all right; let me see your statement.
(Statement handed to the chairman)
MR. STRIPLING. Do you have a copy of that?
MR. CRUM. We can get you copies.
THE CHAIRMAN. I don't care to read any more of the statement. The statement will not be read. I read the first line.
MR. LAWSON. You have spent 1 week vilifying me before the American public————
THE CHAIRMAN. Just a minute————
MR. LAWSON. And you refuse to allow me to make a statement on my rights as an American citizen.
THE CHAIRMAN. I refuse you to make the statement, because of the first sentence in your statement. That statement is not pertinent to the inquiry.

Now this is a congressional committee—a congressional committee set up by law. We must have orderly procedure, and we are going to have orderly procedure.

Mr. Stripling, identify the witness.

MR. LAWSON. The rights of American citizens are important in this room here, and I intend to stand up for those rights, Congressman Thomas.

MR. STRIPLING. Mr. Lawson, will you state your full name, please!

MR. LAWSON. I wish to protest against the unwillingness of this committee to read a statement, when you permitted Mr. Warner, Mr. Mayer, and others to read statements in this room.

My name is John Howard Lawson.

MR. STRIPLING. What is your present address?

MR. LAWSON. 9354 Burnett Avenue, San Fernando, Calif.

MR. STRIPLING. When and where were you born?

MR. LAWSON. New York City.

MR. STRIPLING. What year?

MR. LAWSON. 1894.

MR. STRIPLING. Give us a exact date.

MR. LAWSON. September 25.

MR. STRIPLING. Mr. Lawson, you are here in response to a subpoena which was served upon you on September 19, 1947; is that true?

MR. LAWSON. That is correct....

MR. STRIPLING. What is your occupation, Mr. Lawson?

MR. LAWSON. I am a writer.

MR. STRIPLING. How long have you been a writer?

MR. LAWSON. All my life-at least 35 years-all my adult life.

MR. STRIPLING. Are you a member of the Screen Writers Guild?

MR. LAWSON. The raising of any question here in regard to membership, political beliefs, or affiliation—

MR. STRIPLING. Mr. Chairman—

MR. LAWSON. Is absolutely beyond the powers of this committee.

MR. STRIPLING. Mr. Chairman———

MR. LAWSON. But———

(The chairman pounding gavel)

MR. LAWSON. It is a matter of public record that I am a member of the Screen Writers Guild.

MR. STRIPLING. I ask———

[Applause.]

THE CHAIRMAN. I want to caution the people in the audience: You are the guests of this committee and you will have to maintain order at all times. I do not care for any applause or any demonstrations of one kind or another.

MR. STRIPLING. Now, Mr. Chairman, I am also going to request that you instruct the witness to be responsive to the questions.

THE CHAIRMAN. I think the witness will be more responsive to the questions.

MR. LAWSON. Mr. Chairman, you permitted———

THE CHAIRMAN (pounding gavel). Never mind———

MR. LAWSON (continuing). Witnesses in this room to make answers of three or five hundred words to questions here.

THE CHAIRMAN. Mr. Lawson, you will please be responsive to these questions and not continue to try to disrupt these hearings.

MR. LAWSON. I am not on trial here, Mr. Chairman. This committee is on trial here before the American people. Let us get that straight.

THE CHAIRMAN. We don't want you to be on trial.

MR. STRIPLING. Have you ever held any office in the guild?

MR. LAWSON. The question of whether I have held office is also a question which is beyond the purview of this committee.

(The chairman pounding gavel.)

MR. LAWSON. It is an invasion of the right of association under the Bill of Rights of this country.

THE CHAIRMAN. Please be responsive to the question.

MR. LAWSON. It is also a matter———

(The chairman pounding gavel.)

MR. LAWSON. Of public record———

THE CHAIRMAN. You asked to be heard. Through your attorney, you asked to be heard, and we want you to be heard. And if you don't care to be heard, then we will excuse you and we will put the record in without your answers.

MR. LAWSON. I wish to frame my own answers to your questions, Mr. Chairman, and I intend to do so.

THE CHAIRMAN. And you will be responsive to the questions or you will be excused from the witness stand.

MR. LAWSON. I will frame my own answers, Mr. Chairman.

THE CHAIRMAN. Go ahead, Mr. Stripling.

MR. LAWSON. Correct.

MR. STRIPLING. You have probably written others; have you not, Mr. Lawson?

MR. LAWSON. Many others. You have missed a lot of them.

MR. STRIPLING. You don't care to furnish them to the committee, do you?

MR. LAWSON. Not in the least interested.

MR. STRIPLING. Mr. Lawson, are you now, or have you ever been a member of the Communist Party of the United States?

MR. LAWSON. In framing my answer to that question I must emphasize the points that I have raised before. The question of communism is in no way related to this inquiry, which is an attempt to get control of the screen and to invade the basic rights of American citizens in all fields.

MR. MCDOWELL. Now I must object———

MR. STRIPLING. Mr. Chairman———

(The chairman pounding gavel.)

MR. LAWSON (continuing). Which has been historically denied to any committee of this sort, to invade the rights and privileges and immunity of American citizens, whether they be Protestant, Methodist, Jewish, or Catholic, whether they be Republican or Democrats or anything else.

THE CHAIRMAN (pounding gavel). Mr. Lawson just quiet down again.

Mr. Lawson, the most pertinent question that we can ask is whether or not you have ever been a member of a Communist Party. Now, do you care to answer that question?

MR. LAWSON. You are using the old technique, which was used in Hitler Germany in order to create a scare here———

THE CHAIRMAN (pounding gavel). Oh———

MR. LAWSON. In order to create an entirely false atmosphere in which this hearing is conducted———

(The chairman pounding gavel.)

MR. LAWSON. In order that you can smear the motion-picture industry, and you can proceed to the press, to any form of communication in this country.

THE CHAIRMAN. You have learned———

MR. LAWSON. The Bill of Rights was established precisely to prevent the operation of any committee which could invade the basic rights of Americans.

Now, if you want to know———

MR. STRIPLING. Mr. Chairman, the witness is not answering the question.

MR. LAWSON. If you want to know———

(The chairman pounding gavel.)

THE CHAIRMAN. Mr. Lawson———

MR. LAWSON. You permit me and my attorneys to bring in here the witnesses that testified last week and you permit us to cross-examine these witnesses, and will show up the whole tissue of lie———

THE CHAIRMAN (pounding gavel). We are going to get the answer to that question if we have to stay here for a week.

Are you a member of the Communist Party, or have you ever been a member of the Communist Party?

MR. LAWSON. It is unfortunate and tragic that I have to teach this committee the basic principles of American———

261

THE CHAIRMAN (pounding gavel). That is not the question. That is not the question. The question is: Have you ever been a member of the Communist Party?

MR. LAWSON. I am framing my answer in the only way in which any American citizen can frame his answer to a question which absolutely invades his rights.

THE CHAIRMAN. Then you refuse to answer that question; is that correct?

MR. LAWSON. I have told you that I will offer my beliefs, affiliations, and everything else to the American public, and they will know where I stand.

THE CHAIRMAN (pounding gavel). Excuse the witness——

MR. LAWSON. As they do from what I have written.

THE CHAIRMAN (pounding gavel). Stand away from the stand——

MR. LAWSON. I have written Americanism for many years, and I shall continue to fight for the Bill of Rights, which you are trying to destroy.

THE CHAIRMAN. Officers, take this man away from the stand——

THE CHAIRMAN (pounding gavel). There will be no demonstrations. No demonstrations, for or against. Everyone will please be seated...

Source: House of Representatives, Committee on Un-American Activities, October 20 – 30, 1947
(Washington: Government Printing Office, 1947) 289 -295

HOW WELL DID YOU UNDERSTAND THIS SELECTION?

1. Does the Committee present any evidence to suggest Lawson was a communist?

2. Why did Lawson refuse to directly answer the chairman's question concerning Lawson's alleged membership in the Communist Party?

3. Whose behavior was more "Un-American," that of Lawson, or that of Thomas? Explain.

As the Allies liberated Korea from Japanese control at the end of World War II, the country was divided into two zones of occupation, with the Soviet Union in the North and the United States in the South. After establishing friendly governments, the U.S. and the Soviets withdrew. When Communist North Korean troops invaded the South in June 1950, the U.S. responded decisively. Truman was certain the Soviets were behind the attack. In this address to the American public, Truman outlines the principles of the Truman Doctrine and the necessity of intervening in Korea.

June 27, 1950
Washington, D.C.

PRESIDENT HARRY S. TRUMAN

At noon today I sent a message on the Congress about the situation in Korea. I want to talk to you tonight about that situation, and about what it means to the security of the United States and to our hopes for peace in the world.

Korea is a small country, thousands of miles away, from what is happening there is important to every American.

On Sunday, June 25th, Communist forces attacked the Republic of Korea.

This attack has made it clear, beyond all doubt, that the international Communist movement is willing to use armed invasion to conquer independent nations. An act of aggressions such as this creates a very real danger to the security of all free nations.

The attack upon Korea was an outright breach of the peace and a violation of the Charter of the United Nations. By their actions in Korea, Communist leaders have demonstrated their contempt for the basic moral principles on which the United Nations is founded. This is a direct challenge to the efforts of the free nations to build the kind of world in which men can live in freedom and peace.

This challenge has been presented squarely. We must meet it squarely...

Under the flag of the United Nations a unified command has been established for all forces of the members of the United Nations fighting in Korea. Gen. Douglas MacArthur is the commander of this combined force.

The prompt action of the United Nations to put down lawless aggression, and the prompt response to this action by free peoples all over the world, will stand as a landmark in mankind's long search for a rule of law among nations.

Only a few countries have failed to endorse the efforts of the United Nations to stop the fighting in Korea. The most important of these is the Soviet Union. The Soviet Union has boycotted the meetings of the United Nations Security Council. It has refused to support the actions of the United Nations with respect to Korea. The United States requested the Soviet Government, 2 days after the fighting stated, to use it influence with the North Koreans to have them withdraw. The Soviet Government refused.

The Soviet Government has said many times that it wants peace in the world, but its attitude toward this act of aggression against the Republic of Korea is in direct contradiction of its statements.

For our part, we shall continue to support the United Nations action to restore peace in the world.

Furthermore, the fact that Communist forces have invaded Korea is a warning that there may be similar acts of aggression in other parts of the world. The free nations must be on their guard, more than ever before, against this kind of sneak attack...

When we have worked out with other free countries an increased program for our common defense, I shall recommend to the congress that additional funds be provided for this purpose. This is of great importance. The free nations face a worldwide threat. It must be met with a worldwide defense. The United States and other free nations can multiply their strength by joining with one another in a common effort to provide this defense. This is our best hope for peace.

The things we need to do to build up our military defense will require considerable adjustment in our domestic economy. We have a tremendously rich and productive economy, and it is expanding every year.

Our job now is to divert to defense purposes more of that tremendous productive capacity-more steel, more aluminum, more of a good many things.

In the message which I sent to the Congress today, I described the economic measures which are required at this time.

First, we need laws which will insure prompt and adequate supplies for military and essential civilian use. I have therefore recommended that the Congress give the Government power to guide the flow of materials into essential uses, to restrict their use for nonessential purposes, and to prevent the accumulation of unnecessary inventories.

Second, we must adopt measures to prevent inflation and to keep out Government in a sound financial condition. One of the major causes of inflation is the excessive use of credit. I have recommended that the Congress authorize the Government to set limits on installment buying and to curb speculation in agricultural commodities. In the housing field, where government credit is an important factor, I have already directed that credit be applied, and I have recommended that the Congress authorize further controls.

As an additional safeguard against inflation, and to help finance our defense needs, it will be necessary to make substantial increases in taxes. This is a contribution to our national security that every one of us should stand ready to make. As soon as a balanced and fair tax program can be worked out, I shall lay it before the Congress. This tax program will have as a major aim the elimination of profiteering.

Third, we should increase the production of goods needed for national defense. We must plan to enlarge our defense production, not just for the immediate future, but for the next several years. This will be primarily a task for our businessmen and workers. However, to help obtain the necessary increases, the Government should be authorized to provide certain types of financial assistance to private industry to increase defense production.

We have the sources to meet our needs. Far more important, the American people are unified in their belief in democratic freedom. We are united in detesting Communist slavery.

We know that the cost of freedom is high. But we are determined to preserve our freedom—no matter what the cost.

Our country stands before the world as an example of how free men, under God, can build a community of neighbors, working together for the good of all.

This is the goal we seek not only for ourselves, but for all people. We believe that freedom and peace are essential if men are to live as our Creator intended us to live. It is this faith that has guided us in the past, and it is this faith that will fortify us in the stern days ahead.

From public Papers of the Presidents of the United States: Harry S. Truman
(Government Office, Washington, D.C., 1961 – 1966), 1950: 537 – 540

HOW WELL DID YOU UNDERSTAND THIS SELECTION?

1. How does President Truman justify American intervention in Korea?

2. Why does Truman put so much emphasis on the American economy?

3. How did the Soviet Union respond to American actions?

*On May 17, 1954, the Supreme Court reached a unanimous decision concerning segregation in public schools. This ruling overturned the 1896 **Plessy v. Ferguson** "separate but equal" decision that had been used to justify the segregation of public facilities. The equality of the separate facilities was seldom more than a myth. The National Association for the Advancement of Colored People (NAACP) worked for nearly two decades to argue this case and four other similar cases before the U.S. Supreme Court. Social Scientists offered expert testimony concerning the harmful psychological effects of segregation. Chief Justice Earl Warren led the court in determining that segregated public schools deprived African-American students of equal protection under the law guaranteed by the Fourteenth Amendment. One year after the first **Brown** decision, the Court issued a second ruling, or **Brown II**, on the case instructing the states to desegregate public schools "with all deliberate speed."*

We come then to the question presented: Does segregation of children in public schools solely on the basis of race, even though the physical facilities and other "tangible" factors may be equal, deprive the children of the minority group of equal educational opportunities? We believe that it does...

To separate them from others of similar age and qualifications solely because of their race generates a feeling of inferiority as to their status in the community that may affect their hearts and minds in a way unlikely to ever be undone. The effect of this separation on their educational opportunities as well as stated by a finding in the Kansas case by a court which nevertheless felt compelled to rule against the Negro plaintiffs:

> *Segregation of white and colored children in public schools has a detrimental effect upon the colored children. The impact is greater when it has the sanction of the law, therefore, has a tendency to retard the educational and mental development of Negro children and to deprive them of some of the benefits they would receive in a racially integrated school system.*

Whatever may have been the extent of psychological knowledge at the time of *Plessy v. Ferguson* contrary to this finding is rejected.

We conclude that in the field of public education the doctrine of "separate but equal" has no place. Separate educational facilities are inherently unequal. Therefore, we hold that the plaintiffs and others similarly situated for whom the action have been brought are, by reason of the segregation complained of, deprived of the equal protection of the laws guaranteed by the Fourteenth Amendment. This disposition makes unnecessary any discussion whether such segregation also violates the Due Process Clause of the Fourteenth Amendment.

Because these are class actions, because of the wide applicability of this decision, and because of the great variety of local conditions, the formulation of decrees in these cases presents problems of considerable complexity. On reargument, the consideration of appropriate relief was necessarily subordinated to the primary question – the constitutionality of segregation in public education. We have now announced that such segregation is a denial of the equal protection of the laws.

Source: *Brown v. Board of Education, Topeka*, United States Reports, 347 U.S. 483 [1954]

HOW WELL DID YOU UNDERSTAND THIS SELECTION?

1. Summarize the findings of the *Brown* decision.

2. In what ways did the Court justify reversing *Plessy* v. *Ferguson?*

PRESIDENT EISENHOWER ENFORCES THE *BROWN* DECISION IN LITTLE ROCK, 1957

---

*Following the **Brown** decision in 1954, President Eisenhower was hesitant to compel southern segregationist to implement the Court's ruling. In 1957, Orval E. Faubus, the governor of Arkansas, deployed the state National Guard to prevent nine African-American students from entering Central High School in Little Rock. Eisenhower was obligated to act. In a 1957 televised speech to the American public, Eisenhower explained his reasoning for taking action to ensure the desegregation of the school.*

September 25, 1957,
PRESIDENT DWIGHT D. EISENHOWER

My Fellow Citizens…. I must speak to you about the serious situation that had arisen in Little Rock…In that city, under the leadership of demagogic extremists, disorderly mobs have deliberately prevented the carrying out of proper orders from a federal court. Local authorities have not eliminated that violent opposition and, under the law, I yesterday issued a proclamation calling upon the mob to disperse.

This morning the mob again gathered in front of the Central High School of Little Rock, obviously for the purpose of again preventing the carrying out of the court's order relating to the admissions of Negro children to that school.

Whenever normal agencies prove inadequate to the task and it becomes necessary for the executive branch of the federal government to use its powers and authority to uphold federal courts, the President's responsibility is inescapable.

In accordance with that responsibility, I have today issued and Executive Order directing the use of troops under federal authority to aid in the execution of federal law at Little Rock, Arkansas. This became necessary when my Proclamation of yesterday was not observed, and the obstruction of justice still continues…..

A foundation of our American way of life is our national respect of law.

In the South, as elsewhere, citizens are keenly aware of the tremendous disservice that has been don't to the people of Arkansas in the eyes of the nation, and that has been done to the nation in the eyes of the world.

At a time when we face grave situations abroad because of the hatred that communism bears toward a system of government based on human rights, it would be difficult to exaggerate the harm that is being done to the prestige and influence, and indeed to the safety, of our nation and the world.

Our enemies are gloating over this incident and using it everywhere to misrepresent our whole nation. We are portrayed as a violator of those standards of conduct which the peoples of the world united to proclaim in the Charter of the United Nations. There they affirmed "faith in fundamental human rights" and "in the dignity and worth of the human person" and they did so "without distinction as to race, sex, language or religion."

And so, with deep confidence, I call upon the citizens of the State of Arkansas to assist in bringing to an immediate end all interference with the law and its processes. If resistance to the federal court orders ceases at once, the further presence of federal troops will be unnecessary and the City of Little Rock will return to its normal habits of peace and order and a blot upon the fair name and high honor of our nation in the world will be removed.

Thus will be restored the image of America and of all its parts as one nation, indivisible, with liberty and justice for all.

HOW WELL DID YOU UNDERSTAND THIS SELECTION?

1. In what ways did Eisenhower propose to remedy the situation?

2. How does Eisenhower justify using federal authority against state officials?

3. What does this incident reveal about Eisenhower's attitude toward the issue of civil rights?

When the Soviet Union successfully launched the world's first intercontinental satellite, Sputnik, on October 4, 1957, many felt the Soviet success had damaged American prestige. Eisenhower and his advisors met to discuss the implications.

Memorandum of Conference with the President
October 8, 1957, 8:30 AM

S E C R E T

Declassified: 11-17-76

Others Present: Secretary Quarles
Dr. Waterman
Mr. Hagen
Mr. Holaday
Governor Adams
General Persons
Mr. Hagerty
Governor Pyle
Mr. Harlow
General Cutler
General Goodpaster

Secretary Quarles began by reviewing a memorandum prepared in Defense of the President on the subject of the earth satellite (dated October 7, 1957). He left a copy with the President. He reported that the Soviet launching on October 4th had apparently been highly successful.

The President asked Secretary Quarles about the report that had come to his attention to the effect that Redstone could have been used and could have placed a satellite in orbit many months ago. The Science Advisory Committee had felt, however, that it was better to have the earth satellite proceed separately from military development. One reason was to stress the peaceful character of the effort, and a second was to avoid the inclusion of materiel, to which foreign scientists might be given access, which is used in our own military rockets. He said that the Army feels it could erect a satellite four months prior to the estimated date for the Vanguard. The President said that when this information reaches Congress, they are bound to ask why this action was not taken. He recalled, however, that timing was never given too much importance in our own program, which was tied to the IGY and confirmed that, in order for all scientists to be able to look at the instrument, it had to be kept away from military secrets. Secretary Quarles pointed out that the Army plan would require some modification of the instrumentation in the missile.

He went on to add that the Russians have in fact done us a good turn, unintentionally, in establishing the concept of freedom of international space —this seems to be generally accepted as orbital space, in which the missile is making an inoffensive passage.

The President asked what kind of information could be conveyed by the signals reaching us from the Russian satellite. Secretary Quarles said the soviets say that it is simply a pulse to permit location of the missile through the radar direction finders. Following the meeting, Dr. Waterman indicated that there is some kind of modulation on the signals, which may mean that some coding is being done, although it might conceivably be accidental.

The President asked the group to look ahead five years, and asked about a reconnaissance vehicle. Secretary Quarles said the Air Force has a research program in this area and gave a general description of the project.

Governor Adams recalled that Dr. Pusey had said that we had never thought of this as a crash program, as the Russians apparently did. We were working simply to develop and transmit scientific knowledge. The President thought that to make a sudden shift in our approach now would be to belie the attitude we have had all along. Secretary Quarles said that such a shift would create service tensions in the Pentagon. Mr. Holaday said he planned to study with the Army the back up of the Navy program with the Redstone, adapting it to the instrumentation.

There was some discussion concerning the Soviet request as to whether we would like to put instruments of ours aboard one of their satellites. He said our instruments would be ready for this. Several present pointed out that our instruments contain parts which, if made available to the Russians, would give them substantial technological information.

A. J. Goodpaster
Brigadier General, USA

Source: Memorandum of Conference with President Eisenhower on October 8, 1957, Dwight D. Eisenhower Library, Abilene, Kansas

HOW WELL DID YOU UNDERSTAND THIS SELECTION?

1. What factors does the memorandum suggest kept the Americans from winning the race to launch an artificial satellite?

2. What future actions were recommended?

3. What problems might arise from these proposed actions?

On January 17, 1961, Eisenhower delivered his farewell remarks to the American public in a radio and television address.

January 18, 1961
Washington, D.C.
PRESIDENT DWIGHT D. EISENHOWER

A vital element in keeping the peace is our military establishment. Ours arms must be mighty, ready for instant action, so that no potential aggressor may be tempted to risk his own destruction.

Our military organization today bears little relation to that known by any of my predecessors in peacetime or indeed by the fighting men of World War II or Korea.

Until the latest of our world conflicts, the United States had no armaments industry. American makers of plowshares could, with time and as required, make swords as well. But now we can no longer risk emergency improvisation of national defense; we have been compelled to create a permanent armaments industry of vast proportions. Added to this, three and a half million men and women are directly engaged in the defense establishment. We annually spend on military security more than the net income of all United States corporations.

This conjunction of an immense military establishment and a large arms industry is new in the American experience. The total influence-economic, political, even spiritual-is felt in every city, every statehouse, every office of the federal government. We recognize the imperative need for this development. Yet we must not fail to comprehend its grave implications. Our toil, resources, and livelihood are all involved; so is the very structure of our society.

In the councils of government, we must guard against the acquisition of unwarranted influence, whether sought or unsought, by the military-industrial complex. The potential for the disastrous rise of misplaced power exists and will persist.

We must never let the weight of this combination endanger our liberties or democratic processes. We should take nothing for granted. Only an alert and knowledgeable citizenry can compel the proper meshing of the huge industrial and military machinery of defense with our peaceful methods and goals, so that security and liberty may prosper together.

Akin to, and largely responsible for the sweeping changes in our industrial-military posture, has been the technological revolution during recent decades.

In this revolution, research has become central; it also becomes more formalized, complex, and costly. A steadily increasing share is conducted for, by, or at the direction of, the federal government....

The prospect of domination of the nation's scholars by federal employment, project allocations, and the power of money is ever present-and is gravely to be regarded.

Yet, in holding scientific research and discovery in respect, as we should, we must also be alert to the equal and opposite danger that public policy could itself become the captive of a scientific-technological elite.

It is the task of statesmanship to mold, to balance, and to integrate these and other forces, new and old, within the principles of our democratic system-ever aiming toward the supreme goals of our free society.

Another factor in maintaining balance involves the element of time. As we peer into society's future, we - you and I, and our government – must avoid the impulse to live only for today, plundering, for our own ease and convenience, the precious resources of tomorrow. We cannot mortgage the material assets of our grandchildren without risking the loss also of their political and spiritual heritage. We want democracy to survive for all generations to come, not to become the insolvent phantom of tomorrow.

Down the long lane of the history yet to written America knows that this world of ours, ever growing smaller, must avoid becoming a community of dreadful fear and hate, and be, instead, a proud confederation of mutual trust and respect.

Such a confederation must be one of equals. The weakest must come to the conference table with the same confidence as do we, protected as we are by our moral, economic, and military strength. That table, through scarred by many past frustrations, cannot be abandoned for the certain agony of the battlefield.

Disarmament, with mutual honor and confidence, is a continuing imperative. Together we must learn how to compose differences, not with arms, but with intellect and decent purpose. Because this need is so sharp and apparent I confess that I lay down my official responsibilities in this field with a definite sense of disappointment. As one who witnessed the honor and the lingering sadness of war – as one who knows that another war could destroy this civilization which has been so slowly and painfully built over thousands of years – I wish I could say tonight that a lasting peace is in sight.

Happily, I can say that war has been avoided. Steady progress toward our ultimate goal has been made. But, so much remains to be done. As a private citizen, I shall never cease to do with little I can to help the world advance along that road....

HOW WELL DID YOU UNDERSTAND THIS SELECTION?

1. What are Eisenhower's greatest concerns about the future of the U.S.?

2. What dangers does he foresee associated with the military-industrial complex?

3. What are Eisenhower's concerns about future scientific research?

MULTIPLE CHOICE: Circle the correct response. The correct answers are given at the end.

1. The American policy of containment was designed to
    a. Ration American oil reserves
    b. Halt the Chinese Communist take-over of Vietnam
    c. Stop the expansion of Soviet Communism
    d. Purge the U.S. State Department of Communist officials

2. The Berlin Airlift was a reaction to
    a. Soviet construction of the Berlin Wall
    b. The implementation of the Eisenhower Doctrine
    c. The German refusal to accept the Marshall Plan
    d. The Soviet blockade of Berlin to keep the Allies from having access to West Berlin

3. HUAC investigations of the entertainment industry addressed American concerns about
    a. Racial stereotyping in Hollywood films
    b. The influence of Communists on the industry
    c. Violence and profanity in film
    d. Protecting filmmakers' right to freedom of expression

4. President Truman dismissed General MacArthur because
    a. He failed to drive the Communists out of North Korea
    b. He failed to drive the Communists out of South Korea
    c. Of his erratic and insubordinate behavior
    d. Senator McCarthy revealed that MacArthur was a Communist.

5. The CIA supported a *coup d'etat* in Guatemala in part because the new president
    a. Committed serious human rights violations against the Guatemalan people
    b. Expropriated 225,000 acres of land owned the American corporation United Fruit Company
    c. Cooperated with Fidel Castro and the Soviets
    d. Nationalized the oil fields

6. The Montgomery Bus Boycott
    a. Succeeded in ending segregation on the city bus system
    b. Failed to end segregation on the city bus system
    c. Failed to generate widespread support among African-American residents
    d. Led Eisenhower to intervene and force the integration of the bus system

7. Because of new labor saving devices that were produced in the 1950s,
    a. The time women spent on housework decreased
    b. The time women spent on housework increased
    c. Women were able to devote more time to social activities outside the home
    d. Men helped out more with the housework

8. When the CIA was created in 1947, its purpose was to
    a. Engage in covert operations throughout the world
    b. Investigate alleged communists in the federal government
    c. Monitor the activities of civil rights movement
    d. Coordinate intelligence gathering

9. The five permanent members of the UN Security Council were
   a. U.S., U.S.S.R., Great Britain, France, and Germany
   b. U.S., U.S.S.R., Great Britain, France, and China
   c. U.S., U.S.S.R., Great Britain, France, and Italy
   d. U.S., U.S.S.R., Great Britain, France, and Japan

10. One result of the boom in interstate highway construction was
    a. A dramatic increase in the number of "Mom and Pop" roadside businesses
    b. An increase in the construction of urban light-rail systems
    c. The demise of interurban railway systems
    d. A dramatic reduction in the number of automobiles sold in the U.S.

Answers: 1-c; 2-d; 3-b; 4-c; 5-b; 6-a; 7-b; 8-d; 9-b; 10-c

ESSAYS:

1. What factors contributed to the development of the Cold War? Was one side more to blame than the other for the tension? Explain.

2. Evaluate the social and economic impact of the G. I. Bill of Rights.

3. Evaluate Eisenhower's use of the CIA throughout the Third World. In what ways did CIA activities violate the American commitment to national self-determination?

OPTIONAL ACTIVITIES: (Use your knowledge and imagination when appropriate.)

1. Interview a family member or friend about their experiences during the Cold War. Summarize their responses for the class in an oral presentation

2. View the film "The Crucible," and write a critical analysis of the parallels between the Salem witchcraft trials and the HUAC hearings.

3. Review newspapers and periodicals from the 1950s. Using copies of advertising images and news story photographs, create a poster presentation contrasting the prescribed ideal of suburban life with the actual experience of poor Americans during the 1950s.

WEB SITE LISTINGS:

Containment/War
"The Cold War," CNN series
   http://www.cnn.com/coldwar

"Documents Relating to American Foreign Policy: The Cold War," Vincent Ferraro, Mount Holyoke College
   http://www.mtholyoke.edu/acad/intrel/coldwar.htm

Smithsonian Institution's Soviet Archives Exhibition
   http://www.ibiblio.org/expo/soviet.exhibit/coldwar.html

"Senator Joseph McCarthy," Webcorp Multimedia
   http://webcorp.com/mccarthy/

"Cold War International History Project, Virtual Archive" Woodrow Wilson International Center for Scholars
  http://wwics.si.edu/index.cfm?topic_id=1409&fuseaction=library.Collection

The National Security Archive, George Washington University
  http://www.gwu.edu/~nsarchiv/

Korean War Project
  http://www.koreanwar.org/index1.html

Avalon Project: Yale's Archive for Documents in Law, History, and Diplomacy
  The Cold War: http://www.yale.edu/lawweb/avalon/coldwar.htm

"Truman Doctrine Collection," Harry S. Truman Library & Museum
  http://www.trumanlibrary.org/whistlestop/study_collections/doctrine/large/doctrine.htm

Middle Class Life
Kingwood College Library
  http://kclibrary.nhmccd.edu/decade50.html

"United States Culture and Society in the 1950s," Jessamyn Neuhaus
  http://home.earthlink.net/~neuhausj/1950s/

"The Literature & Culture of the American 1950s," Alan Filreis, University of Pennsylvania
  http://www.english.upenn.edu/~afilreis/50s/home.html

Civil Rights
"The History of Jim Crow,"
  http://www.jimcrowhistory.org/history/transition.htm

"In Pursuit of Freedom & Equality: Brown v. Board of Education of Topeka," Washburn University School of Law,
  http://brownvboard.org/

"Landmark Supreme Court Cases: Brown v. Board of Education," Street Law & the Supreme Court Historical Society
  http://www.landmarkcases.org/brown/

"Little Rock Central High, 40th Anniversary,"
  http://www.centralhigh57.org/

"The Rosa Parks Portal,"
  http://e-portals.org/Parks/

"The Murder of Emmett Till," PBS
  http://www.pbs.org/wgbh/amex/till/filmmore/

"The Martin Luther King, Jr. Papers Project," Stanford University
  http://www.stanford.edu/group/King/

Chapter Twenty-two

HOPE TO DESPAIR:
Kennedy-Johnson Years

John F. Kennedy's election in 1960 launched the decade with a sense of optimism about the future of the United States. Those "high hopes," however, were short lived. After Kennedy's assassination, Lyndon B. Johnson used his influence to secure Kennedy's unfulfilled legislative program and initiated his own domestic agenda, the Great Society. Unfortunately, Johnson's efforts to end poverty and racial injustice would soon be overshadowed by the escalation of the Vietnam War. The earlier sense of hopefulness would be replaced by distrust and frustration.

Kennedy's domestic program, the New Frontier, while promising more than it could deliver, nevertheless had a number of successes. He secured an increase in the minimum wage, Social Security, and moderate urban reforms. He gradually made a commitment to first-class citizenship for African Americans through his support of the desegregation of the University of Alabama, the creation of the President's Committee on Equal Employment Opportunity to eliminate racial discrimination in government hiring, and an executive order prohibiting segregation in federally subsidized housing. He galvanized the American people behind concept of a "peaceful revolution," promoting the Alliance for Progress, intended to spur economic development in Latin America, and Peace Corps activities throughout the Third World. In response to the Soviet launching of Sputnik, Kennedy vowed that the U.S. would be the first to land on the moon, a program that stimulated the American economy.

Kennedy continued Eisenhower's covert efforts to overthrow the government of Fidel Castro. The 1961 invasion, the Bay of Pigs, failed when support from anti-Castro Cubans failed to materialize. The American efforts inadvertently strengthened the relationship between Cuba and the Soviet Union. That conflict culminated with the Cuban Missile Crisis in 1962, when the Soviets installed missiles in Cuba. The conflict, which took the U.S. and the Soviet Union to the brink of war, ended when Soviet Premier Nikita Khrushchev ordered the removal of the missiles. Shortly before his assassination, Kennedy made modest efforts to de-escalate the tension between the U.S. and the Soviet Union. Kennedy also made plans to scale down the American presence in Vietnam and begin a withdrawal of military personnel. After Kennedy's death, Johnson reversed this policy.

Johnson expanded Kennedy's domestic program and developed his own agenda, the Great Society. He aimed to provide abundance and liberty for everyone, and an end to racial injustice and poverty. With the passage of the Economic Opportunity Act, Johnson initiated a war on poverty. Johnson spent billions to wipe out poverty through education and job retraining programs, such as Job Corps, Volunteers in Service to America (VISTA), and Project Head Start. Another priority of the Great Society was the issue of health care, addressed by new legislation creating Medicare health coverage for the elderly and Medicaid coverage for the poor. The Civil Rights Act of 1964, the Voting Rights Act of 1965, and Johnson's appointment of Thurgood Marshall as the first black Supreme Court Justice reflected his commitment to civil rights. These actions, however, intensified the concerns of many white Americans that the civil rights movement was moving too fast.

During Johnson's presidency, the civil rights movement witnessed a radical change in leadership and tactics. Nonviolent, civil disobedience had been promoted by Martin Luther King, Jr. As the head of the Student Non-Violent Coordinating Committee, Stokeley Carmichael drew African Americans to the cause of Black Power, purged white members from the organization, and began to advocate a more radical, separatist message. Prior to his conversion to Islam, Malcolm X urged African Americans to employ "any means necessary," to obtain their freedom.

Other groups adopted the tactics of the Civil Rights movements to press for better treatment. Feminists organized the National Organization for Women and fought for an Equal Rights Amendment and equal pay for comparable work. Mexican Americans also became more militant. César Chávez organized the National Farm Workers' Association and succeeded in improving working and living conditions for Mexican American migrant workers. Encouraged by the Indian Civil Rights Act of 1968, Native Americans asserted their rights. American Indians sought tribal sovereignty and the honoring of treaty agreements.

Johnson's Vietnam policy and the resulting conflict ultimately overshadowed the domestic successes of his presidency. Johnson was a firm believer in American superiority, committed to the containment of Communism. Despite a lack of evidence, Johnson announced to the American public that North Vietnamese patrol boats had attacked American destroyers in the Gulf of Tonkin. Johnson secured the Gulf of Tonkin Resolution from Congress, authorizing him "to take all necessary measures to repel any armed attack against the forces of the United States and to prevent further aggression."

In early 1965, Johnson ordered sustained bombing of the North with Operation Rolling Thunder. Johnson increased the number of American troops from 1965 on, an action that alarmed an ever-growing number of Americans and increased the level of protest against the war. As the war escalated, so too did the cost, consequently funding for Johnson's domestic programs was decreased.

Even with advanced warning from the CIA, the American military was surprised in January 1968 by the Tet Offensive. Vietcong and North Vietnamese forces hit targets all over South Vietnam. This had a dramatic, negative effect on American public opinion. The press, the CIA, the Secretary of Defense, and Johnson's advisors all maintained that the war could not be won. Johnson responded by halting most of the bombing in North Vietnam, and requesting that the North Vietnamese government in Hanoi begin negotiations to conclude the war. Johnson withdrew from the presidential race.

It became clear in 1968 that the war in Vietnam would not end in a decisive victory for the United States. Johnson's dream of a Great Society all but evaporated. His vice president, Hubert Humphrey, would represent the party in the next election. At the Democratic national convention in Chicago, violence erupted between the police and students protesting the war. Television coverage enabled millions of Americans to witness the brutal treatment inflicted on the protestors by the police. In addition, the assassinations of both Martin Luther King, Jr. and Robert Kennedy effectively ended the optimism and idealism that had earlier characterized the 1960s. Conservative Republican candidate Richard M. Nixon easily won the election.

IDENTIFICATION: Briefly describe each term.

Bay of Pigs

Fidel Castro

Great Society

Thurgood Marshall

Nikita Krushchev

Diem Regime

John F. Kennedy

Robert McNamara

Sheriff "Bull" Connor

"I Have a Dream"

Non-violent protest

Rev. Dr. Martin Luther King, Jr.

Malcolm X

Black Power

Student Non-Violent Coordinating Committee (SNCC)

National Organization for Women (NOW)

Equal Rights Amendment

Betty Friedan

Gloria Steinem

Chicana

Woodstock

Lyndon B. Johnson

César Chávez

"The Other America"

Volunteers in Service to America (VISTA)

Head-Start

Medicaid/Medicare

The Civil Rights Act, 1964

Congress of Racial Equality (CORE)

Gulf of Tonkin Resolution

Americanization of the War in Vietnam

Vietcong

Hanoi

Beatles

Tet Offensive

J. Edgar Hoover

THINK ABOUT:

1.   Discuss the factors that influenced Kennedy's decision to withdraw American advisors in Vietnam during the fall of 1963.

2.   Evaluate Johnson's decision to lead the United States into war following the Gulf of Tonkin incident.

3.   Examine the evolution of the civil rights movement from the nonviolent tactics of Martin Luther King, Jr. and SCLC, to the radical approach of the SNCC and Black Power movement. How would you explain this transition?

SENATOR J. WILLIAM FULBRIGHT'S REMARKS ON THE CONCEPT OF TOTAL VICTORY

Speaking before the Senate on July 24, 1961, Senator Fulbright critiques the notion of a "total victory" over international communism.

Mr. President, I should like to comment briefly today on certain themes contained in the remarks concerning our foreign policy made by the junior Senator from Arizona [Mr. GOLDWATER] on July 13. The Senator's views are, as usual, forthright and provocative. They are of special significance, in that the Senator is an acknowledged spokesman and leader of opinion in his party.

The Senator says that our fundamental objective must be "total victory" over international communism. I must confess to some difficulty in understanding precisely what "total victory" means in this age of ideological conflict and nuclear weapons. ...

It would be beneficial and instructive, I think, if those who call for total victory would spell out for us precisely how it might be achieved and, more important, what we would do with a total victory once we had won it. Is it to be won by nuclear war – a war which at the very least would cost the lives of tens of millions of people on both sides, devastate most of our great cities, and mutilate or utterly destroy a civilization which has been built over thousands of years?

Or can total victory be won without war – by some brilliant stroke of diplomacy or b arguments of such compelling logic that the Communists will acknowledge the error of their ways and abandon their grand imperialistic design? Perhaps the advocates of total victory believe that we can achieve it by abandoning our efforts toward disarmament and engaging in an unrestricted nuclear arms race, even though such a policy would provoke similar measures by the Communist powers.

The Senator from Arizona suggest that the periphery of freedom "is growing steadily smaller in direct ratio to our failure to act from strength." What would a policy of strength involve? Does it mean a military invasion of Cuba which would destroy the Castro dictatorship, but which would also alienate the rest of Latin America and necessitate the stationing of Marines in Cuba to protect an American-imposed regime against Fidelista rebels and guerillas? Does it mean the commitment of American forces to interminable guerilla warfare in the jungles of Laos, a war in which all the advantages of geography would be on the side of the Communists?

Even more perplexing than the question of how to win a total victory is the problem of what we would do with it once it was won. Would we undertake a military occupation of Russia and China and launch a massive program to re-educate 200 million Russians and 600 million Chinese in the ways of Western democracy?

Political objectives must be framed in terms of time and circumstance.... We had total victories in the past, and their examples offer little encouragement. We fought the First World War to make the world safe for democracy, and prosecuted the Second World War to achieve the unconditional surrender of our enemies. Both world wars ended in total victory, but the world is far less safe for democracy today than it was in 1914, when the current era of upheavals began. One of the principle lessons of two World Wars is that wars and total victories, generate more problems than they solve. Apparently we have not yet fully accepted the fact that there are no absolute solutions, that we can hope to do, little more than mitigate our problems as best we can and learn to live with them.

As I said in my remarks of June 29, there is a double standard in the struggle between communism and the free nations. While Communist tactics include terror, subversion, and military aggression, the world demands a higher order of conduct from the United States. Our policies must be consistent with our objectives, which are those of constructive social purpose and world peace under world law. Were we to adopt the same mischievous tactics as those employed by the Communists, the principal target of these tactics would be our own principles and our own national style.

The senator says that world opinion "is an area of official concern which has no reason for existing," that world opinion actually countenances international communism. The Senator does an injustice to the hopes and aspirations of peoples throughout the world and he credits communism with a far greater appeal than it actually has. It is not communism, which appeals to the hearts and minds of the emergent peoples of Asia, Africa, and Latin America. These people hope for peace, for a decent material life, and for national self-determination. Only as insofar as communism succeeds in identifying itself with these aspirations does it win prestige, allegiance, and respect.

World opinion is eminently worth courting – because the hopes of millions of people for world order and economic and social reform are our hopes as well. Where world opinion seems to be feeble or ill-informed, our proper task is to seek to develop and inform it, not to dismiss it as unworthy of our concern. ...

World opinion is a civilizing force in the world, helping to restrain the great powers from the worst possible consequences of their mutual hostility. To disavow and override the opinions of other peoples because they do not always agree with our own is to destroy a potentially powerful force for peace and to return to the laws of the jungle. The Senator says that I favor a policy of "non-intervention." I am indeed opposed to policies that would overextend the United States, especially when such policies find little or no support elsewhere in the non-Communist world. By refusing to permit our national strength to be sapped by peripheral struggles, we maximize our power to honor our obligations and commitments all over the world. We are committed to military and political alliances with many nations and we are committed to assist many more nations toward the fulfillment of their legitimate political, economic, and social aspirations. Such policies are the diametric opposite of any doctrine of nonintervention. Their basic concept is one of intervention – but not indiscriminate military intervention in response to every provocation and every disorder, regardless of its character and cause. The latter approach is one of rigid and negative reaction, one which would leave every initiative to our adversaries. The program which I support is one of long range intervention in depth, one which employs all of the instrumentalities of foreign policy, the political and economic as well ads the military. Its object is the realization of our national interests and not merely the piecemeal frustration of Communist ambitions.

There are limitations to foreign policy. We are neither omniscient nor omnipotent, and we cannot aspire to make the world over in our image.

Our proper objective is a continuing effort to limit the world struggle for power and to bring it under civilized rules. Such a program lacks the drama and romance of a global crusade. Its virtue is that it represents a realistic accommodation between our highest purposes and the limitations of human capacity. Its ultimate objective is indeed total victory, not alone for our arms in a nuclear war or for the goal of a world forcibly recast in our image, but rather for the process – a process of civilizing international relations and of bringing them gradually under a world-wide regime of law and order and peaceful procedures for the redress of legitimate grievances.

Source: Senator J. William Fullbright in the United States Senate, July 24, 1961, Congressional Record, 87th Congress, 1st Session, Vol. 107, No. 123, 12280-81.)

HOW WELL DID YOU UNDERSTAND THIS SELECTION?

1. Discuss Fulbright's concerns about the tactics the United States might employ in this Cold War battle with the Soviets.

2. What policies does Fulbright suggest the U.S. adopt to address the Soviet threat?

3. According to Fulbright, what are the American objectives in this contest with the Soviet Union?

When American reconnaissance revealed that the Soviets had installed nuclear missiles in Cuba in October 1962, President Kennedy demanded that the weapons be removed. He responded to the threat by implementing a naval quarantine to block further shipments of Soviet weapons from reaching Cuba. On October 22, Kennedy explained the Cuban situation in a radio and television address to the American public. Within a week, the Soviets accepted the American demands to remove their weapons from Cuba. In exchange, the United States lifted the quarantine and agreed to remove American missiles from Turkey. Although war was ultimately averted, the U.S. and the Soviet Union hovered on the brink of war for several weeks.

October 22, 1962, Washington, D.C.
PRESIDENT JOHN F. KENNEDY

Good evening my fellow citizens:

This Government, as promised, has maintained the closest surveillance of the Soviet military buildup on the island of Cuba. Within the past week, unmistakable evidence has established the fact that a series of offensive missile sites is now in preparation on that imprisoned island. The purpose of these bases can be none other than to provide a nuclear strike capability against the Western Hemisphere.

Upon receiving the first preliminary hard information of this nature last Tuesday morning on 9 A.M., I directed that our surveillance be stepped up. And having now confirmed and completed our evaluation of the evidence and our decision on a course of action, this Government feels obliged to report this new crisis to you in fullest detail.

The characteristics of these new missile sites indicate two distinct types of installations. Several of them include medium range ballistic missiles, capable of carrying a nuclear warhead for a distance of more than 1,000 nautical miles. Each of these missiles, in short, is capable of striking Washington, D.C., the Panama Canal, Cape Canaveral, Mexico City, or any other city in the southeastern part of the United States, in Central America, or in the Caribbean area.

Additional sites not yet completed appear to be designed for intermediate range ballistic missiles-capable of traveling more that twice as far-and thus capable of striking most of the major cities in the Western Hemisphere, ranging as far north as Hudson Bay, Canada, and as far south as Lima, Peru. In addition, jet bombers, capable of carrying nuclear weapons, are now being uncrated and assembled in Cuba, while the necessary air bases are being prepared.

This urgent transformation of Cuba into an important strategic base-by the presence of these large, long-range, and clearly offensive weapons of sudden mass destruction – constitutes an explicit threat to the peace and security of all the Americas, in flagrant and deliberate defiance of the Rio Pact of 1947, the traditions of this Nation and hemisphere, the joint resolution of the 87th Congress, the Charter of the United Nations and my own public warnings to the Soviets on September 4 and 13. This action also contradicts the repeated assurances of Soviet spokesmen, both publicly and privately delivered, that the arms buildup in Cuba would retain its original defensive character, and that the Soviet Union had no need or desire to station strategic missiles, on the territory of any other nation.

The size of this undertaking makes clear that it has been planned for some months. Yet only last month, after I had made clear the distinction between any introduction of ground-to-ground missiles and the existence of defensive antiaircraft missiles, the Soviet Government publicly stated on September 11 that, and I quote, "the armaments and military equipment sent to Cuba are designed exclusively for defensive for defensive purposes," that, and I quote the Soviet Government, "there is no need for the Soviet Government to shift its weapons...for a retaliatory blow to any other country, for instance Cuba," and that, and I quote their government, "the Soviet Union has so powerful rockets to carry these nuclear warheads that there is no need to search for sites for them beyond the boundaries of the Soviet Union." That statement was false.

Only last Thursday, as evidence of this rapid offensive buildup was already in my hand, Soviet Foreign Minister Gromyko told me in my office that he was instructed to make it clear once again, as he said his government had already done, that Soviet assistance to Cuba, and I quote, "pursued solely the purpose of contributing to the defense capabilities of Cuba," that, and I quote him, "training by Soviet specialists of Cuban nationals in handling defensive armaments was by no means offensive, and if it were otherwise," Mr. Gromyko went on, "the Soviet Government would never become involved in rendering such assistance." That statement also was false.

Neither the United States of America nor the world community of nations can tolerate deliberate deception and offensive threats on the part of any nation, large or small. We no longer live in a world where only the actual firing of weapons represents a sufficient challenge to a nation's security to constitute maximum peril. Nuclear weapons are so destructive and ballistic missiles are so swift, that any substantially increased possibility of their use or any sudden change their deployment may well be regarded as a definite threat to peace.

For many years, both the Soviet Union and the United States, recognizing this fact, have deployed strategic nuclear weapons with great care, never upsetting the precarious status quo which insured that these weapons would not be used in the absence of some vital challenge. Our own strategic missiles have never been transferred to the territory of any other nation under a cloak of secrecy and deception; and our history-unlike that of the Soviets since the end of World War II – demonstrates that we have no desire to dominate or conquer any other nation or impose our system upon its people. Nevertheless, American citizens have become adjusted to living daily on the bull's-eye of Soviet missiles located inside the U.S.S.R. or in submarines.

In that sense, missiles in Cuba add to an already clear and present danger – although it should be noted the nations of Latin America have never previously been subjected to a potential nuclear threat.

But this secret, swift, and extraordinary buildup of Communist missiles – in an area well known to have a special and historical relationship to the United States and the nations of the Western Hemisphere, in violation of Soviet assurances, and in defiance of American and hemispheric policy – this sudden, clandestine decision to station strategic weapons for the first time outside of Soviet soil – is a deliberately provocative and unjustified change in the status quo which cannot be accepted by this country, if our courage and our commitments are ever to be trusted again by either friend or foe.

The 1930's taught us a clear lesson: aggressive conduct, if allowed to go unchecked, ultimately leads to war. This nation is opposed to war. We are also true to our word. Our unswerving objective, therefore, must be to prevent the use of these missiles against this or any other country, and to secure their withdrawal or elimination from the Western Hemisphere.

Our policy has been one of patience and restraint, as befits a peaceful and powerful nation, which leads a worldwide alliance. We have been determined not to be diverted from our central concerns by mere irritants and fanatics. But now prematurely or unnecessarily risk the costs of worldwide nuclear war in which even the fruits of victory would be ashes in our mouth – but neither will we shrink from that risk at any time it must be faced.

Acting, therefore, in the defense of our own security and of the entire Western Hemisphere, and under the authority entrusted to me by the Constitution as endorsed by the Resolution of the Congress, I have directed that the following *initial* steps be taken immediately:

First: To halt this offensive buildup, a strict quarantine on all offensive military equipment under shipment to Cuba is being initiated. All ships of any kind bound for Cuba from whatever nation or port will, if found to contain cargoes of offensive weapons, be turned back. This quarantine will be extended, if needed, to other types of cargo and carriers. We are not at this time, however, denying the necessities of life as the Soviets attempted to do in their Berlin blockade of 1948.

Second: I have directed the continued and increased close surveillance of Cuba and its military buildup. The foreign ministers of the OAS, in their communiqué of October 6, rejected secrecy on such matters in this hemisphere. Should these offensive military preparations continue, thus increasing the threat to the hemisphere, further action will be justified. I have directed the Armed Forces to prepare for any eventualities; and I trust that in the interest of both the Cuban people and the Soviet technicians at the sites, the hazards to all concerned of continuing this threat will be recognized.

Third: It shall be the policy of this Nation to regard any nuclear missile launched from Cuba against any nation in the Western Hemisphere as an attack by the Soviet Union on the United States, requiring a full retaliatory response upon the Soviet Union.

Fourth: As a necessary military precaution, I have reinforced our base at Guantanamo, evacuated today the dependents of our personnel there, and ordered additional military units to be on a standby alert basis.

Fifth: We are calling tonight for an immediate meeting of the Organ of Consultation under the Organization of American States, to consider this threat to hemispheric security and to invoke articles 6 and 8 of the Rio Treaty in support of all necessary action. The United Nations Charter allows for regional security arrangements – and the nations of this hemisphere decided long ago against military presence of outside powers. Our other allies around the world have also been alerted.

Sixth: Under the Charter of the United Nations, we are asking tonight that an emergency meeting of the Security Council be convoked without delay to take action against this latest Soviet threat to world peace. Our resolution will call for the prompt dismantling and withdrawal of all offensive weapons in Cuba, under the supervision of U.N. observers, before the quarantine can be lifted.

Seventh and finally: I call upon Chairman Khrushchev to halt and eliminate this clandestine. Reckless, and provocative threat to world peace and to stable relations between our two nations. I call upon him further to abandon this course of world domination, and to join in an historic effort to end the perilous arms race and to transform the history of man. He has an opportunity now to move the world back from the abyss of destruction – by returning to his government's own words that it had no need to station missiles outside its own territory, and withdrawing these weapons from Cuba-by refraining from any action which will widen or deepen the present crisis – and then by participating in a search for peaceful and permanent solutions.

This Nation is prepared to present its case against the Soviet threat to peace, and our own proposals for a peaceful world, at any time and in any forum – in the OAS, in the United Nations, or in any other meeting that could be useful – without limiting our freedom of action. We have in the past made strenuous efforts to limit the spread of nuclear weapons. We have proposed the elimination of all arms and military bases in a fair and effective disarmament treaty. We are prepared to discuss new proposals for the removal of tensions on both sides – including the possibilities of a genuinely independent Cuba, free to determine its own destiny. We have no wish to war with the Soviet Union – for we are a peaceful people who desire to live in peace with all other peoples.

But it is difficult to settle or even discuss these problems in an atmosphere of intimidation. That is why this latest Soviet threat – or any other threat which is made either independently or in response to our actions this week – must and will be met with determination. Any hostile move anywhere in the world against the safety and freedom of peoples to whom we are committed – including in particular the brave people of West Berlin – will be met by whatever action is needed.

Finally, I want to say a few words to the captive people of Cuba, to whom this speech is being directly carried by special radio facilities. I speak to you as a friend, as one who knows of your deep attachment to your fatherland, as one who shares your aspirations for liberty and justice for all. And I have watched and the American people have watched with deep sorrow how your nationalist revolution was betrayed – and how your fatherland fell under foreign domination. Now your leaders are no longer Cuban leaders inspired by Cuban ideals. They are puppets and agents of an international conspiracy which has turned Cuba against your friends and neighbors in the Americas – and turned it into the first Latin American country to become a target for nuclear war – the first Latin American country to have these weapons on its soil.

These new weapons are not in your interest. They contribute nothing to your peace and well-being. They can only undermine it. But this country has no wish to cause you to suffer or to impose any system upon you. We know that your lives and land are being used as pawns by those who deny your freedom. Many times in the past, the Cuban people have risen to throw out tyrants who destroyed their liberty. And I have no doubt that most Cubans today look forward to the time when they will be truly free – free from foreign domination, free to choose their own leaders, free to select their own system, free to own their own land, free to speak and write and worship without fear or degradation. And then shall Cuba be welcomed back to society of free nations and to the associations of this hemisphere.

My fellow citizens: let no one doubt that this is a difficult and dangerous effort on which we have set out. No one can foresee precisely what course it will take or what costs or casualties will be incurred. Many months of sacrifice and self-discipline lie ahead – months in which both our patience and our will will be tested – months in which many threats and denunciations will keep us aware of our dangers. But the greatest danger of all would be to do nothing.

The path we have chosen for the present is full of hazards, as all paths are – but it is the one most consistent with our character and courage as a nation and our commitments around the world. The cost of freedom is always high – but Americans have always paid it. And one path we shall never choose, and that is the path of surrender or submission.

Our goal is not the victory of might, but the vindication of right – not peace at the expense of freedom, but both peace and freedom, here in this hemisphere, and, we hope, around the world. God willing, that goal will be achieved.

Thank you and good night.

HOW WELL DID YOU UNDERSTAND THIS SELECTION?

1. According to Kennedy, how serious is the Soviet threat to American security?

2. Briefly outline Kennedy's proposed response to the threat.

3. Evaluate the possible motives for Kennedy's inclusion of a message to the people of Cuba in this speech.

After the decisive French defeat at Dien Bien Phu and their withdrawal from the region in 1954, President Eisenhower increased support to the South Vietnamese government in their effort to resist reunification with Communist North Vietnam. When Kennedy took office, he continued the containment policy established by the Eisenhower administration. Fearful that the communist threat was escalating throughout the world, Kennedy increased the American presence in Vietnam. In the fall of 1963, however, the situation had deteriorated, and Kennedy reassessed his position. In a televised interview with Walter Cronkite, Kennedy discussed the situation in September 1963. One month after the interview, Kennedy met with Secretary of Defense Robert S. McNamara and Gen. Maxwell D. Taylor to assess the situation in South Vietnam.

September 2, 1963
CBS Television Interview with Walter Cronkite
Washington, D.C.

PRESIDENT JOHN F. KENNEDY

MR. CRONKITE: Mr. President, the only hot war we've got running at the moment is of course the one in Viet-Nam, and we have our difficulties here, quite obviously.

PRESIDENT KENNEDY: I don't think that unless a greater effort is made by the Government to win popular support that the war can be won out there. In the final analysis, it is their war. They are the ones who have to win it or lose it. We can help them, we can give them equipment, we can send our men out there as advisers, but they have to win it-the people of Viet-Nam - against the Communists. We are prepared to continue to assist them, but I don't think that the war can be won unless the people support the effort, and, in my opinion, in the last 2 months the Government has gotten out of touch with the people.

The repression against the Buddhists, we felt, were very unwise. Now we can do is to make it very clear that we don't think this is the way to win. It is my hope that this will become increasingly obvious to the Government, that they will take steps to try to bring back popular support for this very essential struggle.

…[I]n the final analysis it is the people and the government itself who have to win or lose this struggle. All we can do is help, and we are making it very clear. But I don't agree with those who say we should withdraw. That would be a great mistake. I know people don't like Americans to be engaged in this kind of an effort. Forty-seven Americans have been killed in combat with the enemy, but this is a very important struggle even though it is far away.

We took all this-made this effort to defend Europe. Now Europe is quite secure. We also have to participate-we may not like it-in the defense of Asia.

Source: CBS Interview, September 2, 1963, *United States Senate Committee on Foreign Relations, Background Information Relating to Southeast Asia and Vietnam*, 90th Congress 1st Session. (Washington, D.C.: Government Printing Office, 1967), pp. 112-114.

U.S. POLICY ON VIETNAM

Secretary [of Defense Robert S.] McNamara and General [Maxwell D.] Taylor reported to the President this morning and to National Security Council this afternoon. Their report included a number of classified findings and recommendations which will be the subject of further review and action. Their basic presentation was endorsed by all members of the Security Council and the following statement of United States policy was approved by the President on the basis of recommendations received from them and from Ambassador [Henry Cabot] Lodge.

October 2, 1963
Washington, D.C.
WHITE HOUSE STATEMENT

1. The security of South Viet-Nam is a major interest of the United States as other free nations. We will adhere to our policy of working with the people and government of South Viet-Nam to deny this country to communism and to suppress the externally stimulated and supported insurgency of the Viet-Cong as promptly as possible. Effective performance in the undertaking is the central objective of our policy in South Viet-Nam.
2. The military program in South Viet-Nam has made progress and is sound in principle, though improvements are being energetically sought.
3. Major U.S. assistance in support of this military effort is needed only until the insurgency has been suppressed or until the national security forces of the government of South Viet-Nam are capable of suppressing it. Secretary McNamara and General Taylor reported their judgement that the major part of the U.S. military task can be completed by the end of 1965, although there may be a continuing requirement for a limited number of U.S.

training personnel. They reported that by the end of this year, the U.S. program for training Vietnamese should be progressed to the point where 1,000 U.S. military personnel assigned to South Viet-Nam can be withdrawn.

4. The political situation in South Viet-Nam remains deeply serious. The United States has made clear its continuing opposition to any repressive actions in South Viet-Nam. While such actions have not yet significantly affected the military effort, they could do so in the future.

5. It remains the policy of the United States, in South Viet-Nam as in other parts of the world, to support the efforts of the people of that country to defeat aggression and to build a peaceful and free society.

HOW WELL DID YOU UNDERSTAND THIS SELECTION?

1. How does Kennedy explain the deteriorating situation in South Vietnam?

2. According to Kennedy and the White House Statement, what is the role of the United States in South Vietnam?

3. What evidence supports the notion that Kennedy was ready to withdraw American advisors from Vietnam?

OUR DUTY IN SOUTHEAST ASIA

During the Kennedy administration the number of American advisors in South Vietnam had increased from 2,000 in 1961 to 16,000 by 1963. Despite the increased American presence, the situation in South Vietnam had deteriorated. Following Kennedy's assassination, President Johnson reversed the order to withdraw the American advisors. In 1964 Johnson obtained the authority from Congress to intensify American activity in Vietnam with Operation Rolling Thunder, the sustained bombing of North Vietnam. On April 7, 1965, Johnson defended his policy.

April 7, 1965
Johns Hopkins University, Baltimore, Maryland

PRESIDENT LYNDON B. JOHNSON

My fellow Americans: Last week 17 nations sent their views to some dozen countries having interest in Southeast Asia. We are joining these 17 countries in stating our American policy, which we believe will contribute toward peace in this area.

Tonight I want to review once again with my own people the views of your Government.

Tonight Americans and Asians are dying for a world where each people may choose its own path to change.

This is the principle for which our ancestors fought in the valleys of Pennsylvania. It is the principle for which our sons fight in the jungles of Vietnam.

Vietnam is far from this quiet campus. We have no territory there, nor do we seek any. The war is dirty and brutal and difficult. And some 400 young men – born into an America bursting with opportunity and promise – have ended their lives on Vietnam's steaming soil.

Why must we take this painful road?

Why must this nation hazard its ease, its interest and its power for the sake of a people so far away?

We fight because we must fight if we are to live in a world where every country can shape its own destiny. And only in such a world will our own freedom be finally secure.

This kind of a world will never be built by bombs and bullets. Yet the infirmities of man are such that force must often precede reason – and the waste of war, the works of peace.

We wish this were not so. But we must deal with the world as it is, if it is ever to be as we wish.

The world as it is in Asia is not a serene or peaceful place.

The first reality is the North Vietnam has attacked the independent nation of South Vietnam. Its object is total conquest.

Of course, some of the people of South Vietnam are participating in attack on their own Government. But trained men and supplies, orders and arms, flow in a constant stream from North to South. This support is the heartbeat of the war.

And it is a war of unparalleled brutality. Simple farmers are the targets of assassination and kidnapping. Women and children are strangled in the night because their men are loyal to the Government. Small and helpless villages are ravaged by sneak attacks. Large-scale raids are conducted on towns, and terror strikes in the heart of cities.

The confused nature of this conflict cannot mask the fact that it is the new face of an old enemy. It is an attack by one country upon another. And the object of that attack is a friend to which we are pledged.

Over this war - and all Asia – is another reality: the deepening shadow of Communist China. The rulers in Hanoi are urged on by Peking. This is a regime which has destroyed freedom in Tibet, attacked India and has been condemned by the United Nations for aggressions in Korea. It is a nation which is helping the forces of violence in almost every continent. The contest in Vietnam is part of a wider pattern of aggressive purpose.

Why are these realities our concern? Why are we in South Vietnam?

We are there because we have a promise to keep. Since 1954 every American President has offered support to the people of South Vietnam. We have helped to build and we have helped to defend. Thus, over many years, we have made a national pledge to help South Vietnam defend its independence.

I intend to keep our promise.

To dishonor that pledge, to abandon this small and brave nation to its enemy – and to the terror that must follow – would be an unforgivable wrong.

We are also there to strengthen world order. Around the globe – from Berlin to Thailand - are people whose well-being rests, in part, on the belief they can count on us if they are attacked. To leave Vietnam to its fate would shake the confidence of all these people in the value of American commitment. The result would be increased unrest and instability, or even war.

We are also there because there are great stakes in the balance. Let no one think that retreat from Vietnam would bring an end to conflict. The battle would be renewed in one country and then another. The central lesson of our time is that the appetite of aggression is never satisfied. To withdraw from one battlefield means only to prepare for the next. We must say in Southeast Asia – as we did in Europe – in the words of the Bible: "Hitherto shalt thou come, but no further."

There are those who say that all our efforts there will be futile – that China's power is such it is bound to dominate all Southeast Asia. But there is no end to that argument until all the nations of Asia are swallowed up.

There are those who wonder why we have a responsibility for the defense of freedom in Europe. World War II was fought in both Europe and Asia, and when it ended we found ourselves with continued responsibility for the defense of freedom.

Our objective is the independence of South Vietnam, and its freedom from attack. We want nothing for ourselves – only that the people of South Vietnam be allowed to guide their own country in their own way.

We will do everything necessary to reach that objective. And we will do only what is necessary.

In recent months attacks on South Vietnam were stepped up. Thus it became to increase our response and make attacks by air. This is not a change of purpose. It is a change in what we believe that purpose requires.

We do this in order to slow down aggression.

We do this to increase the confidence of the brave people of South Vietnam who have bravely borne this brutal battle for so many years and with so many casualties.

And we do this to convince the leaders of North Vietnam – and all who seek to share their conquest – of a simple fact:

We will not be defeated.

We will not grow tired.

We will not withdraw, either openly or under the cloak of a meaningless agreement.

We know that air attacks alone will not accomplish all these purposes. But it is our best and prayerful judgement that they are a necessary part of the surest road to peace.

We hope that peace will come swiftly. But that is in the hands of others beside ourselves. And we must be prepared for a long, continued conflict. It will require patience as well as bravery – the will to endure as well as the will to resist.

I wish it were possible to convince others with word of what we now   find it necessary to say with guns and planes: Armed hostility is futile. Our resources are equal to any challenge. Because we fight for values and a principal, rather than territory or colonies, our patience and determination are unending.

Once this is clear, then it should be also be clear that the only path for reasonable men is the path of peaceful settlement.

Such peace demands an independent South Vietnam – securely guaranteed and able to shape its own relationships to all others, free from outside interference, tied to no alliance, a military base for no other country.

These are the essentials of any final settlement.

We will never be second in the search for such a peaceful settlement in Vietnam.

There may be many ways to this kind of peace: in discussion or negotiation with the governments concerned; in large groups or in small ones; in the reaffirmation of old agreements or their strengthening with new ones.

We have stated this position over and over again 50 times and more to friend and foe alike. And we remain ready, with this purpose, for unconditional discussions.

And until that bright and necessary day of peace, we will try to keep conflict from spreading. We have no desire to see thousands die in battle – Asians or Americans. We have no desire to devastate that which the people of North Vietnam have built with toil and sacrifice. We will use our power with restraint and with all the wisdom we can command. But we will use it.

This war, like most wars, is filled with terrible irony. For what do the people of North Vietnam want? They want what their neighbors also desire; food for their hunger, health for their bodies and a chance to learn, progress for their country and an end to the bondage of material misery. And they would find all these things far more readily in peaceful association with others than in the endless course of battle.

These countries of Southeast Asia are homes for millions of impoverished people. Each day these people rise at dawn and struggle through weary hours to wrestle existence from the soil. They are often wracked by disease, plagued by hunger, and death comes early, at the age of 40.

Stability and peace do not come easily in such a land. Neither independence nor human dignity will be won by arms alone. It also requires the works of peace.

The American people have helped generously in these works.

Now there must be a much more massive effort to improve the life of man in the conflict-torn corner of the world.

The first step is for the countries of Southeast Asia to associate themselves in a greatly expanded cooperative effort for development. We would hope that North Vietnam will take its place in the common effort just as soon as peaceful cooperation is possible.

The United Nations is already actively engaged in development in this area. I would hope that the Secretary General of the United Nations could use the prestige of his great office-and his deep knowledge of Asia-to initiate, as soon as possible with the countries of the area a plan for cooperation in increased development.

For our part I will ask the Congress to join in a billion-dollar American investment in this effort when it is underway.

And I hope all other industrialized countries-including Soviet Union- will join in this effort to replace despair with hope and terror with progress.

The task is nothing less than to enrich the hopes and existence of more than a hundred million people. And there is much to be done.

The vast Mekong River can provide food and water and power on a scale to dwarf even our own T.V.A.

The wonders of modern medicine can be spread through villages where thousands die for lack of care.

Schools can be established to train people in the skills needed to manage the process of development.

And these objectives, and more, are within the reach of a cooperative and determined effort.

I also intend to expand and speed up a program to make available our farm surplus to assist in feeding and clothing the needy in Asia. We should not allow people to go hungry and naked while our own warehouses overflow with an abundance of wheat and corn, rice and cotton.

I will very shortly name a special team of patriotic and distinguished Americans to inaugurate our participation in these programs. This team will be headed by Mr. Eugene Black, the very able former president of the World Bank.

In areas still ripped by conflict, development will not be easy. Peace will be necessary for final success. But we cannot wait for peace to begin the job.

This will be a disorderly planet for a long time. In Asia, as elsewhere, the forces of the modern world are shaking old ways and uprooting ancient civilizations. There will be turbulence and struggle and even violence. Great social change, as we see in our own country, does not always come without conflict.

We must also expect that nations will on occasions be in dispute with us. It may be because we are rich or powerful, or because we have made mistakes, or because they honestly fear our intentions. However, no nation need ever fear that we desire their land or to impose our will or to dictate their institutions.

But we will always oppose the effort of one nation to conquer another. We will do this because our own security is at stake.

But there is more to it than that. For our generation has a dream. It is a very old dream. But we have the power and the opportunity to make it real.

For centuries nations have struggled among each other. But we dream of a world where disputes are settled by law and reason. And we will try to make it so.

For most of history men have hated and killed one another in battle. But we dream of an end to war. And we will try to make it so.

For all existence most men have lived in poverty, threatened by hunger. But we dream of a world where all are fed and charged with hope. And we will help to make it so.

The ordinary men and women of North Vietnam and South Vietnam, of China and India, of Russia and America, are brave people. They are filled with the same proportions of hate and fear, of love and hope. Most of them want the same things for themselves and their families. Most of them do not want their sons to die in battle, or see the homes of others destroyed.

This can be their world yet. Man now has the knowledge-always before denied-to make this planet serve the real needs of the people who live on it.

I know this will not be easy. I know how difficult it is for reason to guide passion and love to master hate. The complexities of this world do not bow easily to pure and consistent answers.

But the simple truths are there just the same. We must try to follow them as best we can.

We often say how impressive power is. But I do not find it impressive. The guns and bombs, the rockets and warships are all symbols of human failure. They are necessary symbols. They protect what we cherish. But they are witness to human folly.

A dam built across a great river is impressive.

In the countryside where I was born, I have seen the night illuminated the kitchens warmed and the homes heated where once the cheerless night and the ceaseless cold held sway. And all this happened because electricity came to our town along the humming wires of the Rural Electrification Administration. Electrification of the countryside is impressive.

A rich harvest in a hungry land is impressive.

These-not mighty arms-are the achievements which the American nation believes to be impressive.

And-if we are steadfast-the time may come when all other nations will also find it so.

We may well be living in the time foretold many years ago when it was said: "I call heaven and earth to record this day against you, that I have set before you life and death, blessing, and cursing: therefore choose life, that both thou and thy seed may live."

This generation of the world must choose: destroy or build, kill or aid, hate or understand.

We can do all these things on a scale never dreamed of before.

We will choose life. And so doing we will prevail over the enemies within man, and over the natural enemies of all mankind.

HOW WELL DID YOU UNDERSTAND THIS SELECTION?

1. How does Johnson justify the escalation of American involvement in Vietnam?

2. According to Johnson, what are the American objectives in this conflict?

3. How does he propose to achieve these objectives?

In 1961, President Kennedy established the President's Commission on the Status of Women on the recommendation of Esther Peterson, assistant Secretary of Labor. The commission, chaired by Eleanor Roosevelt, was designed to investigate legal and economic discrimination against women. The findings of the commission contributed to the passage of the Equal Pay Act in 1963.

Spring 1963
Washington, D.C.

PRESIDENT KENNEDY

This report is an invitation to action. When President John F. Kennedy appointed our Commission, he said:...*we have by no means done enough to strengthen family life and at the same time encourage women to make their full contribution as citizens...It is appropriate at this time...to review recent accomplishments, and to acknowledge frankly the further steps that must be taken. This is a task for the entire Nation...*

Certain tenets have guided our thinking. Respect for the worth and dignity of every individual and conviction that every American should have a chance to achieve the best of which he-or she-is capable are basic to the meaning of both freedom and equality in this democracy. They have been, and now are, great levers for constructive social change, here and around the world. We have not hesitated to measure the present shape of things against our convictions regarding a good society and to note discrepancies between American life as it is in 1963 and as it might become through informed and intelligent action.

The human and national costs of social lag are heavy; for the most part, they are also avoidable. That is why we urge changes, many of them long overdue, in the conditions of women's opportunity in the United States...

We believe that one of the greatest freedoms of the individual in a democratic society is the freedom to choose among different life patterns. Innumerable private solutions found by different individuals in search of the good life provide society with basic strength far beyond the possibilities of a dictated plan.

Illumined by values transmitted through home and school and church, society and heritage, and informed by present and past experience, each woman must arrive at her contemporary expression of purpose, whether as a center of home and family, a participant in the community, a contributor to the economy, a creative artist or thinker or scientist, a citizen engaged in politics and public service. Part and parcel of this freedom is the obligation to assume corresponding responsibility.

Yet there are social as well as individual determinants of freedom of choice; for example, the city slum and the poor rural crossroad frustrate natural gifts and innate human powers. It is a bitter fact that for millions of men and women economic stringency all but eliminates choice among alternatives...

Economic expansion is of particular significance to women. One of the ironies of history is that war has brought American women their greatest economic opportunities. In establishing this Commission, the President noted: "In every period of national emergency, women have served with distinction in widely varied capacities but thereafter have been subject to treatment as a marginal group whose skills have been inadequately utilized."

Comparable opportunity-and far more varied choice-could be provided by full employment in a period without war.

The Council of Economic Advisers had estimated that between 1958 and 1962 the country's productive capacity exceeded its actual output by some $170 billion, or almost $1,000 per person in the United States. Had this potential been realized, lower rates of unemployment and an impressive supply of additional goods and services would have contributed to national well-being. The currently unused resources of the American economy include much work that could be done by women...

But while freedom of choice for many American women, as for men, is limited by economic considerations, one of the most pervasive limitations is the social climate in which women choose what they prepare themselves to do. Too many plans recommended to young women reaching maturity and only partially suited to the second half of the twentieth century. Such advice is correspondingly confusing to them.

Even the role most generally approved by counselors, parents, and friends-the making of a home, the rearing of children, and the transmission to them in their earliest years of the values of the American heritage-is frequently presented as it is thought to have been in an earlier and simpler society...

Similarly, women's participation in such traditional occupations as teaching, nursing, and social work is generally approved, with current shortages underscoring the nation's need for such personnel. But means for keeping up to date the skills of women who continue in such professions are few. So, too, are those for bringing up to date the skills of women who withdraw in order to raise families but return after their families are grown.

Commendation of women's entry into certain other occupations is less general, even though some of them are equally in need of trained people. Girls hearing that most women find mathematics and science difficult, or that engineering and architecture are unusual occupations for a woman, are not led to test their interest by activity in these fields.

Because too little is expected of them, many girls who graduate from high school intellectually able to do good college work do not go to college. Both they as individuals and the nation as a society are thereby made losers.

The subtle limitations imposed by custom are, upon occasion, reinforced by specific barriers. In the course of the twentieth century many bars against women that were firmly in place in 1900 have been lowered or dropped. But certain restrictions remain...

Some of these discriminatory provisions are contained in the common law. Some are written into statute. Some are upheld by court decisions. Others take the form of practices of industrial, labor, professional, or governmental organizations that discriminate against women in apprenticeship, training, hiring, wages, and promotion. We have identified a number of outmoded and prejudical attitudes and practices.

Throughout it deliberation, the Commission has kept in mind certain women who have special disadvantages. Among head of families in the United States, 1 in 10 is a woman. At least half of them are carrying responsibility for both earning the family's living and making the family's home. Their problems are correspondingly greater; their resources are usually less.

Seven million nonwhite women and girls belong to minority racial groups. Discrimination based on color is morally wrong and a source of national weakness. Such discrimination currently places an oppressive dual burden on millions of Negro women. The consultation held by the Commission on the situation of Negro women emphasized that in too many families lack of opportunity for men as well as women, linked to racial discrimination, has forced the women to assume too large a share of the family responsibility. Such women are twice as likely as other women to have to seek employment while they have preschool children at home; they are just beginning to gain entrance to the expanding fields of clerical and commercial employment; except for the few who can qualify as teachers or other professionals, they are forced into low-paid service occupations.

Hundreds of thousands of other women face somewhat similar situations: American Indians, for instance, and Spanish –Americans, many of whom live in urban centers but are new to urban life and burned with language problems.

While there are highly skilled members of all these groups, in many of the families of these women the unbroken cycle of deprivation and retardation repeats itself from generation to generation, compounding its individual cost in human indignity and unhappiness and its social cost in incapacity and delinquency. This cycle must be broken, swiftly and at as many points as possible. The Commission strongly urges that in the carrying out of its recommendations, special attention be given to difficulties that are wholly or largely the products of this kind of discrimination...

Eight out of ten women are in paid employment outside the home at some time during their lives, and many of these, and others as well, engage in unpaid work as volunteers.

The population contains 13 million single girls and women 14 and over. A 20-year-old girl, if she remains single, will spend some 40 years in the labor force. If after working for a few years, she marries and has a family, and then goes back into the labor force at 30, she is likely to work for some 23 more years. Particularly during the years when her children are in school but have not yet left home permanently, the work she seeks is apt to be part time. Inflexibility with regard to part time employment in most current hiring systems, alike in government and in private enterprise, excludes the use of much able and available trained womanpower; practices should be altered to permit it...

U.S. President's Commission on the Status of Women, American Women: Report of the Presidents Commission (Washington, DC: Government Printing Office, 1963) pp. 1-7

HOW WELL DID YOU UNDERSTAND THIS SELECTION?

1. According to the findings of the commission, what factors contributed to gender inequality in the U.S.?

2. What recommendations does the report make to remedy the situation?

3. According to the report, what role does socio-economic class play in the extent of discrimination experienced by women?

In September 1965, Joseph Lee Jones filed a complaint against the Alfred H. Mayer Company in District Court of the Eighth Circuit. Jones alleged that Mayer refused to sell him a home in St. Louis County, Missouri, because he was African American. He contested their refusal as a violation of the 1866 Civil Rights Act (42 U.S.C. 1982), which guarantees that: "All citizens of the United States shall have the same right, in every State and Territory, as is enjoyed by white citizens thereof to inherit, purchase, lease, sell, hold, and convey real and personal property." The District Court dismissed the charges, as did the Appeals Court. On June 17, 1968, the U.S. Supreme Court reversed the earlier decision and concluded the 1866 statute "bars all racial discrimination, private as well as public, in the sale or rental of property, and that the statute, thus construed, is a valid exercise of the power of Congress to enforce the Thirteenth Amendment."

...We begin with the language of the statute itself. In plain and unambiguous terms, section 1982 grants to all citizens, without regard to race or color, "the same right" to purchase and lease property 'as is enjoyed by white citizens." ...

On its face, therefore, section 1982 appears to prohibit all discrimination against Negroes in the sale or rental of property – discrimination by private owners as well as discrimination by public authorities. Indeed, even the respondents seem to concede that, if section 1982 "means what it says" – to use the words of the respondents' brief – then it must encompass every racially motivated refusal to sell or rent and cannot be confined to officially sanctioned segregation in housing. Stressing what they consider to be the revolutionary implications of so literal a reading of section 1982, the respondents argue that Congress cannot possibly have intended any such result. Our examination of the relevant history, however, persuades us that Congress meant exactly what it said. ...

In light of the concern that led Congress to adopt it and the contents of the debates that preceded its passage, it is clear that the Act was designed to do just what its terms suggest: to prohibit all racial discrimination, whether or not under color of law, with respect to the rights enumerated therein – including the right to purchase or lease property. ...

Against this background, it would obviously make no sense to assume, without any historical support whatever, that Congress made a silent decision in 1870 to exempt private discrimination from the operation of the Civil Rights Act in 1866. ...

The remaining question is whether Congress has power under the Constitution to do what section 1982 purports to do: to prohibit all racial discrimination, private and public, in the sale and rental of property. Our starting point is the Thirteenth Amendment. ...

Negro citizens, North and South, who saw in the Thirteenth Amendment a promise of freedom – freedom to "go and come at pleasure" and to "buy and sell when they please" – would be left with "a mere paper guarantee" if Congress were powerless to assure that a dollar in the hands of a Negro will purchase the same thing as a dollar in the hands of a white man. At the very least, the freedom that Congress is empowered to secure under the Thirteenth amendment includes the freedom to buy whatever a white man can buy, the right to live wherever a white man can live. If Congress cannot say that being a free man means at least this much, then the Thirteenth amendment made a promise the nation cannot keep. ...

The judgment is

Reversed.

Source: The United States Supreme Court, Jones v. Alfred Mayer Co. ,392 U.S. 409, 1967

HOW WELL DID YOU UNDERSTAND THIS SELECTION?

1. How did the respondents, (Alfred H. Mayer Co.) interpret Section 1982 of the statute?

2. How does the Supreme Court respond to their position?

3. How does the Court interpret the meaning of the Thirteenth Amendment?

SOCIAL UNREST

In the summer of 1967, President Johnson created the National Advisory Commission on Civil Disorders to determine the underlying causes of the violent race riots that had erupted in many American cities. The commission presented its findings in 1968.

1968, Washington, D.C.
THE KERNER COMMISSION REPORT ON THE CAUSES OF CIVIL DISORDERS

The summer of 1967 again brought racial disorders to American cities, and with them shock, fear and bewilderment to the nation.

The worst came during a two-week period in July, first in Newark and then in Detroit. Each set off a chain reaction in neighboring communities.

On July 28, 1967, the President of the United States established this Commission and directed us to answer three basic questions:

What happened?

Why did it happen?

What can be done to prevent it from happening again?...

This is our basic conclusion: Our nation is moving toward two societies, one black, one white-separate and unequal.

Reaction to last summer's disorders has quickened the movement and deepened the division. Discrimination and segregation have long permeated much of American life; they now threaten the future of every American.

This deepening racial division is not inevitable. The movement apart can be reversed. Choice is still possible. Our principle task is to define that choice and to press fore a national resolution...

Race prejudice has shaped our history decisively; it now threatens to affect our future.

White racism is essentially responsible for the explosive mixture which has been accumulation in our cities since the end of World War II. Among the ingredients of this mixture are:

Pervasive discrimination and segregation in employment, education and housing, which have resulted in the continuing exclusion of great numbers of Negroes from the benefits of economic progress.

Black in-migration and white exodus, which have produced the massive and growing concentrations of impoverished Negroes in our major cities, creating a growing crisis of deteriorating facilities and services and unmet human needs.

The black ghettos, where segregation and poverty converge on the young to destroy opportunity and enforce failure. Crime, drug addiction, dependency on welfare, and bitterness and resentment against society in general and white society in particular are the result....

Yet these facts alone cannot be said to have caused the disorders. Recently, other powerful ingredients have begun to catalyze the mixture:

Frustrated hopes are the residue of the unfulfilled expectations aroused by the greater judicial and legislative victories of the civil rights movement and the dramatic struggle for equal rights in the South.

A climate that tends toward approval and encouragement of violence as a form of protest has been created by white terrorism directed against nonviolent protest; by the open defiance of law and federal authority by state and local officials resisting desegregation; and by some protest groups engaging in civil disobedience who turn their backs on nonviolence, go beyond the constitutionally protected rights of petition and free assembly, and resort to violence to attempt to compel alteration of laws and policies with which they disagree.

The frustrations of powerlessness have led some Negroes to the conviction that there is not effective alternative to violence as a means of achieving redress of grievances, and of "moving the system." These frustrations are reflected in alienation and hostility toward the institutions of law and government and the white society which controls them, and in the reach toward racial consciousness and solidarity reflected in the slogan "Black Power."

A new mood has sprung up among Negroes, particularly among the young, in which self-esteem and enhanced racial pride are replacing apathy and submission to "the system."

The police are not merely a "spark" factor. To some Negroes police have come to symbolize white power, white racism and white repression. And the fact is that many police do reflect and express these white attitudes.

The atmosphere of hostility and cynicism is reinforced by a wide-spread belief among Negroes in the existence of police brutality and in a "double standard" of justice and protection-one for Negroes and on for whites....

The major goal is the creation of a true nation – a single society and a single American identity. Toward that goal, we propose the following objectives for national action:

Opening up opportunities to those who are restricted by racial segregation and discrimination and eliminating all barriers to their choice of jobs, education and housing.

Removing the frustration of powerlessness among the disadvantaged by providing the means for them to deal with the problems that affect their own lives and by increasing the capacity of our public and private institutions to respond to these problems.

Increasing communication across racial lines to destroy stereotypes, to halt polarization, end distrust and hostility and create common ground for efforts toward public order and social justice.

We propose these aims to fulfill our pledge of equality and to meet the fundamental needs of a democratic and civilized society – domestic peace and social justice.

Report of the National Advisory Commission on Civil Disorders (Washington, D.C.: Government Printing Office, 1968), pp.1-13.

HOW WELL DID YOU UNDERSTAND THIS SELECTION?

1. According to the commission, what were the underlying causes of this urban unrest?

2. What recommendations did the commission suggest to alleviate the problem?

3. According to the report, why were law enforcement authorities part of the problem rather than the solution?

SELF TEST:

MULTIPLE CHOICE: Circle the correct response. The correct answers are given at the end.

1. The United States first got involved in Vietnam during the administration of
    a. Harry S. Truman
    b. Dwight D. Eisenhower
    c. John F. Kennedy
    d. Lyndon B. Johnson

2. A positive consequence of the Black Power movement was
    a. A return to tactics of non-violent civil disobedience
    b. African American pride in their culture and color
    c. That it brought an end to urban unrest
    d. SNCC began to accept white members

3. The Indian Civil Rights Act of 1968 required
    a. The federal government to honor all treaties with Indian nations.
    b. That Native American leave the reservations and assimilate into white society.
    c. Required tribal governments to extend the civil rights guaranteed in the U.S. Constitution to all persons under their jurisdiction.
    d. Theocratic tribes to give up their state religion.

4. In his handling of the Cuban missile crisis, Kennedy
    a. Brought the U.S. to the brink of war with the Soviet Union
    b. Neglected to inform the American public of the potential threat to security
    c. Would not compromise with the Soviets to persuade them remove their missiles
    d. Misjudged the commitment of the Cuban people to a revolution against Castro

5. The administration of Ngo Dinh Diem, the American–supported premier of South Vietnam,
    a. Labored to bring a peaceful conclusion to the conflict with North Vietnam
    b. Purged the South Vietnamese government of corruption
    c. Condoned the persecution of Buddhist monks
    d. Sought to remove the American presence from South Vietnam

6. Due to American failures in the space-race with the Soviets, President Kennedy
    a. Funded efforts to build the first orbiting space station
    b. Withdrew funding from the space program to focus on the Alliance for Progress
    c. Established N.A.S.A.
    d. Pledged that the U.S. would be the first nation to land on the moon

7. The Mississippi Freedom Summer Project involved
    a. Protests against segregation in public schools
    b. Protests against segregation in public transportation
    c. Registering African Americans to vote
    d. Protest against discrimination in public housing

8. Johnson decided to withdraw from his bid for re-election following
    a. The demoralizing Tet Offensive
    b. Revelations of his complicity in the Watergate scandal
    c. The failure of his anti-poverty Great Society programs
    d. The protests at Kent State University

9. The first "Jane Crow" case addressed sexual discrimination in
    a. Jury selection procedures
    b. The workplace
    c. The housing market
    d. The public schools

10. The 1964 Economic Opportunity Act provided
    a. Equal pay for equal work
    b. For the Developmental Loan Fund to assist Latin America
    c. Job training and placement for the poor
    d. $1.5 billion in federal aid to education

Answers: 1-c; 2-a; 3-a; 4-c; 5-b; 6-c; 7-b; 8-a; 9-d; 10-c.

ESSAYS:

1. Evaluate the successes of President Johnson's Great Society programs.

2. Explain why the Tet Offensive was a turning point in the Vietnam War.

3. Compare the concerns of the women's movement with those of the Mexican American and Native American movements during the 1960s.

OPTIONAL ACTIVITIES: (Use your knowledge **and** imagination when appropriate.)

1. After watching the film "Mississippi Burning," review the Douglas Linder's web site, "Mississippi Burning Trial (1967): <http://www.law.umkc.edu/faculty/projects/ftrials/price&bowers/price&bowers.htm>
Write a critique evaluating the historical accuracy of the film.

2. Conduct an oral history interview with a family member or acquaintance about their experiences during the Vietnam War era. (See Judith Moyer's *Step-by-Step Guide to Oral History*, <http://www.dohistory.org/on_your_own/toolkit/oralHistory.html>).   Summarize your findings to the class in an oral presentation.

3.   Examine the founding documents of the Peace Corps, located on the National Archives and Records Administration web site: <http://www.archives.gov/digital_classroom/lessons/peace_corps_documents/peace_corps_documents.html>
Write a comparison of Peace Corps activities during the 1960s with those of Peace Corps today. (See Peace Corps web site: <http://www.peacecorps.gov/>)

WEB SITE LISTINGS:

The Sixties
>   http://history.acusd.edu/gen/classes/20th/sixties.html
>   http://kclibrary.nhmccd.edu/decade60.html
>   http://www.ukans.edu/history/VL/USA/ERAS/20TH/1960s.html
>   http://www.hist.umn.edu/~hist20c/internet/1960s.htm

John F. Kennedy
>   **Assassination:**
>   >   http://mcadams.posc.mu.edu/home.htm
>   **Biography & resources:**
>   >   http://www.ipl.org/div/potus/jfkennedy.html
>   **Cuban Missile Crisis:**
>   >   http://www.gwu.edu/~nsarchiv/nsa/cuba_mis_cri/
>   >   http://www.yale.edu/lawweb/avalon/diplomacy/forrel/cuba/cubamenu.htm
>   >   http://www.mtholyoke.edu/acad/intrel/cuba.htm

Lyndon B. Johnson
>   **Biographical Information:**
>   >   http://www.potus.com/lbjohnson.html
>   >   http://www.lbjlib.utexas.edu/
>   **Vietnam:**
>   >   http://www.cnn.com/US/9702/15/lbj.vietnam/

Great Society:

> http://coursesa.matrix.msu.edu/~hst306/documents/great.html
> http://ci.columbia.edu/0715/index.html

Vietnam, Documents

> http://www.mtholyoke.edu/acad/intrel/vietnam.htm
> http://coombs.anu.edu.au/~vern/van_kien/docs.html
> http://www.ford.utexas.edu/library/exhibits/vietnam/vietnam.htm

Civil Rights:

> http://memory.loc.gov/ammem/aaohtml/exhibit/aopart9b.html
> http://hitchcock.itc.virginia.edu/BlackLeadership/historicalindex.html
> **Martin Luther King, Jr.**
>> http://www.stanford.edu/group/King/
> **Malcolm X**
>> http://www.brothermalcolm.net/

Chapter Twenty-three

THE SEVENTIES: The Crisis of Confidence

The decade of the 1970s witnessed a dramatic erosion of public confidence in government. President Nixon's handling of the Vietnam conflict intensified opposition to the war, and his corruption demonstrated by the Watergate scandal alarmed Americans. After Nixon's resignation Presidents Gerald Ford, and Jimmy Carter worked unsuccessfully to restore confidence in American political leadership. When the decade came to a close, the United States was mired in economic and political difficulties.

The most important issue facing Nixon was the war in Vietnam. Nixon and his Secretary of State, Henry Kissinger, initiated the policy of "Vietnamization," designed to shift the burden of the war onto the South Vietnamese and remove American troops. When peace talks stalled, Nixon increased the bombing in North Vietnam hoping to force Hanoi into making concessions. In April 1970, Nixon announced that American and South Vietnamese forces had invaded Cambodia to search out and destroy North Vietnamese troops and weapons depots. This action seemed to many Americans to be an escalation of the war. The anti-war movement responded with widespread protests. In their effort to contain the protest at Kent State University, National Guardsmen shot and killed four students; at Jackson State College, police shot and killed two African-American students. Public opinion further hardened against the war when the American atrocities at My Lai were revealed in the press. This animosity was compounded when the New York *Times* published the *Pentagon Papers*, which outlined the deception of previous administrations and covert American activities in Southeast Asia. On the eve of the 1972 presidential election, Kissinger and the North Vietnamese foreign minister reached a cease-fire agreement. Although South Vietnamese President Thieu rejected the agreement, Nixon won an overwhelming victory in the election. Further efforts to conclude the war failed. In April 1975, South Vietnam surrendered to the North Vietnamese.

While the war in Vietnam dragged on, Nixon and Kissinger focused their attention on finding success in other areas of foreign policy. They pursued a strategy designed to improve the relationship between China and the United States. Nixon flew to the People's Republic of China in February 1972 and ended two decades of hostility. Nixon and Kissinger were also successful in convincing the Soviets to sign the Strategic Arms Limitation Treaty (SALT I) in May 1972. Beyond Sino-Soviet/U.S. relations, Nixon and Kissinger continued their efforts to curb revolution and nationalism in the Third World. Their policies led many observers to complain about the arrogant American assumption that the U.S. had the right to manipulate the political and economic affairs of Third World countries to suit American interests.

Domestically, Nixon was less engaged than previous presidents. Although Congress defeated his efforts to reform the welfare system, Nixon had limited success in expanding programs like the Job Corps and increasing Medicare and Medicaid benefits. Despite the fact that Nixon's sympathies lay with corporate leaders, demonstrations by environmental advocates convinced him that his administration needed to take some action. As a result, he consistently supported legislation designed to protect the environment and worker safety. In the area of civil rights, Nixon eroded a number of the gains made under Johnson. He appointed conservatives to the Supreme Court and eliminated the Office of Economic Opportunity and the Model Cities Program.

In addition to the Vietnam conflict, Nixon inherited an economic quagmire from the Johnson administration. Foreign competition, high unemployment, staggering inflation, and a declining Gross National Product worsened the crisis. Nixon's response was to devalue the dollar and impose a wage and price freeze. What little this did to help the situation was erased when the 1973 oil embargo drove inflation to uncontrollable levels.

The downfall of Nixon's presidency began before his re-election in 1972. As early as 1969, Nixon abused his position of authority to a shocking degree to combat his opponents, such as civil rights activists and anti-war protestors. After the release of the *Pentagon Papers*, Nixon stepped up his efforts to prevent any future leaks to the press. To ensure Nixon's re-election in 1972, the attorney general established the Committee to Re-elect the President (CREEP). Their activities culminated in the infamous break-in of Democratic national headquarters in the Watergate complex. Nixon's participation in covering up this incident led to his impeachment. He was indicted for obstruction of justice and abuse of power. Nixon resigned in August 8, 1974.

Since Vice President Spiro Agnew had already resigned over his involvement in income tax evasion and the acceptance of bribes, it fell to Agnew's replacement, House minority leader Gerald R. Ford, to assume the presidency. Ford's first major action as president was to grant Nixon a full pardon; an act that inadvertently linked him to the tainted administration. Ford also extended clemency to the men who had evaded the draft during the Vietnam War. Ford's efforts proved inadequate to resolve the nation's economic situation.

Democrat James Earl Carter edged out Ford in the 1976 election. Carter was overwhelmingly supported by not only by his native South, but by African American and Mexican American voters throughout the country as well. Although Carter was honest and hard working, his inexperience limited his ability to successfully address the nation's problems. He responded to "stagflation" by reducing unemployment, however foreign competition, most notably in the automobile industry, along with rapidly increasing energy prices hampered his efforts to reduce inflation.

In the international arena, Carter worked to continue détente with China and the Soviet Union, decelerate the nuclear arms race, eliminate Third World poverty, and champion human rights. Carter sought to shape foreign affairs with his moral authority. He was successful in brokering a peace settlement between Israel and Egypt. He also secured a second SALT agreement with the Soviets to limit nuclear delivery vehicles, warheads and the development of new types of nuclear weapons. The Soviet invasion of Afghanistan in December 1979 led him to shelve SALT-II, suspend shipments of grain and high-technology equipment, boycott the 1980 Summer Olympics in Moscow, and direct the CIA to aid Afghan insurgents. Carter's inability to negotiate the release of Americans held captive by terrorists undermined his bid for re-election.

As the 1980 election approached, divisions within American society became more evident. American Indians, Hispanics, Asian Americans, feminists, and gay pride groups all became much more radical in their struggle for equal rights during the 1970s. Many white ethnic groups mobilized in resistance. Ronald Reagan's victory represented the American desire to restore the nation's "strength and pride."

IDENTIFICATION: Briefly describe each term.

Richard M. Nixon

Henry Kissinger

Palestine Liberation Organization (PLO)

Silent Majority

Vietnamization

Nixon Doctrine

My Lai

Cambodia Invasion

Laos

Kent State University protests

Pentagon Papers

"Ping-Pong" Diplomacy

Committee to Re-elect the President (CREEP)

Leonid Brezhnev

Détente

ICBM

ABM

Salvador Allende

Organization of Petroleum Exporting Countries (OPEC)

Aid to Families with Dependent Children (AFDC)

Environmental Protection Agency (EPA)

Roe v. Wade

Stagflation

Three Mile Island

Watergate Scandal

George McGovern

John Dean

Allan Bakke

White House Tapes

Gerald Ford

Iranian Hostage Crisis

James Earl (Jimmy) Carter

Strategic Arms Limitation Treaty (SALT I)

Menachem Begin

Anwar Sadat

La Raza Unida

Alcatraz Island

Oil Embargo

THINK ABOUT:

1. Who were the members of the "silent majority"? In what ways did Nixon's domestic policies address their concerns?

2. Examine the events that sparked a reinvigoration of the anti-war movement in 1970.

3. Evaluate the impact of the Watergate scandal on public confidence in the federal government

---

JOHN KERRY "STATEMENT"

Early in 1969, President Nixon promised the nation "Vietnamization," a de-escalation of the American presence in Vietnam. Within a year, however, he announced the invasion of Cambodia. This sparked renewed protest against the war. In April 1971, the Senate Foreign Relations Committee conducted hearings into the war. John Kerry testified before the committee, speaking for himself and on behalf of the Vietnam Veterans against the War (VVAW).

April 23, 1971
Washington, D.C.
U.S. Senate Committee of Foreign Relations, Legislative Proposals Relating to the War in Southeast Asia

I would like to talk on behalf of all those veterans and say that several months ago in Detroit we had an investigation at which over 150 honorably discharged, and many very highly decorated, veterans testified to war crimes committed in Southeast Asia. These were not isolated incidents but crimes committed on a day-to-day basis with the full awareness of officers at all levels of command. It is impossible to describe to you exactly what did happen in Detroit - the emotions in the room and the feelings of the men who were reliving their experiences in Vietnam. They relived the absolute horror of what this country, in a sense, made them do.

They told stories that at times they had personally raped, cut off ears, cut off heads, taped wires from portable telephones to human genitals and turned up the power, cut off limbs, blown up bodies, randomly shot at civilians, razed villages in fashion reminiscent of Ghengis Khan, shot cattle and dogs for fun, poisoned food stocks, and generally ravaged the countryside of South Vietnam in addition to the normal ravage of war and the normal and very particular ravaging which is done by the applied bombing power of this country.

We call this investigation the Winter Soldier Investigation. The term Winter Soldier is a play on words of Thomas Paines in 1776 when he spoke of the Sunshine Patriots and summertime soldiers who deserted at Valley Forge because the going was rough.

We who have come here to Washington have come here because we feel we have to be winter soldiers now. We could come back to this country, we could be quiet, we could hold our silence, we could not tell what went on in Vietnam, but we feel because of what threatens this country, not the reds, but the crimes which we are committing that threaten it, that we have to speak out....

In our opinion and from our experience, there is nothing in South Vietnam which could happen that realistically threatens the United States of America. And to attempt to justify the loss of one American life in Vietnam,

Cambodia or Laos by linking such loss to the preservation of freedom, which those misfits supposedly abuse, is to us the height of criminal hypocrisy, and it is that kind of hypocrisy which we feel has torn this country apart.

We found that not only was it a civil war, an effort by a people who had for years been seeking their liberation from any colonial influence whatsoever, but also we found that the Vietnamese whom we had enthusiastically molded after our own image were hard put to take up the fight against the threat we were supposedly saving them from.

We found most people didn't even know the difference between communism and democracy. They only wanted to work in rice paddies without helicopters strafing them and bombs with napalm burning their villages and tearing their country apart. They wanted everything to do with the war, particularly with this foreign presence of the United States of America, to leave them alone in peace, and they practiced the art of survival by siding with whichever military force was present at a particular time, be it Viet Cong, North Vietnamese or American.

We found also that all too often American men were dying in those rice paddies for want of support from their allies. We saw first hand how monies from American taxes were used for a corrupt dictatorial regime. We saw that many people in this country had a one-sided idea of who was kept free by the flag, and blacks provided the highest percentage of casualties. We saw Vietnam ravaged equally by American bombs and search and destroy missions, as well as by Viet Cong terrorism - and yet we listened while this country tried to blame all of the havoc on the Viet Cong.

We rationalized destroying villages in order to save them. We saw America lose her sense of morality as she accepted very coolly a My Lai and refused to give up the image of American soldiers who hand out chocolate bars and chewing gum.

We learned the meaning of free fire zones, shooting anything that moves, and we watched while America placed a cheapness on the lives of Orientals.

We watched the United States falsification of body counts, in fact the glorification of body counts. We listened while month after month we were told the back of the enemy was about to break. We fought using weapons against "oriental human beings." We fought using weapons against those people which I do not believe this country would dream of using were we fighting in the European theater. We watched while men charged up hills because a general said that hill has to be taken, and after losing one platoon or two platoons they marched away to leave the hill for reoccupation by the North Vietnamese. We watched pride allow the most unimportant baffles to be blown into extravaganzas, because we couldn't lose, and we couldn't retreat, and because it didn't matter how many American bodies were lost to prove that point, and so there were Hamburger Hills and Khe Sanhs and Hill Sis and Fire Base 6s, and so many others.

Now we are told that the men who fought there must watch quietly while American lives are lost so that we can exercise the incredible arrogance of Vietnamizing the Vietnamese.

Each day to facilitate the process by which the United States washes her hands of Vietnam someone has to give up his life so that the United States doesn't have to admit something that the entire world already knows, so that we can't say that we have made a mistake. Someone has to die so that President Nixon won't be, and these are his words, "the first President to lose a war."

We are asking Americans to think about that because how do you ask a man to be the last man to die in Vietnam? How do you ask a man to be the last man to die for a mistake. We are here in Washington to say that the problem of this war is not just a question of war and diplomacy. It is part and parcel of everything that we are trying as human beings to communicate to people in this country—the question of racism which is rampant in the military, and so many other questions such as the use of weapons; the hypocrisy in our taking umbrage at the Geneva Conventions and using that as justification for a continuation of this war when we are more guilty than any other body of violations of those Geneva Conventions; in the use of free fire zones, harassment interdiction fire, search and destroy missions, the bombings, the torture of prisoners, all accepted policy by many units in South Vietnam. That is what we are trying to say. It is part and parcel of everything.

An American Indian friend of mine who lives in the Indian Nation of Alcatraz put it to me very succinctly. He told me how as a boy on an Indian reservation he had watched television and he used to cheer the cowboys when they came in and shot the Indians, and then suddenly one day he stopped in Vietnam and he said, "my God, I am doing to these people the very same thing that was done to my people," and he stopped. And that is what we are trying to say, that we think this thing has to end.

We are here to ask, and we are here to ask vehemently, where are the leaders of our country? Where is the leadership? We're here to ask where are McNamara, Rostow, Bundy, Gilpatrick, and so many others? Where are they now that we, the men they sent off to war, have returned? These are the commanders who have deserted their troops. And there is no more serious crime in the laws of war. The Army says they never leave their wounded. The marines say they never even leave their dead. These men have left all the casualties and retreated behind a pious shield of public rectitude. They've left the real stuff of their reputations bleaching behind them in the sun in this country....

We wish that a merciful God could wipe away our own memories of that service as easily as this administration has wiped away their memories of us. But all that they have done and all that they can do by this denial is to make more clear than ever our own determination to undertake one last mission to search out and destroy the last vestige of this barbaric war, to pacify our own hearts, to conquer the hate and fear that have driven this country these last ten years and more. And more. And so when thirty years from now our brothers go down the street without a leg, without an arm, or a face, and small boys ask why, we will be able to say "Vietnam" and not mean a desert, not a filthy obscene memory, but mean instead where America finally turned and where soldiers like us helped it in the turning.

John Kerry, "Statement," April 23, 1971, Senate Committee on Foreign Relations, *Legislative Proposals Relating to the War in Southeast Asia: Hearings* April 20, 21, 22, 28, 1971 (Washington: Government Printing Office, 1971), pp. 180-210.

HOW WELL DID YOU UNDERSTAND THIS SELECTION?

1. How does Kerry interpret Nixon's policy of "Vietnamization"?

2. Why does he describe himself and the other VVAW as "Winter Soldiers"?

3. According to Kerry, how does the reality of the war in Vietnam compare to the version being told to the American public by the Nixon administration?

At the conclusion of the Paris Peace Accords in 1973, President Nixon summarized the arrangement for the American public in a radio and television address. The conflict in Vietnam, however, did not end in 1973. The fighting continued until South Vietnam surrendered to the North in April 1975.

January 23, 1973, Washington, D.C.
PRESIDENT RICHARD M. NIXON

Good evening. I have asked for this radio and television time tonight for the purpose of announcing that we today have concluded an agreement to end the war and bring peace with honor in Vietnam and in Southeast Asia.

The following statement is being issued at this moment in Washington and Hanoi:

At 12:30 Paris time today [Tuesday], January 23 1973, the Agreement on Ending the War and Restoring Peace in Vietnam was initialed by Dr. Henry Kissinger on behalf of the United States, and Special Adviser Le Duc Tho on behalf of the Democratic Republic of Vietnam.

The agreement will be formally signed by the parties participating in the Paris Conference on Vietnam on January 27, 1973, at the International Conference Center in Paris.

The cease-fire will take effect at 2400 Greenwich Mean Time, January 27, 1973. The United States and the Democratic Republic of Vietnam express the hope that this agreement will insure stable peace in Vietnam and contribute to the preservation of lasting peace in Indochina and Southeast Asia.

That concludes the formal statement.

Throughout the years of negotiations, we have insisted on peace with honor. In my addresses to the Nation from this room of January 25 and May 8, [1972] I set forth the goals that we considered essential for peace with honor.

In the settlement that has now been agreed to, all the conditions that I laid down then have been met. A cease-fire, internationally supervised, will begin at 7 p.m., this Saturday, January 27, Washington time. Within 60 days from this Saturday, all Americans held prisoners of war throughout Indochina will be released. There will be the fullest possible accounting for all of those who are missing in action.

During the same 60-day period, all American forces will be withdrawn from South Vietnam.

The people of South Vietnam have been guaranteed the right to determine their own future, without outside interference.

By joint agreement, the full text of the agreement and the protocols to carry it out, will be issued tomorrow.

Throughout these negotiations we have been in the closest consultation with President Thieu and other representatives of the Republic of Vietnam. This settlement meets the goals and has the full support of President Thieu and the Government of the Republic of Vietnam, as well as that of our other allies who are affected.

The United States will continue to recognize the Government of the Republic of Vietnam as the sole legitimate government of South Vietnam.

We shall continue to aid South Vietnam within the terms of the agreement and we shall support efforts by the people of South Vietnam to settle their problems peacefully among themselves.

We must recognize that ending the war is only the first step toward building the peace. All parties must now see to it that this is a peace that lasts, and also a peace that heals, and a peace that not only ends the war in Southeast Asia, but contributes to the prospects of peace in the whole world.

This will mean that the terms of the agreement must be scrupulously adhered to. We shall do everything the agreement requires of us and we shall expect the other parties to do everything it requires of them. We shall also expect other interested nations to help insure that the agreement is carried out and peace is maintained.

As this long and very difficult war ends, I would like to address a few special words to each of those who have been parties in the conflict.

First, to the people and Government of South Vietnam: By your courage, by your sacrifice, you have won the precious right to determine your own future and you have developed the strength to defend that right. We look forward to working with you in the future, friends in peace as we have been allies in war.

To the leaders of North Vietnam: As we have ended the war through negotiations, let us now build a peace of reconciliation. For our part; we are prepared to make a major effort to help achieve that goal. But just as reciprocity was needed to end the war, so, too, will it be needed to build and strengthen the peace.

To the other major powers that have been involved even indirectly: Now is the time for mutual restraint so that the peace we have achieved can last.

And finally, to all of you who are listening, the American people: Your steadfastness in supporting our insistence on peace with honor has made peace with honor possible. I know that you would not have wanted that peace jeopardized. With our secret negotiations at the sensitive stage they were in during this recent period, for me to have discussed publicly our efforts to secure peace would not only have violated our understanding with North Vietnam, it would have seriously harmed and possibly destroyed the chances for peace. Therefore, I know that you now can understand why, during these past several weeks, I have not made any public statements about those efforts.

The important thing was not to talk about peace, but to get peace and to get the right kind of peace. This we have done.

Now that we have achieved an honorable agreement, let us be proud that America did not settle for a peace that would have betrayed our allies, that would have abandoned our prisoners of war, or that would have ended the war for us but would have continued the war for the 50 million people of Indochina. Let us be proud of the 2 1/2 million young Americans who served in Vietnam, who served with honor and distinction in one of the most selfless enterprises in the history of nations. And let us be proud of those who sacrificed, who gave their lives so that the people of South Vietnam might live in freedom and so that the world might live in peace.

In particular, I would like to say a word to some of the bravest people I have ever met-the wives, the children, the families of our prisoners of war and the missing in action. When others called on us to settle on any terms, you had the courage to stand for the right kind of peace so that those who died and those who suffered would not have died and suffered in vain, and so that, where this generation knew war, the next generation would know peace. Nothing means more to me at this moment than the fact that your long vigil is coming to an end.

Just yesterday, a great American, who once occupied this office, died. In his life President [Lyndon B.] Johnson endured the vilification of those who sought to portray him as a man of war. But there was nothing he cared about more deeply than achieving a lasting peace in the world.

I remember the last time I talked with him. It was just the day after New Year's. He spoke then of his concern with bringing peace, with making it the right kind of peace, and I was grateful that he once again expressed his support for my efforts to gain such a peace. No one would have welcomed this peace more than he.

And I know he would join me in asking for those who died and for those who live, let us consecrate this moment by resolving together to make the peace we have achieved a peace that will last.

Thank you and good evening.

HOW WELL DID YOU UNDERSTAND THIS SELECTION?

1. What does Nixon say are the terms of the peace agreement?

2. What is Nixon's evaluation of the American role in the Vietnam War? Do you feel the majority of Americans at the time would have agreed with his assessment? Explain.

3. Do the facts justify calling this a "peace with honor"? Explain.

*After the release of the **Pentagon Papers**, Nixon organized a secret unit within the White House to discredit anyone who leaked confidential or damaging information to the press. E. Howard Hunt, a veteran of the CIA, and G. Gordon Liddy, a former FBI agent, headed the new unit called the "plumbers." To ensure Nixon's re-election in 1972, Attorney General John Mitchell organized the Committee to Re-elect the President (CREEP). They engaged in unethical practices against the Democratic Party. Under the direction of Liddy, five men broke into the Democratic National Headquarters at the Watergate complex. The men were arrested and convicted along with Liddy and Hunt. At their sentencing, it became evident that White House aides had assisted the break-in. When it came to light that the president had been complicit in attempting to cover up the break-in, and that tapes of Nixon's conversations existed, the court ordered Nixon to present the tapes. Nixon resisted. What follows are excerpts from recorded conversations between President Nixon and his advisors in 1972-1973.*

June 23, 1972
The White House

HALDEMAN: Now, on the investigation you know the Democratic break-in thing, we're back in the problem area because the FBI is not under control, because [Director Patrick] Gray doesn't exactly know how to control it and they have-their investigation is now leading into some productive areas. They've been able to trace the money-not through the money itself-but through the bank sources-the banker. And it goes in some directions we don't want it to go. Ah, also there have been some (other) things-like an informant came in off the street to the FBI in Miami who was a photographer or has a friend who is a photographer who developed some films through this guy [Bernard] Barker and the alms had pictures of Democratic National Committee letterhead documents and things. So it's things like that that are filtering in. . . . [John] Mitchell came up with yesterday, and John Dean analyzed very carefully last night and concludes, concurs now with Mitchell's recommendation that the only way to solve this . . . is for us to have [CIA Assistant Director Vernon Walters call Pat Gray and just say, "Stay to hell out of this-this is ah, [our] business here. We don't want you to go any further on it." That's not an unusual development, and ah, that would take care of it.
PRESIDENT: What about Pat Gray-you mean Pat Gray doesn't want to?
HALDEMAN: Pat does want to. He doesn't know how to, and he doesn't have any basis for doing it. Given this, he will then have the basis. He'll call [FBI Assistant Director Mark Felt in, and the two of them-and Mark Felt wants to cooperate because he's ambitious-
PRESIDENT: Yeah.
HALDEMAN: He'll call him in and say, "We've got the signal from across the river to put the hold on this." And that will fit rather well because the FBI agents who are working the case, at this point, feel that's what it is.
PRESIDENT: This is CIA? They've traced the money? Who'd they trace it to?
HALDEMAN: Well, they've traced it to a name, but they haven't gotten to the guy yet.
PRESIDENT: Would it be somebody here?
HALDEMAN: Ken Dahlberg.
PRESIDENT: Who the hell is Ken Dahlberg?
HALDEMAN: He gave $25,000 in Minnesota and, ah, the check went directly to this guy Barker.
PRESIDENT: It isn't from the Committee though, from [Maurice] Stans?
HALDEMAN: Yeah. It is. It's directly traceable and there's some more through some Texas people that went to the Mexican bank which can also be traced to the Mexican bank-they'll get their names today.
PRESIDENT: Well, I mean, there's no way-I'm just thinking if they don't cooperate, what do they say? That they were approached by the Cubans? That's what Dahlberg has to say, the Texans too.
HALDEMAN: Well, if they will. But then we're relying on more and more people all the time. That's the problem and they'll [the FBI] . . . stop if we could take this other route.

PRESIDENT: All right.

HALDEMAN: [Mitchell and Dean) say the only way to do that is from White House instructions. And it's got to be to [CIA Director Richard] Helms and to-ah, what's his name?. . . Walters.

PRESIDENT: Walters.

HALDEMAN: And the proposal would be that... (John) Ehrlichman and I call them in, and say, ah-

PRESIDENT: All right, fine. How do you call him in-I mean you just-well, we protected Helms from one hell of a lot of things.

HALDEMAN: That's what Ehrlichman says.

PRESIDENT: Of course; this [Howard] Hunt [business.] That will uncover a lot of things. You open that scab there's a hell of a lot of things and we just feel that it would be very detrimental to have this thing go any further. This involves these Cubans, Hunt, and a lot of hanky-panky that we have nothing to do with ourselves. Well, what the hell, did Mitchell know about this?

HALDEMAN: I think so. I don't think he knew the details, but I think he knew.

PRESIDENT: He didn't know how it was going to be handled though-with Dahlberg and the Texans and so forth? Well who was the asshole that did? Is it [C. Gordon] Liddy? Is that the fellow? He must be a little nuts!

HALDEMAN: He is.

PRESIDENT: I mean he just isn't well screwed on, is he? Is that the problem?

HALDEMAN: No, but he was under pressure, apparently, to get more information, and as he got more pressure, he pushed the people harder.

PRESIDENT: Pressure from Mitchell?

HALDEMAN: Apparently....

PRESIDENT: All right, fine, I understand it all. We won't second-guess Mitchell and the rest. Thank God it wasn't [special White House counsel Charles] Colson.

HALDEMAN: The FBI interviewed Colson yesterday. They determined that would be a good thing to do. To have him take an interrogation, which he did, and the FBI guys working the case concluded that there were one or two possibilities-one, that this was a White House (they don't think that there is anything at the Election Committee) they think it was either a White House operation and they had some obscure reasons for it-non-political, or it was a-Cuban [operation] and (involved) the CIA. And after their interrogation of Colson yesterday, they concluded it was not the White House, but are now convinced it is a CIA thing, so the CIA turnoff would-

PRESIDENT: Well, not sure of their analysis, I'm not going to get that involved. I'm (unintelligible).

HALDEMAN: No, sir, we don't want you to.

PRESIDENT: You call them in.

HALDEMAN: Good deal.

PRESIDENT: Play it tough. That's the way they play it and that's the way we are going to play it.

PRESIDENT: O.K...Just say (unintelligible) very bad to have this fellow Hunt, ah, he knows too damned much. . . . If it gets out that this is all involved the Cuba thing, it would be a fiasco. It would make the CIA look bad, it's going to make Hunt look bad, and it is likely to blow the whole Bay of Pigs thing which we think would be very unfortunate—both for CIA, and for the country, at this time, and for American foreign policy. Just tell him to lay off Don't you [think] so?

HALDEMAN: Yep. That's the basis to do it on. Just leave it at that.

September 15, 1972

PRESIDENT: We are all in it together. This is a war. We take a few shots and it will be over. We will give them a few shots and it will be over. Don't worry. I wouldn't want to be on the other side right now. Would you?

DEAN: Along that line, one of the things I've tried to do, I have begun to keep notes on a lot of people who are emerging as less than our friends because this will be over some day and we shouldn't forget the way some of them have treated us.

PRESIDENT: I want the most comprehensive notes on all those who tried to do us in. They didn't have to do it. If we had had a very dose election and they were playing the other side I would understand this. No—they were doing this quite deliberately and they are asking for it and they are going to get it. We have not used the power in this first four years, as you know. We have never used it. We have not used the Bureau, and we have not used the Justice Department, but things are going to change now. And they are either going to do it right or go.

DEAN: What an exciting prospect.

PRESIDENT: Thanks. It has to be done. We have been (adjective deleted) fools for us to come into this election campaign and not do anything with regard to the Democratic Senators who are running, et cetera. And who the hell are they after? They are after us. It is absolutely ridiculous. It is not going to be that way any more.

March 13, 1973

PRESIDENT: How much of a crisis? It will be-am thinking in terms of-the point is, everything is a crisis. (expletive deleted) it is a terrible lousy thing it will remain a crisis among the upper intellectual types, the soft heads, our own, to – Republicans and the Democrats and the rest. Average people won't think it is much of a crisis unless it affects them. (unintelligible)

DEAN: I think it will pass. I think after the (Senator Sam] Ervin hearings, they are going to find so much - there will be some new revelations. I don't think that the thing will get out of hand. I have no reason to believe it will.

PRESIDENT: As a matter of fact, it is just a bunch of (characterization deleted). We don't object to such damn things anyway. On, and on and on. No, I tell you this it is the last gasp of our hardest opponents. They've just got to have something to squeal about it.

DEAN: It is the only thing they have to squeal-

PRESIDENT: (Unintelligible) They are going to lie around and squeal. They are having a hard time now. They got the hell kicked out of them in the election. There is not a Watergate around in this town, not so much our opponents even the media, but the basic thing is the establishment. The establishment is dying, and so they've got to show that despite the successes we have had in foreign policy and in the election, they've got to show that it is just wrong, just because of this. They are trying to use this as the whole thing.

March 21, 1973

DEAN: So that is it. That is the extent of the knowledge. So where are the soft spots on this? Well, first of all, there is the problem of the continued blackmail which will not only go on now, but it will go on while these people are in prison, and it will compound the obstruction of justice situation. It will cost money. It is dangerous. People around here are not pros at this sort of thing. This is the sort of thing Mafia people can do: washing money, getting dean money, and things like that. We just don't know about those things, because we are not criminals and not used to dealing in that business.

PRESIDENT: That's right.

DEAN: It is a tough thing to know how to do.

PRESIDENT: Maybe it takes a gang to do that.

DEAN: That's right. There is a real problem as to whether we could even do it. Plus there is a real problem in raising money. Mitchell has been working on raising some money. He is one of the ones with the most to lose. But there is no denying the fact that the White House, in Ehrlichman, Haldeman and Dean, are involved in some of the early money decisions.

PRESIDENT: How much money do you need?

DEAN: I would say these people are going to cost over a million dollars over the next two years.

PRESIDENT: We could get that. On the money, if you need the money you could get that. You could get a minion dollars. You could get it in cash. I know where it could be gotten. It is not easy, but it could be done. But the question is who the hell would handle it? Any ideas on that?

DEAN: That's right. Well, I think that is something that Mitchell ought to be charged with.

PRESIDENT: I would think so too.

From *Hearings before the Committee on The Judiciary*, House of Representatives, 93rd Congress, 2nd Session (Government Printing Office, Washington, D.C., 1974).

HOW WELL DID YOU UNDERSTAND THIS SELECTION?

1. Based on the information in the tapes, assess the degree of Nixon's involvement in the break-in and subsequent cover-up?

2. Make a list of the illegal and/or unethical activities that are discussed by Nixon and his advisors.

3. Why do you think Nixon would have recorded these conversations?

PRESIDENTIAL TELEVISION ADDRESS

By April 1973 the scandal had escalated. In a televised address, President Nixon attempted to dispel suspicions and halt further investigation by addressing the American people and explaining the incident.

April 30, 1973, Washington, D.C.
PRESIDENT RICHARD M. NIXON

I want to talk to you tonight from my heart on a subject of deep concern to every American.

In recent months, members of my Administration and officials of the Committee for the Re-election of the President – including some of my closest friends and most trusted aides – have been charged with involvement in what has come to be known as the Watergate Affair. These include charges of illegal activity during and proceeding the 1972 Presidential election and charges that responsible officials participated in efforts to cover that illegal activity.

The inevitable result of these charges has been to raise serious questions about the integrity of the White House itself. Tonight I wish to address those questions.

Last June 17, while I was in Florida trying to get a few day's rest after my visit to Moscow, I first learned from news reports of the Watergate break-in. I was appalled at this senseless, illegal action, and I was shocked to learn that employees of the Re-election Committee were apparently among those guilty. I immediately ordered an investigation by appropriate government authorities. On September 15, as you will recall, indictments were brought against seven defendants in the case.

As the investigations went forward, I repeatedly asked those conducting the investigation whether there was any reason to believe that members of my Administration were in any way involved. I received repeated assurances that there were not. Because of these continuing reassurances – because I believed the reports I was getting, because I had faith in the persons from whom I was getting them - I discounted the stories in the press that appeared to implicate members of my Administration or other officials of the campaign committee.

Until March of this year, I remained convinced that the denials were true and that the charges of involvement by members of the White House staff were false. The comments I made by my Press Secretary on my behalf, were based on the information provided to us at the time we made those comments. However, new information then came to me which persuaded me that there was a real possibility that some of these charges were true, and suggesting further that there had been an effort to conceal the facts both from the public, from you, and from me.

As a result, on March 21, I personally assumed the responsibility for coordinating intensive new inquiries into the matter, and I personally ordered those conducting the investigations to get all the facts and to report them directly to me, right here in this office.

I again ordered that all persons in the Government or at the Re-election Committee should cooperate fully with the FBI, the prosecutors and the Grand Jury. I also ordered that anyone who refused to cooperate in telling the truth would be asked to resign from government service. And, with ground rules adopted that would preserve the basic constitutional separation of powers between the Congress and the Presidency, I directed that members of the White House staff should appear and testify voluntarily under oath before the Senate Committee investigating Watergate.

I was determined that we should get to the bottom of the matter, and that the truth should fully brought out – no matter who was involved.

At the same time, I was determined not to take precipitate action, and to avoid, if at all possible, any action that would appear to reflect on innocent people. I wanted to be fair. But I knew that in the final analysis, the integrity of this office – public faith in the integrity of this office – would have to take priority over all personal considerations.

Today, in one of the most difficult decisions of my Presidency, I accepted the resignations of two of my closest associates in the White House – Bob Haldeman, John Ehrlichman – two of the finest public servants it has been my privilege to know.

I want to stress that in accepting these resignations, I mean to leave no implication whatever of personal wrongdoing on their part, and I leave no implication tonight of implication on the part of others who have been charged in this matter. But in matters as sensitive as guarding the integrity of our democratic process, it is essential not only that rigorous legal and ethical standards be observed, but also that the public, you, have the total confidence that they are both being observed and enforced by those in authority and particularly by the President of the United States. They agree with me that this move was necessary in order to restore that confidence.

Because Attorney General Kleindienst – through a distinguished public servant, my personal friend for 20 years, with no personal involvement whatever in this matter – has been a close personal and professional associate of some of those who are involved in this case, he and I both felt that it was also necessary to name a new Attorney General.

The Counsel to the President, John Dean, has also resigned.

As the new Attorney General, I have today named Elliot Richardson, a man of unimpeachable integrity and rigorously high principle. I have directed him to do everything necessary to ensure that the Department of Justice has the confidence and trust of every law abiding person in this country.

I have given him absolute authority to make all decisions bearing upon the prosecution of the Watergate case and related matters. I have instructed him that if he should consider it appropriate, he has the authority to name a special supervising prosecutor for matters arising out of the case.

Whatever may appear to have been the case before – whatever improper activities may yet be discovered in connection with this whole sordid affair – I want the American people, I want you to know beyond the shadow of a doubt that during my terms as President, justice will be pursued fairly, fully, and impartially, no matter who is involved. This office is a sacred trust and I am determined to be worthy of that trust.

Looking back at history of this case, two questions arise:

How could it have happened?

Who is to blame?

Political commentators have correctly observed that during my 27 years in politics, I have always previously insisted on running my own campaigns for office.

But 1972 presented a very different situation. In both domestic and foreign policy, 1972 was a year of crucially important decisions, of intense negotiations, of vital new directions, particularly in working toward the goal which has been my overriding concern throughout my political career – the goal of bringing peace to America and peace to the world.

That is why I decided, as the 1972 campaign approached, that the Presidency should come first and politics second. To the maximum extent possible, therefore, I sought to delegate campaign operations, and to remove the day-to-day campaign decisions from the President's office and from the White House. I also, as you recall, severely limited the number of my own campaign appearances.

Who, then, is to blame for what happened in this case?

For specific criminal actions by specific individuals, those who committed those actions, must, of course, beat the liability and pay the penalty.

For the fact that alleged improper actions took place within the White House or within my campaign organization, the easiest course would be for me to blame those to whom I delegated the responsibility to run the campaign. But that would be cowardly thing to do.

I will not place the blame on subordinates – on people whose zeal exceeded their judgement, and who may have done wrong in a cause they deeply believed to be right.

In any organization, the men at the top must bear the responsibility. That responsibility, therefore, belongs here, in this office. I accept that. And I pledge to you tonight, from this office, that I will do everything in my power to ensure that the guilty are brought to justice, and that such abuses are purged from our political processes in the years to come, long after I have left this office….

….I love America. I deeply believe that America is the hope of the world, and I know that in the quality and wisdom of the leadership America gives lies the only hope for millions of people all over the world, that they can live their lives in peace and freedom. We must be worthy of that hope, in every sense of the word. Tonight, I ask for your prayers to help me in everything that I do throughout the days of my Presidency to be worthy of their hopes and of yours.

God bless America and God bless each and every one of you.

HOW WELL DID YOU UNDERSTAND THIS SELECTION?

1. How does Nixon explain his role in the Watergate scandal? Do you find his argument convincing?

2. Who does Nixon hold accountable for the incident?

3. Compare this document with the previous one. Is Nixon being honest with the American people?

President Nixon resigned on August 8, 1974. Special Prosecutor Leon Jaworski weighed the evidence to determine whether Nixon should be indicted on criminal charges for his involvement in the cover-up. The following is a memorandum written for Jaworski, outlining the factors in favor of and those against prosecuting Nixon.

DEPARTMENT OF JUSTICE
MEMORANDUM
TO : Leon Jaworski
Special Prosecutor
DATE: August 9, 1974
FROM : Carl B Feldbaum
Peter M. Kreindler
SUBJECT: Factors to be Considered in Deciding Whether to Prosecute Richard M. Nixon for Obstruction of Justice

In our view there is clear evidence that Richard M. Nixon participated in a conspiracy to obstruct justice by concealing the identity of those responsible for the Watergate break-in and other criminal offenses. There is a presumption (which in the past we have operated upon) that Richard M. Nixon, like every citizen, is subject to the rule of law. Accordingly, one begins with the premise that if there is sufficient evidence, Mr. Nixon should be indicted and prosecuted. The question then becomes whether the presumption for proceeding is outweighed by the factors mandating against indictment and prosecution.

The factors which mandate against indictment and prosecution are:

1. His resignation has been sufficient punishment.

2. He has been subject to an impeachment inquiry with resulting articles of impeachment which the House Judiciary Committee unanimously endorsed as to Article I (the Watergate cover-up).

3. Prosecution might aggravate political divisions in the country.

4. As a political matter, the times call for conciliation rather than recrimination.

5. There would be considerable difficulty in achieving a fair trial because of massive pre-trial publicity.

The factors which mandate in favor of indictment and prosecution are:

1. The principle of equal justice under law requires that every person, no matter what his past position or office, answer to the criminal justice system for his past offenses. This is a particularly weighty factor if Mr. Nixon's aides and associates, who acted upon his orders and what they conceived to be his interests, are to be prosecuted for she same offenses.

2. The country will be further divided by Mr. Nixon unless there is a final disposition of charges of criminality outstanding against him so as to forestall the belief that he was driven from his office by erosion of his political base. This final disposition may be necessary to preserve the integrity of the criminal justice system and the legislative process, which together marshalled the substantial evidence of Mr. Nixon's guilt.

3. Article I, Section 3, clause 7 of the Constitution provides that a person removed from office by impeachment and conviction "shall nevertheless be liable and subject to Indictment, Trial, Judgment, and Punishment, according to Law." The Framers contemplated that a person removed from office because of abuse of his public trust still would have to answer to the criminal justice system for criminal offenses.

4. It cannot be sufficient retribution for criminal offenses merely to surrender the public office and trust which has been demonstrably abused. A person should not be permitted to trade in the abused office in return for immunity.

5. The modern nature of the Presidency necessitates massive public exposure of the President's actions through the media. A bar to prosecution on the grounds of such publicity effectively would immunize all future Presidents for their actions, however criminal. Moreover, the courts may be the appropriate forum to resolve questions of pre-trial publicity in the context of an adversary proceeding.

(National Archives and Records Administration: Records of the Watergate Special Prosecution Force, Record Group 460.)

HOW WELL DID YOU UNDERSTAND THIS SELECTION?

1. Make a list of the pro-indictment and anti-indictment factors.

2. According to the memo, would Article 1, Section 3, clause 7 of the Constitution apply to Nixon at this point? Why or why not?

3. Which side of this debate do you feel is the most persuasive? Explain.

An important goal of the women's movement in the 1970s was to obtain passages of the Equal Rights Amendment (ERA), to ensure that "Equality of rights under the law shall not be denied or abridged by the United States by any state on account of sex." In 1970, the Senate Subcommittee on Constitutional Amendment heard testimony about the ERA. Gloria Steinem testified at the hearings.

Washington, D.C.

I hope this committee will hear the personal, daily injustices suffered by many women-professionals and day laborers, women housebound by welfare as well as suburbia. We have all been silent for too long. We won't be silent anymore.

The truth is that all our problems stem from the same sex-based myths. We may appear before you as white radicals or the middle-aged middleclass or black soul sisters, but we are all sisters in fighting against these outdated myths. Like radical myths, they have been reflected in our laws. Let me list a few:

That Women are Biologically Inferior to Men

In fact, an equally good case can be made for the reverse. Women live longer than men, even when the men are not subject to business pressures.

However, I don't want to prove the superiority of one sex to another; That would only be repeating a male mistake. ...

What we do know is that the difference between two races or two sexes is much smaller than the differences to be found within each group. Therefore, in spite of the slide show on female inferiority's that I understand was shown to you yesterday, the law makes much more sense when it treats individuals, not groups bundled together by some condition of birth....

That Women Are Already Treated Equally in This Society

I'm sure there has been ample testimony to prove that equal pay for equal work, equal chance for advancement, and equal training or encouragement is obscenely scarce in every field, even those - like food and fashion industries- that are supposedly "feminine."

A deeper result of social and legal injustice, however, is what sociologists refer to as "Internalized Aggression." Victims of aggression absorb the myth of their own inferiority, and come to believe that their group is in fact second class.

Women suffer this second class treatment from the moment they are born. They are expected to be rather than achieve, to function biologically rather than learn. A brother; whatever his intellect, is more likely to get the family's encouragement and education money, while girls are often pressured to conceal ambition and intelligence, to a Uncle Tom."

Teachers, parents, and the Supreme Court may exude a protective, well-meaning rationale, but limiting the individual's ambition is doing no one a favor. Certainly not this country. It needs all the talent it can get.

That American Women Hold Great Economic Power

51% of all shareholders in this country are women. That's a favorite malechauvinist statistic. However; the number of shares they hold is so small that the total is only 18% of all shares. Even those holdings are often controlled by men.

Similarly, only 5% of all the people in the country who receive $10,000 a year or more, earned or otherwise, are women. And that includes all the famous rich widows.

The constantly - repeated myth of our economic power seems less testimony to our real power than to the resentment of what little power we do have.

That Children Must Have full-time Mothers

American mothers spend more time with their homes and children than those of any other society we know about....

The truth is that most American children seem to be suffering from too much Mother; and too little Father.

Part of the program of Women's Liberation is a return of fathers to their children.

As for the psychic health of the children, studies show that the quality of time spent by parents is more important than the quantity. The most damaged children were not those whose mothers worked, but those whose mothers preferred to work but stayed home out of a role-playing desire to be a "good mother"

That the Women's Movement Is Not Political, Won't Last, or Is Somehow Not "Serious"

We are 51 % of the population, we are essentially united on these issues across boundaries of class or race or age, and we may well end by changing this society more than the civil rights movement. That is an apt parallel. We, too, have our right wing and left wing, our separatists, gradualists, and Uncle Toms. But we are changing our own consciousness, and that of the country....

I had deep misgivings About discussing this topic when National Guardsmen are occupying our campuses, the country is being turned against itself in a terrible polarization, and America is enlarging an already inhuman and unjustifiable wan But it seems to me that much of the trouble this country is in has to do with the Masculine Mystique; with the myth that masculinity somehow depends on the subjugation of other people. It is a bipartisan problem: both our past and current Presidents seem to be victims of this myth, and to behave accordingly.

Women are not more moral than men. We are only uncorrupted by power. But we do not want to imitate men, to join this country as it is, and I think our very participation will change it. Perhaps women elected leaders-and there will be many more of them-will not be so likely to dominate black people or yellow people or men; anybody who looks different from us.

After all, we won't have our masculinity to prove.

Testimony of Gloria Steinem, U.S. Congress, Senate Committee on the Judiciary, Subcommittee on Constitutional Amendment, 91st Congress, 2nd Session, 1970, pp. 335-337.

HOW WELL DID YOU UNDERSTAND THIS SELECTION?

1. What does Steinem perceive to be the greatest obstacle to equality for women in American society?

2. What are the sex-based myths Steinem attacks? Do you agree with her assessment of the damage they have inflicted on American women? Explain.

3. Evaluate Steinem's analysis of the difference between men and women. Does she see this as a natural difference, or one imposed by society.

MK-ULTRA: The CIA and Radiation

Since the beginning of the Cold War, the CIA had been involved in a secret program to develop methods for controlling human behavior through drugs or psychological techniques. In 1977 a collection of documents was discovered that discussed a top-secret CIA program, code-named MK-ULTRA, which according to one of the documents was "concerned with research and development of chemical, biological, and radiological materials capable of employment in clandestine operations to control human behavior." What follows are the open remarks to the hearing conducted by the Senate to examine the matter.

WEDNESDAY, AUGUST 3, 1977

U.S. SENATE, SELECT COMMITTEE ON INTELLIGENCE, AND SUBCOMMITTEE ON HEALTH AND SCIENTIFIC RESEARCH OF THE COMMITTEE ON HUMAN RESOURCES
Washington, D.C.

The committees met, pursuant to notice, at 9:07 a.m. in room 1202, Dirksen Senate Office Building, Senator Daniel K. Inouye (chairman of the Select Committee on Intelligence) presiding.
Present: Senators Inouye (presiding), Kennedy, Goldwater, Bayh, Hathaway, Huddleston, Hart, Schweiker, Case, Garn, Chafee, Lugar and Wallop.
Also present: William G. Miller, staff director, Select Committee on Intelligence; Dr. Lawrence Horowitz, staff director, Subcommittee on Health and Scientific Research; and professional staff members of both committees.

Senator INOUYE. The Senate Select Committee on Intelligence is meeting today and is joined by the Subcommittee on Health and Scientific Research chaired by Senator Edward Kennedy of Massachusetts and Senator Richard Schweiker of Pennsylvania. Senator Hathaway and Senator Chafee are members of both committees. We are to hear testimony from the Director of Central Intelligence, Adm. Stansfield Turner, and from other Agency witnesses on issues concerning new documents supplied to the committee in the last week on drug testing conducted by the Central Intelligence Agency.

It should be made clear from the outset that in general, we are focusing on events that happened over 12 or as long as 25 years ago. It should be emphasized that the programs that are of greatest concern have stopped and that we are reviewing these past events in order to better understand what statutes and other guidelines might be necessary to prevent the recurrence of such abuses in the future. We also need to know and understand what is now being done by the CIA in the field of behavioral research to be certain that no current abuses are occurring.

I want to commend Admiral Turner for his full cooperation with this committee and with the Subcommittee on Health in recognizing that this issue needed our attention. The CIA has assisted our committees and staffs in their investigative efforts and in arriving at remedies which will serve the best interests of our country.

The reappearance of reports of the abuses of the drug testing program and reports of other previously unknown drug programs and projects for behavioral control underline the necessity for effective oversight procedures both in the executive branch and in the Congress. The Select Committee on Intelligence has been working very closely with President Carter, the Vice President, and Admiral Turner and his associates in developing basic concepts for statutory guidelines which will govern all activities of the intelligence agencies of the United States.

In fact, it is my expectation that the President will soon announce his decisions on how he has decided the intelligence agencies of the United States shall be organized. This committee will be working closely with the President and Admiral Turner in placing this new structure under the law and to develop effective oversight procedures.

It is clear that effective oversight requires that information must be full and forthcoming. Full and timely information is obviously necessary if the committee and the public is to be confident that any transgressions can be dealt with quickly and forcefully.

One purpose of this hearing is to give the committee and the public an understanding of what new information has been discovered that adds to the knowledge already available from previous Church and Kennedy inquiries, and to hear the reasons why these documents were not available to the Church and Kennedy committees. It is also the purpose of this hearing to address the issues raised by any additional illegal or improper activities that have emerged from the files and to develop remedies to prevent such improper activities from occurring again.

Finally, there is an obligation on the part of both this committee and the CIA to make every effort to help those individuals or institutions that may have been harmed by any of these improper or illegal activities. I am certain that Admiral Turner will work with this committee to see that this will be done.

I would now like to welcome the most distinguished Senator from Massachusetts, the chairman of the Health Subcommittee, Senator Kennedy.

Senator KENNEDY. Thank you very much, Mr. Chairman. We are delighted to join together in this very important area of public inquiry and public interest.

Some 2 years ago, the Senate Health Subcommittee heard chilling testimony about the human experimentation activities of the Central Intelligence Agency. The Deputy Director of the CIA revealed that over 30 universities and institutions were involved in an "extensive testing and experimentation" program which included covert drug tests on unwitting citizens "at all social levels, high and low, native Americans and foreign." Several of these tests involved the administration of LSD to "unwitting subjects in social situations."

At least one death, that of Dr. Olson, resulted from these activities. The Agency itself acknowledged that these tests made little scientific sense. The agents doing the monitoring were not qualified scientific observers. The tests subjects were seldom accessible beyond the first hours of the test. In a number of instances, the test subject became ill for hours or days, and effective follow up was impossible.

Other experiments were equally offensive. For example, heroin addicts were enticed into participating in LSD experiments in order to get a reward — heroin.

Perhaps most disturbing of all was the fact that the extent of experimentation on human subjects was unknown. The records of all these activities were destroyed in January 1973, at the instruction of then CIA Director Richard Helms. In spite of persistent inquiries by both the Health Subcommittee and the Intelligence Committee, no additional records or information were forthcoming. And no one — no single individual — could be found who remembered the details, not the Director of the CIA, who ordered the documents destroyed, not the official responsible for the program, nor any of his associates.

We believed that the record, incomplete as it was, was as complete as it was going to be. Then one individual, through a Freedom of Information request, accomplished what two U.S. Senate committees could not. He spurred the agency into finding additional records pertaining to the CIA's program of experimentation with human subjects. These new records were discovered by the agency in March. Their existence was not made known to the Congress until July.

The records reveal a far more extensive series of experiments than had previously been thought. Eighty-six universities or institutions were involved. New instances of unethical behavior were revealed.

The intelligence community of this Nation, which requires a shroud of secrecy in order to operate, has a very sacred trust from the American people. The CIA's program of human experimentation of the fifties and sixties violated that trust. It was violated again on the day the bulk of the agency's records were destroyed in 1973. It is violated each time a responsible official refuses to recollect the details of the program. The best safeguard against abuses in the future is a complete public accounting of the abuses of the past.

I think this is illustrated, as Chairman Inouye pointed out. These are issues, are questions that happened in the fifties and sixties, and go back some 15, 20 years ago, but they are front page news today, as we see in the major newspapers and on the television and in the media of this country; and the reason they are, I think, is because it just continuously begins to trickle out, sort of, month after month, and the best way to put this period behind us, obviously, is to have the full information, and I think that is the desire of Admiral Turner and of the members of this committee.

The Central Intelligence Agency drugged American citizens without their knowledge or consent. It used university facilities and personnel without their knowledge. It funded leading researchers, often without their knowledge.

These institutes, these individuals, have a right to know who they are and how and when they were used. As of today, the Agency itself refuses to declassify the names of those institutions and individuals, quite appropriately, I might say, with regard to the individuals under the Privacy Act. It seems to me to be a fundamental responsibility to notify those individuals or institutions, rather. I think many of them were caught up in an unwitting manner to do research for the Agency. Many researchers, distinguished researchers, some of our most outstanding members of our scientific community, involved in this network, now really do not know whether they were involved or not, and it seems to me that the whole health and climate in terms of our university and our scientific and health facilities are entitled to that response.

So, I intend to do all I can to persuade the Agency to, at the very least, officially inform those institutions and individuals involved.

Two years ago, when these abuses were first revealed, I introduced legislation, with Senator Schweiker and Senator Javits, designed to minimize the potential for any similar abuses in the future. That legislation expanded the jurisdiction of the National Commission on Human Subjects of Biomedical and Behavioral Research to cover all federally funded research involving human subjects. The research initially was just directed toward HEW activities, but this legislation covered DOD as well as the CIA.

This Nation has a biomedical and behavioral research capability second to none. It has had for subjects of HEW funded research for the past 3 years a system for the protection of human subjects of biomedical research second to none, and the Human Experimentation Commission has proven its value. Today's hearings and the record already established underscore the need to expand its jurisdiction.

The CIA supported that legislation in 1975, and it passed the Senate unanimously last year. I believe it is needed in order to assure all our people that they will have the degree of protection in human experimentation that they deserve and have every right to expect.

Senator INOUYE. Thank you very much. Now we will proceed with the hearings. Admiral Turner?

The following outline of methods and substances used by the CIA in experimenting with so-called "brainwashing techniques was one of the many secret documents revealed during the MK-ULTRA hearings.

5 May 1955
A portion of the Research and Development Program of TSS/Chemical Division is devoted to the discovery of the following materials and methods:

1. Substances which will promote illogical thinking and impulsiveness to the point where the recipient would be discredited in public.

2. Substances which increase the efficiency of mentation and perception.

3. Materials which will prevent or counteract the intoxicating effect of alcohol.

4. Materials which will promote the intoxicating effect of alcohol.

5. Materials which will produce the signs and symptoms of recognized diseases in a reversible way so that they may be used for malingering, etc.

6. Materials which will render the indication of hypnosis easier or otherwise enhance its usefulness.

7. Substances which will enhance the ability of individuals to withstand privation, torture and coercion during interrogation and so-called "brainwashing".

8. Materials and physical methods which will produce amnesia for events preceding and during their use.

9. Physical methods of producing shock and confusion over extended periods of time and capable of surreptitious use.

10. Substances which produce physical disablement such as paralysis of the legs, acute anemia, etc.

11. Substances which will produce "pure" euphoria with no subsequent let-down.

12. Substances which alter personality structure in such a way that the tendency of the recipient to become dependent upon another person is enhanced.

13. A material which will cause mental confusion of such a type that the individual under its influence will find it difficult to maintain a fabrication under questioning.

14. Substances which will lower the ambition and general working efficiency of men when administered in undetectable amounts.

15. Substances which will promote weakness or distortion of the eyesight or hearing faculties, preferably without permanent effects.

16. A knockout pill which can surreptitiously be administered in drinks, food, cigarettes, as an aerosol, etc., which will be safe to use, provide a maximum of amnesia, and be suitable for use by agent types on an ad hoc basis.

17. A material which can be surreptitiously administered by the above routes and which in very small amounts will make it impossible for a man to perform any physical activity whatever.

The development of materials of this type follows the standard practice of such ethical drug houses as [deleted]. It is a relatively routine procedure to develop a drug to the point of human testing. Ordinarily, the drug houses depend upon the services of private physicians for the final clinical testing. The physicians are willing to assume the responsibility of such tests in order to advance the science of medicine. It is difficult and sometimes impossible for TSS/CD to offer such an inducement with respect to its products. In practice, it has been possible to use the outside cleared contractors for the preliminary phases of this work. However, that part which involves human testing at effective dose levels presents security problems which cannot be handled by the ordinary contractor.

The proposed facility [deleted] offers a unique opportunity for the secure handling of such clinical testing in addition to the many advantages outline in the project proposal. The security problems mentioned above are eliminated by the fact that the responsibility for the testing will rest completely with the physician and the hospital. [deleted] will allow TSS/CD personnel to supervise the work very closely to make sure that all tests are conducted according to the recognized practices and embody adequate safeguards.

Source: Government Printing Office: Joint Hearings before the Select Committee on Intelligence, 95th Congress 1st Session, August 3, 1977)

HOW WELL DID YOU UNDERSTAND THIS SELECTION?

1. Explain the methods and goals of the MK-ULTRA program.

2. In what ways do these activities represent a violation of the subjects' rights?

3. How could the American government justify employing these methods?

SELF TEST

MULTIPLE CHOICE: Circle the correct response. The correct answers are given at the end.

1. Nixon ordered the invasion of Cambodia in an attempt to
   a. Draw the attention of the North Vietnamese away from South Vietnam
   b. Destroy arms and ammunition depots established there by the North Vietnamese
   c. Placate American demands to withdraw American troops from South Vietnam
   d. "Americanize" the conflict

2. In the wake of the Watergate scandal, Nixon was indicted for
   a. Ordering illegal wiretaps on war protesters
   b. Directing the IRS to audit his political opponents
   c. Ordering CREEP to break into the Democratic national headquarters
   d. Obstruction of justice and presidential abuse of power

3. Nixon and Kissinger worked to establish détente with
   a. China and Korea
   b. The Soviet Union and Iran
   c. Israel and Egypt
   d. The Soviet Union and China

4. OPEC imposed an oil embargo on the U.S. and her allies in 1973 in response to
   a. President Carter's efforts to end the Iranian hostage crisis
   b. C.I.A. attempts to assassinate the President of Egypt, Anwar Sadat
   c. American and allied assistance to Israel during the Yom Kippur War
   d. American assistance to the Shah of Iran

5. President Carter's response to the problem of "stagflation" was
    a. To reduce unemployment
    b. To encourage Americans to "Whip Inflation Now"
    c. To reduce government spending
    d. To raise interest rates

6. President Carter was successful in brokering a peace agreement between
    a. Israel and Palestine
    b. Afghanistan and the Soviet Union
    c. Egypt and Israel
    d. Iran and Syria

7. In November 1979, an Iranian mob took 53 Americans hostage in an effort to
    a. Force the U.S. to return the Shah so he could stand trial in Iran
    b. Force the U.S. to withdraw its support of Israel
    c. Force the U.S. to withdraw its support of the Ayatollah Khomeini
    d. Force the U.S. to nationalize Iranian oil fields

8. In response to the Soviet invasion of Afghanistan, Carter
    a. Reinstated the draft
    b. Banned the sale of high tech materials to the Soviets
    c. Placed an embargo on the exportation of grain to the Soviets
    d. Boycotted the 1980 Moscow Olympic Games

9. The fastest growing minority group in the 1970s was
    a. Asian Americans
    b. Hispanics
    c. African Americans
    d. Arab Americans

10. The 1969 riot at Stonewall Inn in New York City and the civil disobedience that followed marked the beginning of the
    a. Radical feminist movement
    b. Red Power movement
    c. Pan-Asian movement
    d. "Gay Pride" movement

Answers: 1-b; 2-d; 3-d; 4-c; 5-c; 6-c; 7-a; 8-d; 9-b; 10-d

ESSAYS:

1. Discuss the significance of Nixon's foreign policy success in China and the Soviet Union.

2. Examine the economic challenges facing the U.S. in the 1970s. How did each administration attempt to solve them?

3. Explain the increase in white ethnic resistance to the new militancy of women, homosexuals, and racial and ethnic minorities during the 1970s.

OPTIONAL ACTIVITIES: (Use your knowledge **and** imagination when appropriate.)

1. This chapter includes several events that place the U.S. in conflict with Arab nations. Create a time-line that plots American involvement in the Middle East. Highlight American activities there that elicited a negative response from Arab countries.

2.   Create a chart comparing and contrasting the foreign policy approaches of Nixon and Carter. Evaluate the relative success of each president's approach.

2.   This chapter notes that many groups in the U.S. exhibited "new militancy." Select one of these groups (African Americans, women, Asian-Americans, Hispanics, Native Americans, gays & lesbians, etc.), and create a poster presentation that outlines the group's demands and lists their strategy for achieving their goals.

WEB SITE LISTINGS:

The Seventies:
> http://www.super70s.com/Super70s/Timeline/
> http://www.nostalgiacentral.com/seventies.htm
> http://kclibrary.nhmccd.edu/decade70.html

Vietnam War:
> http://www.fsmitha.com/h2/ch26.htm
> http://members.aol.com/veterans/warlib6v.htm

Nixon:
> http://www.archives.gov/nixon/
> http://www.pbs.org/wgbh/amex/presidents/37_nixon/index.html

Pentagon Papers:
> http://www.gwu.edu/~nsarchiv/NSAEBB/NSAEBB48/
> http://www.mtholyoke.edu/acad/intrel/pentagon/pent1.html

Watergate:
> http://www.realhistoryarchives.com/collections/conspiracies/watergate.htm
> http://www.archives.gov/exhibit_hall/american_originals/nixon2.html
> http://www.archives.gov/exhibit_hall/american_originals/contemp.html

Three Mile Island:
> http://www.pbs.org/wgbh/amex/three/

SALT Talks
> http://dosfan.lib.uic.edu/acda/treaties/salt1.htm

Détente:
> http://www.pbs.org/wgbh/amex/china/
> http://www.gwu.edu/~nsarchiv/nsa/publications/DOC_readers/kissinger/nixzhou/

Ford:

http://www.americanpresident.org/history/geraldford/
http://www.pbs.org/wgbh/amex/presidents/38_ford/index.html
Nixon Pardon:
http://www.watergate.info/ford/pardon.shtml

Carter:

http://www.jimmycarterlibrary.org/
http://www.pbs.org/wgbh/amex/presidents/39_carter/index.html
http://odur.let.rug.nl/~usa/H/1990/ch8_p21.htm

Iran Hostage Crisis:
http://www.jimmycarterlibrary.org/documents/hostages.phtml
http://www.jimmycarterlibrary.org/documents/r_ode/index.phtml

SALT II Talks:
http://dosfan.lib.uic.edu/acda/treaties/salt2-1.htm

Chapter Twenty-four

IN OUR TIMES: Reagan to Clinton

After the economic problems of "stagflation" and the international humiliation of the Iran Hostage crisis, Americans seemed ready to return to conservatism with the election of Ronald Reagan as president. He quickly implemented his program of "supply-side economics," which included generous tax cuts for the wealthy and domestic spending cuts, particularly in social welfare programs. The Reagan administration also cut back on government regulation of industries, such as banking and savings-and-loan and in other areas such as consumer protection and the environment. At the same time, defense expenditures increased, including research to develop a Strategic Defense Initiative ("Star Wars"). While the economy stabilized and inflation declined, the budget deficit continued its precipitous growth. In addition, many Americans were never able to enjoy the benefits of "Reaganomics." Poverty increased, particularly among minorities and women, and the gap between the rich and poor dramatically widened. Other problems barely dealt with included the epidemics of AIDS and crack cocaine, the growth of homelessness, and the flood of new immigrants from Asia and Latin America.

In the foreign policy sphere, Reagan began his administration by condemning the "evil empire," the Soviet Union, and promising in the "Reagan Doctrine" to intervene anywhere communism was a threat. Actual interventions were somewhat limited, leading to claims of success in the tiny island of Grenada and disaster in Lebanon. The accession to power of the moderate reformer, Mikhail Gorbachev, in the Soviet Union resulted in better relations between the two nations, culminating in Reagan's visit to Moscow. While the Iran-Contra scandal was somewhat damaging to the Reagan presidency, his personal popularity remained high, partly because, beguiled by his personality, the public tended to disassociate Reagan from the policies and failures of his administration.

After a rough campaign in 1988, Reagan's vice president, George Bush, defeated Democrat Michael Dukakis by activating Americans' fears about crime and liberalism. Bush was far more interested in foreign affairs than in domestic policy. During his administration, the Soviet Union collapsed and the Cold War ended. American troops invaded Panama to remove its dictator and fought a war in the Persian Gulf to turn back the Iraqi invasion of oil-rich Kuwait. Although the dictator Saddam Hussein remained in power, the United States achieved a quick and relatively painless victory. Domestically, however, the Bush administration seemed far less effective. It was plagued by the savings-and-loan scandals, continued growth in the federal deficit, racial unrest demonstrated by the Rodney King riots, urban deterioration, and rising health-care costs. Despite some success with the Federal Clean Air Act and the Americans with Disabilities Act, Bush was perceived by the public to be unconcerned with domestic problems. This was particularly damaging to Bush when the country entered an economic recession and Bush felt forced to agree to tax increases, breaking his promise of "no new taxes."

In the election of 1992, little-known Arkansas Governor Bill Clinton stressed the issues of the faltering economy and health care to win a victory. A third party candidate, billionaire Ross Perot, captured a substantial number of disenchanted voters. Partly as a result of the televised Thomas-Hill hearings and the issues they brought forth, 1992 was also the "Year of the Woman" in which more female candidates were elected than ever before.

The Clinton administration achieved many of its objectives. These included Family Leave legislation, significant trade agreements in NAFTA and GATT, the Brady Bill for gun regulation, and welfare reform. Clinton's greatest success was in the economic area as the country experienced the longest economic boom without inflation in modern American history and budget deficits gave way to unheard-of budget surpluses. He was less successful in realizing some of his other promises. The pledge to end discrimination against gays in the military ended in a "Don't Ask, Don't Tell" compromise that satisfied neither side of the issue. An ambitious attempt to reform the health-care system, led by first lady Hillary Rodham Clinton, fell apart. This failure helped lead to Republican victories in the congressional elections of 1994, resulting in divided government. Clinton was also bedeviled by personal scandals. Independent Counsel Kenneth Starr investigated these. Starr ultimately recommended that the president be impeached for perjury committed in response to inquiries about his relationship with a White House intern. The president was impeached in a party-line vote in the House, but was not convicted in a Senate trial. Many felt that the presidency was badly wounded as a result.

In the area of foreign policy, the president faced a new, unstable world in which the Soviet Union was gone and the United States was the sole super power. The administration attempted to encourage democracy in Russia, peace in the Middle East and Ireland, and an end to ethnic conflicts in the former Yugoslavia with mixed results.

In 2000 an evenly divided nation produced an election in which Congress was split down the middle. George W. Bush, son of the former president, was elected president by a margin of four electoral votes, despite his opponent's 500,000 vote margin in the popular vote. A disputed vote count in Florida was settled by a controversial 5-4 decision by the Supreme Court in Bush's favor. As America entered the new millennium, it faced issues of racism, anti-government extremism, school violence, dramatic demographic changes, and continuing income gaps between the rich and poor. Many worried about disabled government and a decline in morals and community values. Others pointed to continuing economic prosperity and American resilience.

IDENTIFICATION: Briefly describe each term.

Reaganomics

Strategic Defense Initiative ("Star Wars")

Sandra Day O'Connor

Reagan Doctrine

Bombing of U.S. marine headquarters in Lebanon

Iran-Contra scandal

Walter Mondale

Geraldine Ferraro

Mikhail Gorbachev

glasnost and *perestroika*

AIDS

Crack cocaine epidemic

Simpson-Mazzoli Act of 1987

Michael Dukakis

Savings and Loan Crisis

Exxon Valdez

Thomas-Hill hearings

"Year of the Woman"

Rodney King

Americans with Disabilities Act

Collapse of the Soviet system

Persian Gulf War

Ross Perot

"Don't Ask, Don't Tell"

Janet Reno

Ruth Bader Ginsberg

NAFTA and GATT

Brady Bill

Health Care reform attempt

Personal Responsibilities and Work Opportunity Reconciliation Act of 1996 (Welfare Reform)

Dayton Accords

Kosovo

Contract with America

Newt Gingrich

Robert Dole

Kenneth Starr

Monica Lewinsky

Madeleine Albright

Oklahoma City bombing

Alan Greenspan

THINK ABOUT:

1. Some people have argued that Ronald Reagan's push for greater defense expenditures coupled with a vigorous anti-Soviet policy caused the collapse of the Soviet Union. If Reagan had not pushed his policies with such vehemence, would the disintegration of the Soviet Union have occurred anyhow? Was the basic cause of this collapse American pressure or internal problems and issues?

2. Why did Ronald Reagan's popularity seem to be untouched by such negative events as the growing federal budget deficit and the Iran-Contra scandal?

3. If AIDS had not been originally perceived of as the "gay disease," would there have been a greater and more sustained effort to deal with it at its earlier stages?

4. If the Supreme Court had not ruled that Paula Jones could pursue her civil suit against President Clinton while he was still in office, how would the history of his presidency have been different?

THE "SECOND AMERICAN REVOLUTION"
Ronald W. Reagan

Most political observers agree that Ronald Reagan possessed extraordinary skill in expressing his views and rallying support for them. Reagan had clear ideas, many of which conflicted with the direction of American government and policies since the New Deal. He wanted to end the "welfare state," cut taxes, restore a laissez faire economy, and, at the same time, build a larger and stronger new military machine. He hoped to bring about a "new American revolution," to alter American political life. Here in his State of the Union Address in 1985, he outlines that revolution and attempts to build support for his strong ideas.

Mr. Speaker, Mr. President, distinguished members of the Congress, honored guests and fellow citizens. I come before you to report on the state of our union. And I am pleased to report that, after four years of united effort, the American people have brought forth a nation renewed-stronger, freer and more secure than before.

Four years ago, we began to change-forever, I hope-our assumptions about government and its place in our lives. Out of that change has come great and robust growth-in our confidence, our economy and our role in the world . . . .

Four years ago, we said we would invigorate our economy by giving people greater freedom and incentives to take risks, and letting them keep more of what they earned.

We have begun well. But it's only a beginning. We are not here to congratulate ourselves on what we have done, but to challenge ourselves to finish what has not yet been done.

We are here to speak for millions in our inner cities who long for real jobs, safe neighborhoods and schools that truly teach. We are here to speak for the American farmer, the entrepreneur and every worker in industries fighting to modernize and compete. And, yes, we are here to stand, and proudly so, for all who struggle to break free from totalitarianism; for all who know in their hearts that freedom is the one true path to peace and human happiness . . . .

We honor the giants of our history- not by going back, but forward to the dreams their vision foresaw. My fellow citizens, this nation is poised for greatness. The time has come to proceed toward a great new challenge-a Second American Revolution of hope and opportunity; a revolution carrying us to new heights of progress by pushing back frontiers of knowledge and space; a revolution of spirit that taps the soul of America, enabling us to summon greater strength than we have ever known; and, a revolution that carries beyond our shores the golden promise of human freedom in a world at peace.

Let us begin by challenging conventional wisdom: There are no constraints on the human mind, no walls around the human spirit, no barriers to our progress except those we ourselves erect. Already, pushing down tax rates has freed our economy to vault forward to record growth. In Europe, they call it "the American Miracle." Day by day, we are shattering accepted notions of what is possible . . . .

We stand on the threshold of a great ability to produce more, do more, be more. Our economy is not getting older and weaker, it's getting younger and stronger; it doesn't need rest and supervision, it needs new challenge, greater freedom. And that word-freedom-is the key to the Second American Revolution we mean to bring about.

Let us move together with an historic reform of tax simplification for fairness and growth. Last year, I asked then-Treasury Secretary Regan to develop a plan to simplify the tax code, so all taxpayers would be treated more fairly, and personal tax rates could come further down.

We have cut tax rates by almost 25 percent, yet the tax system remains unfair and limits our potential for growth. Exclusions and exemptions cause similar incomes to be taxed at different levels. Low income families face steep tax barriers that make hard lives even harder. The Treasury Department has produced an excellent reform plan whose principles will guide the final proposal we will ask you to enact.

One thing that tax reform will not be is a tax increase in disguise. We will not jeopardize the mortgage interest deduction families need. We will reduce personal tax rates as low as possible by removing many tax preferences. We will propose a top rate of no more than 35 percent, and possibly lower. And we will propose reducing corporate rates while maintaining incentives for capital formation . . . .

Tax simplification will be a giant step toward unleashing the tremendous pent-up power of our economy. But a Second American Revolution must carry the promise of opportunity for all. It is time to liberate the spirit of enterprise in the most distressed areas of our country.

This government will meet its responsibility to help those in need. But policies that increase dependency, break up families and destroy self-respect are not progressive, they are reactionary. Despite our strides in civil rights, blacks, Hispanics and all minorities will not have full and equal power until they have full economic powers . . . .

Let us resolve that we will stop spreading dependency and start spreading opportunity; that we will stop spreading bondage and start spreading freedom. There are some who say that growth initiatives must await final action on deficit reductions. The best way to reduce deficits is through economic growth. More business will be started, more investments made, more jobs created and more people will be on payrolls paying taxes. The best way to reduce government spending is to reduce the need for spending by increasing prosperity . . . .

To move steadily toward a balanced budget we must also lighten government's claim on our total economy. We will not do this by raising taxes. We must make sure that our economy grows faster than growth in spending by federal government. In our fiscal year 1986 budget, overall government program spending will be frozen at the current level; it must not be one dime higher than fiscal year 1985. And three points are key:

First, the social safety net for the elderly, needy, disabled and unemployed will be left intact. Growth of our major health care programs, Medicare and Medicaid, will be slowed, but protections for the elderly and needy will be preserved.

Second, we must not relax our efforts to restore military strength just as we near our goal of a fully equipped, trained and ready professional corps. National security is government's first responsibility, so, in past years, defense spending took about half the federal budget. Today it takes less than a third.... You know, we only have a military industrial complex until a time of danger. Then it becomes' the arsenal of democracy. Spending for defense is investing in things that are priceless: peace and freedom.

Third, we must reduce or eliminate costly government subsidies. For example, deregulation of the airline industry has led to cheaper airfares, but on Amtrak taxpayers pay about $35 per passenger every time an Amtrak train leaves the station. It's time we ended this huge federal subsidy....

In the long run, we must protect the taxpayers from government. And I ask again that you pass, as 32 states have now called for, an amendment mandating the federal government spend no more than it takes in. And I ask for the authority used responsibly by 43 governors to veto individual items in appropriations bills. . . .

Nearly 50 years of government living beyond its means has brought us to a time of reckoning. Ours is but a moment in history. But one moment of courage, idealism and bipartisan unity can change American history forever. . . .

Every dollar the federal government does not take from us, every decision it does not make for us, will make our economy stronger, our lives more abundant, our future more free . . . .

There is another great heritage to speak of this evening. Of all the changes that have swept America the past four years, none brings greater promise than our rediscovery of the value of faith, freedom, family, work and neighborhood.

We see signs of renewal in increased attendance in places of worship: renewed optimism and faith in our future; love of country rediscovered by our young who are leading the way. We have rediscovered that work is good in and of itself; that it ennobles us to create and contribute no matter how seemingly humble our jobs. We have seen a powerful new current from an old and honorable tradition, American generosity . . . .

I thank the Congress for passing equal access legislation giving religious groups the same right to use classrooms after school that other groups enjoy. But no citizen need tremble, nor the world shudder, if a child stands in a classroom and breathes a prayer. We ask you again-give children back a right they had for a century-and-a-half or more in this country.

The question of abortion grips our nation. Abortion is either the taking of human life, or it isn't; and if it is-and medical technology is increasingly showing it is-it must be stopped . . . .

Of all the changes in the past 20 years, none has more threatened our sense of national well-being than the explosion of violent crime. One does not have to have been attacked to be a victim. The woman who must run to her car after shopping at night is a victim; the couple draping their door with locks and chains are victims; as is the tired, decent cleaning woman who can't ride a subway home without being afraid.

We do not seek to violate rights of defendants, but shouldn't we feel more compassion for victims of crime than for those who commit crime? For the first time in 20 years, the crime index has fallen two years in a row; we've convicted over 7,400 drug offenders, and put them, as well as leaders of organized crime, behind bars in record numbers.

But we must do more. I urge the House to follow the Senate and enact proposals permitting use of all reliable evidence that police officers acquire in good faith. These proposals would also reform the habeas corpus laws and allow, in keeping with the will of the overwhelming majority of Americans, the use of the death penalty where necessary.

There can be no economic revival in ghettos when the most violent among us are allowed to roam free. It is time we restored domestic tranquility. And we mean to do just that . . . .

Tonight I have spoken of great plans and great dreams. They are dreams we can make come true. Two hundred years of American history should have taught us that nothing is impossible . . . . Anything is possible in America if we have the faith, the will and the heart.

History is asking us, once again, to be a force for good in the world. Let us begin-in unity, with justice and love.
Thank you and God bless you.

HOW WELL DID YOU UNDERSTAND THIS SELECTION?

1. What did President Reagan believe he had accomplished by 1985?

2. How did Reagan expect to reduce deficits? Did it work?

3. What conservative programs did Reagan advocate in his State of the Union address? What arguments did he use to support these programs?

4. How do you evaluate his "great plans and great dreams"?

One problem that seemed to worsen in the 1980s was the issue of homelessness. The cuts in social welfare programs loosened the already precarious "safety nets" designed to help the most vulnerable members of society. During the 1980s the characteristics of homeless people seemed to change from single people to families headed by women. Homeless people are often ignored by the political system, but this seemed even more true in the 1980s.

You see them now in every American city - the homeless people, who sleep by night in doorways, under highway bridges, in tents, on steaming grates, in bus stations. By day they wander warily from park bench to soup kitchen to abandoned building to public library or museum, watching the long hours slip away into nothingness. On frigid winter nights, they jam into emergency shelters that more closely resemble concentration camps than warm havens. These hundreds of thousands, if not millions, of homeless represent a national epidemic - the most severe housing crisis since the Depression. It is a problem that most agree will only get dramatically worse, growing far faster than the remedies.

Wide disagreement exists over the number of homeless, with the most frequently cited national figures ranging from a low of 250,000 (estimated by the Department of Housing and Urban Development in 1984) to four million (a 1982 estimate by the Community for Creative Non-Violence, an advocacy group located in Washington, D.C.). In a report to the National Governors' Association, New York Gov. Mario Cuomo gave the following estimates for 1983: 20,000 to 25,000, Chicago; 12,000 to 15,000, Baltimore; 2,500, Denver; 8,000 to 10,000, San Francisco; 2,000, Boston; 7,700, St. Louis:; 22,000, Houston.

One difficulty in accurately counting the homeless population is that the number changes constantly in response to such factors as national economic policy, unemployment rates, availability of social services, availability of low-rent housing, season of the year, weather, day of the month. In addition, definitions of homelessness vary, as do counting methodologies. However, as Congressman Bruce Vento (D. Minn.) says, "We shouldn't be diverted by an argument about numbers. The obvious fact is that we have a growing number of homeless."

The real issue is not the precise number of homeless, but the gravity of their situation. The Department of Health and Human Services reports: 'They [the homeless live brutal, debilitating, stressful lives of great hardship." In New York City alone, some 25 to 50 homeless people are thought to die on the streets during each of the winter months. The causes are violence; weather related illnesses (pneumonia, frostbite, gangrene, stroke, heart failure); alcohol-induced illnesses, among others.

Public awareness of the plight of the homeless has heightened. Yet grave misconceptions still abound as to who the homeless are, why they are on the streets, and what is needed to remedy their situation. Some communities acknowledge the problem by shipping the homeless out of town.

Elsewhere, homelessness has become the latest fashion fad: In the spring of 1983, Bloomingdale's department store in New York City opened in its second floor boutique a new display called "Street Couture." The clothing was designed to mimic the dress of the homeless poor: disheveled, wrinkled, patched, and mismatched. A jacket with torn sleeves listed for $190. An employee insisted that the "street look" sells. "Bag ladies are in," she explained.

The insensitivity continues on a daily basis in every city by those who more easily tell a joke about the homeless on the streets than acknowledge the homeless as human beings. D.C. homeless advocates Mary Ellen Hombs and Mitch Snyder offer the following as an example:

"In all of the years that Red and Willie [two homeless men] have spent on the down town [Washington, D.C.] heat grates, millions of people have walked or driven by them, but only a handful have stopped to talk, to see if they could be of any help. Some furtively scan the scene; others stare in amazement. For most, expressions do not change. Red and Willie, their pain and their loneliness, are invisible. If not invisible, then surely untouchable."

Dr. Michael Vergare, a psychiatrist with the Albert Einstein Medical Center in Philadelphia, suggests, "We struggle to comprehend how, in this day and age when so many people are so well off, we have people who cannot find shelter."

John Philips, AIA, 1985 chairman of AIA's housing committee says, "The epidemic of homelessness to some Americans, maybe to many, is so unthinkable that they refuse to recognize the visible homeless although the homeless are all around .... We must acknowledge that homelessness is a major social crisis today."

Often the homeless are identified by their tattered appearance; bizarre behavior; belongings carried in plastic bags or cardboard boxes tied with string or stuffed into shopping carts; swollen, ulcerated legs; apparent aimlessness. But, as Hombs and Snyder describe, "There are also those who have been able to maintain a reasonably good personal appearance and whose behavior betrays no apparent sign of disorder," which allows them to more easily find food, daytime shelter in libraries or museums, and public washroom facilities and to escape threats, violence, and harassment.

Generally, a homeless person is someone who has no stable residence, which is defined as a place to sleep and receive mail. This person is usually destitute and has either minimal or no resources or income. In addition, a homeless person is not likely receiving any government assistance.

Perhaps the first step in understanding the homeless is to dispel the myth that the homeless are on the streets by choice, having voluntarily rejected any available assistance. "It is an overstatement to say even a small minority of these people live on the streets by choice. There is no evidence that people live on the streets by choice," says Robert Hayes, founder and legal counsel of the National Coalition for the Homeless, headquartered in New York City. "It is essential to see the homeless as suffering individuals," Hayes adds, and to illustrate his point offers the following examples:

Alice is an elderly woman who has lived her entire life in quite a normal way. She raised children, then moved out of her home town to the Midwest. Her husband died. Then her rent went up dramatically. She first moved to a cheap hotel, an SRO (single-room-occupancy hotel). She lost that suddenly, at the age of 73, for the first time in her life, Alice could not find a place to live. She wound up in a train terminal. She became confused, and suddenly people were describing her as a "bag lady. "

Joey is a six-year-old boy in New York City. He's been homeless for three years-half of his life. He's been shunted from welfare hotels to what we euphemistically call "barrack shelters" in New York -refugee camps where cots and cribs are lined up on large, open rooms with common sleeping areas. When 1 first met Joey, he was a little fellow He was playful and had that glint in his eyes. And that glint was, to me, something that 1 thought would get him through. But he's six now. The glint's gone. Joey has struggled. Joey has suffered. But most of all, he's lost his playfulness, his right to that commodity that every child should have - his childhood.

Hayes maintains that "if people are offered safe, decent, humane shelters, they will go in off the streets."

A barometer of the problem's seriousness in the incidence of hunger, since hunger is considered the handmaiden of homelessness. In a survey of 181 food pantries and soup kitchens in 12 states, the National Governors' Association found a "dramatic increase" in the numbers seeking emergency food aid between February 1982 and February 1983. In that single year, demand in over half of the programs surveyed rose by 50 percent or more.

In a survey of 25 major cities, the U.S. Conference of Mayors found that hunger and homelessness rose sharply during 1985. Demand rose an average of 28 percent for emergency food and an average of 25 percent for shelter. In fact, the survey of cities ranging in size from New York to Charleston, S. C., found that "in none of the cities surveyed has the economic recovery lessened the problems of homelessness." There are also indications of a growing disparity between the have and have nots. For example, in Chicago "there has been no significant shift in the economic status of the city's poor and near poor." In Salt Lake City, "the national economic recovery has not alleviated the problems of low-income people. In fact, it appears that there are more people in need and that they are worse off, than previously."

Hayes reports, "What we saw in most parts of the country was a 20 to 30 percent increase during 1985 in the number of people seeking help I don't know any place that had spare beds."

Hayes noted last year, "In understanding homelessness, we have to start out by realizing that here we are in 1985 in a period without precedence in the history of the United States. By that I mean, sure there have been a lot of homeless folks in this country over the past few hundred years, but always mass homelessness in this country has been accompanied by system-wide economic dislocations - serious depressions or recessions. But something peculiar is happening because maybe [homelessness was understandable] in the 1930s, maybe even in 1982 or 1983 when there were serious economic problems. But in 1985, it does not seem so simple to understand. It seems that something fairly severe has to be undertaken because the old systems of dealing with mass homelessness in this country aren't working in the 1980s."

What makes the '80s feel like the '30s is the make-up of the homeless population. Now, as in the Depression, the homeless represent a broad cross section of American society - the young and old, single people and families, the mentally and physically disabled, and the ablebodied. The most dramatic change in the last 10 years has been a sharp increase in the number of women, children, young men, and families.

The New York State Department of Social Services reports: "Increasingly, the problem of homelessness is affecting people and families who are in most respects like other poor people, except that they cannot find or afford housing. The homeless transient, the wandering loner who may be alcoholic or mentally disabled, is no longer typical of the great majority of people without shelter. More and more, those sleeping in emergency shelters include parents and children whose primary reason for homelessness is poverty or family disruption. They have arrived in shelters not from the streets but from some dwelling (typically not their own) where they are no longer welcome or where they can no longer afford to stay."

The homeless population is now vastly different from the homogeneous skid row population of the post-World War II era, the majority of whom were older white men suffering from alcoholism and/or drug addiction. Since many cities and states had anti-vagrancy laws (until the 1970s), most skid rowers were actually not homeless, but sheltered - in jails, if not seedy hotels, flophouses, or missions,. But, regardless, many were considered the derelicts of society, as often the homeless are today. Now, though, according to the U.S. General Accounting Office (GAO), the average age of homeless persons is 34. Single women make up 13 percent of the homeless population, minorities 44 percent, and families 21 percent, the GAO reported in 1985. The U.S. Conference of Mayors reported in 1985 that the most significant recent change in the homeless population was the growing number of families with children; the number of young single adults also increased. It is especially poignant to see young children as miniature bag people dragging their toys in plastic bags.

A microcosm of the homeless population is found in Los Angeles County, where the number of homeless in not only large-HUD estimated 33,800 as of July '84- but is thought to be increasing rapidly. The compositional changes in that population parallel shifts in the national homeless population. For example- single males who had became homeless 12 months prior to a survey of homeless shelters (conducted over a six month period ending in May '84) were younger and better educated, and more likely to be non-white, recently unemployed, and veterans than those homeless for more than 12 months. Increased numbers of families with children, single women, and youths were visible throughout the county.

"A whole new wave of homeless people in the U.S. is made up of the young and ablebodied who have little chance of winning a place in a tight [employment] market and consequently no ability to win the competition for housing in a tighter and tighter housing market," Hayes suggests, Marita Dean, of the Washington D.C., office of Catholic Charities, reported in 1984: We're seeing people now that no agency ever saw before, people who never had to beg before. They're frightened, so you help them this month, but they're not going to be any better off next month."

In addition to its demographic diversity, the homeless population varies significantly in duration of homelessness. Vergare and his associate, Dr. Anthony Arce, have suggested three groupings: the chronic, who are homeless for more than 30 continuous days - although many, if not most, have been homeless for months or years; the episodic, who tend to alternate for varying periods of time between being domiciled and homeless, with homelessness usually lasting less then 30 days; and the situational, for whom homelessness is the temporary result of an acute life crisis.

What looms ahead? One clue may be the number of people doubling up (living with one or two other persons or families). The National Coalition for the Homeless estimated at the end of 1985 that there were as many as 10 to 20 million doubling up, with as many as 500,000 in New York City alone. Seattle's Mayor Charles Royer noted in

May 1985, "For every homeless person in Seattle, there are 10 others who are at risk and who need some kind of housing assistance."

A recent needs assessment in New York State found "disturbing information - the numbers of homeless people were far larger than imagined. But even more distressing was the consensus among service providers of the tremendous number of persons and families doubling up," says Nancy Travers, assistant commissioner, New York State Department of Social Services. She suggests that if New York State continued providing shelter to the homeless at the level it did in 1984, "it would take 20 years to meet the needs of the homeless. Clearly this is a housing problem of a scale that is hard to imagine."

Meanwhile, the numbers keep growing. In its Dec. 16, 1985, issue, *Newsweek* reported: "Across the frost belt last week, cities set records in sheltering the homeless: New York, Boston, Philadelphia have emergency policies requiring police and city employees to round up the homeless and take them to shelters after the temperature turns frigid. But the hundreds of shelter beds - in the case of New York City, 23,000 - come nowhere close to meeting the need."

Source: Subcommittee on Housing and Community Development. January 26, 1988.

HOW WELL DID YOU UNDERSTAND THIS SELECTION?

1. How does this reading define a homeless person?

2. What examples are given of homeless people that might not fit your stereotype?

3. How does the homeless population differ from the "skid row" population of the post-World War II era?

4. What problems did the report foresee in the future? Have those predictions come to pass in the last 12 years since the report was written?

Ryan White got AIDS virus from the blood-clotting medicine he took for his hemophilia. He died in 1990, at age eighteen. This is part of his testimony before the Presidential Commission on AIDS, given in 1988. The issue of AIDS was just beginning to become part of the public awareness.

I came face to face with death at thirteen years old. I was diagnosed with AIDS: a killer. Doctors told me I'm not contagious. Given six months to live and being the fighter that I am, I set high goals for myself. It was my decision to live a normal life, go to school, be with my friends, and enjoy day to day activities. It was not going to be easy.

The school I was going to said they had no guidelines for a person with AIDS . . . . We began a series of court battles for nine months, while I was attending classes by telephone. Eventually, I won the right to attend school, but the prejudice was still there. Listening to medical facts was not enough. People wanted one hundred percent guarantees. There are no one hundred percent guarantees in life, but concessions were made by Mom and me to help ease the fear. We decided to meet everyone halfway . . . . Because of the lack of education on AIDS, discrimination, fear, panic, and lies surrounded me. (1) I became the target of Ryan White jokes. (2) Lies about me biting people. (3) Spitting on vegetables and cookies. (4) Urinating on bathroom walls. (5) Some restaurants threw away my dishes. (6) My school locker was vandalized inside and folders were marked FAG and other obscenities.

I was labeled a troublemaker, my mom an unfit mother, and I was not welcome anywhere. People would get up and leave, so they would not have to sit anywhere near me. Even at church, people would not shake my hand.

This brought in the news media, TV crews, interviews, and numerous public appearances. I became known as the AIDS boy. I received thousands of letters of support from all around the world, all because I wanted to go to school . . . . It was difficult, at times, to handle, but I tried to ignore the injustice, because I knew the people were wrong. My family and I held no hatred for those people because we realized they were victims of their own ignorance. We had great faith that, with patience, understanding, and education, my family and I could be helpful in changing their minds and attitudes . . . .

Financial hardships were rough on us, even though Mom had a good job at G.M. The more I was sick, the more work she had to miss. Bills became impossible to pay. My sister, Andrea, was a championship roller skater who had to sacrifice too.. There was no money for her lessons and travel. AIDS can destroy a family if you let it, but luckily for my sister and me, Mom taught us to keep going. Don't give up, be proud of who you are, and never feel sorry for yourself.

HOW WELL DID YOU UNDERSTAND THIS SELECTION?

1. How did Ryan White contract AIDS?

2. Why did both students and adults react to Ryan White the way they did?

3. What caused the attitudes towards Ryan to gradually change?

4. In what ways have public views about AIDS changed since 1988?

On March 2003, President George W. Bush addressed the nation concerning Saddam Hussein.

My fellow citizens, events in Iraq have now reached the final days of decision. For more than a decade, the United States and other nations have pursued patient and honorable efforts to disarm the Iraqi regime without war. That regime pledged to reveal and destroy all of its weapons of mass destruction as a condition for ending the Persian Gulf War in 1991.

Since then, the world has engaged in 12 years of diplomacy. We have passed more than a dozen resolutions in the United Nations Security Council. We have sent hundreds of weapons inspectors to oversee the disarmament of Iraq. Our good faith has not been returned. The Iraqi regime has used diplomacy as a ploy to gain time and advantage. It has uniformly defied Security Council resolutions demanding full disarmament....

Intelligence gathered by this and other governments leaves no doubt that the Iraq regime continues to possess and conceal some of the most lethal weapons ever devised. This regime has already used weapons of mass destruction against Iraq's neighbors and against Iraq's people. The regime has a history of reckless aggression in the Middle East. It has a deep hatred of America and our friends and it has aided, trained and harbored terrorists, including operatives of Al Qaeda. The danger is clear: Using chemical, biological or, one day, nuclear weapons obtained with the help of Iraq, the terrorists could fulfill their stated ambitions and kill thousands or hundreds of thousands of innocent people in our country or any other.

The United States and other nations did nothing to deserve or invite this threat, but we will do everything to defeat it. Instead of drifting along toward tragedy, we will set a course toward safety. Before the day of horror can come, before it is too late to act, this danger will be removed. The United States of America has the sovereign authority to use force in assuring its own national security. That duty falls to me as commander of chief by the oath I have sworn, by the oath I will keep. Recognizing the threat to our country, the United States Congress voted overwhelmingly last year to support the use of force against Iraq.

America tried to work with the United Nations to address this threat because we wanted to resolve the issue peacefully. We believe in the mission of the United Nations...One reason the U.N. was founded after the Second World War was to confront aggressive dictators actively and early, before they can attack the innocent and destroy the peace.

Last September, I went to the U.N. General Assembly and urged the nations of the world to unite and bring an end to this danger. On November 8th, the Security Council unanimously passed Resolution 1441, finding Iraq in material breach of its obligations and vowing serious consequences if Iraq did not fully and immediately disarm. Today, no nation can possibly claim that Iraq has disarmed. And it will not disarm so long as Saddam Hussein holds power.

For the last four and a half months, the United States and our allies have worked within the Security Council to enforce that council's longstanding demands. Yet some permanent members of the Security Council have publicly announced that they will veto any resolution that compels the disarmament of Iraq. These governments share our assessment of the danger, but not our resolve to meet it. Many nations, however, do have the resolve and fortitude to act against this threat to peace, and a broad coalition is now gathering to enforce the just demands of the world.

The United Nations Security Council has not lived up to its responsibilities, so we will rise to ours. In recent days, some governments in the Middle East have been doing their part. They have delivered public and private messages urging the dictator to leave Iraq so that disarmament can proceed peacefully. He has thus far refused.

All the decades of deceit and cruelty have now reached an end. Saddam Hussein and his sons must leave Iraq within 48 hours. Their refusal to do so will result in military conflict commenced at a time of our choosing....

Many Iraqis can hear me tonight in a translated radio broadcast, and I have a message for them: If we must begin a military campaign, it will be directed against the lawless men who rule your country and not against you. As our coalition takes away their power, we will deliver the food and medicine you need. We will tear down the apparatus of terror and we will help you to build a new Iraq that is prosperous and free... The tyrant will soon be gone. The day of your liberation is near...

And all Iraqi military and civilian personnel should listen carefully to this warning: In any conflict, your fate will depend on your actions. Do not destroy oil wells, a source of wealth that belongs to the Iraqi people. Do not obey any command to use weapons of mass destruction against anyone, including the Iraqi people. War crimes will be prosecuted, war criminals will be punished and it will be no defense to say, "I was just following orders." Should Saddam Hussein choose confrontation, the American people can know that every measure has been taken to avoid war and every measure will be taken to win it.

Americans understand the costs of conflict because we have paid them in the past. War has no certainty except the certainty of sacrifice. Yet the only way to reduce the harm and duration of war is to apply the full force and might of our military, and we are prepared to do so...In desperation, he and terrorist groups might try to conduct terrorist operations against the American people and our friends. These attacks are not inevitable. They are, however, possible...

And this very fact underscores the reason we cannot live under the threat of blackmail. The terrorist threat to America and the world will be diminished the moment that Saddam Hussein is disarmed. Our government is on heightened watch against these dangers. Just as we are preparing to ensure victory in Iraq, we are taking further actions to protect our homeland...

Should enemies strike our country, they would be attempting to shift our attention with panic and weaken our morale with fear. In this, they would fail. No act of theirs can alter the course or shake the resolve of this country. We are a peaceful people, yet we are not a fragile people. And we will not be intimidated by thugs and killers...

We are now acting because the risks of inaction would be far greater. In one year, or five years, the power of Iraq to inflict harm on all free nations would be multiplied many times over. With these capabilities, Saddam Hussein and his terrorist allies could choose the moment of deadly conflict when they are strongest. We choose to meet that threat now where it arises, before it can appear suddenly in our skies and cities.

The cause of peace requires all free nations to recognize new and undeniable realities. In the 20th century, some chose to appease murderous dictators whose threats were allowed to grow into genocide and global war. In this century, when evil men plot chemical, biological and nuclear terror, a policy of appeasement could bring destruction of a kind never before seen on this earth. Terrorists and terrorist states do not reveal these threats with fair notice in formal declarations.

And responding to such enemies only after they have struck first is not self defense. It is suicide. The security of the world requires disarming Saddam Hussein now... As we enforce the just demands of the world, we will also honor the deepest commitments of our country. Unlike Saddam Hussein, we believe the Iraqi people are deserving and capable of human liberty, and when the dictator has departed, they can set an example to all the Middle East of a vital and peaceful and self-governing nation...

Free nations have a duty to defend our people by uniting against the violent, and tonight, as we have done before, America and our allies accept that responsibility.

Good night, and may God continue to bless America.

Office of the Press Secretary, Address to the Nation, March 17, 2003.

HOW WELL DID YOU UNDERSTAND THIS SELECTION?

1. What are President Bush's main justifications for military action in Iraq?

2. How does he relate his actions to terrorism?

3. What is his attitude towards the United Nations? Countries opposed to America's position?

4. What are his implicit promises to the Iraqi people?

5. To what extent have the president's justifications and promises proven to be accurate?

African-American fury exploded in the 1992 riots in South Central Los Angeles. After the acquittal of four white police officers accused of beating Rodney King, enraged residents erupted into violence, destroying sections of the city. The riots led to 38 deaths, 3,700 burned-out buildings, and more than $500 million in damages. Congresswoman Maxine Waters, who represented the district, testified about the underlying causes of the riots.

The riots in Los Angeles and in other cities shocked the world. They shouldn't have. Many of us have watched our country-including our government-neglect the problems, indeed the people, of our inner-cities for years-even as matters reached a crisis stage.

The verdict in the Rodney King case did not cause what happened in Los Angeles. It was only the most recent injustice-piled upon many other injustices-suffered by the poor, minorities and the hopeless people living in this nation's cities. For years, they have been crying out for help. For years, their cries have not been heard.

I recently came across a statement made more than 25 years ago by Robert Kennedy, just two months before his violent death. He was talking about the violence that had erupted in cities across America. His words were wise and thoughtful:

> There is another kind of violence in America, slower but just as deadly, destructive as the shot or bomb in the night .... This is the violence of institutions; indifference and inaction and slow decay. This is the violence that afflicts the poor, that poisons relations between men and women because their skin is different colors. This is the slow destruction of a child by hunger, and schools without books and homes without heat in winter.

What a tragedy it is that America has still, in 1992, not learned such an important lesson.

I have represented the people of South Central Los Angeles in the U. S. Congress and the California State Assembly for close to 20 years. I have seen our community continually and systematically ravaged by banks who would not lend to us, by governments which abandoned us or punished us for our poverty, and by big businesses who exported our jobs to Third-World countries for cheap labor.

In LA, between 40 and 50 percent of all African-American men are unemployed. The poverty rate is 32.9 percent. According to the most recent census, 40,000 teenagers-that is 20 percent of the city's 16 to 19 year olds-are both out of school and unemployed ....

We have created in many areas of this country a breeding ground for hopelessness, anger and despair. All the traditional mechanisms for empowerment, opportunity and self-improvement have been closed.

We are in the midst of a grand economic experiment that suggests if we "get the government off people's backs," and let the economy grow, everyone, including the poor, will somehow be better off . . . . The results of this experiment have been devastating. Today, more than 12 million children live in poverty, despite a decade of "economic growth," the precise mechanism we were told would reduce poverty. Today, one in five children in America lives in poverty ....

While the budget cuts of the eighties were literally forcing millions of Americans into poverty, there were other social and economic trends destroying inner-city communities at the same time.

I'm sure everyone in this room has read the results of the Federal Reserve Board's study on mortgage discrimination that demonstrates African Americans . . . are twice as likely as whites of the same income to be denied mortgages ....

In law enforcement, the problems are longstanding and well documented as well.

Is it any wonder our children have no hope? The systems are failing us. I could go on and on .... We simply cannot afford the continued terror and benign neglect that has characterized the federal government's response to the cities since the late 1970s.

Source: Maxine Waters, "Testimony before the Senate Banking Committee," Congressional Record (1992).

HOW WELL DID YOU UNDERSTAND THIS SELECTION?

1. According to Maxine Waters, why shouldn't the 1992 Los Angeles riots have shocked the world?

2. Why was South Central Los Angeles (and other such areas) "a breeding ground for hopelessness, anger and despair"?

3. What government policies of the 1980s did she believe worsened the situation?

4. Do you feel these problems have been solved since then? Can you think of current events that would illustrate similar concerns?

"DON'T ASK, DON'T TELL"

When President Clinton first took office, he attempted to fulfill his promise to gays to end the policy forbidding gays in the military. This position created enormous controversy. As a result, Clinton agreed to a compromise policy known as "Don't Ask, Don't Tell" that permitted homosexuals in the military provided that they did not announce their sexual preference.

U.S. Code – Title 10, Section 654
Policy Concerning Homosexuality in the Armed Forces

(13) The prohibition against homosexual conduct is a long-standing element of military law that continues to be necessary in the unique circumstances of military service.

(14) The armed forces must maintain personnel policies that exclude persons whose presence in the armed forces would create an unacceptable risk to the armed forces' high standards of morale, good order and discipline, and unit cohesion that are the essence of military capability.

(15) The presence in the armed forces of persons who demonstrate a propensity or intent to engage in homosexual acts would create an unacceptable risk to the high standards of morale, good order and discipline, and unit cohesion that are the essence of military capability.

(b) Policy. - A member of the armed forces shall be separated from the armed forces under regulations prescribed by the Secretary of Defense if one or more of the following findings is made and approved in accordance with procedures set forth in such regulations:

(1) That the member has engaged in, attempted to engage in, or solicited another to engage in a homosexual act or acts unless there are further findings, made and approved in accordance with procedures set forth in such regulations, that the member has demonstrated that

(A) such conduct is a departure from the member's usual and customary behavior;

(B) such conduct, under all the circumstances, is unlikely to recur;

(C) such conduct was not accomplished by use of force, coercion, or intimidation;

(D) under the particular circumstances of the case, the member's continued presence in the armed forces is consistent with the interests of the armed forces in proper discipline good order, and morale; and

(E) the member does not have a propensity or intent to engage in homosexual acts.

(2) That the member has stated that he or she is a homosexual or bisexual, or words to that effect, unless there is a further finding, made and approved in accordance with procedures set forth in the regulations, that the member has demonstrated that he or she is not a person who engages in, attempts to engage in, has a propensity to engage in, or intends to en age in homosexual acts.

(3) That the member has married or attempted to marry a person known to be of the same biological sex.

PENTAGON ISSUES NEW GUIDELINES FOR GAYS IN MILITARY

August 13, 1999, Web Posted at: 4:12 p. m. EDT (2012 GMT) From staff and wire reports

WASHINGTON-The U.S. military Friday issued new directives intended to end abuses of the "don't ask, don't tell" policy toward gays and lesbians in the armed forces.

The revised specifications require that troops receive anti-gay harassment training throughout their military careers, starting with boot camp.

"I've made it clear there is no room for harassment or threats in the military," Defense Secretary William Cohen said in issuing the new directives.

The guidelines also mandate that any investigation into the sexual orientation of a soldier be handled at a more senior level of the military justice system than before.

The revisions follow the beating death last month of a soldier at Fort Campbell, Kentucky, who was rumored to be gay. Barry Winchell was bludgeoned to death in his barracks.

The Army conducted a hearing this week to determine whether the murder case against Pvt. Calvin Glover, 18, of Sulphur, Oklahoma, will go to a general court-martial. The decision is expected in about two weeks.

Some activists have charged that gay harassment and investigation of gays have surged to record levels in the military, despite the "don't ask, don't tell" policy.

Last year, 1,145 people were discharged from the armed forces for homosexuality, according to a Pentagon report. In 1997, the total was 997, the highest number since 1987. The number of discharges hit a low of 617 in 1994, the year the "don't ask, don't tell" policy took effect.

Pentagon officials have defended the policy, contending that roughly 80 percent of the discharges occur because the individual has come forward.

The new guidelines do not make any major changes in the procedures that have been followed since 1994, but try to spell them out more clearly, the officials said.

Michelle Benecke, a former Army officer now with the Service members Legal Defense Network, said she "seriously doubts'" the new guidelines will be an adequate response to the problem.

Still, officials said it is hoped that the intended clarifications—and mandatory anti-gay harassment, training — will end what they claim are a relatively small number of abuses.

Under the policy, those who are openly homosexual are still barred from serving in the in the military.

Gays can remain in the services so long as they do not discuss their sexual orientation openly. Commanders and investigators are not permitted to ask troops about their sexual orientation.

The policy was a compromise developed after Congress rejected an earlier proposal by President Clinton for an outright ban on discrimination based on sexual orientation.

Source: CNN, August 13, 1999. Correspondent David Ensor and the Associated Press contributed to this report.

HOW WELL DID YOU UNDERSTAND THIS SELECTION?

1. Why was the government policy called, "Don't Ask, Don't Tell"? What behavior would lead to the "separation" of a homosexual member of the armed forces from the services?

2. What event caused a revision of the policy?

3. What were the "new guidelines"? Do you think these guidelines will be more effective?

LET US STRENGTHEN OUR NATION FOR THE 21ST CENTURY
By Bill Clinton

In 1998, after having won reelection in 1996, a confident President Clinton delivered his annual State of the Union address. Despite the shadow of impending scandal, the president continued to pursue his agenda. He had been particularly adept at occupying the middle ground in American politics and demonstrated his ability to continue to do that in this speech.

January 27, 1998

. . . Community means living by the defining American value-the ideal heard round the world that we are all created equal. Throughout our history, we haven't always honored that ideal and we've never fully lived up to it. Often it's easier to believe that our differences matter more than what we have in common. It may be easier, but it's wrong.

What we have to do in our day and generation to make sure that America becomes truly one nation-what do we have to do? We're becoming more and more and more diverse. Do you believe we can become one nation? The answer cannot be to dwell on our differences, but to build on our shared values. We all cherish family and faith, freedom and responsibility. We all want our children to grow up in a world where their talents are matched by their opportunities.

I've launched this national initiative on race to help us recognize our common interests and to bridge the opportunity gaps that are keeping us from becoming one America. Let us begin by recognizing what we still must overcome. Discrimination against any American is un-American.

We must vigorously enforce the laws that make it illegal. I ask your help to end the backlog at the Equal Employment Opportunity Commission. Sixty thousand of our fellow citizens are waiting in line for justice, and we should act now to end their wait.

We also should recognize that the greatest progress we can make toward building one America lies in the progress we make for all Americans, without regard to race. When we open the doors of college to all Americans, when-we rid all our streets of crime, when there are jobs available to people from all our neighborhoods, when we make sure all parents have the child care they need, we're helping to build one nation.

We, in this chamber and in this government, must do all we can to address the continuing American challenge to build one America. But we'll only move forward if all our fellow citizens-including every one of you at home watching tonight-is also committed to this cause.

We must work together, learn together, live together, serve together. On the forge of common enterprise Americans of all backgrounds can hammer out a common identity. We see it today in the United States military, in the Peace Corps, in AmeriCorps. Wherever people of all races and backgrounds come together in a shared endeavor and get a fair chance, we do just fine. With shared values and meaningful opportunities and honest communication and citizen service, we can unite a diverse people in freedom and mutual respect. We are many; we must be one.

In that spirit, let us lift our eyes to the new millennium. How will we mark that passage? It just happens once every thousand years. This year, Hillary and I launched the White House Millennium Program to promote America's creativity and innovation, and to preserve our heritage and culture into the 21st century. Our culture lives in every community, and every community has places of historic value that tell our stories as Americans. We should protect them. I am proposing a public/private partnership to advance our arts and humanities, and to celebrate the millennium by saving American's treasures, great and small.

And while we honor the past, let us imagine the future. Think about this-the entire store of human knowledge now doubles every five years. In the 1980s, scientists identified the gene causing cystic fibrosis-it took nine years. Last year, scientists located the gene that causes Parkinson's Disease-in only nine days. Within a decade, "gene chips" will offer a road map for prevention of illnesses throughout a lifetime. Soon we'll be able to carry all the phone calls on Mother's Day on a single strand of fiber the width of a human hair. A child born in 1998 may well live to see the 22nd century.

Tonight, as part of our gift to the millennium, I propose a 21st Century Research Fund for path-breaking scientific inquiry-the largest funding increase in history for the National Institutes of Health, the National Science Foundation, the National Cancer Institute.

We have already discovered genes for breast cancer and diabetes. I ask you to support this initiative so ours will be the generation that finally wins the war against cancer, and begins a revolution in our fight against all deadly diseases.

As important as all this scientific progress is, we must continue to see that science serves humanity, not the other way around. We must prevent the misuse of genetic tests to discriminate against any American.
And we must ratify the ethical consensus of the scientific and religious communities, and ban the cloning of human beings.

We should enable all the world's people to explore the far reaches of cyberspace. Think of this-the first time I made a State of the Union speech to you, only a handful of physicists used the World Wide Web. Literally, just a handful of people. Now, in schools, in libraries, homes and businesses, millions and millions of Americans surf the Net every day. We must give parents the tools they need to help protect their children from inappropriate material on the Internet. But we also must make sure that we protect the exploding global commercial potential of the Internet. We can do the kinds of things that we need to do and still protect our kids.

For one thing, I ask Congress to step up support for building the next generation Internet. It's getting kind of clogged, you know. And the next generation Internet will operate at speeds up to a thousand times faster than today.

Even as we explore this inner space in a new millennium we're going to open new frontiers in outer space. Throughout all history, humankind has had only one place to call home---our planet Earth. Beginning this year, 1998, men and women from 16 countries will build a foothold in the heavens-the international space station. With its vast expanses, scientists and engineers will actually set sail on an unchartered sea of limitless mystery and unlimited potential.

And this October, a true American hero, a veteran pilot of 149 combat missions and one, five-hour space flight that changed the world, will return to the heavens. Godspeed, John Glenn.

John, you will carry with you America's hopes. And on your uniform, once again, you will carry America's flag, marking the unbroken connection between the deeds of America's past and the daring of America's future.

Nearly 200 years ago, a tattered flag, its broad stripes and bright stars still gleaming through the smoke of a fierce battle, moved Francis Scott Key to scribble a few words on the back of an envelope-the words that became our national anthem. Today, that Star Spangled Banner, along with the Declaration of Independence, the Constitution and the Bill of Rights, are on display just a short walk from here. They are America's treasures and we must also save them for the ages.

I ask all Americans to support our project to restore all our treasures so that the generations of the 21st century can see for themselves the images and the words that are the old and continuing glory of America; an America that has continued to rise through every age, against every challenge, of people of great works and greater possibilities, who have always, always found the wisdom and strength to come together as one nation-to widen the circle of opportunity, to deepen the meaning our freedom, to form that "more perfect union." Let that be our gift to the 21st century.

God bless you, and God bless the United States.

Bill Clinton, "Let us Strengthen our Nation for the 21st Century," The 1998 State of the Union, January 27, 1998 (Vital Speeches of the Day, February 15, 1999).

HOW WELL DID YOU UNDERSTAND THIS SELECTION?

1. What issues did President Clinton consider to be most important in his 1998 State of the Union address?

2. How did his views of what was most important differ from those of President Reagan thirteen years earlier?

3. Why does the president speak of and introduce John Glenn?

4. What unspoken issue existed at this time? How might it affect the president's program?

SELF TEST

MULTIPLE CHOICE: Circle the correct response. The correct answers are given at the end.

1. Part of President Reagan's supply-side economics was a push to
   a. lower military expenditures
   b. increase taxes on the rich
   c. cut domestic social program expenditures
   d. increase the power of federal government agencies

2. The first woman to be on a major party ticket as a vice presidential candidate in 1984 was
   a. Janet Reno
   b. Sandra Day O'Connor
   c. Hillary Rodham
   d. Geraldine Ferraro

3. The people who profited most from the economic policies of the 1980s were
   a. wealthy businessmen
   b. skilled workers
   c. black inner-city residents
   d. small farmers

4. One result of Reagan's economic policies was that the national debt
   a. stayed the same because of reductions in the budget for social welfare programs
   b. declined a bit due a combination of budget cuts and tax increases
   c. declined substantially as a result of prosperity and increased federal revenues
   d. doubled due to a combination of tax cuts and increased defense expenditures

5. Like the 1880s, the 1980s was an era characterized by
   a. government regulation of all aspects of the economy
   b. powerful union movements asserting workers' demands
   c. an emphasis on personal wealth and greed
   d. a strong idealistic push for community involvement

6. The main reason for the dramatic changes in the Soviet Union from the late 1980s to early 1990s was
   a. the reforms launched by Soviet leader Mikhail Gorbachev
   b. the brilliant diplomacy instituted by Ronald Reagan
   c. the fears caused by the American Strategic Defense Initiative
   d. the constant worries about an imminent western invasion

7. What led some people to wonder if President Bush was trustworthy in keeping his promises?
   a. his attempt to end all affirmative action
   b. his characterization of the Soviet Union as an "evil empire"
   c. the breaking of his, "Read my lips, no new taxes" pledge
   d. his belated embrace of a pro-choice stance on abortion

8. The American public supported the Persian Gulf War for all these reasons EXCEPT
   a. It seemed a matter of the forces of democracy against an evil dictatorship.
   b. There were genuine fears that the Soviet Union would seize control of the region.
   c. People worried that Saddam Hussein would have too much control over oil production.
   d. Some people wanted to see America demonstrating that it could use its military might.

9. The deciding issue in the 1992 presidential election was the soundness of America's
    a. military preparedness
    b. moral and spiritual ideals
    c. politics
    d. economy

10. President Clinton suffered a serious defeat regarding his plans for
    a. reform of the welfare system
    b. overhaul of the health care system
    c. reducing the federal deficit
    d. "Family Leave" legislation

Answers: 1-c; 2-d; 3-a; 4-d; 5-c; 6-a; 7-c; 8-b; 9-d; 10-b.

ESSAYS:

1. Describe the impact on American life and society in the last twenty years of
    A) the drug epidemic   B) the AIDS epidemic
    C) the changing lives and status of women   D) the problems of the poor and minorities

How has America attempted to deal with these issues? Discuss the success or failure of these attempts.

2. Compare and contrast the ideologies and actions of the three presidents of this era (Reagan, Bush, and Clinton). Who was the most successful? The least successful? Why?

3. Why do commentators talk of a "new world order" that arose in the late 1980s to the present? What caused such a basic change in international relations? What are the consequences of this change?

OPTIONAL ACTIVITIES: (Use your knowledge **and** imagination when appropriate.)

1. Find someone who voted for Reagan in 1980 and/or 1984. Ask him or her to describe the reasons for this vote. What does that person think of the Reagan administration today? How does the answer you received compare to what you have learned about the Reagan presidency?

2. Write your own brief autobiography (2-3 pages). Relate the events of your life to American history at the same time.

3. If you were born after 1976, describe the first important historical event you can remember. Why do you think this was the first event to stick in your mind? How do your memories compare to what you have learned about the event?

WEB SITE LISTINGS:

Official Site of Ronald Reagan Presidential Library:
http://www.reagan.utexas.edu/

White House home page – source on recent presidents:
http://www.whitehouse.gov

History of AIDS:
http://www.library.ucsf.edu/collres/archives/ahpl

Iran/Contra:
http://www.Realhistoryarchives.com/collections/conspiracies/irancontra.htm

House Judiciary Impeachment Report:
http://www.house.gov/judiciary/report5

Document Center including Documents on Poverty, Crime, Terrorism, Impeachment and War:
http://www.lib.umich.edu/govdocs/usterror.html
/impeach.html
/census2/
/iraqwar.html

Recent and Older Supreme Court Decisions:
http://www.findlaw.com/casecode/supreme.html

Recent Elections:
http://www.pbs.org/newshour/election98
/election2000

9/11:
http://911digitalarchive.org
http://www.911ashistory.org

Iraq War 2003 Links to Many Sources:
http://www.library.umass/edu/subject/iraqwar

Best Sources for Current Events:
http://www.nytimes.com
http://www.cnn.com